DOCU

ILLUSTRATING
PAPAL AUTHORITY
A.D. 96 – 454

EDITED AND INTRODUCED

by

E. GILES

PREFACE

I EXPRESS my thanks to Dr William Telfer, Master of Selwyn College, Cambridge, for looking through my MS., and causing this book to have fewer amateurish blunders than it would have had but for his kind help. I also thank my friends Mr H. S. Buss, M.A., and Mr G. H. Newsom, B.A., for their help in some of the translations, and Canon E. Evans, D.D., for translating Document 69.

My grateful acknowledgements are due to the following, who have permitted me to reproduce passages from the works indicated: George Allen & Unwin, Ltd (A. B. Teetgen, *The Life of St Pulcheria*); Geoffrey Bles, Ltd (A Religious, C.S.M.V., *The Incarnation of the Word of God*); Columbia University Press (E. M. Sanford, *On the Government of God*; J. T. Shotwell and L. R. Loomis, *The See of Peter*); The Right Rev. The Abbot of Downside (John Chapman, *Bishop Gore and the Catholic Claims* and *Studies on the Early Papacy*); The English Province of the Redemptorists (O. R. Vassall-Phillips, *St Optatus*). I have also found *The See of Peter*, noted above, most helpful when revising the nineteenth-century translations.

E. GILES

CONTENTS

Contents

CHAPTER VI. TWO ANTI-POPES HIPPOLYTUS AND NOVATIAN

CHAPTER VII. ORIGEN

CHAPTER VIII. CYPRIAN

CHAPTER IX. BAPTISM BY HERETICS

CHAPTER X. A.D. 260 TO 314

Contents

Contents

Contents

Chapter XVI. JOHN CHRYSOSTOM

Chapter XVII. AUGUSTINE

Contents

Contents

Contents

INTRODUCTION

That they may be one

John 17. 11

THERE is unfortunately a wide gulf between the Roman Catholic and Anglican views on Church authority. Roman Catholics claim universal jurisdiction for the Pope as by divine law,[1] and the Anglican Article 37 denies such jurisdiction. Further, Roman Catholics believe that a divided Church is impossible, and go on to assume that their communion, which claims to be the whole Church, must be so. Anglicans believe that the Church militant ought not to be divided, but in fact is. They frequently express their faith in "one Catholick and Apostolick Church", and suppose, for example, that the provinces of Canterbury and York are provinces of that Church and that Christians all over the world who are in communion with the see of Canterbury are bona fide members thereof, in spite of their separation from the Roman see. "The divisibility of the Church", says Dom Chapman, "is the cardinal doctrine of Anglicanism and its most fundamental heresy."[2]

During the last hundred years a vast number of controversial books have been published on this dispute. They often turn on the authority held by the early bishops of Rome, both sides quoting from the fathers in support of their views. This is sometimes called "the appeal to history". The most popular of such works are *Roman Catholic Claims* by Charles Gore, 1st edition 1888, 11th edition 1921, and the reply to the 9th edition by Dom John Chapman, called *Bishop Gore and the Catholic Claims*, 1905. The chief excuse for my book is that extracts from the fathers, when seen in their context, so often give a different picture from that which they give when quoted

---

[1] *Pastor Aeternus* § 3, in C. Butler, *The Vatican Council*, 2. 284.
[2] *Bishop Gore and the Catholic Claims*, 20.

briefly by controversial writers. Most readers of controversy have neither the time nor the knowledge to enable them to go to libraries, check the references, and translate into English. Yet it is obvious that an author with an axe to grind must never be taken at his own valuation. He needs to be checked at every turn. Our Documents are therefore collected to put at the disposal of the English reader the raw material necessary for the study of this dispute. Most of them are quoted or cited in one or both of the two books just mentioned, and reference to these is given in all such cases at the end of the Document, the author's name and page number only being printed. By using these two works mainly for the selection of the Documents, I have kept the book within bounds, and I hope I have been balanced in my selection. I should have liked to avoid all notes and comments, but this seemed impossible. It has been necessary to link the Documents to the history of the Church, and in some cases to show how they have been used by the axe-grinders. To do this fairly is not easy.

The largest and most important controversial books on our subject were written about fifty years ago : Luke Rivington, *The Primitive Church and the See of Peter*; F. W. Puller, S.S.J.E., *Primitive Saints and the See of Rome*; Edward Denny, *Papalism*, and John Chapman, *Studies on the Early Papacy*. This last, though published in 1928, is really a collection of articles written some twenty to thirty years earlier. These four writers were unrepentant axe-grinders and went for each other vigorously. Dr Adrian Fortescue's smaller and later work, *The Early Papacy*, I would also mention because he pours scorn on this appeal to ancient documents.[1] I realize that such an appeal will not by itself solve the problem of disunity, but I do not see how the historical field can be ignored, especially in view of a remark of Pope Leo XIII quoted below. Fortescue's alternative seems to be to accept what the Roman Catholic Church teaches now,[2] which is not helpful to those whose convictions prevent this. In his Bampton Lectures, 1942, Dr Trevor Jalland[3] has made a serious attempt at

---

[1] Page 3.   [2] Page 4 and note.
[3] *The Church and the Papacy*, London, 1944.

objective study of papal authority, and in so doing has found it necessary to make short work of many of the arguments by which Anglicans have sought to defend their position. The lectures cover the whole of the Christian era, but are most detailed when dealing with the period covered by this book.

Two special points must be mentioned before we begin to call our witnesses, namely the use of the title Pope, and the difficult question of development. The earliest indication of the use of *Papa* at Rome for the bishop of Rome is an inscription dated about 303: "Double cubicle with arched tombs and light made by Severus the deacon with the permission of his Pope Marcellinus (JUSSU PP SUI MARCELLINI) for himself and his relations."[1] Marcellinus occupied the see from 296 to 304. I would have preferred to use the title Pope for the Roman bishop in my notes and comments right from the beginning, but this might seem to some to be prejudging the issue. I have therefore seldom used it until we come to the fourth century. Even then the documents will show that it was by no means in general use, but it seems a pity to use three words when one will do. It is worth noting that the bishop of Carthage was called Pope in 203[2] and 250,[3] likewise the bishop of Alexandria about 250.[4] The African Tertullian *may* be using it of the Roman bishop in 220.[5]

We are often asked to bear in mind "that the primacy was never as a ready made system traced out for the constitution of the ancient Church, but was deposited in it like a fructifying germ which developed with the life of the Church".[6] "So we ought not to represent the situation as if the Roman see clearly foresaw all for which she was destined",[7] and "Reflexion on the real implications of the original data [of the Roman primacy] was needed before their full significance was generally appreciated."[8] Opinions differ as to whether this

[1] J. S. Northcote, *Roma Sotteranea*, London, 1869, p. 93.
[2] *Passio S. Perpetuae* 4 § 3 (*P.L.* 3. 44).
[3] Cyprian, *Ep.* 23, title, etc.   [4] Eus. *H.E.* 7. 7 § 4.
[5] Doc. 18 § 13.
[6] Cardinal Hergenrother, *Anti Janus*, E.T., Dublin, 1870, p. 118.
[7] F. Walter, *Kirchenrechts*, 1842, pp. 41, 42.
[8] Jalland, *Papacy*, 542.

approach to the subject can be reconciled with the official statement of Pope Leo XIII, that present beliefs about papal authority are not new, but are "the venerable and constant belief of every age".[1]

Finally may I remind readers that the text for this book is our Lord's own prayer "That they may be one"? One Jesuit, the Rev. Albert Gille, went so far as to say that "excessive Anglican freedom amalgamating with excessive Catholic discipline would, by tempering each other, result in a combination which the separate elements could never rival".[2] Desire for reunion has been expressed officially by both sides of the Anglo-Roman cleavage, though reunion is conceived by them in very different ways. In 1895 Pope Leo XIII, with special reference to England, humbly prayed "for the return of Christian nations now separated from us"[3]; and in 1948 the Lambeth Conference Committee affirmed like its three predecessors that "there can be no fulfilment of the Divine purpose in any scheme of reunion which does not ultimately include the great Latin Church of the West, with which our history has been so closely associated in the past, and with which we are still bound by many ties of common faith and tradition".[4]

[1] *Satis Cognitum* § 15.
[2] *A Catholic Plea for Reunion*, London, 1934, p. 67.
[3] *Ad Anglos.*
[4] *The Lambeth Conference, 1948*, Pt II, p. 66.

ABBREVIATIONS AND SIGNS

A.N.C.L.	*Ante-Nicene Christian Library.* English translations published by T. & T. Clark, Edinburgh, from 1867.
Bagster.	*The Greek Ecclesiastical Historians,* published by Samuel Bagster, London, 1843–1846.
Batiffol.	*Primitive Catholicism,* 1911, E.T. of *L'Église Naissante et le Catholicisme,* by P. Batiffol.
Chapman.	*Bishop Gore and the Catholic Claims,* by John Chapman, London, 1905.
C.S.E.L.	*Corpus Scriptorum Ecclesiasticorum Latinorum,* Vienna, 1886 *et seq.*
D.C.B.	*Dictionary of Christian Biography,* 1877–1887.
Denny.	*Papalism,* by E. Denny, London, 1912. All references are to Denny's pages.
Duchesne.	*Early History of the Christian Church,* by L. Duchesne, E.T., 3 vols., London, 1909–1924.
E.T.	English translation.
Eus.	Eusebius.
Gore.	*Roman Catholic Claims,* by Charles Gore, 11th Edition, London, 1921.
H.E.	*Historia Ecclesiastica.*
Hefele.	*A History of the Christian Councils,* by C. J. Hefele, E.T. Vols. 1–3, Edinburgh, 1894–1896.
Jalland, *Leo.*	*The Life and Times of St Leo the Great,* by T. G. Jalland, London, 1941.
Jalland, *Papacy.*	*The Church and the Papacy,* by T. G. Jalland, London, 1944.
J.T.S.	*Journal of Theological Studies.*
Kidd, *Docs.*	*Documents Illustrative of the History of the Church,* edited by B. J. Kidd, vols. 1 and 2, London, 1920–1923. References are to Kidd's volumes and pages.

Kidd, *Hist. Ch.*	*A History of the Church to A.D. 461*, by B. J. Kidd, 3 vols., Oxford, 1922.
L. & O.	*Eusebius: Ecclesiastical History*, Vol. 1, translation by H. J. Lawlor and J. E. L. Oulton, London, 1927.
L.C.L.	*The Loeb Classical Library*. Texts and translations.
L.F.	*Library of the Fathers*. English translations published at Oxford from 1838.
Mansi.	*Sacrorum Conciliorum . Collectio*, by J. D. Mansi, Florence, from 1759.
M.D.	*The Works of Aurelius Augustine: A New Translation*, edited by Marcus Dods the Younger; published by T. & T. Clark, Edinburgh, 1871–1876.
P.G.	*Patrologia Graeca*. Edited by J. P. Migne, Paris.
P.L.	*Patrologia Latina*. Edited by J. P. Migne, Paris.
P.N.F.	*Nicene and Post Nicene Fathers*. English translations, Oxford and New York, 1896–1900.
Puller.	*Primitive Saints and the See of Rome*, by F. W. Puller, 3rd Edition, London, 1900.
Rivington.	*The Primitive Church and the See of Peter*, by L. Rivington, London, 1894.
Schwartz.	*Acta Conciliorum Oecumenicorum*, edited by E. Schwartz, Berlin, 1928–1938.
S.E.P.	*Studies on the Early Papacy*, by John Chapman, London, 1928.
Turner.	*Ecclesiae Occidentalis Monumenta Juris Antiquissima*, edited by C. H. Turner, Tom. 1, Oxford, 1899–1939.
†	Slightly revised.
‡	Revised.

EDITOR'S NOTE

NUMBERS in references normally refer to pages, or to volumes and pages.

References in brackets below the titles of Documents:

(1) The first reference is to some edition of the Greek or Latin text: in the majority of the Documents, to Migne's *Patrologia*. Migne is unique in giving almost the entire body of patristic writings, and his collection still provides the most universally accessible and convenient means of referring to the fathers. But the text Migne gives has inevitably, in some cases, ceased to be the best critical text, and where reference is made to it, it does not follow that it is the text translated. Most of the Greek texts will be found in *Griechischen Christlichen Schriftsteller* (Leipzig, 1897 ff.), and for Latin works the Vienna *Corpus* (*C.S.E.L.*) is now commonly used. In other cases separate works by various editors are accepted as giving the standard texts.

(2) The second reference is to the English translation reproduced. Where there is no second reference, the translation is my own. Where I have slightly revised the E.T., the second reference is followed by the sign † ; where my revision is more than slight, the sign ‡ is used. I have, however, felt free to conform punctuation and spelling to a consistent modern usage throughout, without making any special note of the alterations thereby involved.

To make it clear that my own remarks are of secondary importance, they appear in smaller print than the Documents. Italics are used within the Documents to draw attention to those passages which seem to me to be specially relevant to the matter in hand, or have been considered by Gore, Chapman, or other controversial writers to be relevant to their cause. For such emphasis I alone am responsible. Some of the dates in the book are necessarily conjectural.

CHAPTER I

THE APOSTOLIC FATHERS

I. CLEMENT OF ROME

OUR earliest witness outside the New Testament is a letter written by the church of Rome to the church of Corinth. References in our Documents 6 § 11, 7 § 1, and 9. 3 § 3 have caused scholars to assign the letter to Clement who was bishop of Rome about A.D. 90 to 100.

DOCUMENT 1——*The First Epistle of Clement.* A.D. 96.
(Lightfoot[1] 5; Lowther Clarke[2] 49.)

The church of God which sojourns at Rome to the church of God which sojourns at Corinth, to those who are called, and sanctified by the will of God through our Lord Jesus Christ. Grace and peace be multiplied to you from Almighty God through Jesus Christ.

1. Owing to the sudden and repeated misfortunes and calamities which have befallen us, brethren, we are somewhat late, we think, in concerning ourselves with the matters disputed among you, beloved, and with the sedition, so alien and out of place in God's elect .

5. But, to finish with these ancient examples, let us come to the athletes of the recent past; let us take the noble examples of our own generation. Through jealousy and envy the greatest and most righteous pillars [of the Church] were persecuted, and contended unto death. Let us set before our eyes the good apostles: *Peter,* who through unrighteous jealousy endured not one or two but many labours, and so having borne witness proceeded to his due place of glory. Through jealousy

[1] J. B. Lightfoot, *Apostolic Fathers*, Part I, Vol. II, London, 1890.
[2] W. K. Lowther Clarke, *The First Epistle of Clement to the Corinthians*, London, 1937.

and strife *Paul* displayed the prize of endurance; Then he passed from the world and went to the holy place. . . .

56. Therefore let us too intercede on behalf of those who fall into any trespass, that gentleness and humility may be given them, so that they may yield not to us but to God's will.

58. . Receive our counsel, and you will have no cause to regret. . .

59. *But if any disobey the words spoken by him through us, let them know that they will involve themselves in transgression and no small danger.* But we shall be innocent of this sin; and we shall ask with earnest prayer and supplication that the Creator of all may keep unbroken the fixed number of his elect in all the world through his beloved servant Jesus Christ.

63. It is right, then, that, confronted by so many examples, we should bow the neck and take the seat of obedience, and submit to those who are leaders of our souls, that ceasing from vain sedition we may reach the mark set before us in truth, free from all blame. For you will give us joy and gladness if, *obedient to what we have written through the Holy Spirit,* you root out the lawless anger of your jealousy, according to the prayer for peace and concord which we have made in this letter. We are sending faithful and discreet men, who have lived amongst us without blame from youth to old age; they will be witnesses between you and us. This we do that you may know that all our care has been, and still is, that you may soon be at peace.

(Gore 94, 95; Chapman 62, 63, 70 note.)

The apology for delay at the beginning of the letter suggests that the Corinthian Christians had written to Rome for advice in their dispute about the authority of the ministry. The church of Corinth was founded by Paul, and John the apostle was probably still alive, but it is Rome, some 600 miles away, which intervenes, and Gore admits that the letter is written with a tone of considerable authority (see §§ 59, 63). The force of this may be a little weakened by the fact that Julius Caesar had repopulated Corinth with Italian freedmen in 46 b.c., so that it was racially in close touch with Rome.

Roman Catholics are fond of quoting the great Anglican authority Lightfoot, who wrote, "It may perhaps seem strange to describe this noble remonstrance as the first step towards papal domination. And yet undoubtedly this is the case".[1] But Lightfoot also says that Clement writes as the mouthpiece of the Roman Church, and on terms of equality with the Corinthians, not as successor of Peter.[2]

II. IGNATIUS OF ANTIOCH

About twenty years after Clement, Ignatius, bishop of Antioch, wrote seven letters to various local churches as he was on his way to martyrdom at Rome. This writer is well known for his insistence on the authority of the bishop.

DOCUMENT 2——Ignatius, *To the Smyrnaeans.* A.D. 115. (*P.G.* 5. 708; Srawley[3] 90.)

Ignatius . . to the church which is at Smyrna in Asia, in a blameless spirit and in the word of God heartiest greeting.

8. Avoid divisions, as the beginning of evil. Follow, all of you, the bishop, as Jesus Christ followed the Father; and follow the presbytery as the apostles. Moreover reverence the deacons as the commandment of God. Let no man do aught pertaining to the Church apart from the bishop. Let that eucharist be considered valid which is under the bishop or him to whom he commits it. Wheresoever the bishop appears, there let the people be, even as wheresoever Christ Jesus is, there is the Catholic Church. It is not lawful apart from the bishop either to baptize or to hold a love-feast. But whatsoever he approves, that also is well-pleasing to God, that everything you do may be secure and valid.

12. The love of the brethren who are at Troas salutes you. . . . (Chapman 71A note.)

On the above Monseigneur Batiffol is content to follow Lightfoot and to say "In other words the bishop constitutes the unity of the local church and Jesus Christ the unity of all the local churches, the unity of all the dispersed bishops".[4] The authority of the bishop is also emphasized in the letter to Philadelphia.

[1] *Apostolic Fathers*, Part I, Vol. I, p. 70.
[2] Ibid., pp. 69, 70.
[3] J. H. Srawley, *The Epistles of St Ignatius*, London, 1919.
[4] Batiffol, 139.

Document 3——Ignatius, *To the Philadelphians.* A.D. 115.
(*P.G.* 5. 697; Srawley 81.)

Ignatius, who is also Theophorus, to the church of God the Father and Jesus Christ which is at Philadelphia in Asia, to her who has received mercy and is established in godly concord and rejoices in the passion of our Lord and in his resurrection without wavering, being fully persuaded in all mercy; her I salute in the blood of Jesus Christ; seeing that it is eternal and enduring joy, especially if they be at one with the bishop and with the presbyters who are with him. . . .

4. Therefore give heed to keep one eucharist. For there is one flesh of our Lord Jesus Christ, and one cup unto union with his blood. There is one altar, as there is one bishop, together with the presbytery and the deacons, my fellow-servants; that whatsoever you do, you may do according to God.

11. . The love of the brethren who are at Troas salutes you, whence also I write unto you. . (Gore 33.)

Our next Document shows the special honour Ignatius paid to the church of Rome.

Document 4——Ignatius, *To the Romans.* A.D. 115.
(*P.G.* 5. 685; Srawley 70 †.)

Ignatius . . to the church that is beloved and illuminated by the will of him that willed all things which exist, in faith and love towards Jesus Christ our God; to her that presides in the district of the region of the Romans,[1] being worthy of God, worthy of honour, worthy of congratulation, worthy of praise, worthy of success, worthy in purity, and having the presidency of the love,[2] following the law of Christ, bearing the Father's name; which church also I salute in the name of Jesus Christ, Son of the Father; to them that are united in flesh and spirit with every one of his commandments, being wholly filled with the grace of God, without wavering, and strained *clear from*

[1] προκάθηται ἐν τόπῳ χωρίου Ῥωμαίων.
[2] προκαθημένη τῆς ἀγάπης.

every foreign stain, warmest greeting in Jesus Christ our God without blame.

3. You have never envied anyone; you have taught others, but I wish that what you enjoin in your teaching may endure.

4. . entice the wild beasts to become my tomb, and to leave naught of my body, that I may not, when I have fallen asleep, prove a burden to any man. Then shall I be truly a disciple of Jesus Christ, when the world shall not see even my body. Entreat the Lord for me, that by these instruments I may be found a sacrifice unto God. I do not enjoin you *as Peter and Paul did*. They were apostles, I am a convict. They were free, but I am a slave to this hour.

9. Remember in your prayer the church in Syria, since it has God as its shepherd in my place. Jesus Christ alone shall be its bishop, *and your love.* . My spirit salutes you, as also does the love of the churches which received me.

(Gore 95 note; Chapman 63A, 65A, 70B note.)

Here is early witness to the planting of the Roman church by Peter and Paul, but our main interest lies in the preface. Contrast the magnificent array of words with the simpler salutations to the other churches (Docs. 2 and 3). What is the meaning of "presides in the district of the region of the Romans"? Does it indicate the place where the presiding church of Christendom is situated,[1] or does it describe the limits of the jurisdiction of the Roman church?[2] Tertullian says "The very seats of the apostles preside over their own places" (Doc. 12 § 36). Again, "having the presidency of the love" may mean that the Roman church presides over the whole Church,[3] because at the end of Docs. 2 and 3 "the love" could easily mean the Church. But against this we see that at the end of Doc. 4 the love and the Church are distinct. ἡ ἀγάπη seems in some sense to denote the unity of the faithful.

Newman found no difficulty in the fact that the Pope is never mentioned by Ignatius. He thought that the occasion for the exercise of papal authority had not yet arisen.[4] Chapman thought the Pope's name was concealed for fear of persecution.[5]

[1] L. J. Tixeront, *History of Dogmas*, E.T., 1. 129.
[2] Lightfoot, op. cit., Part II, Vol. II, p. 190.
[3] F. X. Funk, *Manual of Ch. Hist.*, E.T., 1. 60.
[4] *Development of Christian Doctrine*, London, 1845, p. 167.
[5] *J.T.S.*, Vol. V, pp. 530–532.

CHAPTER II

IRENAEUS

IRENAEUS is the most important witness of the second century. He was taught the faith by Polycarp, bishop of Smyrna, who in his turn had been taught by John the apostle. He became bishop of Lyons in A.D. 178, and soon after began his five books against the heresies. First, however, three earlier documents, preserved by Eusebius the historian, come forward for consideration. The comments of Eusebius are of course much later, say A.D. 311.

I. DIONYSIUS OF CORINTH

DOCUMENT 5——Dionysius of Corinth, *To the Romans.* A.D. 171.
   In Eusebius, *H.E.* 2. 25 § 8. (*L.C.L.* 1. 182; L. & O. 60 †.)

And that they [Peter and Paul] were martyred both at the same time, Dionysius, bishop of the Corinthians, proves as follows in a passage written to the Romans.

"In these ways you also, by such an admonition, have united *the planting that came from Peter and Paul, of both the Romans and the Corinthians.* For indeed both planted also in our Corinth, and likewise taught us; and likewise they taught together also in Italy, and were martyred at the same time."

(Gore 94; Chapman 66B.)

DOCUMENT 6——Dionysius of Corinth, *To Soter.* A.D. 171.
   In Eusebius, *H.E.* 4. 23. (*L.C.L.* 1. 380; L. & O. 130 ‡.)

9. Moreover, there is also extant a letter of Dionysius to the Romans, addressed to Soter, the then bishop . ., in which he writes thus commending the custom of the Romans which was observed down to the persecution in our day:

10. "For this has been your practice from the beginning: to

6

do good in various ways to all the brethren, and to send supplies to the many churches in every city, thus relieving the want of the needy, now making provision, by the supplies which you have sent from the beginning, for brethren in the mines; and thus as Romans you observe the hereditary custom of Romans, which your blessed bishop Soter has not only maintained, but even added to, by providing an abundance of supplies to the saints, and by exhorting with blessed words, *as a loving father his children*, the brethren who come up." [1]

11. Now in this same letter, he also mentions the letter of Clement to the Corinthians, showing that it was an ancient custom dating from primitive times to read it in church. At all events he says: "'To-day we have passed the Lord's holy day, in which we read your letter; from the reading of which we shall always be able to draw advice, as also from the former letter written to us through Clement."

(Gore 94; Chapman 63.)

Evidently the churches in Rome and Corinth kept in close touch. We saw in Doc. 1 that Clement of Rome wrote to the Corinthian church with a tone of considerable authority. This tone was far from being resented by Corinth; on the contrary, about 76 years later the letter is still being read aloud in church on Sundays. The Roman "presidency of love" (Doc. 4) takes the practical form of almsgiving extending far beyond the bounds of Italy and right into the fourth century. I cannot agree with Chapman that the "blessed words, as a loving father his children," refer to the letter written by Soter. When Christians from overseas came up to Rome, the bishop encouraged them "with blessed words, etc.". His letter like that of his predecessor is also read in church on Sunday.

II. HEGESIPPUS

DOCUMENT 7——Hegesippus, *Memoirs.* About A.D. 175.
  In Eusebius *H.E.* 4. 22. (*L.C.L.* 1. 374; L. & O. 127 †.)

1. Now Hegesippus, in the five memoirs which have come down to us, has left a complete record of his personal views. In them he tells us that on a journey as far as Rome he associated

---

[1] τοὺς ἀνιόντας ἀδελφούς.

with many bishops, and that he had received the same teaching from all. In fact we may listen to what he says, when after some remarks on the epistle of Clement to the Corinthians, he adds as follows:

2. "And the church of the Corinthians continued in the true doctrine until Primus was bishop of Corinth.   . With them I associated on my voyage to Rome, and I abode with the Corinthians many days; during which we were refreshed together in the true word.

3. But when I came to Rome, I made for myself a succession-list as far as Anicetus; whose deacon was Eleutherus. Soter succeeded Anicetus, after him Eleutherus. *In every succession, and in every city*, things are as the law and the prophets and the Lord preach."   (Gore 97.)

III. IRENAEUS

DOCUMENT 8——Irenaeus, *Against the Heresies,* Book 1.
        A.D. 185.

Chapter 10.   (*P.G.* 7. 552; Hitchcock[1] 1. 29 †.)

2. This kerygma and this faith the Church, although scattered over the whole world, observes diligently, as if it occupied but one house, and believes as if it had but one mind, and preaches and teaches as if it had but one mouth. And *although there are many dialects in the world, the force of the tradition is one and the same.* For the same faith is held and handed down by the churches established in the Germanies, the Spains, among the Celtic tribes, in the East, in Libya, and in the central portions of the world.

Chapter 25.   (*P.G.* 7. 685; Hitchcock 1. 40 ‡.)

6. Certain of them [Carpocratians] brand their disciples behind the lobe of the right ear. Marcellina, who *came to Rome* in the time of Anicetus, since she was of this school, led many astray.

---

[1] F. R. M. Hitchcock, *St Irenaeus: Against the Heresies,* London, 1916.

Chapter 27. (*P.G.* 7. 687; *L.F.* 42. 78 †.)

1. One Cerdon, too, taking his beginning from Simon and his set, *sojourned in Rome under Hyginus,* who occupied the ninth place in the episcopal succession from the apostles, and taught that the God proclaimed by the law and the prophets is not the Father of our Lord Jesus Christ, the one being revealed, the other unknown; the one again being just, the other good.

2. And Marcion of Pontus *came in his place,* and extended his school, shamelessly blaspheming him who is called God by the law and the prophets.

(Gore 41; Chapman 22B, 37B, 65B.)

DOCUMENT 9——Irenaeus, *Against the Heresies,* Book 3. A.D. 185.

Chapter 3. (*P.G.* 7. 848; Hitchcock 1. 84 ‡.)

1. Any one who wishes to discern the truth may see in every church in the whole world the apostolic succession clear and manifest. We can enumerate those who were appointed as bishops in the churches by the apostles and their successors to our own day, who never knew or taught anything like their foolish doctrine. Had the apostles known any secret[1] mysteries which they taught privately to the perfect, they would surely have entrusted this teaching to the men in whose charge they placed the churches. For they wished them to be without blame and reproach to whom they handed over their own position of authority.   .

2. But (as it would be very long, in a book of this kind, to enumerate the successions of all the churches) by pointing out the apostolic tradition and faith announced to mankind,[2] which has been brought down to our time by successions of bishops, in the greatest, most ancient, and well known church, founded and established by the two most glorious apostles, Peter and Paul, at Rome, we can confound all who in any other way, either for self-pleasing or vainglory, or by blindness or perversity, gather more than they ought. *For to this church on account of her more powerful principality it is necessary* (? *inevitable*)

[1] Cf. Innocent, Doc. 180 § 2.   [2] Rom. 1. 8.

that every church should come together (? agree), that is the faithful from all sides, in which, always, that which is the tradition from the apostles has been preserved by those who are from all parts. [Ad hanc enim ecclesiam propter potentiorem (or potiorem) principalitatem necesse est omnem convenire ecclesiam, hoc est, eos qui sunt undique fideles, in qua semper ab his qui sunt undique conservata est ea quae est ab apostolis traditio.]

3. The blessed apostles after founding and building up the church entrusted the office of bishop to Linus. Paul speaks of this Linus in his epistles to Timothy. Anencletus followed him. After him, in the third place after the apostles, Clement was appointed bishop. He not only saw the blessed apostles, but also had intercourse with them, and had their preaching ringing in his ears and before his eyes. He was not alone in this, for there were still many left at the time who had been instructed by the apostles. When Clement was bishop a great dissension arose in Corinth among the brethren, and the church in Rome sent a powerful letter[1] to the Corinthians, urging them to have peace, renewing their faith and announcing to them the tradition they had lately received from the apostles.

Euarestos succeeded this Clement, and Alexander Euarestos, and then Sixtus, the sixth after the apostles, was appointed. After him came Telesphorus, who had a glorious martyrdom. Then came Hyginus, Pius, Anicetus, Soter and Eleutherus, the twelfth from the apostles who now occupies the see. In the same order and in the same succession the tradition of the apostles in the Church and the preaching of the truth have come down to us. And this is a most complete proof that it is one and the same life-giving faith which has been preserved in the Church from the apostles until now, and handed down in truth.

4. And Polycarp was not only instructed in the faith by the apostles, and personally acquainted with many who had seen the Lord, but he was also appointed by the apostles for Asia as bishop in the church at Smyrna. Him even I saw early in my youth. For he remained a long time with us and was exceedingly old. And after a glorious and conspicuous martyrdom he passed away, having always taught these things which he

[1] Doc. 1.

learnt from the apostles, which also the Church hands down and which alone are true. All the churches throughout Asia, and the successors of Polycarp, . add similar testimony.

In the time of Anicetus, *when staying at Rome, Polycarp* converted many of these heretics to the Church of God, declaring that this was the one and only truth he had received from the apostles, and this had been handed down to us by the Church.
. The church in Ephesus, founded by Paul, and where John lived until the days of Trajan, is also a witness of the tradition of the apostles.

Chapter 4. (*P.G.* 7. 855; Hitchcock 1. 88 †.)

1. . If there was a question about any trifling matter, would it not be necessary to have recourse to the oldest churches, in which the apostles lived, and obtain from them some clear and definite ruling on the present subject of dispute? And if the apostles had not left us the Scriptures, should we not need to follow the order of tradition which they handed on to those to whom they entrusted the churches?

2. Many nations of barbarians who believe in Christ and have their salvation not written on paper with ink, but by the Spirit on their hearts, assent to this order, and carefully keep the old tradition, believing in one God, the maker of heaven and earth. .

3. Before Valentinus there were none of his way of thinking, and before Marcion there were none of his. For *Valentinus came to Rome* in the days of Hyginus, flourished under Pius, and lived until Anicetus. But Cerdon, who was before Marcion, also lived in the days of Hyginus, the eighth bishop. He often came to church and professed his faith, at one time teaching secretly and at another confessing openly, and at last being convicted of false teaching, he forsook the Christian congregation. Marcion, who succeeded him, flourished in the days of Anicetus the tenth bishop.

(Gore 94, 96, 97, 98; Chapman 37B, 61B, 64, 65, 68B.)

In these two Documents Irenaeus records the visit of Polycarp and four heretics to Rome. This is considered in Chapter V. Our concern now is with the famous passage about the "more powerful principality" of the Roman Church (3. 3 § 2). It is preserved only in Latin, and the Latin has been translated in many different ways. Abandoning any attempt at good English, I have followed Gore and Chapman where they agree, otherwise adhering close to the Latin, but giving alternatives in two places.

There seem to be three insoluble problems in this difficult passage. It is agreed "that in the time of Irenaeus the see of Rome was the first see of the Catholic Church".[1] But in what sense? For the meaning of *principalitas* is ambiguous: in due course it changed its meaning from the idea of seniority in time to that of supremacy. We do not know the date of the Latin translation. The phrase *potentiorem principalitatem* could mean "superior origin" as suggested by Jalland,[2] or it could mean "greater supremacy" as most R.C. scholars assume. Secondly, the two meanings of the words *convenire ad* both find support in the Vulgate. In Mark 1. 45 we get *conveniebant ad eum undique*, "they came to him from everywhere". But in 2 Cor. 6. 15, there is *quae conventio Christi ad Belial?*, "what agreement has Christ with Belial?". Thirdly, it is not clear whether "the faithful from all sides" are kept steadfast in their faith by their visits to the Roman church, or whether the Roman church is kept firm by having her faith checked by the visits of "those who are from all parts".

The extreme R.C. view was that the passage is evidence for the infallibility[3] of the Roman church, since "all orthodox churches are in agreement with her".[4] Other Roman Catholics do not go so far as this; for example Francis Bacchus[5] wrote: "The primacy of the Roman church is for St Irenaeus's purpose the token that all the churches are agreed with her. It is not the reason why they are unanimous with her." To refute the suggestion of Roman infallibility, Anglicans[6] point out that Irenaeus appeals also to the churches of Smyrna and Ephesus, as reliable witnesses of the truth (3. 3 § 4).

IV. CELSUS

A hostile work by Celsus probably belongs to this period.[7]

DOCUMENT 10——Celsus, *True Account.* About A.D. 176.
In Origen, *Contra Celsum*, Book 3 § 12. (*P.G.* 11. 933; *A.N.C.L.* 23. 94 ‡.)

When Christians had greatly increased in numbers, they were divided and split up into factions, each individual

[1] Puller, 33.   [2] *Papacy*, 111.
[3] Chapman in *Revue Bénédictine*, 1895, p. 64.
[4] Rivington, 37.   [5] *Dublin Review*, April 1899, p. 383.   [6] Puller, 33.
[7] J. Lebreton, S.J., and J. Zeiller, *History of the Primitive Church*, E.T., 4. 821 (London, 1948).

desiring to have his own party. Being thus separated through their numbers they confute one another, still having, so to speak, one name in common, if indeed they still retain it. And this is the only thing which they are yet ashamed to abandon, while other matters are determined in different ways by the various sects. (Gore 51.)

Gore asks why the bishop of Rome did not clear up the party quarrels pointed out by Celsus. (See also page 20 below.) Chapman's reply to this line of attack is that "the clear rule of faith was there" and "the voice of the Church collective was perfectly certain and well known, and the heretics despised it". If the sectaries declined to heed their local bishop, "they would not have attended any better to the voice of the Church's head".[1]

[1] Chapman, 37B.

CHAPTER III

THE DISPUTE ABOUT EASTER
A.D. 190

DOCUMENT 11——Eusebius, *H.E.*, Book 5. A.D. 311.

Chapter 23. (*L.C.L.* 1. 502; L. & O. 168 †.)

1. Now a question of no small importance arose in their time. For the communities of the whole of Asia, relying on a tradition of great antiquity, thought that they ought to observe the fourteenth day of the moon (the day on which the Jews were ordered to sacrifice the lamb) as the day for the festival of the Saviour's Pascha; since they deemed it necessary at all costs to put an end to their fast on that day, no matter on what day of the week it should fall. But it was not the custom for the churches throughout all the rest of the world thus to celebrate it, preserving as they did by an apostolic tradition the custom which had obtained hitherto, that it was not proper to end the fast on any other day than on the day of the resurrection of our Saviour.

2. So then, synods and assemblages of bishops came together, and unanimously drew up in letters an ecclesiastical decree for the faithful everywhere, to the effect that the mystery of the Lord's resurrection from the dead should never be celebrated on any other but the Lord's day, and that on that day alone we should observe the close of the paschal fast.

3. Now there is still extant to this day a letter from those who were then assembled in Palestine, over whom Theophilus, bishop of the community at Caesarea, and Narcissus, of Jerusalem, presided; and likewise another also from those at Rome, on the same question, which indicates that Victor was bishop; one too from the bishops in Pontus, over whom Palmas, as the oldest, had presided; and also one from the communities in Gaul, over which Irenaeus was bishop.

14

4. Moreover one from the bishops in Osrhoëne and the cities in that part; as well as a personal letter from Bacchyllus, bishop of the church of the Corinthians, and from great numbers of others who pronounced one and the same opinion and judgement, and gave the same decision. And the one decree which they made was that which we have stated.

Chapter 24.

1. But of those bishops in Asia who confidently affirmed that they ought to keep to the custom which they had received from days of yore, Polycrates was the leader. And he too sets forth the tradition which had come down to him, in the letter he penned to Victor and the church of the Romans, in the following words:

2. "As for us, then, we keep the day without tampering with it, neither adding, nor subtracting. For indeed in Asia great lights have fallen asleep, such as shall rise again on the day of the Lord's appearing, when he comes with glory from heaven to seek out all his saints: to wit, Philip, one of the twelve apostles, who has fallen asleep in Hierapolis, also his two daughters who grew old in virginity, and his other daughter who lived in the Holy Spirit and rests at Ephesus.

3. "And, moreover, [there is] John too, he who leant back on the Lord's breast, who was a priest, wearing the sacerdotal plate, both martyr and teacher. He has fallen asleep at Ephesus.

4. "Moreover, Polycarp too at Smyrna, both bishop and martyr; and Thraseas, both bishop and martyr, of Eumenia, who has fallen asleep at Smyrna.

5. "And why need I mention Sagaris, bishop and martyr, who has fallen asleep at Laodicea? or the blessed Papirius, or Melito the eunuch who in all things lived in the Holy Spirit, who lies at Sardis, awaiting the visitation from heaven, when he shall rise from the dead?

6. "These all observed the fourteenth day for the Pascha according to the gospel, in no way deviating therefrom, but following the rule of faith. And moreover I also, Polycrates,

the least of you all, [do] according to the tradition of my kinsmen, some of whom also I have followed closely. Seven of my kinsmen were bishops, and I am the eighth. And my kinsmen always kept the day when the people put away the leaven.

7. "Therefore I for my part, brethren, who number sixty-five years in the Lord and have conversed with the brethren from all parts of the world and traversed the entire range of holy Scripture, *am not affrighted by threats*. For those better than I have said, 'We must obey God rather than men'."

8. Then he goes on to add as follows, with reference to the bishops present at his writing who held the same view as he did: "But I could mention the bishops present with me, whom I summoned when ye yourselves desired [1] that I should summon them. And if I were to write their names, the number thereof would be great. But they who know my littleness approved my letter, knowing that I did not wear my grey hairs in vain, but that I have ever lived in Christ Jesus."

9. Thereupon Victor, the president of the [church] of the Romans, *endeavoured to cut off* by a single stroke the communities of the whole of Asia, together with the neighbouring churches, *from the common union*, on the ground of unorthodoxy; and, indeed, denounced them in letters, proclaiming that the brethren in those parts *were all wholly excommunicate*.

10. Howbeit this did not please all the bishops without exception. On the contrary, they exhorted him in reply to have a mind for the things which make for peace and neighbourly union and charity. And their words are extant also, in which they *censure Victor* somewhat sharply.

11. One of these was Irenaeus, who wrote in the name of the brethren in Gaul, whose leader he was; and, while holding that the mystery of the Lord's resurrection should be celebrated on the Lord's day and on that alone, he nevertheless suitably gives Victor much counsel besides, not to cut off whole churches of God for observing an ancient custom handed down to them. Then he goes on to add, in these very words:

12. "For not only is there a controversy about the day, but

1 ἠξιώσατε.

also about the very manner of the fast. For some think they ought to fast a single day, but others two, others again even more. And in the opinion of others, the 'day' amounts to forty continuous hours.

13. "And this variety of observance did not originate in our time, but much further back, in the times of those before us, who, no doubt mistakenly, held closely, in their simplicity and ignorance, to this custom, and have transmitted it to posterity. Yet none the less they all lived in peace, and we live in peace, with one another; and the difference concerning the fast enhances the unanimity of our faith."

14. To these remarks he also adds the following account, which it will not be out of place for me to quote: "And the elders before Soter, who presided over the church of which you are now the leader (we mean Anicetus and Pius, Hyginus and Telesphorus and Xystus), neither themselves observed it nor permitted those [residing] with them [to do so]; and none the less, though themselves not observing it, were they at peace with the members of those communities where it was observed, when the latter came to them. And yet the observance was the more obnoxious to those who did not observe it.

15. "And none were ever cast out because of this course of action, but those very elders before you, though they did not observe it, would send the eucharist to members of those communities who observed it.

16. "And when the blessed Polycarp stayed at Rome in the time of Anicetus, although they had some trifling disagreements on other matters, they immediately made peace, nor did they care to quarrel on this head. For neither could Anicetus persuade Polycarp not to observe what he had always observed with John the disciple of our Lord and the other apostles with whom he consorted; nor yet did Polycarp persuade Anicetus to observe it, for he said that he ought to hold to the custom of the elders before him.

17. "And though such was the case, they held communion with one another, and in the church Anicetus yielded the [celebration of the] eucharist to Polycarp, manifestly out of respect. So they parted from one another in peace, and the

whole Church was at peace, both they who observed and they
who did not observe."

18. Thus, then, did Irenaeus entreat and negotiate on behalf of the peace of the churches—a man well named, for he
was a peace-maker both in name and character. And he corresponded by letter not only with Victor, but also with very
many and various rulers of churches, in a fitting manner, on
the question which had been raised.

(Gore 95, 96, 133; Chapman 66, 67.)

Professor G. La Piana[1] argues that Victor's pontificate was a
struggle for full control over the different Christian congregations in
Rome. He was resisted by an Asiatic congregation led by the presbyter
Blastus, whose different paschal custom had been tolerated by Victor's
predecessors. Victor, by excommunicating these Asiatics, became
embroiled with the episcopate of Asia and sympathizers. By enlisting
against them the support of bishops of the other paschal tradition he
turned the controversy into one regarding authority in the universal
Church. Dr N. Zernov,[2] accepting this account of the facts, argues
that Eusebius has given an anachronistic interpretation of them,
owing to his interest in the paschal controversy of the fourth century.
We shall therefore be wise first to study the second century documents
quoted, separately and on their own merits. From these we glean little
about papal authority. We learn that a Roman council desired or
demanded [3] of the bishop of Ephesus that he should summon a provincial council in the province of Asia (24 § 8), and that an earlier
bishop of Rome was unable to persuade Polycarp to alter his "obnoxious" customs (24 §§ 14, 16). Then from the comments of Eusebius
we at least learn what a Palestinian bishop, in the time of Pope
Miltiades,[4] thought might have been the relationship between the
bishop of Rome and other bishops.

Eusebius' opinion seems to be that Victor's council wrote a threatening (24 § 7) letter to the bishop of Ephesus, desiring or demanding
him to call together the local bishops to consider the Easter question.
This provincial synod, relying on an apostolic tradition, refused to
come into line with the rest of the Church. Whereupon Victor did
two things: he tried to excommunicate the Asiatics from the Catholic
Church, and he declared that they were excommunicate (24 § 9).
This has been said to mean that he cut them off from the Roman
church, but that his attempt to cut them off from the common union

[1] *Harvard Theol. Review*, July 1925, pp. 213–221, 233–235.
[2] *Church Quarterly Review*, April 1933, pp. 24–41.
[3] Liddell and Scott give this as a possible meaning of ἀξιόω.
[4] See below, p. 84 ff.

failed. Irenaeus and some other bishops disapproved of his action (24 § 10). They exhorted, censured, counselled, entreated, and negotiated (24 §§ 10, 11, 18) with him to be more peaceable, Irenaeus appealing to the tolerance of earlier bishops of Rome. No one says that Victor's action was *ultra vires*.[1] Harnack thought that the bishop of Rome must have been recognized "as the special guardian of the common unity".[2]

[1] Rivington, 43.   [2] *History of Dogma*, E.T., 2. 161.

CHAPTER IV

TERTULLIAN

TERTULLIAN, the son of a centurion, was born in Carthage about A.D. 155. He was well educated and became an advocate in Rome. At about the age of forty he was baptized and ordained priest, and he wrote with ability in defence of the faith, being concerned in refuting Gnostic heresies. Like Irenaeus he believed that "the faith . . . was once for all delivered unto the saints",[1] and so he had no use for the idea of a secret tradition by which the Gnostics were working havoc among the weaker Christians. In quoting § 3 of the next Document, Gore[2] asks why the situation was not put right by a "papal voice" or "infallible teacher" at the centre of Christendom. The Document shows what Tertullian believed to be the genuine tests of truth.

DOCUMENT 12———Tertullian, *De Praescriptione.*   A.D. 200.
   (*P.L.* 2. 14; *L.F.* 10. 436 ‡.)

2.   . Heresies derive their strength from the infirmities of certain men; they have no vigour if they attack a good strong faith.

3. These weaker vessels are also built up into ruin by the victims of heresy. *How is it that this or that man, the most faithful, the most prudent, the most practised in the Church has gone over to that side?* Who, so speaking, does not reply to himself, that those whom heresies have been able to change should be reckoned neither prudent nor faithful nor experienced?

20. .   These large and numerous churches are but the one primitive and apostolic Church, from which they all derive. Thus all are primitive and apostolic, whilst all are one. The salutation of peace,[3] the fact that it is called a brotherhood, and the bond of guest friendship[4] are all proofs of unity. The

---

[1] Jude 3.   [2] Gore, 51. See also p. 13 above.
[3] Probably *Pax vobiscum.*
[4] *contesseratio hospitalitatis.* Tertullian presumably invented the word *contesseratio*; but the text of this passage is doubtful. See also § 36.

principle underlying these three practices is none other than the uniform tradition, the holy mystery which is everywhere the same.

21. . And I will here point out that what they preached, namely what Christ revealed to them, can only be proved by the same churches which those apostles founded. . . Therefore it follows that every doctrine which agrees with these apostolic churches, the wombs and originals of the faith, must be considered true, as without doubt containing what the churches have received from the apostles, the apostles from Christ, Christ from God; and that every other doctrine must indeed be considered false, being contrary to the truth of the churches, and of the apostles, and of Christ, and of God.

22. . Was anything hidden from *Peter who was called the rock on which the Church would be built,* who received the keys of the kingdom of heaven, and the power of loosing and binding in heaven and on earth? *Was anything hidden from John,* the most beloved of the Lord, who leaned upon his breast, to whom only, the Lord foretold the treachery of Judas?

26. . . . The Lord spoke openly, without hint of any hidden mystery. He commanded that what they heard in darkness and in secret, they should preach in light and on the housetops.

Even if they spoke of certain things among those of their own household as it were, we cannot believe that they were such as would superimpose another rule of faith, diverse from and contrary to that which the catholics proclaimed in public.

30. Where then was Marcion, the Pontic ship-owner and zealous Stoic? Where Valentine the follower of Platonism? It is agreed that they lived not so long ago, in the reign of Antonine, and that they first believed in the doctrine of the Catholic Church, in the Roman church under the episcopate of the blessed Eleutherus, until by reason of their ever restless curiosity, with which they infected the brethren also, they were once and again expelled. . . . Apelles also is as far from being an ancient as Marcion his instructor and trainer; but deserting the continency of a Marcionite, and falling for a woman, he retired from the eyes of his most holy master to Alexandria. Thence years after he returned no better. . . .

31. From this digression, I come back to point out that truth belongs to an earlier date [1] and falsehood to a later date, [2] which is borne out by the parable in which the original good seed is imposed by the Lord, and afterwards the mixture of barren weed is imposed upon it by the hostile devil. [3]   On these grounds all later heresies will be refuted. . .

32. Besides, if any heresies dare to plant themselves in the apostolic age, that they may seem to have been handed down from the apostles, because they existed under the apostles, we can say: "Let them make known the originals of their churches; let them *unfold the roll of their bishops*, so running down in succession from the beginning, that *their first bishop had for his ordainer and predecessor some one of the apostles*, or of apostolic men who continued steadfast with the apostles." For in this way do the apostolic churches reckon their origin; as the church of Smyrna reports that Polycarp was placed by John; so that of the Romans, that Clement was ordained by Peter. Just so can the rest show the men they have, who, being appointed by the apostles to the episcopate, are transmitters of the apostolic seed. Let the heretics fabricate something of the kind, for after blasphemy what is illicit to them? But even if they fabricate they will make no headway, for their doctrine, when compared with the apostolic, will declare by diversity and contradiction that it had no apostle for its author, nor any apostolic man.   .   To this test then will they be challenged.

36. . . Run through *the apostolic churches in which the very seats of the apostles preside* over their own places, in which their own authentic writings are recited, sounding the voice and expressing the face of each one. Is Achaia near you? you have Corinth. If you are not far from Macedonia, you have Philippi and the Thessalonians. If you can travel into Asia, you have Ephesus. But if you are near Italy, you have Rome, where authority is at hand for us too. What a happy Church is that, *on which the apostles poured out their whole doctrine with their blood*; where Peter had a like passion with the Lord; where Paul was crowned with the death of John [the Baptist]; where the apostle John was plunged into boiling oil, and suffered nothing, and

[1] *principalitatem.*   [2] *posteritatem.*   [3] Matt. 13. 37, 39.

was banished to an island! Let us see what she has learnt, and taught, what personal bonds of friendship she has formed[1] with the African churches also. She acknowledges one God, the creator of the universe, and Christ Jesus from the Virgin Mary, Son of God the creator, and the resurrection of the flesh. She joins the law and the prophets with the evangelic and apostolic writings, and from them she drinks in the faith, which she seals with water, clothes with the Holy Ghost, feeds with the eucharist, exhorts to martyrdom, and so she receives no one who opposes these principles.

(Gore 40, 41, 45 note, 51, 94 note, 96; Chapman 37, 65, 71A.)

Tertullian's five tests of truth then are: widespread consent (§ 20), apostolic foundation (§§ 21, 36), antiquity (§ 31), episcopal succession from the apostles, and apostolic authorship (§ 32).

It is in the work of Tertullian and his contemporary, Clement of Alexandria, that we have the Church's earliest extant comments on the famous Petrine texts. See above, Doc. 12 § 22, and below, Doc. 18 § 21, and also:

DOCUMENT 13——Clement of Alexandria, *Quis Dives Salvetur?* A.D. 203.
(*P.G.* 9. 625.)

21. . When he heard these things, blessed Peter, the elect, the one picked out, the first of the disciples, for whom only and for himself the Saviour pays the tribute, quickly learnt and understood the saying. (Chapman 47A.)

DOCUMENT 14——Tertullian, *Scorpiace.* A.D. 208.
(*P.L.* 2. 142; *A.N.C.L.* 11. 403 †.)

10. .. No delay or inquest will meet Christians on the threshold.. For though you think that heaven is still shut up, remember that the Lord left the keys of it to Peter here, and *through him* to the Church, which keys everyone will carry with him, if he has been questioned and made confession [of faith]. (Chapman 50B.)

[1] *contesserarit.* See above, p. 20, n. 4.

Later Tertullian lapsed into Montanism, a heresy that had arisen in Phrygia in the second century. Montanists claimed to possess a free, pure religion of the Spirit, in contrast to the institutional religion of the Church. In about the year 172 they were condemned by the "faithful throughout Asia" meeting in synods.[1] Hoping to get recognition in Rome, they appealed to the martyrs who were in prison awaiting trial at Lyons and Vienne. These martyrs wrote to the church in Asia, A.D. 177, and also to Eleutherus, bishop of Rome, the latter letter being carried by Irenaeus.

DOCUMENT 15——Martyrs of Lyons, *To Eleutherus*. A.D. 177. In Eusebius, *H.E.*, Book 5. (*L.C.L.* 1. 442; L. & O. 149 †.)

Chapter 3.

4. . Just then for the first time the disciples of Montanus . . in the region of Phrygia were winning a wide reputation for prophecy. . And when a dissension arose about these said people, the brethren in Gaul once more submitted a pious and most orthodox judgement of their own on this matter also, issuing as well various letters of martyrs who had been perfected among them, letters that they penned, while still in bonds, to the brethren in Asia and Phrygia, and moreover to Eleutherus, who was then bishop of the Romans, negotiating[2] for the peace of the churches.

Chapter 4.

1. And the same martyrs too commended Irenaeus, already at that time a presbyter of the community at Lyons, to the said bishop of Rome, rendering abundant testimony to the man, as the following expressions show:

2. "Once more and always we pray that you may rejoice in God, father[3] Eleutherus. This letter we have charged our brother and companion Irenaeus to convey to you, and we beg you to receive him as zealous for the covenant of Christ."

(Chapman 66.)

[1] Eus. *H.E.* 5. 16 § 10.
[2] πρεσβεύοντες (plural: it is the martyrs who were negotiating).
[3] *pater*.

Eleutherus took no action in favour of the Montanists, and some twenty years later Proclus arrived in Rome to propagate the same heresy.

DOCUMENT 16——Gaius, *Dialogue with Proclus.*
In Eusebius, *H.E.* 6. 20. (*L.C.L.* 2. 64; L. & O. 194 †.)

3. There has reached us also a dialogue of Gaius, a very learned person, which was set a-going at Rome at the time of Zephyrinus with Proclus, the champion of the heresy of the Phrygians.

H.E. 2. 25. (*L.C.L.* 1. 180; L. & O. 60 †.)

6. . Gaius in fact when discussing in writing with Proclus speaks as follows .
7. "But I myself can point out the trophies of the apostles. For if you will go to the Vatican, or to the Ostian Way, you will find the trophies of those who founded this church." [1]

(Chapman 66A.)

Proclus, however, made some headway, and the Roman bishop was on the point of recognizing the Montanist movement, and of advising the Asiatics to do the same, and so reversing "the authoritative acts of his predecessors". However, another heretic, whom Tertullian calls Praxeas, arrived in Rome and caused the bishop to change his mind. Tertullian the Montanist was naturally annoyed.

DOCUMENT 17——Tertullian, *Adversus Praxean.* A.D. 213.
(Evans [2] 89; Evans [2] 130.)

1. . . . like Praxeas. For this person was the first to import to Rome out of Asia this kind of wrongheadedness For at that time the bishop of Rome was on the point of recognizing the prophecies of Montanus and Prisca and Maximilla, and as a result of that recognition was offering peace to the churches of Asia and Phrygia; but this man, by false assertions con-

[1] See p. 27 below.
[2] E. Evans, *Tertullian's Treatise against Praxeas*, London, 1948.

cerning the prophets themselves and their churches, and by insistence on the decisions of the bishop's predecessors, forced him both to recall the letters of peace already issued and to desist from his project of receiving the spiritual gifts. Thus Praxeas at Rome managed two pieces of the devil's business: he drove out prophecy and introduced heresy; he put to flight the Paraclete and crucified the Father.

(Chapman 66A note.)

The discipline of the Church was too lax for Tertullian the Montanist. His later treatise *On Modesty* is marked throughout by intense bitterness.

DOCUMENT 18——Tertullian, *De Pudicitia*. About A.D. 220.
   (*P.L.* 2. 980; *A.N.C.L.* 18. 57 ‡.)

1.   . It is the system of Christian modesty which is being shaken.   . . I hear that there has even been an edict set forth, and a peremptory one too. *The sovereign pontiff, that is the bishop of bishops*, pronounces: "I remit the crimes of adultery and fornication, to those who have done penance." O edict on which cannot be inscribed "Well done!"

13. .   . And to produce the aforesaid effect in a person, you make fine speeches with every possible allurement of pity in the roll of kind shepherd and blessed Pope.[1]

(Chapman 37B note, 67B.)

Most scholars whether Roman Catholic[2] or Anglican[3] suppose that the *De Pudicitia* is aimed at either Zephyrinus or Callistus, for we know that Hippolytus (Doc. 22 § 12) accused these bishops of laxity. This view finds some support from Jerome's remark 170 years later that Tertullian was driven into Montanism "by the envy and abuse of" the Roman clergy.[4] Notice also, for what it is worth, the expression *apostolice* in § 21 below. But Archbishop Benson[5] saw no reason why other bishops should not be accused of laxity as well as the Roman ones, and he believed that Tertullian was more likely to be attacking his own bishop, Agrippinus of Carthage; and this opinion is held by

---

[1] *benedictus Papa.*
[2] E.g. Tixeront, *History of Dogmas*, E.T., 1. 320.
[3] E.g. Fuller, in *D.C.B.*, 4. 859.   [4] Doc. 126 § 53.
[5] *Cyprian*, 30, 31.

many French scholars.[1] We saw in the Introduction[2] that the title *Papa* was used of at least two other bishops of Carthage. If, however, we accept the majority view, it follows that the papal edict had referred to the Roman primacy, and that it had made itself felt in Africa. The bishop, whoever he was, had evidently based his authority on our Lord's words to Peter in Matt. 16. 19; and the heretic goes on to assert that this authority died with Peter.

Doc. 18 continued. (*P.L.* 2. 1024; *A.N.C.L.* 18. 117 ‡.)

21. . Now then, apostolic sir,[3] show me samples of your prophetic gifts, and I will recognize their divine origin. Secondly, justify your claim to the power of remitting such sins. Now with reference to your decision, I ask: how do you come to usurp the prerogatives of the Church? If it is because the Lord said to Peter, "Upon this rock I will build my Church, to thee I have given the keys of the heavenly kingdom"; or "Whatsoever thou shalt bind or loose on earth, shall be bound or loosed in heaven"; do you for that reason presume to have diverted the power of binding and loosing to yourself, that is to every sister church of Petrine origin?[4] What a fellow you are, subverting and wholly changing the obvious intention of the Lord, who conferred this on Peter personally! He says, "on *thee* will I build my Church and I will give the keys to *thee*", not to the Church.

(Gore 83; Chapman 50.)

We must not close this chapter without some remark on the important words of Gaius quoted as part of Document 16: "But I myself can point out the trophies[5] of the apostles. For if you will go to the Vatican, or to the Ostian Way, you will find the trophies of those who founded this church." This famous statement of about A.D. 200 is the earliest literary source for the veneration of the graves of Peter and Paul at Rome. τρόπαια might mean tablets erected at the places of execution, but it was the opinion of a Protestant scholar, Professor Hans Lietzmann, that the context demands the meaning "graves".[6] Were these graves pointed out by Gaius genuine or fakes? After a

---

[1] See Lebreton and Zeiller, *The History of the Primitive Church*, E.T., 3. 580, n. 2 (1945) and 4. 995 (1948).
[2] Page xvii.
[3] *apostolice.*
[4] *id est ad omnem ecclesiam Petri propinquam.*
[5] τρόπαια.
[6] *Petrus und Paulus in Rom*, edit. 1927, p. 210.

study of the evidence of the ancient liturgies commonly reckoned to be Roman, and of the excavations under S. Peter's at Rome, and under the Basilica of S. Paul on the Ostian Way, Lietzmann concludes that one who was careless or a cheat would be likely to "find" the remains in the catacombs near those of other Christians, where Christian sentiment was dominant, where Christian worship was easy. The relics might have been "invented", lying side by side. The ancient and unanimous tradition, however, finds the graves of Peter and Paul widely separated, hard by well-used roads, each alone in the midst of heathen graves. The natural explanation is that the ancient sites are genuine.[1]

1 *Petrus und Paulus in Rom*, pp. 245–247.

CHAPTER V

VISITORS TO ROME

HISTORIANS and controversial writers alike refer to the large number of fathers and heretics who visited the Roman church between the years 140 and 220. On the visits of the heretics a Lutheran scholar, C. P. Caspari, a professor of theology in Norway, wrote: "Teachers and disciples, or at any rate the latter, flocked thither in order to make converts from within and without the Roman Christian community, after the manner of all sectarians, seeking their adherents chiefly among Christians, or in the existing churches. They also wanted to gain weight in the large, highly esteemed, and very influential congregation of the world capital, yes and perhaps in part even recognition, in order thereby to find entrance more easily elsewhere, and to be able to spread more effectively. The respect enjoyed by the church of Rome was to second them in their aspirations: she was, so to speak, to stamp them with the hall-mark of being truly Christian, ecclesiastically respectable, and orthodox. During their stay, which was often fairly long, and sometimes very long, they would cause unrest in the congregation, would lead members astray, some more some less; and more than once they approached the leaders and clergy, not always without success."[1]

The following is a list of these visitors, many of whom are noted in our Documents. They are approximately in chronological order.

Cerdon from Syria	Docs. 8, 9.
Valentine from Egypt	Doc. 9, 12 § 30.
Justin Martyr from Palestine	Eus. *H.E.* 4. 11 § 11.
Euelpistus and Hierax, slaves from Cappadocia and Iconium	*Acta Justini* § 3 (*P.G.* 6. 1569).
Tatian	Tatian, *Oratio ad Graecos* § 35 (*P.G.* 6. 877).
Marcion from Pontus	Docs. 8, 9, 12 § 30.
Marcellina	Doc. 8.
Hegesippus from Jerusalem	Doc. 7.
Abercius, bishop of Hierapolis	Doc. 19.
Irenaeus from Lyons	Doc. 15.

[1] *Quellen zur Geschichte des Taufsymbols*, Vol. III, p. 309, A.D. 1875.

29

Rhodo from Asia	Eus. *H.E.* 5. 13 § 1.
Florinus from Lower Asia	Doc. 20.
Blastus from Greece	Doc. 20.
Theodotus from Byzantium	Doc. 21.
Proclus from Phrygia	Doc. 16.
Praxeas from Asia	Doc. 17
Noetus, Epigonus, and Cleomenes from Smyrna	Doc. 22 § 7.
Origen from Egypt	Doc. 34.
Sabellius from Africa	Doc. 22 § 12.
Alcibiades from Syria	Doc. 22 § 13.

DOCUMENT 19——Epitaph of Abercius of Hierapolis. About A.D. 180.

In *Vita S. Abercii* 77. (Nissen[1] 121.)

77. I, the freeman of an elect city, made this when living, that I might have in due time a place here for my body. My name is Abercius and I am the disciple of the holy shepherd, who feeds flocks of sheep upon the hills and plains, who has great eyes looking everywhere, for this man taught me faithful scriptures. He sent me to royal Rome to consider and to behold the queen with garment and sandals of gold; there I beheld a people having a shining seal. And I saw the plain of Syria and all towns including Nisibis, crossing over Euphrates. Everywhere I had companions with Paul. . Standing by, I Abercius ordered these things to be written here, I truly being in my seventy-second year. Let everyone who is like-minded pray for Abercius when he thinks on this. Let not any man place another above my tomb; whoever does so shall pay to the treasury of the Romans two thousand gold pieces and a thousand gold pieces to my worthy fatherland Hierapolis.

Lightfoot[2] thought that the queen with golden sandals was the Roman church; and Lawlor and Oulton[3] suppose that the visit of Abercius to Rome was to uphold the catholic cause against Montanism. (See Doc. 15.)

[1] T. Nissen, *S. Abercii Vita*, Leipzig, 1912. (See W. Lüdtke and T. Nissen, *Abercii Titulus Sepulcralis*, Leipzig, 1910.)
[2] *Apostolic Fathers*, Part II, Vol. I, p. 482.
[3] *Eusebius: Ecclesiastical History*, 2. 172.

DOCUMENT 20———Eusebius, *H.E.* 5. 15.
   (*L.C.L.* 1. 470; L. & O. 158 †.)

But others flourished at Rome, led by Florinus, who had fallen from the presbyterate of the Church, and, with him, Blastus, who had suffered a similar fall. These drew away more of the Church and enticed them to their opinion, each trying to innovate upon the truth in his own way.

(Chapman 65B.)

DOCUMENT 21.   *The Little Labyrinth.*[1]   About A.D. 211.
   In Eus. *H.E.* 5. 28.   (*L.C.L.* 1. 516; L. & O. 172.)

3. For they say that all the men of former days, and the apostles themselves, received and taught the things which these men now say and that the truth of the preaching was preserved until the times of Victor, who was the thirteenth bishop of Rome from Peter; but that the truth was falsified from the days of his successor, Zephyrinus.

6. . . . And how are they not ashamed to ascribe these things falsely to Victor, when they certainly know that Victor excommunicated Theodotus the cobbler, the prime mover and father of this God-denying apostasy, when he was the first to say that Christ was a mere man? For if Victor was of their way of thinking, as their slander affirms, how could he have cast out Theodotus, the inventor of this heresy?

8. For example, I shall remind many of the brethren of an event which took place in our day, the which, if it had been done in Sodom, would, in my opinion, have perchance admonished even that people. There was a certain confessor named Natalius, who lived not long ago, but in our own time.

9. Once upon a time this man was deceived by Asclepiodotus and another Theodotus, a banker. Both these last were pupils of Theodotus the cobbler, who was the first to be excommunicated by Victor, as I said, the then bishop, on account of this sentiment or, rather, senselessness.

10. So Natalius was persuaded by them to take the title of

[1] For title, date, and author see R. H. Connolly in *J.T.S.*, Jan. 1948, pp. 73–79. He assigns it to Hippolytus.

bishop of this heresy at a salary, and to be paid by them one hundred and fifty denarii a month.

11. When, therefore, he became one of them, he was frequently admonished by the Lord in visions. For our compassionate God and Lord, Jesus Christ, did not wish that a witness to his own sufferings should perish outside the Church.

12. But when he paid less regard to the visions, being ensnared by having the first place among them, and by the greed of filthy lucre which destroys many, he was finally scourged by the holy angels, and suffered no light punishment the whole night long; insomuch that he arose at dawn, put on sackcloth, covered himself with ashes, and with all haste prostrated himself in tears before Zephyrinus, the bishop; and, rolling at the feet not only of the clergy but also of the laity, he moved with his tears the compassionate Church of the merciful Christ. And though he used much entreaty and showed the weals of the stripes he had received, scarcely was he taken back into communion.   (Chapman 65B.)

CHAPTER VI

TWO ANTI-POPES
HIPPOLYTUS AND NOVATIAN

I. HIPPOLYTUS

OUR next Document comes from a work discovered in 1851. The author is now recognized to be Hippolytus, a bishop, a pupil of Irenaeus, and the most learned member of the Roman church of his day. Our interest lies in the writer's condemnation of Zephyrinus and Callistus, who were bishops of Rome during his time. There is a good edition of the Greek text published by Paul Wendland.[1]

DOCUMENT 22——Hippolytus, *Philosophumena*, Book 9.   About
    A.D. 235.
    (Wendland 240; Legge[2] 2. 118 †.)

7. . . . A certain man named Epigonus became the minister and disciple of Noetus, and while he was living in Rome broadcast the godless doctrine. Cleomenes, who was alien to the Church in life and manners, confirmed his teaching when he had become his disciple. At that time Zephyrinus, an ignorant and greedy man, *thought* that he ruled the church, and, persuaded by the gain offered, gave leave to those coming to him to learn from Cleomenes. He himself also was in time beguiled and ran into the same errors; his fellow-counsellor and comrade in this wickedness was Callistus, whose life and the heresy by him invented I shall shortly set forth. The school of these successive [teachers] continued to grow stronger, and increased through the help given to it by Zephyrinus and Callistus. Yet *we never yielded*, but many times withstood them to the face, refuted them, and compelled them perforce to confess the truth.

[1] In *Die Griechischen Christlichen Schriftsteller der Ersten Drei Jahrhunderte*, Leipzig, 1916.
[2] F. Legge, *Hippolytus: Philosophumena* (London, 1921), a translation of the text of R. Cruice (Paris, 1860).

33

They, being ashamed for a season, and being brought by the truth to confess it, before long returned to wallowing in the same mire.

(Wendland 248; Legge 2. 128 †.)

12.   Victor sends Callistus to abide in Antium, making him a certain monthly allowance for his support. After [Victor's] falling asleep, Zephyrinus, having had [Callistus] as a coadjutor in the management of the clergy, honoured him to his own detriment, and, sending for him from Antium, set him over the cemetery. And Callistus, being ever with [Zephyrinus] and, as I have said before, serving him with hypocrisy, put him in the background as able neither to judge what was said to him nor to comprehend the counsel of Callistus when talking to him of those things that pleased him. So, after the death of Zephyrinus, [Callistus], thinking that he had succeeded in his pursuit, *put away Sabellius* as one who did not hold right opinions. For [Callistus] *was afraid of me,* and deemed that he could thus wipe off the charge against him before the churches, just as if he held no different opinions from theirs. Now Callistus was a sorcerer and a trickster and in time snatched many away; and harbouring the poison in his heart, he devised nothing straight, and was ashamed to declare the truth because he had reproached us in public.

Notice how the author, whilst doing all he can to implicate Callistus in the Sabellian heresy, is nevertheless obliged to declare it was he, Callistus, who pronounced the condemnation.

Doc. 22 continued.   (Wendland 249; Legge 2. 130 †.)

The sorcerer, having dared such things, set up *a school against that of the Church,* thus to teach. And first he contrived to make concessions to men in respect of their pleasures, telling everyone that their sins were remitted by himself. For if anyone should transgress who has been received by another and calls himself a Christian, he says that his transgression will not be reckoned against him if he hastens to the school of Callistus. And many were pleased at this idea, for they had been stricken with conscience and also cast out for many heresies. And some even, after they had been *cast out of the Church by our judgement*, joined with these last and filled the school of Callistus. He laid it down that if even a bishop commits any sin, though it should be one unto death, he ought not to be deposed. In his time bishops and priests and deacons who had married twice and even three times began to keep their places among the clergy. For if anyone who was in the clerical order should marry, he decided that he should remain in the order as if he had not sinned. .. His hearers, being attracted by these doctrines, continue, and delude themselves and many others, crowds of whom flock *into the school*. And thus they are multiplied and rejoice in the crowds, by reason of the pleasures which Christ did not permit. Thinking slightly of him, they forbid no one to sin, affirming that they themselves remit sins to those with whom they are well pleased.

The author goes on to accuse Callistus of permitting well-born women to commit fornication. As a result of this, he says, such women began to attempt abortions; and he continues:

Doc. 22 continued.   (Wendland 250; Legge 2. 131 †.)

See now what impiety the lawless one has reached, when he teaches adultery and murder at the same time! And in the face of these audacities the shameless ones attempt to call themselves a catholic church, and some think they do well to join with them. Under this [Callistus too], a second baptism has been ventured upon by them for the first time. These things the most amazing Callistus has set on foot, whose school still persists and preserves the customs and tradition, not discerning with whom it should communicate, but offering communion indiscriminately to all. From him also they are called by a name that they share with him, and because the protagonist of such works is Callistus, they are called Callistians.

13. *When the teaching of this* [Callistus] *had been dispersed over the whole world*, a certain man called Alcibiades, dwelling at Apamea in Syria, who was crafty and full of impudence, and, having looked into the matter, deemed himself more forcible

and expert in tricks than Callistus, *arrived in Rome* bringing with him a book. He pretended that Elchasai, a righteous man, had received it from the Seres of Parthia and gave it to one called Sobiae, as having been revealed by an angel, whose height was 24 schoeni, which is 96 miles.

(Gore 98, 99; Chapman 66A, 67B note.)

DOCUMENT 23——Hippolytus, *Philosophumena*, Book 10. About A.D. 235.
(Wendland 283; Legge 2. 168 ‡.)

27.   . Callistus, whose life we have set forth faithfully, confirmed the heresy of these people [Noetus, Epigonus, and Cleomenes]. Taking his start from them, he also gave birth to a heresy himself.

Anglicans, led by Canon C. Wordsworth in 1853,[1] were quick to seize on this work to show how some early bishops of Rome were regarded by a contemporary. Gore points out how Hippolytus calls Callistus a leader of heresy, and thinks no more of it than if he were abusing any bishop. How can papal infallibility be claimed as a third-century doctrine?

These remarks lose their force when it is seen that the author recognized neither Zephyrinus nor Callistus as lawful bishops. According to him Zephyrinus imagined he was bishop of Rome (9 § 7), and Callistus wanted to be, and supposed that he had got what he wanted, but was really the leader of a lax school which received those whom the author had excommunicated (9 § 12). In fact the author reckoned himself to be the true bishop. This view was advanced by Döllinger[2] in 1853 and is now widely accepted.[3]

This serious schism in the Roman church appears to have had no effect outside Rome. We learn from the Filocalian Catalogue (A.D. 354) that the successor of Callistus, "Pontian the bishop and Hippolytus the presbyter were deported as exiles to the noxious island of Sardinia" in A.D. 235, and that Pontian resigned his see in September that year.[4] Pontian and Hippolytus were both buried at Rome on 13 August, the latter on the Tiburtine Way.[5] About 140 years later Pope Damasus put an inscription on the tomb of Hippolytus describing him as a Novatianist, and telling how he had heard that just before his martyrdom he had told those who asked him that

[1] *St Hippolytus and the Church of Rome*, 1853; 2nd edit., 1880.
[2] *Hippolytus and Callistus*, E.T., 301 ff.
[3] Cf. Jalland, *Papacy*, 552, but see also Prestige, *Fathers and Heretics*, 49.
[4] *P.L.* 13. 450.   [5] *P.L.* 13. 465.

they "all should follow the catholic faith".[1] About the year 400 Prudentius copied out this inscription and improved on it.[2] Hippolytus is commemorated as a saint on 22 August by the R.C. church.

II. NOVATIAN

With the next anti-pope, about twenty years later, it is a different story. After the martyrdom of Fabian, on 20 January 250, the Roman see was vacant for over a year, during which time Novatian was leader of the Roman clergy.[3] According to Pacian,[4] a fourth-century Spanish bishop, the real instigator of the Novatianist schism in Rome was a depraved African presbyter called Novatus. He is mentioned by Cyprian in our Doc. 26 and elsewhere. But when Eusebius in Doc. 30 speaks of Novatus, he means, not the African of that name, but the anti-pope himself whom Cyprian and others call Novatian. Our next Document was penned by this Novatian[3] writing in the name of the Roman clergy to Cyprian, bishop of Carthage. The subject of the letter was how to deal with those who had lapsed during the persecution under the emperor Decius.

DOCUMENT 24——Novatian, *Ad Cyprianum.* A.D. 250.
    In Cyprian,[5] *Ep.* 30. (*C.S.E.L.* 3. 550.)

To Pope Cyprian, the Presbyters and Deacons abiding at Rome greeting.

2. . . . The apostle would not have given us such praise, saying "your faith is spoken of throughout the world", *unless the aforesaid discipline had derived its roots of faith even from that early date,* from which praise and glory it would be a very great crime to have degenerated.

5.   On us, however, there lies a further need for delay, in that, since the death of Fabian of most honoured memory, on account of the difficulties of circumstances and times, we have no bishop yet appointed who should settle all these matters, and who might, with authority and counsel, take account of those who have lapsed. However, in so important a

---

[1] C. Kirch, S. J., *Enchiridion,* Friburg, 1910, p. 339.
[2] *Peristephanon,* Hymn 11 (*P.L.* 60. 535).
[3] See Doc. 28 § 5.   [4] *Ep.* 3. 6 (*P.L.* 13. 1067).
[5] For all Cyprian's works I have made use of *L.F.* and *A.N.C.L.* in compiling my own translation.

matter, we agree with you that the peace of the Church must be awaited, and then, in a full conference of bishops, presbyters, deacons, and confessors, with the laity also who have stood fast, account be taken of the lapsed. For it seems to us invidious and oppressive to examine without the advice of many what many have committed, and for one to pass sentence, when so great a crime is known to have spread itself among great numbers; neither indeed can a decree be established which does not appear to have the consent of numbers.   (Chapman 71B.)

In March 251 Cornelius was elected bishop of Rome and consecrated by sixteen bishops,[1] but Novatian allowed himself to be consecrated as his rival.

DOCUMENT 25——Cyprian, *Ep.* 69.   A.D. 254.
   (*C.S.E.L.* 3. 757.)

8.   These [Novatianists] now rend the Church, and rebel against the peace and unity of Christ, and attempt to set up a chair for themselves and to assume the primacy, and to claim the right of baptizing and offering.
(Chapman 55B.)

The context shows that the primacy here means the bishopric. Like Hippolytus, Novatian became the leader of a party of rigorists, but unlike Hippolytus he made things worse by baptizing again all who came over to his side.[2] The effect of this was to harden his school into a definite schism. This schism began in Rome, but the danger of it was quickly felt in Africa, and Cyprian, bishop of Carthage, wrote to Cornelius recognizing him as the true bishop.

DOCUMENT 26——Cyprian, *Ep.* 47.   A.D. 251.
   (*C.S.E.L.* 3. 605.)

Cyprian to Cornelius his brother, greeting.

I have thought it both obligatory on me and needful for you, dearest brother, to write a short letter to the confessors who are with you, and who, seduced by the obstinacy and depravity of Novatian and Novatus, have withdrawn from the Church;

[1] Doc. 28 § 24.   [2] Cyprian, *Ep.* 73. 2.

in which letter I would prevail with them, from mutual affection, to return to their mother, that is, to the Catholic Church.

(Chapman 24A.)

Cyprian then sent to Rome to investigate the schism, and to ascertain on the spot who was the properly constituted bishop. The messengers brought back their report that the true bishop of Rome was Cornelius, and Cyprian urged all the bishops of his province to support him.

DOCUMENT 27——Cyprian, *Ep.* 48. A.D. 251.
(*C.S.E.L.* 3. 607.)

Cyprian to Cornelius his brother, greeting.

3. However, certain people sometimes disturb the minds and souls of men by their reports, representing things falsely. To be sure, we furnish all who sail hence with a rule [of faith], lest in sailing they meet with temptation,[1] and we well know that we have exhorted them to acknowledge and hold to the womb and root of the Catholic Church. Our province is somewhat scattered, for it includes Numidia and Mauritania, and the fact of a schism in the city might perplex and unsettle the minds of those absent. Accordingly with the aid of those bishops we ascertained the exact truth and got better authority for the proof of your ordination. Then at length, all scruples being removed from the minds of everyone, we decided to send, and are sending, a letter to you from all throughout the province; so that all our colleagues might give their decided approval and support to you and your communion, that is,[2] to both the unity and the charity of the Catholic Church.

(Gore 199; Chapman 56B, 116A.)

We see from the above two letters, and from the opening words of the next Document, that to uphold and communicate with Cornelius and to reject his rival was to be loyal to the Catholic Church. Puller[3] asserts and Chapman[4] denies that these words could have been written about the legitimate bishop of any see.

[1] Presumably, lest they be beguiled by schismatics on landing.
[2] The words "that is" are absent from some MSS.
[3] Page 85, n. 5.   [4] Page 24A.

Novatian had shaken the confidence of an African bishop called Antonian, to whom Cyprian wrote fully on the subject of the schism.

DOCUMENT 28——Cyprian, *Ep.* 55.   A.D. 252.
     (*C.S.E.L.* 3. 624.)

Cyprian to Antonian, his brother, greeting.

1. I received your first letter, dearest brother, which firmly stood by the unity of the priestly college, and agreed with the Catholic Church. In your letter you pointed out that you did not communicate with Novatian, but followed our advice, and agreed with Cornelius, our fellow bishop. You wrote, also, that I should forward a copy of the same letter to our colleague Cornelius, that, so laying aside all anxiety, he might at once know that you held communion with him, that is, with the Catholic Church.

2. . There arrived, however, afterwards your other letter, sent by Quintus, our fellow presbyter, in which I perceive that your mind, influenced by a letter of Novatian, has begun to waver.

5. I wrote fully to Rome to the clergy, then still acting without a bishop. . That I wrote this you may learn from their answer;[1] for they wrote as follows: "However, in so important a matter, we agree with you that the peace of the Church must be awaited, and then, in a full conference of bishops, presbyters, deacons, and confessors, with the laity also who have stood fast, account be taken of the lapsed." It was added also (Novatian then writing) .. that peace should be granted to the lapsed who were sick and at the point of death. *Which letter was sent throughout the whole world* and made known to all the churches and all the brethren.

6. However, in accordance with a previous decision, when the persecution was lulled and opportunity given for meeting together, a large number of bishops assembled. These had been preserved safe and sound by their own faith and the care of the Lord. And, Holy Scripture being cited on both sides, we balanced our resolution [about the lapsed] with healthy

---

[1] Doc. 24.

moderation. . And *lest the number of bishops in Africa should seem insufficient,* we wrote to Rome also on this subject to our colleague Cornelius, who himself likewise, in a council held with very many fellow bishops, agreed in the same opinion with us.

8. I come now, dearest brother, to the character of Cornelius, our colleague, that you with us may know him more truly, not from the lies of envious and disparaging men, but from the judgement of God who made him a bishop and from the witness of fellow bishops, the whole company of whom, throughout the entire world, have consented with unanimity. . . He too was made bishop . when *the place of Fabian, that is, when the place of Peter,*[1] and the rank of the priestly chair were vacant. This chair being occupied by God's will, and ratified by the consent of all of us, whoever now wishes to be made bishop . . . whoever he be, although greatly boasting of himself and claiming very much for himself, is profane, an alien and without the pale. And as after the first there cannot be a second, whoever is made after one who ought to be alone is no longer second, but none at all.

9. He [Cornelius] sat fearless at Rome in the priestly chair, at that time when a tyrant, hostile to God's priests, was threatening whatever can or cannot be uttered: one who would with much more patience and endurance hear that a rival prince was raised against himself than that a priest of God was established at Rome. .

24. . . When a bishop has been made in the Church by sixteen fellow bishops, Novatian tries by intrigue to be made an adulterous and strange bishop by deserters;[2] and whereas there is one Church from Christ throughout the whole world divided into many members, and *one episcopate, diffused through a harmonious multitude of many bishops,* he, in spite of the tradition of God and the unity of the Catholic Church everywhere compacted and joined together, attempts to make a human church, and *sends his new apostles through very many cities,* that he may establish certain recent foundations of his own institution. And although there have already been ordained, through all

---

[1] Cf. Optatus 1 § 10 (Doc. 83).
[2] See Eus., *H.E.* 6. 43 § 8.

provinces and through every city, bishops, in age venerable, in faith sound, in trials proved, in persecution banished, he dares to create other false bishops over them, as if he could wander over the whole world with the obstinacy of his new attempt.   (Chapman 55B, 56B.)

Points to notice in the above letter are: that important decisions of the Roman church about the lapsed were broadcast to all the faithful everywhere (§ 5), that according to Cyprian authority was in the hands of the multitude of bishops (§§ 6, 24), and that the anti-pope claimed something like universal jurisdiction (§ 24). To him the bishop of Alexandria wrote a letter of protest.

DOCUMENT 29——Dionysius of Alexandria, *To Novatian.*
      A.D. 252.
   In Eusebius, *H.E.* 6. 45.   (*L.C.L.* 2. 126; L. & O. 214 †.)

Dionysius to Novatian, a brother, greeting.

If you were led on unwillingly, as you say, you will prove it by retiring willingly. For *a man ought to suffer anything and everything, rather than divide the Church of God,* and it is no less glorious to incur martyrdom to avoid schism than to avoid idolatry; in fact in my opinion it is more so. For in the one case a man is a martyr for the sake of his own single soul, but in the other for the sake of the whole Church.

                                   (Gore 128.)

Our next document shows that Novatian's attempt to make his schism universal was not without effect.

DOCUMENT 30——Dionysius of Alexandria, *To Stephen, Bishop of Rome.*   About A.D. 256.
   In Eusebius, *H.E.* 7. 4, 5.   (*L.C.L.* 2. 138; L. & O. 220 †.)

4. Dionysius, therefore, having communicated with him on this point at very great length in a letter, at its close shows that with the abatement of the persecution the churches everywhere, rejecting the innovation of Novatus, had resumed peace among themselves. He writes thus:

5. "But know now, brother, that all the churches in the

East, and still further away, which were formerly divided have been united, and all their presidents everywhere are of like mind, rejoicing above measure at the unexpected arrival of peace: Demetrian at Antioch, Theoctistus at Caesarea, Maza banes at Aelia, Marinus at Tyre (Alexander having fallen asleep), Heliodorus at Laodicea (for Thelymidres has entered into his rest), Helenus at Tarsus and all the churches of Cilicia, Firmilian and all Cappadocia. For I name only the more eminent bishops to avoid making my letter long and my discourse tedious. Nevertheless the Syrias as a whole and Arabia, which you constantly help and to which you have now written, and Mesopotamia and Pontus and Bithynia, and, in a word, all everywhere rejoice exceedingly in their concord and brotherly love, giving glory to God." (Chapman 57A, 63B.)

Chapman[1] supposes that the Novatianist schism became thus wide-spread because it originated in the see of Rome.

[1] Pages 57A, 99A.

CHAPTER VII

ORIGEN

DURING the period of the two anti-popes of the last chapter, there lived in Egypt and Palestine one of the most notable Christians of the third century. Origen was the eldest of seven sons of Christian parents. His father was killed in a persecution[1] in A.D. 202, and the family was left poor. The next year, when not quite eighteen, Origen was appointed by bishop Demetrius to be head of the catechetical school at Alexandria.[2] The next two bishops, Heraclas and Dionysius, were both his pupils. In about the year 231 he migrated to Caesarea in Palestine, where he lived till his death in 253. He was a prolific writer, and in our discussion he is called as a witness by Pope Leo XIII as well as by Chapman and Gore.

Newman wrote in 1845 that "it is a less difficulty that the papal supremacy was not formally acknowledged in the second century, than that there was no formal acknowledgement of the doctrine of the Holy Trinity till the fourth. No doctrine is defined until it is violated."[3] Our Document 21 shows that the doctrine of the Trinity was violated by Theodotus the cobbler when Origen was a boy. In the next Document we see the same doctrine clearly set out and claimed as apostolic.

DOCUMENT 31——Origen, *De Principiis*, Book 1, Pref. A.D. 230.
  (*P.G.* 11. 116; Butterworth[4] 2 ‡.)

2.   The teaching of the Church, handed down in unbroken succession from the apostles, is still preserved and continues to exist in the churches up to the present day. .

4. The particular points clearly delivered in the teaching of the apostles are as follows:

First, that God is one, who created and arranged all things, and who, when nothing existed, caused the universe to be. He is God from the first creation and foundation of the world, the God of all just men, of Adam, Abel . . . Moses and the pro-

---

[1] Eus., *H.E.* 6. 1.   [2] Ibid., 6. 3 § 3.
[3] *Development of Christian Doctrine*, 167.
[4] G. W. Butterworth, *Origen on First Principles*, London, 1936.

.phets. This God, in the last days, as he announced beforehand
by his prophets, sent the Lord Jesus Christ, first to call Israel,
and secondly, after the unbelief of the people of Israel, to call
the Gentiles also. This just and good God, the Father of our
Lord Jesus Christ, himself gave the law, the prophets, and the
gospels, and he is God both of the apostles and also of the Old
and New Testaments.

Secondly, Jesus Christ, he who came to earth, was begotten
of the Father before every creature. And after he had ministered
to the Father in the foundation of all things, for "through him
all things were made", in these last times he emptied himself
and was made man, and was incarnate although God; and
while made man remained the God that he was. He assumed
a body like our body, differing in this alone, that it was born
of a virgin and of the Holy Ghost. And this Jesus Christ was
born and suffered in truth and not merely in appearance, and
truly died our common death. Moreover he truly rose from
the dead, and after his resurrection he conversed with his
disciples and was taken up.

Thirdly, the apostles related that the Holy Ghost is united
in honour and dignity with the Father and the Son.

(Gore 45, 46.)

The above Document is an example of what Gore calls "the
summary of the catholic tradition" or "historical Christianity", to
which the Church of England makes her appeal. In the next Document we see the same writer's exposition of Matt. 16. 16–19, the chief
of the famous Petrine texts on which the R.C. doctrine of papal
jurisdiction is based.

DOCUMENT 32——Origen, *Commentary on Matthew*, Book 12.
    A.D. 247.
    (*P.G.* 13. 997; *A.N.C.L.* 456A ‡.)

10.   . . And if we too have said like Peter, "Thou art the
Christ, the Son of the living God", not as if flesh and blood
had revealed it to us, but because light from the Father in
heaven had shone in our hearts, we become a Peter, and to us
also he who was the Word might say, "Thou art Peter and

upon this rock I will build my Church". For every imitator of
Christ is a rock, of Christ, that is, who is the spiritual rock that
followed them[1] that drank of him. And upon every such rock
is built every word of the Church, and the whole order of life
based thereon; for whosoever is perfect, having the sum of
words and deeds and thoughts which fill up the state of
blessedness, in him is the Church that God is building.

11. But if you suppose that God builds the entire Church
upon Peter and on him alone, what would you say about John,
the son of thunder, or any particular apostle? In other words,
are we to be so bold as to say that it is against Peter in particular
that the gates of Hades shall not prevail, but that they shall
prevail against the other apostles and the perfect? Does not
the above saying "The gates of Hades shall not prevail against
it" hold in regard to all, and in the case of each of them? And
likewise with regard to the words "Upon this rock I will build
my Church"? Are the keys of the kingdom of heaven given by
the Lord to Peter only, and will no other of the blessed receive
them? But if this promise, "I will give unto thee the keys of
the kingdom of heaven", applies likewise to the others, how
shall not all the things previously mentioned, and also the
following sayings spoken to Peter, apply likewise to them? For
in the passage before us, the words "Whatsoever thou shalt
bind on earth shall be bound in heaven" and what follows do
appear to be addressed to Peter individually; but in the Gospel
of John, the Saviour, having given the Holy Spirit to the
disciples by breathing on them, says "Receive ye the Holy
Ghost" and what follows.[2] For all the imitators of Christ are
surnamed "rocks" from him, the spiritual rock which follows
those who are being saved;   but from the very fact that
they are members of Christ, they are called Christians by
a name derived from him. And those called after the rock are
called Peter, and taking our line from these, you will say that
the righteous are named after the righteousness of Christ, and
the wise after the wisdom of Christ. And so in regard to all
Christ's other names, you will apply them as surnames to the
saints; and the Saviour's words "Thou art Peter" and so on

[1] 1 Cor. 10. 4.   [2] Cp. Cyprian four years later: Doc. 37 § 4.

down to the words "prevail against it" might be addressed to all such persons. But [1] what is the "it"? Is it the rock upon which Christ builds the Church, or is it the Church? For the phrase is ambiguous. This I think to be the correct answer: the gates of Hades will not prevail either against the rock on which Christ builds the Church, or against the Church; [1] just as "the way of a serpent upon a rock",[2] according to the passage in Proverbs, cannot be found. Now if the gates of Hades prevail against anyone, he cannot be a rock on which Christ builds the Church, nor can he be the Church built by Christ upon the rock. For the rock is inaccesible to the serpent, and it is stronger than the gates of Hades which are opposing it, so that because of its strength the gates of Hades do not prevail against it. But the Church, as a building of Christ, who built his own house wisely upon the rock,[3] makes the gates of Hades irrelevant. These gates do prevail against every man who is outside the rock and the Church, but against the Church they have no power.

(Gore 86, 87, 199; Chapman 57B note, 115B.)

Pope Leo XIII, in common with reputable Anglican scholars,[4] considered that our Lord meant by the rock the apostle Peter. He also supposed that our Lord's words "the gates of hades shall not prevail against it" proclaim and establish the universal jurisdiction of Peter.[5] Origen gives no support to either of these doctrines, except that, by disputing the former one, he implies that someone had suggested it. § 11 cannot be used to deny the authority of Peter over the other apostles, unless we are prepared to go further and to say he had no authority over any Christian.[6]

DOCUMENT 33——Origen, *Commentary on Matthew*, Book 13. A.D. 247.
  (*P.G.* 13. 1129; *A.N.C.L.* 482B ‡.)

14. . . . Jesus . . . sends Peter to drag up the fish into the net, in the mouth of which he said that a stater would be found which was to be given for himself and Peter. It seems to me, then, that they thought that this was *a very great honour*

[1] . . . [1] Quoted Leo XIII, *Satis Cognitum* § 12. [2] Prov. 30. 19.
[3] Matt. 7. 24. [4] E.g. H. L. Goudge in *New Commentary*, N.T., 168B.
[5] *Satis Cognitum* § 12. [6] Chapman, 57B, n. 4.

which had been bestowed on Peter by Jesus (judging him greater than the rest of his friends), and wished to verify what they suspected by asking Jesus and hearing from him whether, as they supposed, he had judged Peter the greatest of them. At the same time they hoped to learn why Peter had been preferred to the rest of the disciples.

31. And indeed if we were to attend carefully to the Gospels, we should also find, in relation to those things which seem to be common to Peter and those who have three times admonished the brethren, a great difference and a pre-eminence in the things said to Peter, compared with the second class. For it is no small difference that Peter received the keys *not of one heaven but of more*, and in order that whatsoever things he binds on the earth may be bound not in one heaven but in them all, as compared with the many who bind on earth and loose on earth, so that these things are bound and loosed not in the heavens, as in the case of Peter, but in one only; for *they do not reach so high a stage, with power as Peter to bind and loose in all the heavens*. The better, therefore, is the binder, so much more blessed is he who has so been loosed that in every part of the heavens his loosing has been accomplished.

(Gore 86, note 4; Chapman 46, 57B note.)

Here Origen definitely believes that Peter held some sort of primacy. His conclusion from the tribute money incident is reasonable, but though his ideas expressed in § 31 are unscriptural and absurd, they show that he is determined to establish a Petrine primacy somehow or other. But from his writings we learn that the doctrine of the Trinity was clearly expressed by the third century, whereas he shows no knowledge of the doctrine of papal jurisdiction derived from Peter. He tells us how he wanted to see the Roman church, and Eusebius says that he went to Rome.

DOCUMENT 34——Eusebius, *H.E.* 6. 14 § 10.
   (*L.C.L.* 2. 48; L. & O. 190.)

Now Adamantius (for this also was Origen's name), when Zephyrinus was at that time ruling the church of the Romans, himself states in writing somewhere that he stayed at Rome. His words are: "Desiring to see the most ancient church of the Romans".   (Chapman 67B.)

CHAPTER VIII

CYPRIAN

THASCIUS CYPRIANUS, a wealthy advocate of Carthage, was baptized in the year 246, being 47 years old. Two years later he was made bishop of Carthage, and during his ten years' episcopate he suffered under the Decian persecution of 250–251. He died a martyr's death under the Emperor Valerian on 14 September 258. He is an important witness in regard to Church government and Church unity. F. W. Puller confidently asserts that "The defenders of the English Church may safely stake their case, so far as it relates to the papal claims, on the witness born by Cyprian".[1]

I. THE PRIMACY OF PETER

Cyprian is clearer than Origen[2] about the meaning of our Lord's words to Peter (Matt. 16. 18). To him the rock is Peter, and our Lord built his Church on Peter. He says this so often that no one doubts that it is his view. Cyprian also claims that this text gives the bishops their authority, for the Church is settled upon them.

DOCUMENT 35——Cyprian, *Ep.* 33. A.D. 250.
(*C.S.E.L.* 3. 566.)

1. Our Lord, whose precepts we ought to fear and observe, determines the honour of a bishop and the order of his Church, when he speaks in the Gospel, and says to Peter, "I say unto thee, that thou art Peter, and on this rock I will build my Church; and the gates of hell shall not prevail against it. And I will give unto thee the keys of the kingdom of heaven; and whatsoever thou shalt bind on earth shall be bound in heaven; and whatsoever thou shalt loose on earth shall be loosed in heaven". Thence, through the changes of times and successions, the ordination of bishops and the plan of the Church flow on, so that the Church is settled upon the bishops, and every act of the Church is regulated by these same prelates.

[1] Puller, 95.   [2] Doc. 32.

Since then this is founded on divine law, I marvel that some, with bold daring, have ventured to write to me as if they wrote in the name of the Church; whereas the Church is established in the bishop, and clergy, and all who stand fast.

(Chapman 54B, 55A.)

DOCUMENT 36——Cyprian, *Ep.* 43. A.D. 251.
(*C.S.E.L.* 3. 594.)

5.   They, who have departed from the Church, do not allow the Church to recall and bring back the lapsed. There is one God, and one Christ, and one Church, and one chair founded by the voice of the Lord on the rock.[1] Another altar cannot be set up, nor a new priesthood made, besides the one altar and the one priesthood. Whoever gathers elsewhere scatters.   (Gore 117 note; Chapman 54B, 55A.)

II. THE TREATISE ON UNITY

We saw in Chapter VI how Cyprian supported bishop Cornelius of Rome against his rival Novatian. But the two letters above are concerned not with the schism at Rome, but with the writer's own troubles at Carthage. When he was made bishop, he was opposed by five presbyters. After the Decian persecution the bishop's first task was to consider on what terms those who had lapsed from the faith could be restored to communion. On this point there was scope for disagreement, and Cyprian's five opponents decided to renew their hostility by taking a more lenient line than he did. These people formed a party under the leadership of Felicissimus the deacon. The anti-pope Novatian also had followers at Carthage, and the two opposition parties gave the occasion for Cyprian's tract on Church unity, which was read at the council of Carthage in A.D. 251, and also sent to Rome.[2]

DOCUMENT 37——Cyprian, *De Catholicae Ecclesiae Unitate.*
      A.D. 251.
   (*C.S.E.L.* 3. 212.)

4.   . There is an easy proof for faith in a summary of truth. The Lord says to Peter, "I say unto thee", says he, "that

1 Or "on Peter".   2 *Ep.* 54. 4.

thou art Peter, and upon this rock I will build my Church, and the gates of Hades shall not prevail against it. And I will give unto thee the keys of the kingdom of heaven, and whatsoever thou shalt bind on earth shall be bound in heaven, and whatsoever thou shalt loose on earth shall be loosed in heaven". *Upon one he builds the Church*, and though *to all the apostles*, after his resurrection, *he gives an equal power* and says, "As the Father sent me, even so send I you; receive the Holy Ghost: whose sins ye remit, they are remitted to them: whose ye retain, they shall be retained", yet in order that he might make clear the unity,[1] by his authority, *he has placed the source of the same unity, as beginning from one.* Certainly the other apostles were what Peter was, endowed with *equal fellowship both of honour and of power*, but a beginning is made from unity, that one Church of Christ may be shown. This one Church, also, the Holy Ghost in the person of the Lord describes in the Song of Songs and says: "My dove, my spotless one, is but one; she is the only one of her mother, elect of her that bare her." He who does not hold this unity of the Church, does he think that he holds the faith? He who opposes and resists the Church, does he trust himself to be in the Church? For the blessed apostle Paul teaches this same thing, and expounds the sacrament of unity saying, "One body and one spirit, one hope of your calling, one Lord, one faith, one baptism, one God"

5. We ought firmly to hold and assert this unity, especially we bishops who preside in the Church, that we may prove that the episcopate itself also is one and undivided. Let no one deceive the brotherhood by lies; let no one corrupt the truth of the faith by a faithless treachery. The episcopate is one, part of which is held by each one in solidity.[2]

(Gore 89, 117 note; Chapman 53, 54A.)

The above version has been considered by many scholars to be the original if not the only authentic text of Cyprian. Throughout the treatise there is no reference to Rome, or to any papal jurisdiction

[1] See Doc. 43 § 3.
[2] *cujus a singulis in solidum pars tenetur.*
Tenere in solidum is a legal phrase denoting the possession of something by several persons without division.

derived from Peter.[1] "The treatise was written to meet special needs, and . . papal authority did not come into the question."[2] Disputes based on this version have therefore turned on the question whether in Cyprian's view the primacy of Peter was a permanent factor in the Church or not. On the one hand it is suggested that " Peter is not the real ground, not the cause nor the centre, but only the starting point in time, and the means of recognition of Church unity".[3] If this is not so, why does Cyprian quote our Lord's words to the eleven in John 20, and twice assert that all the apostles, Peter included, had equal power? Against this view Dom Chapman stresses the words "Upon one he builds the Church". That one is Peter: Peter is the rock, and the idea of a temporary rock is absurd. There is no mention of priority in time in *Epistles*.33 and 43,[4] and from these letters it seems clear to Chapman that Cyprian means Peter, like the bishop, to be "a permanent not a transient guarantee of the unity of the edifice which rises upon a single rock".[5]

The text from which the above translation was made was published by G. Hartel in the Vienna Corpus in 1868. This version follows the earliest printed editions, many of which were published between 1471 and 1547. It has a better manuscript backing than any other version, some of the MSS. going back to the sixth or seventh century. But in 1937 Maurice Bévenot,[6] S.J., published a photograph of the same passage in one MS. of the twelfth century.[7] This version exalts the primacy of Peter and the necessity of union with his see. The following is translated from the photograph:

Document 37A——Cyprian, *De Catholicae Ecclesiae Unitate.*
(Bévenot, frontispiece.)

The Lord says to Peter, "I say unto thee", says he, "that thou art Peter .. shall be loosed in heaven". And to the same after his resurrection, he says to him "Feed my sheep". Upon him he builds the Church, and he commits to him the sheep to feed, and though to all the apostles he gives an equal power, yet he founded one chair, and by his authority appointed the source and system of unity. Certainly the rest were as Peter was, but *primacy is given to Peter* and one Church and one chair is shown: and they are all shepherds, but one flock is exhibited, which is fed by all the apostles with unanimous consent. And

[1] Puller, 88.   [2] Rivington, 50, n. 3.
[3] Hugo Koch, *Cyprian und der Römische Primat*, 43.
[4] Docs. 35, 36.   [5] *S.E.P.*, 33.
[6] *St Cyprian's De Unitate*, London, 1937.
[7] Paris National Library: Lat. 15282, folio 22v.

he who does not hold this unity of his Church, does he think he holds the faith? *He who deserts the chair of Peter, upon whom the Church was founded, does he trust himself to be in the Church?* The episcopate is one, part of which is held by each one in solidity.

A quotation from the above version is found in a letter of Pope Pelagius II, A.D. 590. He writes: "Blessed Cyprian, noble martyr, in the book which he called by the name of unity, among other things says thus: 'The beginning sets out from unity: and primacy is given to Peter, that one Church of Christ and one chair may be shown: and all are shepherds, but one flock is exhibited, to be fed by the apostles with unanimous consent', and a few words later 'He that does not hold this unity of the Church, does he think he holds the faith? He who deserts and resists the chair of Peter, upon which the Church was founded, does he trust himself to be in the Church?'"[1]

The authority for this letter of Pelagius II is one tenth-century MS.

Though the version in Document 37A appears alone in only one MS., it appears in other MSS. followed by the version in Document 37. The earliest MS. of this type belongs to the ninth century. The following is an example given by Hartel:

DOCUMENT 37B——Cyprian, *De Catholicae Ecclesiae Unitate.* (*C.S.E.L.* 3. 212 note.)

The Lord says to Peter, "I say unto thee", says he, "that thou art Peter . . shall be loosed in heaven". And to the same after his resurrection he says "Feed my sheep". Upon that one he builds the Church, and he commits to him his sheep to feed, and though to all the apostles he gives an equal power, yet he founded one chair, and appointed the origin of unity by the authority of his utterance. Certainly the rest were as Peter, but primacy is given to Peter that one Church and one chair may be shown: and they are all shepherds, but one flock is exhibited, which is fed by all the apostles with unanimous consent. And he who does not hold this unity of Paul, does he think he holds the faith? He who deserts the chair of Peter upon which the Church was founded, does he trust himself to be in the Church? Upon one he builds the Church, and though to all the apostles

[And so on as in Doc. 37.]

[1] *Ep.* 4 (*P.L.* 72. 713).

Yet a fourth type is the text of Baluze given by Migne, Doc. 37c. This is a combination of our two Documents 37 and 37A. The italics follow Doc. 37, the bold type Doc. 37A, and the words in ordinary type are common to both sources.

DOCUMENT 37C——Cyprian, *De Unitate Ecclesiae.*
   (*P.L.* 4. 498; *A.N.C.L.* 8. 380 ‡.)

4.   The Lord says to Peter, "I say unto thee", says he, "that thou art Peter   . shall be loosed also in heaven". **And again to the same after his resurrection he says " Feed my sheep ".** Upon **that** *one* he builds his Church, **and he commits to him his sheep to feed.** And though to all the apostles *after his resurrection* he gives an equal power *and says,* "*As the Father sent me, even so send I you ; receive the Holy Ghost : whose sins ye remit, they are remitted to them : whose ye retain, shall be retained*", *yet in order that he might make clear the unity,* **he founded one chair ;** by his authority he has placed the source of *the same* unity *as beginning from one.* Certainly the other apostles were what Peter was, *endowed with equal fellowship both of honour and of power, but a beginning is made from unity,* **and primacy is given to Peter,** that one Church *of Christ* **and one chair** may be shown : **and they are all shepherds and one flock is exhibited, which is fed by all the apostles with unanimous consent,** that one Church *of Christ* may be shown. *This one Church, also, the Holy Ghost in the person of the Lord describes in the Song of Songs and says :* " *My dove, my spotless one, is but one ; she is the only one of her mother, elect of her that bare her.*" He who does not hold this unity of the Church, does he think that he holds the faith? *He who opposes and resists the Church,* **he who deserts the chair of Peter on whom the Church is founded,** does he trust himself to be in the Church? *For the blessed apostle Paul teaches this same thing, and expounds the sacrament of unity saying,* "*One body and one spirit, one hope of your calling, one Lord, one faith, one baptism, one God*"

5. *We ought firmly to hold and assert this unity, especially we bishops*   [And so on as in Doc. 37.]

(Gore v; Chapman 96ʙ note.)

The oldest MS. of this type is of the tenth century. It was the standard edition for 300 years and found its way into Migne's *Patrologia* with Benedictine authority. It will be seen that the special contribution of Doc. 37 to this version consists in three quotations from the Bible, and some remarks at the beginning of § 5 about the need for bishops to stick together.

With such conflicting evidence, we cannot be sure of objective facts, and it is not surprising that scholars have upheld the versions which support their own views on what Cyprian ought to have said.

In 1839 J. H. Newman[1] thought the Benedictine version arose by the incorporation of marginal notes into the original (Doc. 37), without intentional dishonesty. He sees little doctrinal difference in the versions, because "the chair of Peter" is a figurative name for any see, a designation of the one bishop, and applicable against anyone who opposed his lawful bishop anywhere. The difficulty about this is that in one passage Cyprian, writing of a journey from Carthage to Rome, says that the travellers sailed "to the chair of Peter".[2]

In 1868 Hartel published his version (Doc. 37), and in the same year R. E. Wallis of Wells Cathedral translated Baluze's text (Doc. 37C), asserting without argument that the words which are printed above in bold type are "undoubtedly spurious".[3] Twenty years later, Gore, in his *Roman Catholic Claims*, calls them "interpolations", and assumes without argument that to print or quote them is to carry on the dirty work of falsification. This attitude he kept up through nine editions.[4] In 1896 E. W. Benson, Archbishop of Canterbury, thought that these words in bold type "taught the cardinal doctrine of the Roman see".[5] He therefore had to prove that they were forgeries, which he endeavoured to do in twenty-four pages. He does show that the powers at Rome in the sixteenth century and in France early in the eighteenth century were determined that the passages which exalt the primacy of Peter, and the necessity of communion with his see, should be upheld in the printed editions. The French went to the extent of substituting pages after the index had been printed.[6]

At the turn of the century Chapman concludes that the words in bold type cannot be later than about A.D. 350. He thinks they are in fact the work of Cyprian. When certain Roman confessors seceded from Novatian and returned to communion with Cornelius, Cyprian wrote *Ep.* 54 to congratulate them, and mentioned his tract *De Unitate* which he had sent. This was, according to Chapman, a copy of the revised form (Doc. 37A), the changes being made to suit the Novatianist schism at Rome.[7] Dr E. W. Watson, whilst rejecting Chapman's conclusion, admits that the words in bold type in Doc. 37C are

1 *L.F.* 3. 150–152.
2 *Ep.* 59 § 14 (Doc. 38).
3 *A.N.C.L.* 8. 381 note.
4 1st edition, 108; 9th edition, 112.
5 *Cyprian*, 203.
6 Ibid. 214, 215.
7 *Revue Bénédictine*, 1903, p. 40 f.

consistent in style and thought with Cyprianic authorship.[1] This is an important point in establishing the validity of Doc. 37A, and since it was taken up later by Chapman[2] and is accepted by Jalland,[3] I quote here the parallels in other works of Cyprian.

1. "Peter also, to whom the Lord *commends his sheep to be fed* and guarded, on whom he placed and founded the Church, denies that he has any gold or silver." (*De Hab. Virg.* 10.)
2. "There is one God and one Christ and one Church and *one chair* founded by the voice of the Lord on the rock." (*Ep.* 43 : Doc. 36.)
3. ". . . or say that he held *the primacy* . . ." (*Ep.* 71 § 3 : Doc. 44.)
4. "Although we are many *shepherds*, yet we *feed one flock*." (*Ep.* 68. 4.)
5. ". . fellow bishops, the whole company of whom, throughout the entire world, have *consented with unanimity*." (*Ep.* 55 § 8 : Doc. 28.)
6. ". . to *the chair of Peter* and to the principal church . ." (*Ep.* 59 § 14 : Doc. 38.)

These original views of Chapman were quickly accepted by two German protestant scholars, A. Harnack[4] and H. Von Soden,[5] and in 1909 P. Batiffol[6] argued that whilst both versions of the *De Unitate* were by Cyprian, the original was that sent to Rome (Doc. 37A). So in his tenth edition Gore is forced to remove his remarks about falsification and leave the subject alone.[7] Hugo Koch argues against Cyprianic authorship,[8] and Chapman's last word in 1910 is to the effect that a forger could never have combined passages "from different MSS. with such simplicity and success".[9] And why should a forger in favour of the papacy include the words about the equality of the apostles? However, Denny believed that there was no limit to the ingenuity of forgers,[10] but he admits the words in bold type may be as early as A.D. 330.[11]

In 1921 Dr B. J. Kidd reverted to Benson's view that the "interpolator" intended to claim universal jurisdiction for the Roman bishop. If Cyprian did support this claim, he soon contradicted it by opposing Pope Stephen over the matter of rebaptism[12] (see Chapter IX). This it seems, according to Maurice Bévenot, is just what happened. This Jesuit scholar, after studying over 100 MSS. in which the treatise on Unity appears, concludes that our Doc. 37A represents the original work of Cyprian, which he altered to Doc. 37 when he quarrelled with Stephen. He points out that the quotation from

1 *J.T.S.* 5. 433. 2 *S.E.P.*, 36, 37.
3 *Papacy*, 163. 4 *Theol. Litztg.*, 1903, p. 262.
5 *Texte und Untersuchungen*, 1904, Band 25, pt 3, p. 21 note.
6 Page 372. 7 Page v.
8 *Texte und Unt.*, 1910, Band 35, p. 158.
9 *S.E.P.*, 38, 39. 10 Page 655.
11 Page 662. 12 *Hist. Ch.*, 1. 458, 459.

Paul and the appeal for episcopal unity which follows it are found in Doc. 37 but not in Doc. 37A. This quotation was used in the baptismal controversy by Cyprian himself,[1] by Firmilian,[2] and by two other bishops.[3] This view is ably worked out.[4] The outcome seems to be that, even according to such an ardent Anglican controversialist as Edward Denny, a writer as early as A.D. 330 asserted that "he who deserts the see of Peter" could not with certainty claim to be a member of the Church. A number of world-famous scholars, catholic and protestant, believe this remark to have emanated from Cyprian.

Doc. 37 continued.
(*C.S.E.L.* 3. 214.)

5.   The episcopate is one, part of which is held by each one in solidity. The Church is one, though it is widely spread into a multitude by an increase of fruitfulness.   Of her womb we are born, with her milk we are fed, with her spirit we are made alive.

6. The spouse of Christ cannot become adulterate; she is undefiled and pure. She knows one home.   And *does anyone think that this unity* coming from the divine strength, and cohering in the heavenly sacraments, *can be severed in the Church*, and split by the divorce of contending wills? He who does not hold this unity does not hold the law of God, or the faith of the Father and the Son, or life and salvation.

8. Who then is so wicked, faithless, or insane with the madness of discord, as to think he can rend or dare to rend God's unity, the Lord's robe, Christ's Church? He himself warns us in his gospel, and teaches saying, "And there shall be one flock and one shepherd". And does anyone think there can be *in one place* either many shepherds or many flocks?   .
Do you think you can stand and live, withdrawn from the Church, building for yourself other seats and different homes?   .

23.   There is one God, and one Christ, and his Church is one, and the faith is one, and there is one people joined in solid unity of the body by the glue of agreement. *Unity cannot*

[1] *Ep.* 74. 11.   [2] In Cyprian, *Ep.* 75. 24.
[3] *Sententiae episcoporum* 1, 5 (*C.S.E.L.* 3. 436, 439).
[4] M. Bévenot, op. cit., 55–61.

be severed, nor can' the one body be separated by a division of its structure, or be torn with its entrails extracted by laceration. Parted from the womb, a thing cannot live and breathe separately; it loses the substance of health.

(Chapman 22B, 23A, 123B and note, 124A.)

In § 5 we get the important doctrine of the solidity of the episcopate. The other three passages are quoted by Chapman to refute what he calls the cardinal Anglican heresy, that the Church can be divided.[1] The words "in one place" (§ 8) show that Cyprian is not dealing with the unity of the whole Church.

III. THE CHAIR OF PETER THE PRINCIPAL CHURCH

From Cyprian's 59th Letter we learn that Felicissimus was excommunicated (§ 1), and that a gang of five heretics belonging to his faction had ordained one Fortunatus as rival bishop of Carthage (§ 10). Felicissimus then went with them to Rome to gain recognition from the bishop there (§ 14). At first they were rejected (§ 1), but later, under vicious threats from the gang, Cornelius seemed to hesitate (§ 2).

DOCUMENT 38——Cyprian, *Ep.* 59. A.D. 252.
    (*C.S.E.L.* 3. 666.)

Cyprian to his brother Cornelius, greeting.

1. I have read your letter, dearest brother, which you sent by our brother Saturus the acolyte, so full of brotherly love, church discipline, and priestly reproof. In it you point out that Felicissimus (no new enemy of Christ, but long ago excommunicated for his very many and grave crimes, and condemned not only by my sentence, but by that of many fellow bishops) has been rejected by you over there; and although he came thronged by a crowd and faction of desperadoes, he was expelled from the Church with the full vigour with which bishops ought to act. . .

2. But when I read your other letter, brother, which you joined to the first, I was surprised to notice that you were to

---

[1] Chapman, 20A. But see Doc. 236.

some extent moved by the menaces and threats of those who came and, as you wrote, assailed you, and with the utmost desperation threatened that if you would not receive the letter they brought, they would read it publicly, and would utter many base and disgraceful things, worthy of their lips. But if it is the case, dearest brother, that the audacity of the most wicked is to be feared, and what evil men cannot do by right and equity they can do by daring and desperation, well then so much for the vigour of episcopacy, and for the majestic and divine power of governing the Church. Nor can we any longer continue, or in fact now be, Christians, if it is come to this, that we dread the menaces and snares of outcasts. .
The strength of our faith, dearest brother, must remain immovable; and our courage, firm and unshaken, should endure against all the inroads and violence of the roaring waves, even as the strength and mass of a resisting rock. .   .

5. .   What sort of people do you think they are, those enemies of the priests and rebels against the Catholic Church, who are alarmed neither by the severe warning of the Lord, nor by the vengeance of future judgement? *For this has been the source from which heresies and schisms have arisen, that God's priest is not obeyed, nor do people reflect that there is for the time one priest in the church, who for the time is judge instead of Christ,*[1] and if the whole brotherhood would obey him, according to divine teaching, no one would stir up anything against the college of priests; no one after the divine judgement, after the votes of the people, after the consent of the fellow bishops, would make himself a judge, not now of the bishop but of God.

7.   Peter, however, on whom the Church has been built by the same Lord, speaking one for all, and answering with the voice of the Church, says, "Lord to whom shall we go?" .

9. But I did not immediately write to you, dearest brother, about Fortunatus, that false bishop who was set up by a few inveterate heretics, because *the matter was not one which must at once and in haste be brought to your notice, as though it were great and serious*; especially as you already knew the name of Fortunatus

[1] This passage in italics was cited by Leo XIII in *Satis Cognitum* § 15.

well enough. He is one of the five presbyters who, sometime back, deserted from the Church, and were recently excommunicated by the decision of many of our fellow bishops, men of considerable influence, who wrote to you on this subject last year. . .

10. But I informed you, brother, by Felician, that Privatus, an old heretic of the colony of Lambesa, had come to Carthage. He was condemned many years ago for numerous and serious crimes, by the sentence of ninety bishops, and, as you will remember, he was very severely noted by our predecessors Fabian [1] and Donatus [2]. .   These five, with a few who either had sacrificed or had evil consciences, chose Fortunatus to be their false bishop, that, their crimes agreeing, the ruler might be such as the ruled.

11. Hence too, dearest brother, you may at once discern the other lies which desperate and abandoned men have there spread around. . .

14. For these too it was not enough to have departed from the gospel, to have deprived the lapsed of the hope of satisfaction and penance. .   . After all this, they yet in addition, having had a false bishop ordained for them by heretics, dare to set sail, and to carry letters from schismatic and profane persons *to the chair of Peter, and to the principal church, whence the unity of the priesthood took its rise.*[3] They fail to reflect that those Romans are the same as those whose faith was publicly praised by the apostle, to whom unbelief cannot have access. But why do they come and announce that a false bishop has been made against the bishops? Either they are pleased with what they have done, and persist in their wickedness; or if it displeases them and they withdraw, they know whither they may return. For it has been decreed by all of us, and is alike fair and just, that every cause should there be heard where the crime has been committed.[4] And since a portion of the flock has been assigned to the individual shepherds, which each is to rule and gvoern, having to give account of his ministry to the Lord, so

---

[1] Of Rome.   [2] Of Carthage.
[3] *ad ecclesiam principalem unde unitas sacerdotalis exorta est.*
[4] See Doc. 208 § 3.

those over whom we are set ought not to run about, or break the harmonious concord of bishops by their crafty and deceitful rashness, but there to plead their cause where they will have both accusers and witnesses of their crime; *unless perhaps to some few desperate and abandoned men the authority of the bishops appointed in Africa seems to be inferior.* These African bishops have already judged their case, and have recently by the weight of their judgement condemned their moral sense, which is entangled by many criminal snares.

19. Now, though I know, dearest brother, that for the mutual love which we owe and hold out towards each other, you always read our letters to the very eminent clergy who there preside with you, and to your most holy and large congregation; yet now I both exhort and beg you to do at my request what on other occasions you do of your own accord and courtesy, and read this my letter, so that if any contagion of poisoned language or pestilent propaganda has crept in over there, it may be completely removed from the ears and hearts of the brethren, and the sound and sincere affection of good men may be cleansed from all the dirt of heretical slander.

(Gore 117, 118 note, 199; Chapman 54B, 55B, 71B, 116A.)

This long letter contains a number of points bearing on our inquiry. In § 2 Cyprian seems politely to rebuke the bishop of Rome for being intimidated by threats. In § 14 the see of Peter is clearly at Rome. As regards *ecclesiam principalem*: Duchesne[1] and Rivington[2] render it "sovereign church"; Koch[3] and Puller[4] make it mean the first church in order of time. There are difficulties in either of these interpretations. In order to reckon Rome as the earliest of all local churches, we have to rule out the church of Jerusalem for the reason that it ceased to exist after the destruction of the city in A.D. 70, and further to suppose that the church of Rome was founded before any of the Pauline churches, perhaps by those "sojourners from Rome"[5] who were at Jerusalem on the first Whitsunday. On the other hand it is doubtful whether *principalis* carried the meaning "principal" or "sovereign" as early as Cyprian's day. It has been claimed that Tertullian so uses it in his *De Anima* § 13,[6] where he argues that the

1 *The Churches Separated from Rome*, E.T., 1907, p. 97.
2 Page 58.   3 *Texte und Unt.*, 1910, Band 35, p. 96.   4 Pages 51, 446.
5 Acts 2. 10.   6 *P.L.* 2. 667, 668; *A.N.C.L.* 15. 437.

soul is superior to the mind, but even here the meaning may be that the soul is created before the mind; and in our Doc. 12 § 31, also by Tertullian, *principalitas* clearly means "prior date". Both sides in our dispute appeal to Tertullian, because he was a favourite author of Cyprian.[1]

De Marca, a French lawyer, explained the latter half of § 14 as follows: "Cyprian openly sets forth to Cornelius the rights of the bishops of each province, which consist in this, that to them belong the examination and decision of causes, and the rule of the flock, they having to return an account of their administration to God, and that it is not lawful to appeal to Rome or elsewhere, and that the authority of the African bishops is not less than that of the rest."[2] On the other hand, if these principles were so clearly established in the third century, one wonders why Felicissimus and his party thought it worth while to seek recognition in Rome.

In § 14 Cyprian says that the Roman church is impervious to heresy, but in § 19 he is less sure, and urges the public reading of his letter as a safeguard.

The same year, 252, Cornelius was banished to Civitavecchia[3] and Cyprian writes to congratulate him and his church on their stand against persecution.

DOCUMENT 39——Cyprian, *Ep.* 60.   A.D. 252.
  (*C.S.E.L.* 3. 692.)

Cyprian to Cornelius his brother, greeting.

1.   Over there [i.e. in Rome], the courage of the bishop who leads has been publicly tested, and the unity of the brethren who accept his leadership has been displayed. Since *there is one mind and one voice among you Romans, your whole church has confessed.*

2. Dearest brother, the faith which the blessed apostle praised in you has been evident. This excellence of courage and firmness of strength he even then foresaw in the Spirit.

.   the examples of agreement and bravery which you have given to the other brethren are magnificent.

(Chapman 71B.)

[1] Jerome, *De Viris Illustribus* 53.
[2] *De Concordia* 7. 1 § 3, A.D. 1641 (3. 285, edit. 1788).
[3] *Filocalian Catalogue* (*P.L.* 13. 451).

IV. UNITY AND SCHISM

Those who believe that the Catholic Church can be divided find no support from Cyprian. As we have seen, he asserts the exact opposite (Doc. 37 § 23). But Dr E. B. Pusey,[1] writing about the Anglican view of Church unity, quotes the next Document.

DOCUMENT 40——Cyprian, *Ep.* 63.　A.D. 253.
　　(*C.S.E.L.* 3. 712.)

13.　. The cup of the Lord is not water alone, or wine alone, unless both are mingled together, so also the body of the Lord cannot be flour alone, or water alone, unless both be united and joined together and compacted in the structure of one loaf. In this·very sacrament our people are shown to be made one; so that just as many grains collected into one, and ground and mingled together make one loaf, so in Christ, who is the heavenly bread, we may know that there is one body, in which our whole company is joined and united.

(Gore 32.)

If this sacramental conception of Church unity makes papalism unnecessary as Gore implies, it can also presumably dispense with episcopacy or any other form of Church government. But there can be no doubt that Cyprian believed in bishops as much as did Ignatius.[2]

DOCUMENT 41——Cyprian, *Ep.* 66.　A.D. 254.
　　(*C.S.E.L.* 3. 732.)

8. ... "We believe and are sure that thou art the Son of the living God." There speaks Peter, upon whom the Church was to be built. He teaches and shows in the name of the Church that although a rebellious and proud multitude of heedless men may withdraw, yet the Church does not depart from Christ. And *they are the Church who are a people united to the priest*, and a flock sticking to its shepherd. From this you ought to realize that the bishop is in the Church, and the Church in the bishop; and *if any one is not with the bishop, he is not in the Church*. Further, they flatter themselves in vain who creep in

[1] *Eirenicon*, 1865, p. 57.　　　　[2] Doc. 2.

and imagine that they communicate secretly with some people, without having peace with the priests of God. In actual fact the Church which is catholic and one *is not cut or divided*, but is undoubtedly connected and joined together by the cement of priests mutually cleaving to each other.

(Chapman 22B, 54B.)

V. THE SPANISH APPEAL

The story revealed by Cyprian's next letter is a favourite of the Anglicans. Two Spanish bishops, Basilides and Martial, were accused of having denied the faith in persecution, and were deposed (§ 1). Basilides confessed his crime and other sins, resigned his see, and gladly accepted lay communion (§ 6). Martial further involved himself in paganism and buried his sons in a pagan cemetery (§ 6). The people of Merida chose Sabinus to be their bishop instead of Basilides (§ 5). The election was approved by neighbouring bishops in council, and he was consecrated to fill the vacancy (§ 5). After a time Basilides went to Rome and asked Stephen, the new bishop there, to restore him to his bishopric. Stephen accepted the view of the case presented to him by the suppliant, and declared both the fallen bishops to be restored (§ 5). This was awkward, for the opinion given by the bishop of Rome caused some of the Spanish bishops to communicate with Basilides and Martial (§ 9), thus creating a local schism. The two churches wrote to Cyprian, putting the case before him, and asking for his opinion (§ 1), and a third letter from Felix of Saragossa confirmed their view of the case. The three letters were carried by Sabinus, the new bishop of Merida, and by a Bishop Felix, probably the successor of Martial (§ 6). On receipt of the correspondence, thirty-seven African bishops met in council in the autumn of A.D. 254. Our Document is the council's reply. The removal of Basilides and the consecration of Sabinus are upheld. In Cyprian's view, the appeal of Basilides to Rome makes no difference, because Stephen, residing at a distance, "was through negligence imposed upon" (§ 5). Stephen only had Basilides' side of the question, and Cyprian believed himself to be more accurately informed by the two churches concerned, and by a third independent witness.

DOCUMENT 42——Cyprian, *Ep.* 67.   Autumn, A.D. 254.
    (*C.S.E.L.* 3. 735.)

Cyprian, Caecilius, Primus . . . [37 names in all], to Felix the presbyter and the people abiding at Legio and Asturica, also to Aelius the deacon and the people abiding at Emerita, brethren in the Lord, greeting.

1. When we had met together, dearest brethren, we read your letter which . . you sent to us by Felix and Sabinus, our fellow bishops, intimating that Basilides and Martial, being defiled with certificates of idolatry and bound by the guilt of dreadful crimes, ought not to hold the episcopate and administer the priesthood of God. And you wished us to write to you an answer on this point, and to relieve your . . . anxiety by giving our opinion. . But it is not our advice but the divine precepts which make reply, for in them it has long ago been ordered by a heavenly voice, and laid down by the law of God, what sort of persons ought to serve the altar, and celebrate divine sacrifices. .

2. . . . Keeping these things before our eyes   we ought, in the ordinations of priests, to choose only unstained and upright ministers who, holily and worthily offering sacrifices to God, may be heard in the prayers which they make for the safety of the Lord's people, since it is written, "God heareth not a sinner. .   ".

3. Do not let the people flatter themselves that they can be free from contamination when communicating with a sinful priest.   .

5.   . This practice, we note, was followed among you in the ordination of our colleague Sabinus, so that the bishopric was conferred on him by the votes of the whole brotherhood and by the judgement of the bishops who had met together at that time, or who had written to you about him, and hands were laid on him to take the place of Basilides. *The ordination, being rightly performed, cannot be annulled by the fact that Basilides,* after his crimes had been detected and further laid bare by the confession of his own conscience, *went to Rome and deceived Stephen our colleague* (who was far away and ignorant of the facts and of the truth), and contrived to be unjustly replaced in the episcopate from which he had been justly deposed. The effect of this is not to efface but to swell the crimes of Basilides, for to his former sins he has also added the guilt of deceit and fraud. For he is not so much to be blamed who

through negligence was imposed upon, as he is to be execrated who through fraud imposed upon him. But if Basilides could impose upon men, on God he could not.

6. Wherefore since (as you, dearest brother, have written, and as also Felix and Sabinus ʼbur colleagues assert, and as another Felix of Caesaraugusta, devout in faith, and defender of the truth, intimates in his letter) Basilides and Martial have been defiled with the profane certificate of idolatry　　And since there are many other and grievous crimes in which Basilides and Martial are implicated, it is vain for such men to attempt to usurp the episcopate; for it is evident that men of that kind cannot preside over the Church of Christ, nor ought they to offer sacrifices to God. But, more especially, *our colleague Cornelius*, a peaceable and righteous priest, and by the favour of the Lord honoured with martyrdom, long since decreed with us, and with all the bishops throughout the whole world, that such men might be admitted to do penance, but were prohibited from the ordination of the clergy and from the priestly honour.

9. And so, dearest brothers, although amongst our colleagues are some who think that the godly discipline may be neglected, and who rashly communicate with Basilides and Martial, this thing ought not to disturb our faith.

　　　　　　(Gore 113, 114 note; Chapman 56A, 99.)

The main point of all this is that Cyprian, a most illustrious bishop, saint, and martyr, overrides the opinion of the bishop of Rome. Chapman says that Cyprian and his council "concluded (rightly or wrongly) that Stephen had been deceived, and that on this ground his decision need not be obeyed". Batiffol[1] points out the writers' mistake, in § 3, in supposing that the unworthiness of the minister pollutes the sacrament, but this scarcely weakens the Anglican case. Rivington[2] infers, from the words about Cornelius in § 6, that "our saint is avowedly acting under the shelter of a papal decision to which the whole Church had agreed". Cardinal Hergen-rother[3] says, "From Stephen, Basilides obtained restoration to his See; an act in which Cyprian disputed not the right of the Pope, but blamed only the special exercise of that right".

[1] Page 377.　　　[2] Page 74.　　　[3] *Anti Janus*, E.T., 111.

CHAPTER IX

BAPTISM BY HERETICS

CYPRIAN's relations with Rome deteriorated on the accession of Stephen in A.D. 254. We saw in the last Document how the two bishops disagreed over the Spanish appeal. The next year a dispute arose between them over the method of admitting reformed heretics into the Church. Cyprian believed that all baptism outside the Church was no baptism, and so he insisted that heretics and schismatics should be baptized on admission to the Church, unless they were lapsed churchmen previously baptized by the Church.[1] He was only able to trace his authority back to the local custom of one of his predecessors about forty or fifty years earlier.[2] This was the time of Tertullian's *De Baptismo*, which maintains the same view.[3] Cyprian did not think the lateness of this tradition was of much consequence, for he held that reason and truth were more important than custom.[4]

Stephen said that baptism in the name of Christ was efficacious,[5] regardless of the faith of the baptizer or the baptized; therefore heretics were to be admitted by the laying on of hands.[6] He claimed that his custom was apostolic,[7] and he called the practice of Cyprian "rebaptism". Cyprian denied that it was rebaptism, and assumed throughout that since the apostles condemned heresy, they must have regarded heretical baptism as invalid.

Roman Catholics and Anglicans agree that Rome was right and Carthage wrong. Our contemporary authorities are the letters of Cyprian (69–75), the acts of the seventh council of Carthage, and some letters of Dionysius of Alexandria preserved by Eusebius. Our first Document is a letter from the fifth council of Carthage, consisting of thirty-two bishops, who wrote to eighteen bishops of Numidia.

DOCUMENT 43——Cyprian, *Ep.* 70. A.D. 255.
(*C.S.E.L.* 3. 767.)

1. . We do not bring out our judgement as original, but we join with you in mutual harmony in a judgement settled by

---

[1] *Ep.* 74. 12 (Doc. 48).   [2] *Ep.* 71. 4 (Doc. 44); *Ep.* 73. 3 (Doc. 46).
[3] § 15 (*P.L.* 1. 1325).   [4] *Ep.* 71. 3 (Doc. 44); *Ep.* 73. 13 (Doc. 46).
[5] *Ep.* 75. 18 (Doc. 49).   [6] *Ep.* 74. 1 (Doc. 48).
[7] Cyprian, *Ep.* 75. 5 (Doc. 49).

our predecessors long ago and observed by us. We consider it
to be obvious and we hold for certain that no one can be
baptized outside the Church, for there is one baptism appointed
in the holy Church.

3. To admit that they have baptized is to approve the
baptism of heretics and schismatics. For it cannot be partly
void and partly valid. If he could baptize, he could also give
the Holy Ghost. But if he cannot give the Holy Ghost, because,
standing without the pale, he is not with the Holy Ghost,
neither can he baptize anyone who comes [to him], because
there is one baptism and one Holy Ghost and *one Church
founded by Christ our Lord upon Peter for the origin and principle of
unity.*[1] So it comes about that all among them is empty and
false, and that nothing which they have done ought to have
our approval.   (Chapman 54B.)

DOCUMENT 44——Cyprian, *Ep.* 71, to Quintus.   A.D. 255.
    (*C.S.E.L.* 3. 771.)

1. . . Baptism indeed is one in the Catholic Church, because the Church is one, and baptism cannot be beyond the
Church.   .

3. Nor should we be governed by custom, but reason should
prevail. For even Peter, *whom the Lord chose first,* and on whom
he built his Church, when Paul later disputed with him about
circumcision, *did not claim anything insolently for himself,* or assume
anything arrogantly, or say that he held the primacy and ought
to be obeyed the more by novices and new-comers.   His
Church should know that remission of sins can only be given
in the Church, and that the enemies of Christ cannot claim
for themselves any share in his grace.

4. This is what the late Agrippinus[2] established and confirmed when he had duly pondered the matter with the rest
of his bishops who then governed the Lord's Church in the
provinces of Africa and Numidia.   (Chapman 54B, 55B.)

---

[1] See Doc. 37 § 4.
[2] Cp. Vincent of Lerins, *Commonitorium* 6 (Doc. 237).

The reference to Peter in § 3 above could mean that he claimed no primacy over Paul at all, in spite of his much earlier call by Christ. Döllinger[1] thought that the words meant that Peter had a primacy but did not assert it on this occasion, and Tixeront[2] sees here an allusion to the claims of Pope Stephen.

Accepting, with N. Zernov,[3] the traditional order of Cyprian's letters as correct, we learn that in the following year, seventy-one bishops[4] met for the sixth council of Carthage, and wrote to the bishop of Rome as follows:

DOCUMENT 45——Cyprian, *Ep.* 72. A.D. 256. (*C.S.E.L.* 3. 775.)

Cyprian and the rest, to Stephen their brother, greeting.

1. . The chief subject to be reported from our council to you, and referred to your gravity and wisdom, is one which has more bearing on priestly authority and on the unity and dignity which by divine order belong to the Church catholic. It is that they who have been dipped abroad outside the Church, and have been polluted by the stain of profane water among heretics and schismatics, ought to be baptized when they come to us and to the Church, which is one. For it is not enough to lay hands on them that they may receive the Holy Ghost, unless they also receive the baptism of the Church. I enclose copies of a letter written to Quintus[5] our colleague, settled in Mauritania, and of the letter written by our colleagues to the fellow bishops in Numidia.[6] These letters explain that what heretics use is no baptism, and that none of those who are opposed to Christ can profit by his grace.

3. We have brought these things to your notice, dearest brother, for the general honour and for single-hearted affection. We believe that what is both devout and true will be truly pleasing to your devotion and faith. But we know that there are some who will not lay aside what they have once imbibed, or easily change their position, but, whilst keeping the bond of peace and concord with their colleagues, retain

[1] *Ch. Hist.*, E.T., 1. 259 n. (1840).
[2] *History of Dogmas*, E.T., 1. 369, n. 3.
[3] *Church Quarterly Review*, Jan. 1934, pp. 322, 323.
[4] Cyprian, *Ep.* 73. 1.
[5] Doc. 44. [6] Doc. 43.

certain practices of their own which have once been adopted among them. In this matter, we coerce no one, nor do we lay down the law, *for each prelate has the right of his free will in the administration of the church, and he will give an account of his actions to the Lord.* (Gore 117 note, 119.)

Bernardo Jungmann[1] thought that in § 3 above, Cyprian was suggesting to Stephen that he should treat the matter as one of discipline, "in which anyone could follow the policy which seemed to him to be right". But Zernov[2] supposes that Cyprian meant that he did not impose his will on the other African bishops.

DOCUMENT 46——Cyprian, *Ep.* 73, to Jubian.   A.D. 256.
   (*C.S.E.L.* 3. 780.)

3. With us it is no new or sudden thing to decide that those who come to the Church from heresy are to be baptized. It is now many long years since this was settled by many bishops who were brought together under the late Agrippinus.[3]

7. But it is plain where and by whom remission of sins can be given, that is to say, the remission that is given in baptism. First the Lord gave that power to Peter, on whom he built the Church and whom he appointed and declared the origin of unity, that what he loosed should be loosed. And after the resurrection he speaks to the apostles also saying, "As the Father sent me, so I send you". When he had said this he breathed and said to them, "Whose sins ye remit, they are remitted to them; whose sins ye retain, they shall be retained".[4]

11.   Whither shall he come who thirsts? To heretics, where there is no fount and river of living water at all, or to the Church which is one, and was, by the voice of the Lord, founded upon one, who also received the keys? She it is alone who holds and possesses the whole power of her Spouse and Lord.

13. Some people, when overcome by reason, vainly fall back on precedent, as if precedent was greater than truth.

[1] *Dissertationes* 4. 71 (Tome I, p. 325, edit. 1880).
[2] Op. cit., 328–330.
[3] See Doc. 44 § 4 and note.
[4] Cp. Doc. 37 § 4.

26. We have written to you briefly about these things, dearest brother, to the best of our poor ability, directing no one nor prejudging the case so as to prevent any bishop from acting as he thinks fit, for each one has a free control over his own decision.   Patiently and gently we uphold a spirit of charity, the honour of the college, the bond of faith and agreement among priests.

(Gore 119; Chapman 53A note, 54B.)

Our next two Documents are the acts of the seventh council of Carthage, reaffirming Cyprian's view of the question, and Cyprian's letter to Pompey, which quotes Stephen's view. The order of these two Documents is disputed. Hefele[1] is doubtful, but inclines to the opinion that the council comes first. The matter is important, because if the council was held after Stephen's decree had been received, it means that the Africans unanimously agreed in council that he was wrong. Benson[2] and Kidd[3] put the council second, and Rivington[4] puts it first.

DOCUMENT 47——Council of Carthage, 1 September 256, *Sententiae Episcoporum.*
(*C.S.E.L.* 3. 435.)

The judgement of eighty-seven bishops on the baptism of heretics.

When, on the first of September, many bishops from the provinces of Africa, Numidia, and Mauritania had met together with the presbyters and deacons and in the presence of a large number of the laity, first of all the letter from Jubian to Cyprian about the baptism of heretics was read, and then Cyprian's reply to Jubian,[5] after which Cyprian said: "You have heard, dearest colleagues, what Jubian our fellow bishop has written to me, consulting our humble opinion about the unlawful and profane baptism of heretics, and also how I replied to him to the effect that we have once and again frequently decided that heretics coming to the Church ought to be baptized and sanctified with the baptism of the Church.

---

[1] Hefele, 1. 101, 102; 3. 434.   [2] *Cyprian*, 361.
[3] *Hist. Ch.*, 1. 468, 469.   [4] Pages 89, 90.
[5] Doc. 46.

Another letter of Jubian in reply to our letter has also been read to you. Agreeably to his sincerity and devotion, in this letter he not only assents but gives thanks and admits that he has been instructed. It remains for each one of us to say what he thinks on this subject, *judging no one, nor depriving anyone of the right of communion, if he should think differently. For no one of us sets himself up as a bishop of bishops, or by tyranny and terror forces his colleagues to the necessity of obedience; since every bishop, in the free use of his liberty and power, has the right to his own opinion, and can no more be judged by another than he himself can judge another.* But we all await the judgement of our Lord Jesus Christ, who alone has the power to set us in the government of his Church, and to judge our acts therein."

8. Crescens of Cirta said: "The letter of our most beloved Cyprian to Jubian and also that to Stephen have been read. . ."

63. Likewise another Felix from Buslacene said: "In admitting heretics without the baptism of the Church, no one should prefer custom to reason and truth: for reason and truth always exclude custom."[1]   (Gore 119, 134.)

Three other bishops dealt with this question of custom, reason, and truth in the same way (§§ 28, 30, 77).

Both Puller[2] and Batiffol[3] have read into these remarks of Cyprian the idea that the bishop of Rome had claimed to be "bishop of bishops". But all that Cyprian actually says is that no African bishop claims such a position. If this is all he means, he seems to be under-lining what he had previously written to Stephen[4] and to Jubian,[5] to the effect that he did not wish to impose his convictions on his colleagues.

Pompey, a bishop in Tripolitania, voted by proxy at the September council (§ 84), but he may have been present at the earlier one which produced *Ep.* 72 to Stephen. He wanted to know how Stephen replied, so Cyprian tells him in *Ep.* 74, the first paragraph of which contains what Batiffol calls "the papal edict": "In answer to [Cyprian's] imprudent words [about not laying down the law[4]], Rome intimated to him the law."[6]

[1] On this point see Tertullian, *De Corona* § 4.
[2] Page 65.   [3] Page 391.
[4] *Ep.* 72. 3 (Doc. 45).   [5] *Ep.* 73. 26 (Doc. 46).
[6] Batiffol, 389.

DOCUMENT 48——Cyprian, *Ep.* 74, to Pompey.   A.D. 256.
(*C.S.E.L.* 3. 799.)

1.   Since you have asked to be informed how our brother Stephen replied to our letter, I have sent you a copy of his reply. If you read it you will more and more realize his mistake in trying to uphold the cause of heretics against Christians, and against the Church of God. For among the other arrogant or irrelevant or inconsistent things which he wrote awkwardly and carelessly, he has even inserted this: "If then anyone comes to you from any heresy whatever, let nothing be innovated beyond what has been handed down, namely that hands be laid on them to repentance; for the heretics themselves do not baptize those who specially come to them from another [heresy], but simply communicate them."

2. He has forbidden anyone coming from any heresy whatever to be baptized in the Church, that is, he has judged the baptism of all heretics to be right and lawful.   . .

4. Truly an excellent and legitimate tradition has been proposed by our brother Stephen's teaching, supplying us with an adequate authority! For to the same passage of his letter, he has thrown in these words: "For the heretics themselves do not baptize those who specially come to them from another [heresy], but simply communicate them."[1] To this depth of evil the Church of God and spouse of Christ has sunk, that she is to follow the example of heretics, that in celebrating the heavenly sacraments, light must borrow her discipline from darkness.[1] .

7.   The stubborn hardness of our brother Stephen has burst out to such an extent, that he insists that sons are born to God even from the baptism of Marcion, of Valentine, or Apelles, or other blasphemers against God the Father.   .

8. . . Does he give glory to God who is the friend of heretics and the enemy of Christians, and who thinks that the priests of God who guard the truth are to be excommunicated?[2]

---

1   1 Quoted by R. Hooker, *Of the Laws of Ecclesiastical Polity* 4. 11 (A.D. 1593).

2 *abstinendos.*

10.   Among religious and simple minds there is a short way by which to put off error and elicit the truth. For if we return to the head and origin of divine tradition, human error ceases, the nature of the heavenly sacraments is evident, and whatever lay hid under the gloom and cloud of darkness is laid open in the light of truth. Even so, if a channel carrying water, which before flowed abundantly and freely, suddenly fails, do we not go to the spring to discover the reason there?   if the truth has in any respect tottered or faltered, we should go back to its source in the Lord and to the gospel and the apostolic tradition, so that the grounds for our conduct might spring from these, where both our rank and origin took its rise.

12. This, dearest brother, is our practice and our conviction after exploration and scrutiny of the truth, that all who are converted to the Church from any heresy must be baptized with the only lawful baptism of the Church, except those who had been baptized before in the Church and had then gone over to heretics. These on their return, after doing penance, should be received by imposition of hands only, and restored by the shepherd to the fold from which they have strayed.

(Gore 39, 119, 133.)

Commenting on § 10 of the above letter an Irish Anglican, George Salmon, writes: "The question is, not who was right in that particular dispute, but what were the principles on which the fathers of the Church argued. . . . Plainly Cyprian here maintains, that the way to find out what traditions are genuine, is not to take the word of the bishop of Rome, but to search the scriptures as the only trustworthy record of apostolic tradition." [1]

In the first paragraph of the above letter, Cyprian quotes Stephen's decree on the subject of heretical baptism: heretics were not to be baptized again, but, on conversion to the Church, they were to be received, after repentance, by the laying on of hands alone. The Council of Carthage in September 256 unanimously accepted the opposite view, that they were to be baptized again (see Doc. 47). Hence, as we have already mentioned, arises the dispute on the chronological order of these two Documents. If the Roman decree was received in Carthage before September, then obviously the African bishops ignored it. Hence the anxiety of R.C. scholars to

[1] *The Infallibility of the Church*, 1888, p. 144.

date the Roman decree, or at any rate its arrival in Africa, after
1 September. There is no certain answer to this point of chronology.
We have placed the council first, because nowhere in its minutes is
Stephen's letter mentioned. The letters from and to Jubian were read
(see Preface), and also the letter of the previous council to Stephen
(§ 8). Since this previous council had thought fit to report their find-
ings to Rome, it seems reasonable to suppose that the African bishops
would have insisted on hearing Rome's reply, if it had come, and that
it would have been mentioned along with the other correspondence.
Puller[1] conjectured that the bishops may have known about the
letter, but that it was not publicly read for fear of causing scandal to
the inferior clergy and laity who, we are told, were present. Puller
also points out that in the September council four bishops dealt with
the Roman argument from custom; but we know that this argument
was being discussed in Africa earlier.[2]

The African church was not content merely to write to Stephen.
One of the two councils of A.D. 256 sent a deputation of bishops to
him. The way this deputation was treated we learn from the sarcastic
pen of Firmilian, in the next Document, § 25. Firmilian was a pupil
of Origen who, about the year 232, became bishop of Caesarea in
Cappadocia, a city of 400,000 people. He was therefore a bishop of
long standing when Cyprian appealed for his support in his quarrel
with Rome.

DOCUMENT 49——Firmilian, *To Cyprian*. A.D. 256.
   In Cyprian, *Ep.* 75. (*C.S.E.L.* 3. 813.)

5. .   With reference to what Stephen has said, that the
apostles forbade those who came from heresy to be baptized,
and transmitted this custom to be observed by posterity, you
have answered most fully that no one is so foolish as to believe
that the apostles did transmit this, for it is a certain fact that
these accursed and detestable heresies arose at a later date.   .

6. Those who are at Rome do not in all respects observe the
things handed down from the beginning; and anyone may see
that *their claim to apostolic authority is a vain one*, from the fact that
in the celebration of Easter and many other sacraments and
divine things there are certain divergencies among them, and
that all things are not observed there as they are at Jerusalem.
So in most of the other provinces too, there are many varia-
tions due to the difference in places and names; and yet on
this account there is no departure from the peace and unity

1 Page 455.   2 See Doc. 44 § 3.

of the Catholic Church. Such a departure Stephen has now dared to make by breaking the peace against you which his predecessors always kept with you in mutual love and honour. In this way he defames the blessed apostles Peter and Paul, declaring that they had handed down this custom, who in fact execrated heretics in their letters, and warned us to avoid them. From this it is apparent that this tradition [of Stephen] is human, for it supports the heretics and asserts that they have the baptism which belongs to the Church alone.

7. For as a heretic may not lawfully ordain or lay on hands, neither may he baptize or perform any holy or spiritual act, since he is alien to spiritual and godly holiness. Some time ago we confirmed that all this should be held fast and maintained against the heretics. We were assembled with those from Galatia, Cilicia, and other nearby regions at a place in Phrygia called Iconium, because some people were doubtful about these things.

17. In view of this, I am rightly indignant at the folly of Stephen so open and conspicuous. He who so boasts about the place of his bishopric and *insists that he holds his succession from Peter*, on whom the foundations of the Church were laid, is introducing many other rocks and is building many new churches, as long as he supports their baptism with his authority.

Stephen, who declares that he has the chair of Peter by succession, is roused by no zeal against the heretics. . . .

18. "But", says he [Stephen], "the name of Christ avails so much for the faith and for the holiness of baptism, that whoever is anywhere baptized in Christ's name at once receives Christ's grace."

19. You Africans can say this against Stephen, that when you discovered the truth you abandoned the error of custom. But we join truth and custom together, and *to the custom of the Romans we oppose a custom based on truth*, and thus we maintain the tradition which has been handed down from the beginning by Christ and by the apostles. We only know the one Church of God, and we reckon no baptism holy except that of the holy Church, neither do we remember that these convictions ever had a beginning with us.

22.   And Stephen is not ashamed to assert that remission of sins can be given by those who are set fast in all kinds of sin.

23.   Yea, thou [Stephen] art worse than all the heretics; for when the multitude discovers its mistake and comes to thee to receive the true light of the Church, thou abettest the errors of those who come, and heapest up the darkness of heretical night by obscuring the light of the truth of the Church.   .

24.   . Of no one more than of thee [Stephen] do the divine scriptures say "An angry man stirreth up strife, and a wrathful man heapeth up sins". For what great strifes and dissensions hast thou stirred up throughout the churches of the whole world! And how great a sin hast thou heaped up, when thou cuttest thyself off from so many flocks! For *thou didst cut thyself off*; be not deceived; for he who has made himself an apostate from the communion of the united Church is truly the schismatic. *For while thou thinkest that all may be excommunicated by thee, thou hast excommunicated thyself alone from all.* [After quoting Ephesians 4. 1–6 he continues:]

25. With what diligence has Stephen obeyed these saving commands and warnings of the apostle, keeping in the first place lowliness and meekness! For what is more lowly or meek than to disagree with so many bishops all over the world, breaking peace with each one by various kinds of quarrel, now with the Orientals, as we are sure you know, now with yourselves who are in the south? From you he received episcopal legates with such longsuffering and meekness that he would not even admit them to the common intercourse of speech. So mindful was he of love and charity that he commanded the whole brotherhood that no one should admit them to his house, so that when they came, not only peace and communion, but even shelter and hospitality were denied them. This is to keep the unity of the Spirit in the bond of peace: to cut himself off from the unity of love, to alienate himself from the brethren in everything, and to rebel in furious anger against the sacrament and bond of peace. With such a man can there be one body, one Spirit, when perhaps he has not even one mind, so slippery is he, so shifting, so unstable?

. It is plain that we cannot have a baptism in common with heretics, with whom we have nothing in common at all. And yet Stephen is not ashamed to give his patronage to such men against the Church, or to divide the brotherhood for the sake of upholding heretics and above all to call Cyprian a false Christ, a false apostle, and a deceitful workman. He is conscious that all these qualities are in himself, and has been beforehand with lies accusing another of those things which he deserves to hear himself. (Gore 91, 119, 133.)

The reasons for which the Anglicans appeal to this letter are obvious. It shows what a leading eastern bishop thought of a Roman bishop with whom he disagreed, and how he answered his attempt to excommunicate his opponents. But we also find embodied in the letter the claims of Stephen. He claimed to be the successor of Peter, and to sit in his chair (§ 17). In this dispute he claimed to be the mouthpiece of the apostles (§§ 5, 6), and especially of Peter and Paul (§ 6). He appealed not only to custom (§ 19), but also to reason (§ 18). And he claimed the right to excommunicate those who did not accept his ruling (§ 24).

I will now let two eminent biographers of Cyprian sum up the discussion with which this chapter is concerned.

Mgr Freppel, bishop of Angers, wrote in 1865: "A dispute arises in Asia Minor and Africa on a point of discipline, both sides equally appealing to custom. It is a new question, which touches both the idea of the Church, and the general theory of the sacraments. Two great bishops resolve it in an erroneous sense: around them people hold to their opinion; they have the prestige of knowledge and saintliness. Further, one must say that their solution fascinates the intellect: for at first it seems to safeguard catholic unity more, by drawing a clearer line between heresy and the Church. Very well! some lines from the Pope's pen are enough to upset all the scaffold of texts and reasoning. The partisans of innovation may resist as they please, write letter upon letter, assemble councils; the five lines of the sovereign Pontiff will become the rule of conduct for the universal Church. Oriental and African bishops, all those who at first had rallied to the opposite opinion will retrace their steps, and the entire catholic world will follow the decision of the bishop of Rome. If this is an argument against the primacy of the Pope, we can only desire one thing, namely that our opponents may discover many similar ones in history."[1]

E. W. Benson, Archbishop of Canterbury, wrote in 1896: "We have done justice to Stephen's correct judgement on the particular

---

[1] *St Cyprien*, 443.

point, and to the soundness of his reasons. But . . be it first observed that of all who asked Cyprian's counsel, of all his own councillors, of prelates assembled from Africa, Numidia, Mauretania, of Firmilian and Dionysius the Great, not one suggests the least reference to the Roman see, nor mentions its estimate of itself as an element in the question, or as a scruple to be borne in mind. Augustine,[1] who marshals every argument in refutation of his opinion, never suggests that obedience to Rome's speaking would have saved him from his error."[2]

For the later judgement of the Church on this question see Council of Arles, Doc. 60 § 8; Augustine, Docs. 171–173; Vincent of Lerins, Doc. 237 § 6.

[1] See Docs. 171 § 28, 172 §§ 2–8, 173.
[2] *Cyprian*, 434.

CHAPTER X

A.D. 260 TO 314

CYPRIAN was martyred in the year 258; two years later the Valerian persecution was over, and there was an interval of forty-two years of peace before the outbreak of the last and fiercest persecution, which ended in the West with the rescript of toleration in 311.[1] Our information about this period is scanty, depending mainly on fourth-century documents, which throw a few shafts of light on papal authority at the time.

I. DIONYSIUS OF ALEXANDRIA

About the year 260, Dionysius of Alexandria was anxious to refute the heresy of Sabellius, and he wrote a letter of doubtful orthodoxy to two bishops of Pentapolis (Cyrenaica). He spoke of the Son as "one made of God", and added that he could not have existed before he was made.[2] He was charged with heresy before Dionysius, bishop of Rome, who first held a council in Rome, and in the name of the council wrote a treatise on the doctrine of the Trinity.

DOCUMENT 50——Dionysius of Rome, *Adversus Sabellianos.*
  About A.D. 260.
  In Athanasius, *De Decretis Nicaenae Synodi.* (*P.G.* 25. 461;
  L.F. 8. 45 ‡.)

26. Next I naturally turn to those who divide and cut into pieces and destroy that most sacred doctrine of the Church of God, the monarchy.   So we may not divide into three godheads the wonderful and divine unity; nor disparage as a created being the dignity and exceeding majesty of the Lord; but we must believe in God the Father Almighty, and in Christ Jesus his Son, and in the Holy Ghost, and that the word is united to the God of the universe. For he says "I and the Father are one" and "I am in the Father and the Father is in me". In

[1] Lactantius, *De Mortibus Persecutorum* 48 (*P.L.* 7. 267).
[2] Athanasius, *De Sent. Dion.* § 4 (*P.G.* 25. 485).

80

this way both the divine Trinity and the holy doctrine of the monarchy will be preserved.

The bishop of Alexandria, hearing that he had been accused of heresy at Rome, sends his defence to the bishop of Rome.

DOCUMENT 51——Athanasius, *De Synodis.* A.D. 359.
  (*P.G.* 26. 769; *L.F.* 8. 142 ‡.)

43. . *A charge had been laid by some people against the bishop of Alexandria before the bishop of Rome*, as he had said that the Son was made, and not one in substance with the Father. This had given great pain to the Roman council; and the bishop of Rome expressed their united sentiments in a letter to his namesake. This led to his writing an explanation which he called *The Book of Refutation and Defence*; and it runs thus:

44. "And I have written in another letter a refutation of the false charge which they bring against me, that I deny that Christ is one substance with God. For though I say that I have not found or read this term anywhere in Holy Scripture, yet my remarks which follow, which they have not noticed, are not inconsistent with this belief. For I instanced a human production, which is evidently homogeneous, and I observed that undeniably fathers differed from their children, only in not being the same individuals; otherwise there could be neither parents nor children. And my letter, as I said before, owing to present circumstances, I am unable to produce, or I would have sent you the very words I used, or rather a copy of it all; which, if I have an opportunity, I will do still. . . ."
  (Gore 99; Chapman 68A.)

Athanasius, writing ninety years later, sums up the episode as follows:

DOCUMENT 52——Athanasius, *De Sententia Dionysii.* A.D. 352.
  (*P.G.* 25. 500; *P.N.F.* 4. 181A †.)

13. When Dionysius the bishop had heard of the affairs in Pentapolis, and in zeal for religion had, as I said, written the

letter to Euphranor and Ammonius against the heresy of
Sabellius, some of the brethren in the Church, of orthodox
views, went up to Rome, but without asking him, so as to learn
from himself what he had actually written; and they spoke
against him in the presence of his namesake, Dionysius bishop
of Rome. The latter, on hearing it, wrote both against the
Sabellians and against those who held views for which Arius
was ejected from the Church. He called it an equal and
opposite impiety to follow Sabellius, or those who say that the
Word of God is a creature and was made and had a beginning.
He also wrote to Dionysius to explain how he was accused by
them. And he at once replied and inscribed the books *A Refutation and Defence.* Notice here the foul gang of anti-Christians,
and how they have brought on their own disgrace. *For since
Dionysius bishop of Rome wrote against those who said that the Son of
God was a creature and made, it is clear that, not now for the first time,
but years ago, the heresy of the Arian anti-Christians has been anathematized by all.* And since Dionysius the bishop of Alexandria made
his defence about the letter he had written, it shows that he
neither thought as they allege, nor ever held the infamy of
Arius.   (Gore 99; Chapman 68a.)

II. PAUL OF SAMOSATA

DOCUMENT 53——Eusebius, *H.E.* 7. 30.
    (*L.C.L.* 2. 222; L. & O. 245.)

18. When Paul had fallen from the episcopate, as well as
from his orthodoxy in the faith, Domnus succeeded to the
ministry of the church at Antioch.

19. But as Paul refused on any account to give up possession
of the church building, the emperor Aurelian, on being peti-
tioned, gave an extremely just decision regarding the matter,
ordering the assignment of the building *to those with whom the
bishops of the doctrine in Italy and Rome should communicate in
writing.* Thus was the aforesaid man driven with the utmost
indignity from the church by the ruler of this world.

                              (Chapman 68a.)

Either "it was notorious enough even to the heathen, that the mark of true Christians was communion with the Roman church".[1] Or perhaps "Aurelian was desirous of restoring and cementing the dependence of the provinces on the capital by every means which could bind the interests or prejudices of any part of his subjects".[2]

III. THE DICE-PLAYERS

The anonymous tract against gambling, which is usually printed with Cyprian's works, probably belongs to this period.

DOCUMENT 54——*De Aleatoribus.*
    (*C.S.E.L.* 3 pt 2. 93; Shotwell & Loomis[3] 426 †.)

1.   Whereas divine and fatherly affection has conferred upon us the *apostolic leadership*[4] and has ordained by divine dignity *the see of the vicar of the Lord*[5] and we bear *the original authentic apostolate upon which Christ founded the Church* in the person of our predecessor, who received at the same time the power of loosing and binding, and the responsibility of forgiving sins, we are warned by the doctrine of salvation that while we are continually pardoning sinners we ourselves must not be perverted equally with them.

2. . . . So, inasmuch as he has appointed *us, that is the bishops, to be shepherds* of the spiritual sheep, that is the faithful who are placed under our care, let us see to it that no sore of vice be found among them, and let us watch carefully every day that after the heavenly medicine has been applied, their fleece may grow in beauty as they approach the radiance of the garments of heaven.

3. In the gospel the Lord spoke to Peter. "Peter," he said "lovest thou me?" And Peter answered: "Yea, Lord; thou knowest that I love thee." And he said: "Feed my sheep." Wherefore since we have received into the heart's guestchamber this bishopric, that is, the Holy Spirit through the imposition of hands, let us show no harshness to our neighbour.

[1] Fleury, *Hist. Ecclésiastique* 8. 8 (2. 375, edit. 1720).
[2] Gibbon, *Decline and Fall* c. xvi (2. 124, edit. Bury, 1909).
[3] J. T. Shotwell and L. R. Loomis, *The See of Peter*, Columbia Univ. Press, 1927.
[4] *apostolatus ducatum.*   [5] *vicariam Domini sedem.*

The Lord warns us and says: "Grieve not the Holy Spirit that is within you   ."

10. And *that blessed apostle Paul, the agent, the vicar of Christ,* discharging his office in the Church, asserts and says: "Ye are the temple of God, and Christ dwelleth in you."[1]

(Gore v, 118; Chapman 82.)

For the author we have to choose between Pope Miltiades,[2] an anti-pope,[3] and an African bishop.[4] The text is not inconsistent with any of these choices.

IV MILTIADES OR MELCHIADES

The last persecution gave rise to the Donatist schism in Africa. In 311 Caecilian was chosen by the vote of the whole people to be bishop of Carthage, and was consecrated by Felix, bishop of Aptunga. Two priests who were disappointed of the bishopric said that Felix was a traditor, that is one who had surrendered the sacred scriptures during the persecution, whence they inferred that the consecration was invalid. Soon after, Majorinus was consecrated as rival bishop. When the persecution ended, all Church property was restored, and a grant of money was made by the Emperor Constantine to the African clergy. In carrying out these regulations, the proconsul of Africa dealt with Caecilian and ignored Majorinus. The rival party complained to the emperor, and asked for an investigation by judges from Gaul. The emperor wrote to Pope Miltiades and to Mark, whoever he was.

DOCUMENT 55——Constantine, *To Miltiades.* A.D. 313.
   In Eusebius, *H.E.* 10. 5. (*L.C.L.* 2. 454; *P.N.F.* 1. 381A ‡.)

18. Constantine Augustus to Miltiades, bishop of Rome, and to Mark. Since many such documents have been sent to me by Anulinus, the most illustrious proconsul of Africa, in which it is said that Caecilian, bishop of the city of Carthage, has been accused by some of his colleagues in Africa, in many matters; and since it seems to me a very serious thing that in those provinces which divine providence has freely entrusted

[1] 1 Cor. 3. 16.
[2] E. Jacquier, *Dict. Théol. Cath.*, 1. 704 (1903).
[3] A. Harnack, *Chronologie*, 2. 370 f. (1904).
[4] P. Monceaux, *L'Afrique Chrétienne*, 2. 115 (1902).

to my devotedness, and in which there is a great population, the multitude are found following the baser course, and dividing, as it were, and the bishops are at variance, [§ 19] it seemed good to me that Caecilian himself with ten bishops who appear to accuse him, and with ten others whom he may consider necessary for his defence, should sail to Rome, that there, in the presence of yourselves and of Rheticius and Maternus and Marinus your colleagues, whom I have commanded to hasten to Rome for this purpose, he may be heard as you may understand to be in accordance with the most holy law. [§ 20] But in order that you may be able to have most perfect knowledge of these things, I have subjoined to my letter copies of the documents sent to me by Anulinus, and have sent them to your above-mentioned colleagues. When your firmness has read these, you will consider in what way the above-mentioned case may be most accurately investigated and justly decided. For it does not escape your diligence that I have such reverence for the legitimate Catholic Church that I do not wish you to leave schism or division in any place. May the divinity of the great God preserve you, most honoured sirs, for many years.

The council was held at Rome on 2 October 313, and besides the Pope and the three Gallic bishops, it included fifteen Italian bishops.[1] The case against Caecilian was conducted by Donatus, bishop of Casae Nigrae.

DOCUMENT 56——Optatus, *De Schismate Donatistorum*, Book 1.
    A.D. 370.
    (*C.S.E.L.* 26. 27; Vassall-Phillips[2] 45 †.)

24. When these nineteen bishops had taken their seats together, the case of Donatus and of Caecilian was brought forward. This judgement was passed against Donatus by each of the bishops. . . *Caecilian was pronounced innocent by the sentence of all the above-named bishops, and also by the sentence of Miltiades, by which the judgement was closed* in these words: "Since it is certain that those who came with Donatus have

---

[1] Optatus 1. 23.
[2] O. R. Vassall-Phillips, *St Optatus*, London, 1917.

failed to accuse Caecilian in accordance with their undertaking, and since it is also certain that Donatus has not proved him guilty on any account, I judge that, according to his deserts, he be maintained in the communion of the Church, continuing to hold his position unimpaired."

DOCUMENT 57——Augustine, *Ep.* 43.   A.D. 397.
(*P.L.* 33. 161 ; M.D. 6. 141 †.)

4.   . Caecilian and those who sailed to meet him were present. The case was tried by Melchiades, who was then bishop of Rome, and with him were the assessors whom the emperor had sent at the request of the Donatists. Nothing could be proved against Caecilian, and so he was confirmed in his see, and Donatus, who was there as his opponent, was condemned. After all this, they still persevered in the obstinacy of their most sinful schism ; so an appeal was made to the emperor, and he took pains to have the matter *examined more carefully and concluded* at Arles. They, however, declined a decision of the Church, and appealed to Constantine to hear their cause himself. When this trial came on, both parties were present ; Caecilian was pronounced innocent, and they retired vanquished, and yet continued in their wickedness.

16. . . . And yet what a *decision was finally pronounced by the blessed Melchiades himself* : how fair, how complete, how prudent, and how fitted to make peace ! For he did not presume to depose from his own rank those peers against whom nothing had been proved ; and, laying blame chiefly upon Donatus, whom he had found the cause of the whole disturbance, he gave to all the others restoration if they chose to accept it, and was prepared to send letters of communion even to those who were known to have been ordained by Majorinus ; so that wherever there were two bishops, owing to their number being doubled by this dissension, he decided that the one who was prior in the date of ordination should be confirmed in his see, and a new congregation found for the other. O excellent man ! O son of Christian peace, *father of the Christian people* !

20.   It was not before other bishops, but at the bar of

the emperor, that they dared to bring the charge of wrong judgement against ecclesiastical judges of so high authority as the bishops by whose sentence the innocence of Caecilian and their own guilt had been declared. *He granted them the second trial at Arles,* before other bishops; not because this was due to them, but only as a concession to their stubbornness, and from a desire by all means to restrain so great effrontery. For this Christian emperor did not presume so to grant their unruly and groundless complaints as to make himself the judge of the decision pronounced by the bishops who had sat at Rome; but he appointed, as I have said, other bishops, from whom, however, they preferred again to appeal to the emperor himself; and you have heard the terms in which he disapproved of this. . . . When the prudent emperor was aware of this, he compelled the rest to come to Milan in charge of his guards. Caecilian having come thither, he brought him forward in person, as he has written; and having examined the matter with diligence, caution, and prudence, which his letters on the subject indicate, he pronounced Caecilian perfectly innocent, and them most criminal.

The last two Documents are quoted by Rivington[1] to illustrate the authority of Pope Miltiades. The investigation at Rome did not settle the complaints of the Donatists: three more were held in the next three years at Carthage, Arles, and Milan,[2] all of them set on foot by the emperor. Notice at this point the entry of the Christian emperor as executive officer in Church affairs. This new factor should be borne in mind when studying the documents which follow, for it causes considerable disturbance in ecclesiastical constitution and authority.

V COUNCIL OF ARLES

DOCUMENT 58——Constantine, *To Chrestus of Syracuse,* A.D. 314.
    In Eusebius, *H.E.* 10. 5.   (*L.C.L.* 2. 457; L. & O. 318 †.)

21.   Constantine Augustus to Chrestus, bishop of Syracuse. Already on a former occasion, when some in a base

[1] Pages 141, 142.
[2] Optatus, Appendix II and III (*C.S.E.L.* 26. 197–206), and Doc. 57 § 20.

and perverse manner began to create divisions with regard to the worship of the holy and heavenly power, and the catholic religion, in my desire to cut short such dissensions among them, I had given orders to the effect that certain bishops should be sent from Gaul, nay further, that the opposing parties, who were contending stubbornly and persistently together, should be summoned from Africa; that so, in the presence also of the bishop of Rome, this question which appeared to have been raised might through their coming receive a right solution by means of a careful examination in every particular.

22. But since, as it happens, some, forgetful both of their own salvation and of the reverence they owe to their most holy religion, even now do not cease to perpetuate their private enmities, being unwilling to conform to the judgement already passed, and affirming that after all it was a few persons who gave their opinions and decisions, or that they were in a hurry to pass judgement very speedily and sharply without having first accurately examined all those matters that ought to have been investigated; and since, as a result of all this, it has come to pass that even those very persons who ought to be of one mind in brotherly concord are separate from each other in a disgraceful, nay rather in an abominable, fashion, and give to those men whose souls are strangers to this most holy religion an occasion to scoff, it became incumbent upon me to provide that that which ought to have ceased by voluntary agreement, after the judgement already passed, may even now, if possible, be ended by the presence of many persons.

23. We have therefore commanded that very many bishops from various and numberless places should assemble at the city of Arles by the first of August.

DOCUMENT 59——Council of Arles, *To Silvester.* A.D. 314.
   (*C.S.E.L.* 26. 206; Vassall Phillips 389 †.)

To the most beloved Pope Silvester: Marinus .   [33 names], eternal life in the Lord.

Being united by the common tie of charity, and by that unity which is the bond of our mother, the Catholic Church, we have been brought to the city of Arles by the wish of the most pious emperor, and *we salute you with due reverence, most glorious Pope.* Here we have suffered from troublesome men, dangerous to our law and tradition—men of undisciplined mind, whom both the authority of our God, which is with us, and our tradition and the rule of truth reject, because they have neither reason in their argument, nor any moderation in their accusations, nor was their manner of proof to the point. Therefore *by the judgement of God and of Mother Church,* who knows and approves her own, *they have been either condemned or rejected.* Would, most beloved brother, that you had thought it well to be present at this great spectacle! We believe surely that in that case a more severe sentence would have been passed against them; and our assembly would have rejoiced with a greater joy, had you passed judgement together with us; but since you were by no means able to leave[1] *that region where the apostles daily sit,*[2] and their blood[2] without ceasing bears witness to the glory of God, . . . it did not seem to us, most well-beloved brother, that we ought to deal exclusively with those matters on account of which we had been summoned, but we judged that we also should take counsel on our own affairs; because, as the countries from which we have come are different, so events of various kinds will happen which we think that we ought to watch and regulate. Accordingly, we thought well, in the presence of the Holy Ghost and his angels, that concerning the various matters which occurred to each of us, we should make some decrees to provide for[3] the present state of peace. We also agreed to write first to you who hold the greater dioceses[3] that by you especially they should be brought to the knowledge of all. What it is that we have determined on, we have appended to this poor letter of ours.

In the first place we were bound to discuss a matter that concerned the usefulness of our life. Now since One died and rose again for many, the same season should be observed with a religious mind by all at the same time, lest divisions or dis-

[1] Cp. Letter to Pope Julius, Doc. 73 § 9.
[2] Cp. Tertullian, Doc. 12 § 36.
[3]   [3] Doubtful text. See Turner, 383B.

sensions arise in so great a service of devotion. We judge therefore that the Easter of the Lord should be observed throughout the world upon the same day.　　　　(Chapman 94B.)

"The greater dioceses" are extensive civil divisions. The whole
tone of the letter shows the Pope as the acknowledged leader of the
western Church and "the centre of communications".[1]

DOCUMENT 60——Council of Arles: Canons.　A.D. 314.
　　(Turner 381A.)

The assembly of bishops, who were gathered together in the
city of Arles, to the most holy brother Silvester.　　What we
have decreed with one consent, we have reported to your
charity, that the bishops may know what ought to be observed
in future.

　1. In the first place, concerning the observance of Easter,[2]
it shall be observed by us on one day and at one time, throughout all the world, *when you, according to custom, direct letters to all.*

　8. Since the Africans are used, according to their law, to
rebaptize,[3] we decree that if anyone comes to the Church from
heresy they shall interrogate him concerning his creed; and
if they perceive that he was baptized in the Father and the
Son and the Holy Ghost, only the hand shall be laid upon
him,[4] that he may receive the Holy Ghost. But if on being
questioned, he does not answer this Trinity, he shall be
baptized.

VI. THE PRIMACY OF PETER

DOCUMENT 61——Eusebius, *H.E.* 2. 14.　A.D. 314.
　　(*P.G.* 20. 172; L. & O. 47.)

　6. .　　In the reign of Claudius, the all-good and gracious
Providence of the universe led Peter, the strong and great
apostle, marked out by his qualities as the spokesman of all the
rest, on Simon's heels to Rome, as if to oppose this mighty bane

---

[1] B. J. Kidd, *The Roman Primacy*, 44.
[2] See Chapter III.　　　　　　　　　[3] See Chapter IX.
[4] Cp. Stephen in Doc. 48 § 1.

of the world. Having protected himself with divine armour like a noble captain of God, Peter conveyed the precious merchandise of the spiritual light from the East to western folk. (Chapman 47A.)

This record of Peter in Rome should be compared with earlier Documents which always couple him with Paul : Dionysius of Corinth, Doc. 5; Irenaeus, Doc. 9. 3 § 2; and Tertullian, Doc. 12 § 36.

CHAPTER XI

ARIAN TROUBLES

THE era of persecution ended in 313, and the history of the Church in the middle of the fourth century hinges on the attack on the doctrine of the Trinity by the heresy of Arius. For earlier attacks on this doctrine see *The Little Labyrinth* § 6, Doc. 21; *Philosophumena* 9. 12, Doc. 22; and Doc. 50.

I. THE COUNCIL OF NICAEA

As is well known, the heresy of Arius was condemned at Nicaea by the First General Council in A.D. 325. "Praises of the council of Nicaea, in the records of the Church are infinite. Those who have spoken of this holy assembly have always born marvellous witness to its esteem and respect."[1]

DOCUMENT 62——Council of Nicaea: Canons. A.D. 325. (*P.L.* 67. 41; Kidd, *Docs.* 2. 17 †.)

5. Concerning those, whether of the clergy or laity, who have been excommunicated by the bishops in the different provinces, let the sentence of the canon prevail which pronounces that those persons who have been cast out by some bishops are not to be accepted by any other. Inquiry should, however, be made whether they have been excommunicated through the peevishness or contentiousness, or other such-like bitterness, of the bishop. And in order that this inquiry may be conveniently made, it is decreed to be proper that synods should be assembled twice every year in every province, that, all the bishops of the province being assembled together, such questions may be examined. In this way those who have confessedly offended against the bishop may appear to everyone to be with reason excommunicated, until it shall seem fit to

---

1 Tillemont, *Mémoires*, 6. 687 (A.D. 1704).

their general assembly to pronounce a more lenient sentence upon them.   .[1]

6. Let the ancient customs prevail which are in Egypt and Libya and Pentapolis, according to which the bishop of Alexandria has authority over all these places. For this is also customary to the bishop of Rome. In like manner in Antioch and in the other provinces, the privileges are to be preserved to the churches. But this is clearly to be understood that if anyone be made a bishop without the consent of the metropolitan, the great synod declares that he shall not be a bishop. If, however, two or three bishops shall, from private contention, oppose the common choice of all the others, it being a reasonable one and made according to the ecclesiastical canons, let the choice of the majority hold good.

(Gore 101, 102 ; Chapman 77A.)

This famous Canon 6 throws less light on the nature of the Roman primacy and the extent of Rome's jurisdiction than does the letter of the council of Arles in Doc. 59. This is either because the assembled bishops "knew nothing of the papal claims",[2] or because such claims were so well established as to require no confirmation.[3] The Nicene fathers clearly had no use for Cyprian's theory that "each prelate has the right of his free will in the administration of the church".[4] It was seen to be unworkable ; and the organization into metropolitan areas is further emphasized in our next Document.

DOCUMENT 63——The "Apostolic" Canons.   Fourth century. (*P.L.* 67. 145; *P.N.F.* 14. 596A.)

35. The bishops of every nation must acknowledge him who is first among them, and account him as their head, and do nothing of consequence without his consent; but each may do those things only which concern his own parish, and the country places which belong to it. But neither let him who is first do anything without the consent of all; for so there will be unanimity, and God will be glorified through the Lord in the Holy Ghost. (Gore 103 note.)

[1] This canon is considered in Chapter XX, pp. 235-237.
[2] Kidd, *Hist. Ch.*, 2. 48.
[3] G. Phillips, *Kirchenrecht*, Band 2, p. 36 (Regensburg, 1845).
[4] Doc. 45 § 3.

The above canon is given because of the use made of it by Gore, but the ninth canon of the synod of Antioch[1] (held probably within a year or two of Nicaea)[2] covers the same ground, and makes it clear that the head bishop of the province is he who presides in the civil capital of that province.

II. JULIUS, BISHOP OF ROME

Athanasius, the champion of the Nicene or orthodox faith, was ordained bishop of Alexandria in A.D. 328. Two years later the Emperor Constantine moved his capital from Rome to Byzantium, calling the latter place Constantinople. Julius became Pope on 6 February 337, and the following May the emperor died. The empire was divided and Constantius II ruled at Constantinople over the East and developed sympathy with Arian doctrines. This gave impetus to a reaction towards Arianism, led by Eusebius of Nicomedia, who in A.D. 339 got himself translated to the see of Constantinople, whose rightful bishop was in exile. His Arianizing party, which had the backing of the emperor's court, were called Eusebians.

In the year 338 the Eusebians accused Athanasius of misappropriating charitable supplies,[3] and of other irregularities, and declared that he was no longer the rightful bishop of Alexandria.[4] They also wrote to Julius and "requested him to call a council, and to be himself the judge, if he so pleased" (Doc. 66). The following January they appointed an Arian called Gregory to succeed Athanasius, "and sent him to Alexandria with a military force" (Doc. 67 § 29). Athanasius then sailed to Rome.

DOCUMENT 64——Athanasius, *Historia Arianorum.* A.D. 358.
(*P.G.* 25. 705; *L.F.* 13. 227 ‡.)

11. As soon as Athanasius heard, he, knowing the fury of the heretics, sailed to Rome, that the synod might be held as arranged. And Julius wrote and sent presbyters, Elpidius and Philoxenus, and fixed a time by which they must come or consider themselves to be altogether under suspicion. But as soon as the Eusebians realized that the trial was to be an ecclesiastical one, at which no count would be present, no soldiers stationed before the doors, and that the proceedings would not be regulated by royal order (for they have always

[1] Hefele, 2. 69.
[2] H. Chadwick in *J.T.S.*, Jan. 1948, p. 34.
[3] Athan. *Apol.* § 18.　　　[4] Ibid. § 7.

depended on these things to support them against the bishops, and without them they dare not even speak), they were so alarmed that they detained the presbyters till after the appointed time, and invented this preposterous excuse, that they were not able to come now on account of the war which was begun by the Persians. (Chapman 38A note.)

Instead of going to Rome as they were asked to do, the Eusebians wrote to the Pope, but their letter is only extant in the paraphrase of Sozomen a century later.

DOCUMENT 65——Sozomen, *Church History*, Book 3. A.D. 450. (*P.G.* 67. 1052; Bagster 114 ‡.)

8. . [The Roman bishop] wrote to the bishops of the East, rebuking them for their wrong judgement of these men, and for disturbing the peace of the Church by abandoning the Nicene doctrines. He bade a few of them to come to him on a certain day to show that they had now reached a just decision about them, and threatened to bear with them no longer should they introduce more innovations. . The partisans of Athanasius and Paul were reinstated in their sees, and they forwarded the letter of Julius to the bishops of the East. These bishops were highly indignant at these [letters] and met at Antioch and framed a reply to Julius, replete with elegance and the graces of rhetoric, but couched in a tone of irony and defiance. They confessed therein that *the Roman church was entitled to the honour of all*, because it was the school of the apostles and was from the beginning the metropolis of religion, although those who imported the doctrine came to her from the East. But they ought not to take second place because their church was small in size and numbers, for they excelled in virtue and wisdom. *They called Julius to account* for communicating with the partisans of Athanasius and were indignant against him for insulting their synod and *abrogating their sentence*. And they *rejected his action as unjust and opposed to ecclesiastical law*. After these complaints and protests, they offered peace and communion to Julius, if he would sanction

the deposition of those whom they had expelled, and the ordination of those whom they had elected instead; and they threatened the contrary, if he opposed their decrees. They added that the priests of the East before them had raised no objection when Novatian was expelled by the church of Rome.
(Gore 101 note; Chapman 38B note.)

At the council of Rome in the autumn of 340, more than fifty bishops declared Athanasius to be innocent.

DOCUMENT 66——Athanasius, *Apologia contra Arianos.* A.D. 351.
 (*P.G.* 25. 280; *L.F.* 13. 39 ‡.)

20. The Egyptians wrote to everyone and to Julius, bishop of Rome. The Eusebians also wrote to Julius and, thinking to frighten me, requested him to call a council, and to be himself the judge, if he so pleased. So, when I went up to Rome, Julius wrote to the Eusebians a suitable reply, and sent two of his own presbyters, Elpidius and Philoxenus. But they, when they heard of me, were thrown into confusion, not expecting that I would go up, and they begged to be excused. They offered unsatisfactory reasons, but really they were afraid that they would be convicted of those things which Valens and Ursacius confessed later. However, more than fifty bishops assembled in the place where Vito held his congregation, and they accepted my defence, and admitted me to their communion and their love. They were indignant against the Eusebians, and asked Julius to write to that effect to those who had written to him. This he did, and sent his letter by Gabian the count. "Julius to the beloved brethren . ."
(Chapman 38A note.)

DOCUMENT 67——Julius, *To the Eusebians.* A.D. 340.
 In Athan. *Apol.* 20–36. (*P.G.* 25. 281; *L.F.* 13. 39 ‡.)

20.   . Julius to the beloved brethren, Danius,[1] Flacillus,[2] Narcissus, Eusebius, Maris, Macedonius, Theodorus, and their

[1] Dianius, bishop of Caesarea in Cappadocia 340–362.
[2] Bishop of Antioch 333–342.

friends, who have written to us from Antioch, greeting in the Lord.

21. I have read the letter which was brought by my presbyters Elpidius and Philoxenus, and I am surprised that whereas we wrote in charity and conscious sincerity, you have replied with contention and impropriety; for the pride and arrogance of the writers is exhibited in the letter. These things are alien to the faith in Christ; for what was written in charity should also have a reply in charity.   But we are obliged to infer that the words by which you seem to honour us are transformed by irony.

26.   . I must inform you that although I alone wrote, yet the view I expressed is not only mine, but that of *all the bishops throughout Italy and in these parts.* Indeed I was unwilling to make them all write, lest they should have the pressure of numbers. Of course the bishops assembled on the day fixed, and agreed in these views which I again write to signify to you; so that, beloved, although I alone write, be sure that this is the opinion of all. So much then for the unreasonable, unjust, and suspicious excuses which some of you have devised.

29. Now when these things were so spoken, and there were so many witnesses for him [Athanasius], and so much in justification was advanced for him, what did it bind us to do? What did the ecclesiastical canon require, but that we should not condemn the man, but rather receive and treat him as a bishop, as we have done? And besides all this, he stayed here a year and six months, awaiting the arrival of you, or of those who wanted to come. His presence shamed everyone, for he would not have been here, if he had not had confidence; and he came not of his own accord, but *he was summoned by letter from us,* as we wrote to you. But after all this, you complain that we acted against the canons. Now consider: who are they that have done so? We who received the man after so many proofs, or they who, being at Antioch thirty-six halts away, appointed a stranger to be bishop, and sent him to Alexandria with a military force?

33. Not only the bishops Athanasius and Marcellus came here and complained of the injustice that had been done to

them, but many other bishops also, from Thrace, from Coele–Syria, from Phoenicia and Palestine, and not a few presbyters; and others from Alexandria and elsewhere were present at the council here, and besides the other things which they said, they lamented before all the assembled bishops the violence and injustice which the churches had suffered.

34. . . . Now as men with hearts of pity, take care to remedy, as I said before, the things done against the canons, so that if any [harm] has been done, it may be healed by your care. And do not write that I have preferred the communion of Marcellus and Athanasius to yours, for such things are not marks of peace, but of contention and brotherly hatred. I have written the above for this reason, that you may realize that we did not receive them unjustly, and this strife may cease.

35.   O beloved, the decisions of the Church are no longer according to the gospel, but tend only to exile and death. Supposing, as you assert, that there was some charge against them, the case ought not to have been conducted thus, but according to the ecclesiastical canon. You should have written to us all, *so that justice might be determined by all.* For the sufferers were bishops, and prominent churches, which the apostles themselves had governed. And why were we not written to especially about the church of the Alexandrians? Are you ignorant that the custom was *first to write to us, and then for justice to be determined from here?* If then the bishop there was at all suspect, it should have been reported in writing to the church here. As it is they failed to inform us, but acted as they pleased, and now want to obtain our concurrence, though we have not condemned him. Not so the statutes of Paul,[1] not so have the fathers handed down; this is another model, and a new procedure. I beseech you, readily bear with me: what I write is for the common good. For *what we have received from the blessed apostle Peter,* that I point out to you; and as I believe these things to be obvious to all, I should not have written if the events had not distracted us.

(Chapman 38A note, 73B note, 94B.)

[1] 1 Tim. 5. 19, 20.

Athanasius, bishop of Alexandria, came to Rome on a summons from the Pope (§ 29). The Pope wrote on behalf of the fifty [1] western bishops assembled with him (§ 26). He appealed to the authority of Peter and Paul, and claimed to hand on the word of Peter (§ 35). When the bishops of apostolic sees are accused, the matter must be reported to all the bishops, who should jointly pass sentence. Where the bishop of Alexandria is concerned, custom demands that the investigation takes place at Rome [2] (§ 35).

III. THE COUNCIL OF SARDICA, A.D. 342

By permission of the emperors, [3] the case of Athanasius was further considered at the council of Sardica, the modern Sofia in Bulgaria. This council was attended by bishops from all over the empire, including places as far apart as Arabia and Britain. It is not known how many bishops attended. In his *Apologia*, Athanasius says that over 300 passed sentence in his favour, [4] and he gives 281 signatures [5]; elsewhere he says about 170 were present. [6] Eusebius of Nicomedia had died the previous year, but bishops of his party came to Sardica, and then, avoiding the council, they retired to Philippopolis, [7] eighty miles to the east. From there they wrote as follows:

DOCUMENT 68——The Eusebians, *Letter from Philippopolis.* A.D. 342.
In Hilary, *Fragmentum* 3. 27. (*P.L.* 10. 674.)

To Gregory, bishop of Alexandria, Amphion, bishop of Nicomedia, Donatus, bishop of Carthage, Wherefore the whole council, following ancient law, condemned Julius of the city of Rome, Hosius, Protogenes, Gaudentius, and Maximin of Trèves, as originators of the communion of Marcellus, Athanasius, and other miscreants, . for it was Julius of the city of Rome, as *chief and leader of the wicked*, who first opened the door of communion to infamous and condemned men. (Chapman 73B.)

The orthodox majority confirmed the decisions of the council of Rome, A.D. 340, pronounced the Arian Gregory at Alexandria to be a usurper, and passed important canons, which have given rise to

[1] Doc. 66.
[2] See Docs. 51, 52.
[3] Hilary, *Fragm.* 2. 11 (Doc. 73). [4] *Apol.* 1.
[5] Doc. 72 § 50. [6] *Hist. Arian.* 15.
[7] Socrates, *H.E.* 2. 20, and Doc. 236.

much dispute. There are Greek and Latin versions of these canons, and they vary considerably. I have followed the *Authenticum Latinum* which Turner and others[1] believe to be original. Hefele gives both versions, believing them both to be original.

DOCUMENT 69——Council of Sardica: Canons. A.D. 342.
(Turner 494A.)

3. The bishop Hosius said: But if a bishop has had sentence pronounced against him in some action, and thinks he has good cause for the judgement to be reconsidered, let us, if you agree,[2] do honour to the memory of the holy apostle Peter: let letters be written to the bishop of Rome, either by those who have conducted the examination or by the bishops living in the nearest province; if he decides that the sentence must be reconsidered, let it be reconsidered and let him appoint judges; but if he concludes that the case is such that it is inexpedient to reopen old wounds by raking up the past, his [own] decision shall stand confirmed. Are all agreed?" The council answered: "Agreed."

4. The bishop Gaudentius said: "A rider, if you agree, to this very holy decision you have made: When a bishop has been deposed by the judgement of the bishops living in neighbouring places and has announced that he must transact [the] business in the city of Rome, let another bishop on no account be ordained in his stead in the same see after the appeal of him who appears to have been deposed, except the case shall have been determined by the judgement of the bishop of Rome."

5. The bishop Hosius said: "But it has been agreed that if a bishop has been accused, and the assembled bishops of that region have passed judgement and have ejected him from his degree, and it turns out that he has appealed and taken flight to the most blessed bishop of the church of Rome, and he has consented [for him] to be heard, and has thought it just that the inquiry should be reopened: let him vouchsafe to write to the bishops in the adjacent and neighbouring province [that]

[1] W. Telfer in *Harvard Theological Review*, 1943, Vol. 36, p. 182, n. 32.
[2] *si vobis placet* or εἰ δοκεῖ.

they search out all things with diligence and make decision according to fidelity of truth. But if anyone asks for his case to be heard again, and by his own petition has moved the bishop of Rome to send a presbyter with a special mission, it shall be in the bishop's power [to say] what he wishes or what he judges best; [and] if he decides that he ought to send such persons as, being present with the bishops, may give judgement as having the authority of him by whom they have been dispatched, [this] will be within his discretion; if, however, he considers the bishops are competent to make a final decision on the matter, he shall do what in his most wise counsel he judges [best]."

(Gore 113, 114; Chapman 73–75.)

These canons either grant considerable powers to the Pope, or recognize such powers as already existing. A condemned bishop may appeal to the Pope. The Pope decides whether there is a case for rehearing or not. If he grants a re-opening of the case, he appoints as judges the bishops who are neighbours to the province of the accused. He may also send priests of his own to act with his authority in the new court. Meantime the see of the accused bishop must not be filled by a fresh appointment.

Anglican scholars maintain that these are new powers granted to the Pope for the first time. The words "if you agree" in Canon 3, imply that the Canon need not be passed.[1] In this they follow the Gallican P. Quesnel, who wrote: "This power of decreeing a rehearing in the province itself, although it is far less than the right of appeals, was nevertheless proposed with extreme caution and hesitation by Hosius, who begged almost as a suppliant, and on the pretext that the memory of St Peter should be honoured, for an innovation, by no means in accordance with the canons of Nicaea, which ran counter to very definite precedent."[2]

But Chapman and other Roman Catholics do not admit that the powers are new. The right of appeal to the Pope is recognized as by divine law, and Canon 5 merely outlines the procedure to be adopted if such right is exercised by a bishop. The words "if you agree" are just a formula. "No doubt a new honour would have been paid to St Peter even by a canon which merely sanctioned the existing custom of appeals to Rome."[3] This right of appeal to Rome had recently been exercised by Athanasius (see Doc. 64).

[1] Gore, 114; Kidd, *Roman Primacy*, 52.
[2] *Opera S. Leonis*, Vol. II, 257A (edit. 1700).
[3] Chapman, 75 and note.

We shall see, however, in Chapter XX that when an African priest appealed to Pope Zosimus against a condemnation by an African court, the Pope based his right to interfere not on divine law, but on the above Canon 5, which he believed to be Nicene. Again as regards the meaning of the phrase "if you agree" (εἰ δοκεῖ) Athanasius in the following passage shows how the same verb was used at the council of Nicaea, when that council made a decision about the keeping of Easter, and he contrasts it with the expression they used when dealing with matters of faith.

DOCUMENT 70——Athanasius, *De Synodis.*   A.D. 359.
   (*P.G.* 26. 688; *L.F.* 8. 79 ‡.)

5. As to the Nicene council, it was not a common meeting, but convened upon a pressing necessity, and for a reasonable object. The Syrians, Cilicians, and Mesopotamians were out of order in celebrating the feast, and kept Easter with the Jews; on the other hand, the Arian heresy had risen up against the Catholic Church, and found supporters in the Eusebians, who both were zealous for the heresy, and conducted the attack upon religious people. This gave occasion for an ecumenical council, that the feast might be everywhere celebrated on one day, and that the heresy which was springing up might be anathematized. It took place then; and the Syrians submitted, and the fathers pronounced the Arian heresy to be the forerunner of antichrist, and drew up a suitable formula against it. And yet in this, many as they were, they ventured on nothing like the proceedings of these three or four men. Without prefixing consulate, month, and day, they wrote concerning Easter "It seemed good [1] as follows", for it did then seem good that there should be a general compliance; but about the faith they did not write "It seemed good", but "Thus believes the Catholic Church"; and thereupon they confessed how they themselves believed *in order to show that their own sentiments were not new*, but apostolic.   (Gore 43.)

Gore quotes from this passage to show that the Church cannot make new articles of faith.

Before disbanding, the Council of Sardica wrote four letters.

[1] ἔδοξε.

DOCUMENT 71——Council of Sardica, *To the Church of Alexandria*. A.D. 342.
  In Athan. *Apol.* (*P.G.* 25. 312; *L.F.* 13. 60 ‡.)

36.   . The holy council, by the grace of God assembled at Sardica, from Rome and Spain, Gaul, Italy, Campania, Calabria, Apulia, Africa, Sardinia, Pannonia, Mysia, Dacia, Noricum, Siscia, Dardania, the other Dacia, Macedonia, Thessaly, Achaia, Epirus, Thrace, and Rhodope, and Palestine, and Arabia, and Crete, and Egypt, to their dearly beloved brethren, the presbyters and deacons, and to all the holy church of God abiding at Alexandria, greeting in the Lord.

37. We were not ignorant, but the fact was well known to us, even before we received the letters of your piety, that the supporters of the abominable heresy of the Arians were practising many dangerous schemes   when they came to the city of Sardica, they were unwilling to meet the council of all the holy bishops. From this *it became evident that the decision of our brother and fellow bishop Julius was a just one*; for after cautious deliberation and care he had determined that we ought not to hesitate at all about holding communion with our brother Athanasius. For he had the credible testimony of eighty bishops, and was also able to advance this fair argument in his support, that by the mere means of our dearly beloved brethren his own presbyters, and by correspondence, he had defeated the designs of the Eusebians, who relied more upon violence than upon a judicial inquiry.

And so all the bishops from all parts determined to hold communion with Athanasius on the ground that he was innocent. . .

39. .   . As for Gregory, who has the reputation of being illegally ordained by the heretics, and has been sent by them to your city, we wish you all to realize that he has been degraded *by a judgement of the whole sacred synod*, although in fact he has never at any time been considered to be a bishop at all.   (Chapman 73B, 75B.)

A similar letter was sent to the bishops of Egypt and Libya.[1]
[1] Athan. *Apol.* 41, 42.

DOCUMENT 72——Council of Sardica, *To the Whole Church.*
        A.D. 342.
    In Athan. *Apol.* (*P.G.* 25. 324; *L.F.* 13. 69 ‡.)

43.   The holy council by the grace of God assembled at
Sardica, to their dearly beloved brethren in the Lord, the
bishops and fellow-ministers of the Catholic Church everywhere.

44. The Arian fanatics have dared repeatedly to attack the
servants of God who hold the right faith; they tried to sub-
stitute a spurious doctrine, and to drive out the orthodox.
Indeed their slanders were clearly proved by the fact that, when they
were called by our dearly beloved fellow minister Julius, they would
not come, and also by the writings of Julius himself. For had
they had confidence in the measures in which they were
engaged against our fellow ministers, they would have come.
And besides they gave a more evident proof of their conspiracy
by their conduct in the great and holy synod. For when they
reached Sardica and saw our brothers Athanasius, Marcellus,
Asclepas and the rest, they were afraid to come to a trial, and
though they were repeatedly invited to attend, they would
not obey the summons.

49.   *We have therefore pronounced* our dearly beloved
brethren and fellow ministers Athanasius, Marcellus, and
Asclepas, and those who minister to the Lord with them, to be
innocent and clear of offence, and have written to the district
of each, that the people of each church may know the innocence
of their own bishop, and may accept him as their bishop, and
expect his coming. As for those who have invaded their
churches like wolves, Gregory at Alexandria, Basil at Ancyra,
and Quintian at Gaza, no one should call them bishops, or
hold any communion at all with them, or receive letters from
them or write to them.   Those who separate the Son and
alienate the Word from the Father ought themselves to be
separated from the Catholic Church and to be alien from the
Christian name. They should therefore be anathema to you,
because they have adulterated the word of truth. The order is
apostolic, "If any man preach any other gospel unto you than
that ye have received, let him be anathema".

50. Signed: Hosius from Spain, Julius of Rome by Archidamus and Philoxenus presbyters, Protogenes of Sardica   . [and 277 others from Gaul, Africa, Egypt, Italian Canale, Cyprus, and Palestine].   (Chapman 73B.)

We notice in the above two letters, that the council claims to decide on questions of faith, and to decide also who is the rightful bishop of Alexandria.

DOCUMENT 73——Council of Sardica, *To Julius*. A.D. 342.
   In Hilary, *Fragmentum* 2. (*P.L.* 10. 639; editor, and
      Shotwell & Loomis, 528.[1])

9.   Paul the apostle said concerning himself: "Or do you seek a proof of the Christ that speaks in me?" Yet, of a truth, since the Lord Christ dwelt in him, it would be impossible to doubt that the Holy Ghost spoke through his soul, and resounded through the organ of his body. Accordingly you too, most beloved brother, though separated in the body were present in a harmony of mind and will. The excuse for your absence was both honourable and necessary lest either schismatic wolves might steal and rob by stealth, or heretical dogs bark madly in the wild fury of excitement, or even the crawling devil pour forth the poison of blasphemy; for this will appear best and fittest, that *the priests of the Lord from all the provinces should report to the head, that is to the see of Peter the apostle*.[2]

10. But inasmuch as our written reports contain every event and transaction and resolution of ours and as the voices of our dear brothers and fellow priests, Archidamus and Philoxenus, and of our dear son Leo, the deacon, can describe them to you accurately and faithfully, it seems almost superfluous to rehearse these same things in this letter. It has been clear to everyone that those who came here from the East, who call themselves bishops, although some of their leaders have

---

[1] §§ 10, 11, 13 from J. T. Shotwell and L. R. Loomis, *The See of Peter*, Columbia Univ. Press, 1927; § 9 added by editor.

[2] *Hoc enim optimum et valde congruentissimum esse videbitur, si ad caput, id est ad Petri apostoli sedem, de singulis quibusque provinciis Domini referant sacerdotes.*

impious minds, tainted by the baleful poison of the heresy of Arius, have long been raising cowardly objections and out of distrust refusing to appear for trial and abjuring communion with you and us, although our communion is blameless, for we have believed in the testimony of more than eighty bishops together as to the innocence of Athanasius. But when these others were summoned by your priests and your letter to the council which was to be held at Rome, they would not come. And it was exceedingly unjust for them to condemn Marcellus and Athanasius and to deny them fellowship in the face of the testimony of so many bishops.

11. There were three subjects for us to discuss. For our devout emperors themselves gave us permission to debate thoroughly everything under dispute, and first of all the holy faith and sound truth, which are being assailed. . .

13. You, then, in your excellent wisdom, should provide that our brethren in Sicily, Sardinia, and Italy may learn by a communication from you what has been done and decreed, that they may not accept in ignorance letters of communion or certificates from men who have been degraded by a just verdict. (Chapman 73B.)

Some Anglicans[1] have found it convenient that the words in § 9 of the above letter for which I have given the Latin[2] were rejected by certain scholars in the eighteenth century, e.g. Archibald Bower, Counsellor of the Inquisition, 1748: "I agree with Blondel[3] that this passage is foisted in; but cannot acquiesce to the only reason he alleges to support his opinion, viz. the barbarity of the Latin expression 'valde congruentissimum esse'; for such a slip might easily escape . . . besides we are not certain the letter was originally written in Latin. The want of connection between that sentence and what is said before and after it, is I think a more convincing proof of forgery."[4] Chapman, however, thinks that "The connection is not difficult to see; Julius was right to be unwilling to leave Rome, for there would have been no head there who could keep in order from thence the schismatic wolves and heretic dogs, and hear appeals".[5] Kidd accepts the passage as genuine, but tries to weaken its force by saying that "this was a Western Council, and the Pope is admittedly 'head' of

[1] E.g. Denny, 630.   [2] Page 105, n. 2.
[3] *De la Primauté en l'Eglise*, p. 106 (A.D. 1641).
[4] *Hist. of Popes*, Vol. I, p. 121.
[5] *S.E.P.*, 63 n.

Western Christendom".[1] Reference to the beginning of Doc. 71 and the end of Doc. 72 shows, however, that bishops were present from Greece, Palestine, Egypt, and Arabia. Apparently these also addressed the Pope as their head.

Notice in § 11 how the civil power controls ecclesiastical discussion. And with § 13 compare the request to Pope Silvester in Doc. 59.

IV POPE LIBERIUS

The Arian heresy was condemned at the ecumenical council of Nicaea, A.D. 325 (Doc. 70). Athanasius, the champion of orthodoxy, was confirmed in his see by Pope Julius and the council of Rome in 340 (Doc. 67). Again at the council of Sardica, A.D. 342, Athanasius was declared orthodox, and the Nicene creed upheld (Doc. 72 § 49). But the enemies of truth would not own themselves beaten, and relying on Constantius, who became sole emperor in 351, they continued to bully the bishops who remained loyal.

The emperor brought pressure to bear on Pope Liberius to make him sign against Athanasius and to communicate with the Arians. When he refused he was sent into exile, A.D. 355. Jerome, writing some thirty years later, says that Liberius, "giving in to the irksomeness of exile", subscribed to the heretical and false doctrine.[2] The evidence for this fall of the Pope is weighty. It consists of three letters of the Pope himself, preserved in Hilary's fragments, two statements of Athanasius in Docs. 75 § 89 and 77 § 41 below, two statements of Jerome,[3] and one of Sozomen.[4] The most important of the three papal letters is:

DOCUMENT 74——Liberius, *To the Eastern Presbyters and Bishops.*
    A.D. 357.
In Hilary, *Frag.* 6 (*Pro deifico timore*) § 5. (*P.L.* 10. 689.)

. . . I did not defend Athanasius, but because my predecessor Julius, of good memory, had received him, I was afraid lest I might be judged a dissembler in some sort. But when, by God's will, I realized that you had justly condemned him, I at once assented to your opinions; and I have given letters, about that very man (that is about his condition), to be carried to the emperor Constantius by our brother Fortunatian. So then, Athanasius being removed from communion with all of us, and since I am not even to receive his letters, I say that I am quite

---

[1] *Hist. Ch.*, 2. 87.   [2] *Chron. ad Ann.* 352 (Doc. 119).
[3] Ibid. and *De Viris Ill.* § 97 (Doc. 126).   [4] *H.E.* 4. 15.

at peace with all of you, and in peace and harmony with all
the eastern bishops throughout the provinces.

Bishop Hefele believed that all the letters of Liberius in which he
implicates himself are forgeries,[1] but he is refuted by another Roman
Catholic, P. Le Page Renouf.[2] And more recent scholars have
accepted them as genuine.[3] J. H. Newman agrees that the Pope subscribed to Arian confessions, and is concerned only to show that a
signature under duress cannot be a decision of the Pope *ex cathedra*;[4]
and even Chapman does not deny the fall of Liberius.[5] It seems therefore unnecessary to set out in detail the documentary evidence for the
fact; besides, it is not really relevant to our inquiry. What we want to
know is how the contemporary Church, and Athanasius in particular,
regarded the Pope's fall. On this point opinions differ.

"If anything in the world can be certain, it is certain that St Athanasius, had he had any idea of the bishop of Rome being in a unique sense the guardian of the faith, much more any notion of his infallibility, must have adopted another tone in regard to his fall. He must have quivered at the awful shock of finding himself deserted by the 'Holy Father' on the central dogma of the faith. It must have been much more to him than his desertion by Hosius. There is no avoiding or palliating this conclusion."[6]

"It is certain, 'if anything in the world can be certain,' that Athanasius regarded the Pope as 'being in a unique sense the guardian of the faith', and I cannot see that there is any room for controversy on this point . .

"Though Hosius was personally of extraordinary influence and fame, yet it will be found that St Athanasius always treats Liberius as the more important, whenever the two are mentioned."[7]

Gore is wrong to drag in the question of infallibility, which is
irrelevant here, but some light is thrown on the main point in dispute
by the three works of Athanasius which follow.

DOCUMENT 75——Athanasius, *Apologia contra Arianos.* A.D. 358.
   (*P.G.* 25. 409; *L.F.* 13. 122 ‡.)

89.   . Now if the true bishops had resisted by words
alone those who plotted against us and wished to undo

[1] Hefele, 2. 242.   [2] *Condemnation of Pope Honorius*, 44 (A.D. 1868).
[3] See Jalland, *Papacy*, 229, n. 3.   [4] *Historical Sketches*, 3. 340 note.
[5] Chapman, 38A.   [6] Gore, 100.
[7] Chapman, 72B note.

what had been done for us, or if they had been ordinary men, and not the bishops of notable cities, and the heads of so great churches, one might suspect that now they too had acted contentiously in order to court favour. But they both tried reasoning and also endured exile, and one of them is Liberius, bishop of Rome, for although he did not endure to the end the distress of exile, yet he remained banished for two years, knowing of the conspiracy against us. And there is also the great Hosius and the bishops of Italy, and of Gaul, and others from Spain, and from Egypt, and Libya, and all those of Pentapolis. For although Hosius, for fear of the threats of Constantius, seemed for a short time not to resist, yet the great violence and tyranny of the emperor, and the many insults and stripes, prove that he yielded to them for a time, not because he gave us up, but because the weakness of old age did not bear the stripes.

90. Now if anyone wishes to learn about our case, and about the Eusebian slander, he should read what has been written for us, and let him hear the witnesses, not one or two or three, but such a number of bishops; and again let him attend to the witnesses on the affairs of Liberius and Hosius and those with them, who, when they saw the attempts made against us, submitted to suffer all things rather than renounce the truth, and the judgement on our behalf. (Chapman 72B note.)

DOCUMENT 76——Athanasius, *Apologia de Fuga Sua.* A.D. 358. (*P.G.* 25. 649; *L.F.* 13. 191 ‡.)

4. . Even now, while the churches were at peace, and the people worshipping publicly, Liberius bishop of Rome, Paulinus metropolitan of Gaul, Dionysius metropolitan of Italy, Lucifer metropolitan of the Sardinia islands, and Eusebius of Italy, all good bishops and preachers of the truth, were seized and banished on no pretext, except that they would not unite with the Arian heresy, or subscribe to the false accusations and slanders which they had invented against us.

5. *Of the great*, happily aged, and well named *Hosius it*

is superfluous for me to speak; for probably everyone knows that
they banished him also; for he is no obscure person, but *most
famous of all* and more, the notable old man! For in what
council did he not lead the way, and convince everyone by
his orthodoxy? Where is any church which does not possess
some glorious monuments of his leadership?

DOCUMENT 77——Athanasius, *Historia Arianorum*.   A.D. 358.
   (*P.G.* 25. 733; *L.F.* 13. 248 ‡.)

35.   . From the outset, they [the Arians] did not even
spare Liberius bishop of Rome, but extended their fury even
to that place; they did not respect it because it is an apostolic
throne, nor were they cautious because Rome is the metropolis
of Romania; they did not remember that formerly they had
written to them as apostolic men. But confusing all things
together, they forgot everything entirely, and only considered
their zeal for evil. For when they saw that he was orthodox
and hated the Arian heresy, and that he tried hard to persuade
everyone to renounce it and withdraw from it, these profane
men reasoned thus: "*If we persuade Liberius we shall soon prevail
over all.*" And they imposed upon the emperor, and he,
expecting quickly to draw all men over to his side by means of
Liberius, writes to him, and sends a certain eunuch called
Eusebius with letters and gifts, to flatter him with the gifts and
to threaten him with the letters. So the eunuch went to Rome,
and first invited Liberius to subscribe against Athanasius, and
to communicate with the Arians, saying: "The emperor wishes
it, and orders you to do so." And then showing him the gifts,
he took him by the hand, and again besought him, saying:
"Comply with the emperor and take these."

36. But to convince him, the bishop said: "How can this be
done against Athanasius? How can we condemn a man who
has been fairly acquitted first by one council, then by another
assembled from all parts of the world, and whom the church of
Rome dismissed in peace? Who will approve of us if we reject
in his absence one whose presence we welcomed and admitted
to communion? There is no such ecclesiastical canon; nor

have we ever received such a tradition from the fathers, which tradition they might have received from the blessed and great apostle Peter."

37.　　. The emperor therefore writes to Rome, and again palace officials, notaries, and counts are sent with letters to the prefect, that they may either lead Liberius away from Rome by craft, and send him to himself at the camp, or else persecute him by violence.

38. Such being the letters, fear and treachery prevailed throughout the city. How many families were threatened! How many people were bribed to denounce Liberius in public! . . How strictly did they guard the harbour and the gateways, that no orthodox person might come to visit Liberius! Rome also experienced the enemies of Christ and knew at last what she would not believe when told how the other churches in every city were ravaged by them.　　Constantius plotted against all, and banished Liberius.

39. After the emperor had frequently written to Rome, had threatened, sent legates, and schemed, the persecution spread to Alexandria. Liberius was dragged before him, but boldly speaking out, he said to him : "Stop persecuting the Christians ; do not try to bring profanity into the Church through me. We are ready to endure anything, rather than to be called Ariomaniacs. We are Christians ; do not force us to become Christ's enemies. We also advise you not to fight against him who gave you this rule, nor to show impiety to him instead of thankfulness. Do not persecute those who believe in him."

41.　　Thus they tried at first to corrupt the church of the Romans, wishing to introduce impiety into it. But Liberius, after he had been exiled for two years, gave way, and from fear of threatened death he subscribed. But this also shows their violence, and the hatred of Liberius against the heresy, and his support of Athanasius, whilst he had a free choice. For what is done under torture against a man's first judgement is not the willing deed of those who fear, but that of the tormentors. These latter attempted everything to support the heresy, while the people in every church, holding the faith they had learnt, waited for the return of their teachers. And they all rejected the anti-Christian heresy, and avoided it like a serpent.

42. But although the ungodly had done all this, yet they thought *they had accomplished nothing, so long as the great Hosius escaped their knavish tricks.* And now they set out to extend their fury to that venerable old man. They felt no shame that he is the father of the bishops, nor did they care that he had been a confessor, nor respect the length of his episcopate, in which he had continued more than sixty years, but they set aside everything and only looked at the heresy, truly men who neither "fear God nor regard man".[1] So they went to Constantius and again argued as follows: "We have done everything; we have banished the bishop of the Romans, and before him many other bishops, and we have filled every place with alarm. But these strong measures of yours are nothing to us, *nor have we succeeded at all, so long as Hosius remains.* While he is in his own place, they all also are in their churches, for he is competent in reason and in faith to persuade all against us. He is the president of councils, and his letters are heard everywhere, and he put forth the faith in Nicaea, and proclaimed everywhere that the Arians were heretics. If therefore he remains, the banishment of the rest is superfluous, for our heresy will be put out. Begin, then, to persecute him also, and spare him not, old as he is. Our heresy does not recognize the honourable grey hairs of the aged."   (Gore 52, 100; Chapman 72B note.)

V. HILARY OF POITIERS

Anglicans like Pusey[2] and Gore[3] believed that the unity of the Church is not primarily a matter of outward government. It is God and not man who makes Christians to be "of one heart and soul".[4] He does this by infusing into them the Holy Ghost in baptism, so that they become one in nature. It is true that only through the visible organ of his Church has God covenanted to give us this new nature, but it is possible to emphasize the outward government in such a way as to weaken the essential unity of nature. This line of thought is supported by an appeal to Hilary, bishop of Poitiers. He was a contemporary of Athanasius, and one of the few leading bishops who

---

[1] Luke 18. 4.   [2] *Eirenicon* (1865), p. 56 f.
[3] Page 30.   [4] Acts 4. 32.

withstood the Arian persecutions. His two works from which we quote were written towards the end of three years' exile from his see.

DOCUMENT 78——Hilary, *De Trinitate*, Book 8. A.D. 360.
  (*P.L.* 10. 240; *P.N.F.* 9. 139A ‡.)
  5.   . The Arians try to refer his words "I and the Father are one" to a consent of unanimity, so that there may be in them a unity of will, not of nature, that is, "that they may be one" not through that which they are, but by identity of will. And they quote in their defence the passage in the Acts of the Apostles, "Now the multitude of believers were one soul and heart", that a diversity of souls and hearts may be united into one heart and soul, through conformity of the same will.
  7. . . As to those whose soul and heart were one, I ask whether they were one through faith in God. Certainly through faith, for through this the soul and heart of all were one. Again I ask: is the faith one, or is there another? One indeed, and that on the authority of the apostle himself, who proclaims one faith even as one Lord, and one baptism, and one hope, and one God. If then it is through faith, that is, through the nature of one faith, that all are one, how is it that you do not understand a natural unity in those who through the nature of one faith are one? For all were born again to innocence, to immortality, to the knowledge of God, to the faith of hope.   .
If, however, they have been begotten again into the nature of one life and eternity, then inasmuch as their soul and heart are one, the unity of assent is inactive in those who are one in rebirth of the same nature.
  8.   The apostle shows that this unity of faith arises from the nature of the sacraments, when he writes to the Galatians: "For as many of you as were baptized into Christ did put on Christ. There is neither Jew nor Greek, there is neither bond nor free, there is neither male nor female; for ye are all one in Christ Jesus." That they are one amid so great a diversity of race, condition, and sex, is it from assent of will or from the unity of the sacrament, since these have one baptism and have all put on one Christ? What therefore will an agreement of

minds avail here, when they are one because they have put on one Christ through the nature of one baptism?

(Gore 211, 212.)

But the view that the visible Church can be divided for a long time, finds no support from the fathers.[1] This is admitted by Gore, who explains that the fathers were not prophets of the future. He cites an early work of Athanasius to show how he optimistically supposed that Christian nations would never go to war against each other.

DOCUMENT 79——Athanasius, *Oratio de Incarnatione Verbi Dei.* A.D. 318.
　　　(*P.G.* 25. 188; C.S.M.V.[2] 91 ‡.)

52. . . The barbarians of to-day are naturally savage in their habits, and as long as they sacrifice to idols, they furiously rage against each other, and cannot bear to be a single hour without weapons. But when they hear the teaching of Christ, forthwith they turn from fighting to farming, and instead of arming with swords, they raise their hands in prayer. In a word, instead of fighting each other, they take up arms against the devil and against evil spirits, subduing the demons by self-restraint and virtue, and overcoming them by their self-command and integrity of soul. These facts are a proof of the godhead of the Saviour, for he has taught men what they could never learn among idols.　　　　　　(Gore 139.)

DOCUMENT 80——Hilary, *Second Letter to Constantius.*　A.D. 360.
　　　(*P.L.* 10. 566; *The Rambler*, July 1859, 218.)

5. Since the Nicene council, we have done nothing but write the creed. While we fight about words, inquire about novelties, take advantage of ambiguities, criticize authors, fight on party questions, have difficulties in agreeing, and prepare to anathematize each other, there is scarce a man who belongs to Christ. For we are wandering, blown by variable winds of doctrine; and either we cause confusion when we

[1] But see Doc. 236.
[2] A Religious of C.S.M.V., *The Incarnation of the Word of God*, London, 1944.

teach; or when we are taught we go astray. Take, for instance, last year's creed; what alteration is there not in it already? First, we have the creed which forbids us to touch the Homoousion; then comes another which decrees and preaches Homoousion; next the third excuses the word substance, as adopted by the fathers in their simplicity; lastly the fourth, which instead of excusing condemns . . The partial or total resemblance of the Father and of the Son is a subject of dispute for these unhappy times of ours. . Every year, and moon, we determine creeds; we change decrees, we prohibit our changes, we anathematize our prohibitions. Thus we either condemn others in ourselves, or ourselves in others, and while we bite one another, we are already consumed by each other. (Gore 212, 213.)

It is clear that Tillemont's remark quoted at the beginning of this chapter[1] needs some revision. The Nicene creed had not as yet acquired the respect it did in later years. The dissensions mentioned by Hilary are further revealed by the numerous councils, Arian, semi-Arian, and orthodox, which were held during his period of banishment: Sirmium in 357, Ancyra and Sirmium in 358, in Gaul, at Ariminum, at Nice, and at Seleucia in 359. Gore[2] wants to know why Pope Liberius, when he returned from exile in 358, did not settle the whole question by stating clearly what was the true faith. We have seen how he suffered for the faith; but these wrangling Arian heretics with the emperor supporting them would listen neither to the universal council of Nicaea, nor to the Pope.

VI. THE PRIMACY OF PETER

DOCUMENT 81——Cyril of Jerusalem, *Catechetical Lectures.* A.D. 348.
(*P.G.* 33. 408; *L.F.* 2. 24 ‡.)

Lecture 2. § 19.   Let no one then despair of his own salvation. Peter, the chiefest[3] and first of the apostles, before a little maid thrice denied the Lord; but when remorse touched him he wept bitterly; and to weep shows a heartfelt penitence. And so he not only received forgiveness for the denial, but was spared his apostolic dignity.

[1] Page 92.   [2] Page 52.   [3] κορυφαιότατος.

Lecture 6. § 15. The error spreading, that goodly pair, Peter and Paul, the rulers[1] of the Church, being present, set matters right again.

Lecture 11. § 3. And when all were silent, for it was beyond man's reach to learn, Peter, the leader[2] of the apostles, and chief[3] herald of the Church, uttering no refinement of his own, nor persuaded by man's reasoning, but having his mind enlightened from the Father, says to him: "Thou art the Christ."   (Chapman 47.)

DOCUMENT 82——Ephrem the Syrian,[4] *Eulogy on Peter, Paul, Andrew, etc.*: Works, Class 5, Sermon 11.
(*Collectio Ecclesiae Patrum* [5] 37. 446.)

3. Hail, O Peter: gate of sinners, firm trust of penitents, encouragement of converts, recalling those who deny, consolation of the lapsed. Hail, O Peter: tongue of the disciples, voice of the heralds, eye of the apostles, keeper of the heavens, firstborn of the key-bearers. Hail, O Peter: who plays out the devil's contest, and after injury brings back victory with violence, who overthrows the greatest enemy, who after being wounded brought back honour and after a fall erected a trophy and ripped off the crown from the head of the adversary.
                              (Chapman 47A.)

---

[1] προστάται.   [2] πρωτοστάτης.
[3] κορυφαῖος.   [4] Died about 373
[5] D. A. B. Caillau, Paris, 1842.

CHAPTER XII

THE TIME OF POPE DAMASUS

ON the death of Pope Liberius in A.D. 366, he was succeeded by a Spaniard called Damasus, who governed the Roman church for eighteen years. His period provides us with many illustrations of papal authority. I leave the matter of the schism at Antioch and the writings of Jerome for later chapters, and here gather up the other contemporary documents which have been cited in our controversy.

I. OPTATUS OF MILEVE

Little is known of this African bishop, apart from his one extant work which we have already quoted in Doc. 56. When Optatus wrote, the Donatist schism had pursued its course for fifty-eight years, and Parmenian was the third Donatist bishop of Carthage; the schism was strongly established in Africa, and had intruded into Rome with Macrobius as rival to Damasus. The Donatists did not believe that the Church was outwardly divided; they claimed to be the whole of the true Church of Christ, and they aimed at presenting the Church "without spot or wrinkle".[1] To prove their schismatic character, Optatus appeals to the apostolic succession, and to the much wider communion of the catholics.

DOCUMENT 83——Optatus, *De Schismate Donatistorum*, Book 1.
    A.D. 370, revised 385.
    (*C.S.E.L.* 26. 12; Vassall-Phillips 20 †.)

10.   I see that you are ignorant that the schism at Carthage was begun by your chiefs. Search out the origin of these things, and you will find that in associating heretics with schismatics, you have pronounced judgement against yourselves. For it was not Caecilian who went forth from Majorinus, your father's father, but it was Majorinus who deserted Caecilian; nor was it Caecilian who separated himself from *the chair of Peter or of Cyprian*,[2] but Majorinus, on whose chair you sit, which had no existence before Majorinus himself.

[1] Eph. 5. 27.   [2] Cp. Cyprian, *Ep.* 55 § 8 (Doc. 28).

DOCUMENT 84——The Same, Book 2.
   (*C.S.E.L.* 26. 36; Vassall-Phillips 64 ‡.)

2. So we have proved that the Catholic Church is the Church which is diffused throughout the world. We must now mention its ornaments.   For one who knows, to err is sin; those who do not know may sometimes be pardoned. You cannot deny that you know that *upon Peter first in the city of Rome was conferred the episcopal chair, on which sat Peter, the head of all the apostles,* whence he was called Cephas, *that in this one chair unity should be preserved by all, lest the other apostles might uphold each for himself separate chairs, so that he who should set up a second chair, against the unique chair, would already be a schismatic and a sinner.*

3. Well, then, on the one chair, which is the first of the endowments, Peter first sat, to whom succeeded Linus; to Linus succeeded Clement, Anacletus, Evaristus, Sixtus, Telesphorus, Iginus, Anicetus, Pius, Soter, Victor, Zephyrinus, Calixtus, Urban, Pontian, Anterus, Fabian, Cornelius, Lucius, Stephen, Sixtus, Dionysius, Felix, Marcellinus, Eusebius, Militades, Silvester, Mark, Julius, Liberius, Damasus; to Damasus Siricius, *who to-day is our colleague, and he, with the whole world, agrees with us in one bond of communion through the intercourse of letters of peace.* Now do you show the origin of your chair, you who wish to claim the holy Church for yourselves.

4. But you say that you too have some sort of a party in the city of Rome. It is a branch of your error growing out of a lie, not from the root of truth. In a word, were Macrobius to be asked where he sits in that place, could he say "In Peter's chair"?   . Since then Claudian has succeeded to Lucian, Lucian to Macrobius, Macrobius to Encolpius, Encolpius to Boniface, Boniface to Victor. Victor would not have been able, had he been asked where he sat, to show that anyone had been there before him; nor could he have pointed out that he held any chair, save that of pestilence. For pestilence sends down its victims, destroyed by diseases, to the lower regions, which are known to have their gates, against which gates we read that Peter, namely our chief, received the saving keys, to

whom it was said by Christ: "To thee I will give the keys of the kingdom of heaven, and the gates of hades do not conquer them." . . .

6. So, of the aforesaid endowments, the chair is, as we have said, the first, which we have proved to be ours, through Peter, and which draws to itself the angelus, unless perchance you, claiming him for yourselves, have him shut up in a little place. Send him out if you can, and let him exclude the seven angeli who are amongst our colleagues in Asia, to whose churches writes John the apostle, churches with which it is proved that you have no intercourse of communion. Whence is your angelus; who amongst you is able to move the waters, or to be numbered with the other endowments of the Church? *Whatever is outside the seven churches is alien.* Supposing then that you really had even one, through that one you would be in communion with the other angeli too, and through the angeli with the above-mentioned churches, and through these churches with us.   (Gore 119; Chapman 24A, 47B, 55, 56A.)

DOCUMENT 85——The Same, Book 6.
    (*C.S.E.L.* 26. 147; Vassall-Phillips 254 ‡.)

3.   We have followed the will and command of God, by loving peace and communicating with the whole world, united to the Easterns, where Christ was born   where is the seven-fold church, from which you not only do not grieve that you have been cut off, but in a sort of way rejoice. You call us defiled, because we have loved unity well-pleasing to God; because *we agree and communicate with the Corinthians, Galatians and Thessalonians,* and because we have not, with you, read corrupt books. Deny, if you can, that you read alien books. How dare you read the epistles written to the Corinthians, who are unwilling to communicate them? How can you read those written to the Galatians and Thessalonians in whose communion you are not? Since all these things are so, understand that you are cut off from the holy Church, and we are not polluted.
                    (Gore 119; Chapman 22B.)

From Book 2 § 2 of this work, Pope Leo XIII claimed that "bishops are deprived of the right and power of ruling, if they deliberately secede from Peter and his successors".[1] Gore points out how Optatus stresses in 2 § 6 and 6 § 3 the necessity of communion with the apostolic churches of Asia, Corinth, and Galatia.[2]

The classic article on the parallels between the Donatist and Anglican "schisms" was written more than a century ago by Bishop Nicholas Wiseman, D.D.[3] There are two lines of defence. First Donatism was founded on the heresy that the wickedness of the minister invalidates the sacrament, which heresy is rejected by the Church of England.[4] Secondly, Anglicans do not attempt to set up a rival bishop of Rome, a Donatist action which Optatus especially condemns (2 § 4).[5]

II. OPTATUS ON THE KEYS

DOCUMENT 86——Optatus, *De Schismate*, Book 7.
(*C.S.E.L.* 26. 170; Vassall-Phillips 283 †.)

3.   You have not wished to bring forward the examples to be found in the gospel, as for instance what has been written concerning the person of the most blessed Peter, where we may read a description of the way in which unity is to be obtained or procured. Without doubt it is evil to do anything against a prohibition, but it is worse not to have unity when you can. We see that this unity was preferred to punishment by Christ himself, who chose that all his disciples should be in unity, rather than punish a sin against himself. For, as he did not wish to be denied, he declared that whosoever should deny him before men would he deny before his Father. And though this has been thus written, nevertheless *for the good of unity blessed Peter*, for whom it would have been enough if after his denial he had obtained pardon only, *deserved to be placed before all the apostles, and alone received the keys of the kingdom of heaven, to be communicated to the rest.*[6] So from this example it is given us to

---

[1] *Satis Cognitum* § 15.   [2] Page 119 and n. 2.
[3] *Dublin Review*, August 1839, pp. 139–180.
[4] Article 26.   [5] Denny, 440.
[6] *tamen bono unitatis beatus Petrus, cui satis erat, si post quod negavit, solam veniam consequeretur, et praeferri apostolis omnibus meruit et claves regni caelorum communicandis ceteris solus accepit.*

understand that for the sake of unity sins should be buried, since the most blessed apostle Paul says that charity can cover a multitude of sins. (Chapman 50B.)

The question arises whether, in the opinion of Optatus, the keys were "to be communicated to the rest" by our Lord or by Peter. The most interesting and contradictory comments are by Bossuet, bishop of Meaux in 1682, and by O. R. Vassall-Phillips in 1917.

Bossuet: "In fact to be sure, those things which are given to Peter (Matt. 16) were communicated afterwards to the apostles (Matt. 18, John 20), but communicated not by Peter, but by Christ, as is clear."[1]

Vassall-Phillips: "The meaning is clear beyond all doubt. . . St Peter had to impart to the other apostles, for them to use also, the keys which as their head, he had himself alone received from Christ."[2]

Chapman and Vassall-Phillips both stress the statement that "Peter . . . alone received the keys", a statement which agrees with the Bible, for neither in Matt. 18. 18 nor in John 20. 23 are the keys mentioned, but only the power of binding and loosing. It is argued that if Optatus had wanted to say that Christ gave the keys to the rest, after he had given them to Peter, he would have said, "Peter first received the keys". If anyone should imagine that to receive the power of binding and loosing is exactly the same as to receive the keys, he has been answered as long ago as 1595 by Francis of Sales, who thought that to possess the keys is to possess authority as "head and permanent officer"; but to bind and loose is to exercise authority "as delegates and agents" of the key-holder.[3] Compare Pacian, *Ep.* 3 (Doc. 89); Augustine, *Sermo* 295 (Doc. 155).

III. THE PRIMACY OF PETER

A contemporary of Optatus, known as Ambrosiaster, asserts that Peter was the head, set over the other apostles.

DOCUMENT 87—Ambrosiaster, *Quaestiones ex Novo Testamento*. A.D. 370.
(*P.L.* 35. 2272.)

75. . . . So the collectors of the half-shekel say to the apostle Peter, "Does not your master pay the half-shekel?" Having

---

[1] *Defensio Dec. Cleri Gallicani* 8. 12 (*Opera*, 9. 383B; Paris, 1836).
[2] *St Optatus*, 285 n.
[3] *Les Controverses*, E.T., 255, 256 (edit. 1886).

said which, they agreed that the master pays for all the disciples. Now the Saviour, when he orders it to be given for himself and Peter, seems to have paid out for all; so just as all were included in the Saviour, by virtue of his office as teacher, likewise after the Saviour all were included in Peter. For *he appointed him to be their head*,[1] that he might be the shepherd of the Lord's flock. For amongst other things he says to the disciples: "Watch and pray lest ye enter into temptation"; and he says to Peter, "Behold, Satan hath desired to have you, that he may sift you as wheat; but I have prayed for thee, that thy faith fail not, and do thou later, being converted, strengthen thy brethren". What ambiguity is there? Did he pray for Peter, but not pray for James and John, not to mention the others? It is clear that all are included in Peter, for by praying for Peter, he is seen to have prayed for all. For always a people is blamed and praised *in him that is set over*.[2]

(Chapman 59B note.)

On the other hand the same writer[3] thinks it necessary also to emphasize the primacy of Paul.

DOCUMENT 88——Ambrosiaster, *Commentaria in XIII Epistolas Beati Pauli.*
   On Gal. 2. 9, 10.   (*P.L.* 17. 349.)

. By the apostles who were somewhat distinguished among their colleagues, whom also he, Paul, because of their constancy calls "pillars", and who had always been intimate with the Lord, even beholding his glory on the mount, by them he [Paul] says the gift which he received from God was approved; so that he would be worthy to have primacy[4] in preaching to the Gentiles, even as Peter had the primacy in preaching to the circumcision. And even as he gives colleagues to Peter, outstanding men among the apostles, so he also joins to himself Barnabas, who was associated with him by divine choice; yet he claims the privilege of primacy granted by God for himself

---

[1] *caput.*   [2] *praeposito.*
[3] See *D.C.B.*, 1. 90B and A. Souter in *Texts and Studies*, Vol. VII, No. 4.
[4] *primatum.*

alone, even as it was granted to Peter alone among the apostles, in such a way that the apostles of the circumcision stretched out their right hands to the apostles of the Gentiles to manifest a harmony of fellowship, that both parties, knowing that they had received from the Lord a spirit of completeness in the imparting of the gospel, might show that they were in no way appointing one another.

Pacian, bishop of Barcelona, follows Cyprian (Doc. 37 § 4) in placing "the foundation of unity" in our Lord's words to Peter.

DOCUMENT 89——Pacian, *Ep.* 3, to Sympronianus. About
    A.D. 375.
    (*P.L.* 13. 1071; *L.F.* 17. 347 ‡.)

11.   . All you seek then, you have in Matthew. Why did not you, who teach a bishop, read it all? Look at the opening words of that precept. As Matthew himself reports, the Lord spoke to Peter a little earlier; he spoke to one, that from one he might found unity, soon delivering the same to all. Yet he still begins just as to Peter: "And I say also unto thee", he says "that thou art Peter   "

(Gore 199; Chapman 115B.)

We shall see in Chapter XVI that Chrysostom frequently uses the word κορυφαῖος (leader) of Peter and the other apostles, but in the next Document there is a stronger word, κορυφαιότατος (super-leader), which is used only of Peter.   (See also Doc. 81.)

DOCUMENT 90——Epiphanius, *Against the Heresies*, Heresy 59.
    A.D. 372
    (*P.G.* 41. 1029.)

7.   . as Manasseh the son of Hezekiah was converted and received by the Lord, and as Saint Peter, the very chiefest[1] of the apostles, who had at one stage denied the Lord, has become for us in truth a solid rock, bearing the weight of the faith of the Lord, on which the Church is, in all ways, built.

(Chapman 47B.)

[1] κορυφαιότατος.

IV BASIL

In the year 330 Basil was born of Christian parents at Caesarea in Cappadocia; he was one of ten children and two of his brothers became bishops and one of his sisters, Macrina, is a canonized saint. He was educated at Constantinople and Athens and baptized at the age of twenty-seven. The following year he retired from the world, but discovered that community life was more in accordance with the divine will than solitary life, and so became the founder of monasticism in Asia Minor. He was ordained deacon in 359 and priest in 362, and on and off for eight years he was the right-hand man of his bishop, whom he succeeded in 370. During his episcopate Arian persecutions were renewed under the Emperor Valens (364–378), but when the emperor visited Caesarea early in 372 this great bishop stood up to him and even secured his support. Worn out by excessive asceticism and the conflicts of the time Basil died at an early age on 1 January 379.

These conflicts against the faith, within the eastern church, are brought to our notice by the two extracts below from Basil's writings. In *Epistle* 90 he contrasts the chaotic condition of the East with the unity of the western bishops.

DOCUMENT 91——Basil, *Epistle* 90.   A.D. 372.
(*P.G.* 32. 473; *P.N.F.* 8. 176B ‡.)

To the holy brethren, the bishops of the West.

1. . . . Since we account your mutual sympathy and unity an important blessing to us, so we implore you to pity our dissensions; and not to part us from you because we are separated by distance, but to admit us to the unison of one body, because we are united in the fellowship of the Spirit.

2. Our distresses are notorious, even though we do not tell them, for now "their sound is gone out into all the world". The doctrines of the fathers are despised; apostolic traditions are set at naught; the devices of innovators are in vogue in the churches; now men are word-makers, not theologians; the wisdom of this world wins the first places and has rejected the glory of the cross. Shepherds are banished and grievous wolves substituted, who scatter the flock of Christ. Prayer-houses are empty; the deserts are full of weepers. The elders weep when they compare the present with the past. The younger are more to be pitied, not knowing what they have lost.   (Gore 170.)

DOCUMENT 92——Basil, *On the Holy Ghost*, Ch. 30. A.D. 374. (*P.G.* 32. 212; *P.N.F.* 8. 48B ‡.)

77. When from lengthy and bitter strife, the struggle passed to open hostility against us, then the war divided in endless ways into many parts, so that both through common enmity and through private suspicion there was intense hatred by all. But what storm at sea was ever more fierce than this tempest of the churches? In it every landmark of the fathers has been moved; every foundation, every bulwark of opinion has been shaken; everything, buoyed up on the unsound, is dashed about and shaken down. We attack one another; we are overthrown by one another. If our enemy does not strike us first, we are wounded by the comrade at our side. . So all men alike, each as best he can, lift the hand of murder against one another. Harsh rises the cry of the combatants encountering each other in dispute; already all the Church is almost full of the inarticulate screams, the unintelligible noises, rising from the ceaseless agitations that divert the right rule of the doctrine of true religion, now in the direction of excess, now in that of defect. On the one hand are they who confound the Persons and are carried away into Judaism; on the other hand are they who, through the opposition of the natures, pass into paganism. Neither can inspired scripture mediate, nor can the apostolic traditions arbitrate, between the opponents. Plain speaking is fatal to friendship, and differing opinions are sufficient cause for hostility. The likeness in error is a more effective bond of union than any sworn allegiance. Everyone is a theologian, though his soul be branded with countless stains. Hence many join in sedition with the revolutionaries. And so, in fact, self-appointed men and sons of place-hunters share out the high places of the churches, rejecting the government of the Holy Ghost. The rules of the gospel are now everywhere thrown into confusion; there is an indescribable pushing for the chief places, while every advertiser tries to force himself into high office. This lust for power is followed by anarchy, and the commands of those in authority are ineffective and idle, for everyone in his ignorant pride thinks he is more bound to command than to obey.

78. So since, in such a din, no human voice has power to be heard, I consider silence more use than speech. . . .

(Gore 212.)

Gore quotes from the above two Documents to show doctrinal confusion and lack of discipline within the Catholic Church as a deplorable fact of history.

V. THE ROMAN SEE

Our next Document shows what ninety bishops of Italy and Gaul thought of papal authority in matters of faith.

DOCUMENT 93——Damasus, *Ep.* 1 (*Credimus sanctam fidem*).
　　A.D. 371.
　　In Theodoret, *H.E.* 2. 17. (*P.G.* 82. 1052; *P.N.F.* 3. 83A ‡.)

The bishops assembled at Rome in sacred synod, Damasus and Valerian and the rest, to their beloved brethren the bishops of Illyria, send greeting in God.   When first the wickedness of the heretics began to flourish, and when, as now still more, the blasphemy of the Arians was creeping abroad, our fathers, 318 bishops,[1] the holiest bishops in the Roman empire,[1] deliberated at Nicaea. The wall which they set up against the weapons of the devil, and the antidote wherewith they repelled his deadly poisons, was their confession that the Father and the Son are of one substance, one godhead, one virtue, one power, one likeness, and that the Holy Ghost is of the same essence and substance. Whoever did not thus think was judged separate from our communion. Their deliberation was worthy of all respect, and their definition sound. But certain men have intended by other later discussions to corrupt and befoul it. Yet at the very outset, error was so far set right by the bishops on whom the attempt was made at Ariminum[2] to compel them to manipulate or innovate in the faith, that they confessed themselves seduced by opposite arguments, or owned that they had not perceived any contradiction to the opinion

[1] . . [1] Some MSS. omit these words. The *Collectio Romana* reads "*atque ex parte sanctissimi episcopi urbis Romae directi*", thus adding the legates of Silvester to the 318 bishops.
[2] A.D. 359.

of the fathers delivered at Nicaea. No prejudice could arise from the number[1] of bishops gathered at Ariminum, since it is well known that *neither the bishop of the Romans,*[2] *whose opinion ought before all others to have been waited for, nor Vincent,*[3] whose stainless episcopate had lasted so many years, nor the rest gave in their adhesion to such doctrine.   (Chapman 115A.)

DOCUMENT 94——Council of Rome, A.D. 378, *To the Emperors* (*Et hoc gloriae*).
   (*P.L.* 13. 575.)

   1. This also, most merciful sovereigns is a clear example of your glory and piety that, when we gathered in considerable numbers from the different parts of Italy, to the sublime sanctuary of the apostolic see, and were considering what request we should make to you on behalf of the churches, we could find nothing better than that which you, in your spontaneous forethought, have bestowed. We now realize that there ought to be no shame in asking, or need to obtain by petition, favours which you have already granted. For as regards the fairness of our petition, long ago we gained what we now request; but, as regards the need of renewing our prayer, since we have not received the effect of your favours, we wish to obtain them again. .

   9.   We request your clemency to make an order, that if anyone shall have been condemned by the judgement of Damasus or of ourselves, who are catholics, and shall unjustly wish to retain a church, or when called by a priestly judgement is absent through insolence, that he be summoned to Rome either by the illustrious men the prae-

DOCUMENT 95——Gratian, *To Aquilinus, Vicar of the City* (*Ordinariorum sententiae*). A.D. 378.
   (*P.L.* 13. 586.)
   6. We will that if anyone has been condemned by the judgement of Damasus, which he had given with the advice of five or seven bishops, or by the judgement or advice of those who are catholics, if he

[1] "Over 400 western bishops": Athan. *De Synod.* 8 (*P.G.* 26. 691).
[2] Liberius.
[3] Bishop of Capua.

torian prefects of your Italy or by the vicar.

But if a question of this kind arises in more distant parts, let the examination be transferred by the local courts to the metropolitan; or if he is a metropolitan himself, he should be ordered of necessity to journey to Rome without delay, or to those judges whom the Roman bishop may appoint, so that those who shall have been deposed be kept away from the bounds of the city in which they exercised the priesthood, lest they again impudently usurp that which they have been deprived of by law. Certainly, if either the metropolitan or any other priest be suspected of favour or iniquity, it is lawful to appeal either to the Roman bishop or to a council of fifteen neighbouring bishops.

unjustly wishes to retain the church, so that he through insolence does not come when called to a priestly judgement, he be summoned with authority, either by the illustrious men the praetorian prefects *of Gaul* and Italy, or by the proconsuls or vicars, *and be sent to the episcopal judgement,* or else come under prosecution at Rome. Or if such arrogance should arise in more distant parts, let the whole pleading of the cause be submitted to the examination of the metropolitan in the same province as the bishop; or if he is a metropolitan himself, he should of necessity journey to Rome without delay or to those judges whom the Roman bishop may appoint; so that they who have been deprived be kept away from the bounds of the town in which they were priests. For we punish people less severely than they merit, and we avenge sacrilegious obstinacy more leniently than it deserves. But if the iniquity or favour of the metropolitan bishop or other priest is suspected, it is lawful for the accused to appeal to the Roman bishop, or to a council of fifteen neighbouring bishops.

The italics show where Gratian has departed from the wording of the petition. In so far as the rescript deals with the Gallic or Italian bishops it is straightforward. That part dealing with the rest of the western empire, should be compared with the Sardican canons (Doc. 69). The chief difference is that the canons deal with the cases of bishops who appeal against their local church courts, but the rescript, whilst touching on appeals in certain cases, mainly has in mind culprits who ignore the local court. These, if metropolitans, can be made to stand trial in Rome. The young Christian emperor gives civil force to a decision of the Pope and his council. The following year we find the eastern emperor, Theodosius I, legislating in favour of orthodoxy.

DOCUMENT 96——*Theodosian Code* 16. 1. 2 (*Cunctos populos*), 27 February 380.
(*P.L.* 13. 530; Gibbon [1] 3. 148 †.)

We wish all nations which are governed by the measure of our kindness to abide in that religion which is declared to have been introduced by S. Peter, the apostle to the Romans, and by him to have been handed down to this day, and which is followed by the pontiff Damasus, and by Peter, bishop of Alexandria, a man of apostolic holiness. This is, that according to the apostolic discipline, and the doctrine of the gospel, we should believe the sole deity of the Father, the Son, and the Holy Ghost, under an equal majesty and a pious Trinity. We authorize the followers of this law to embrace the name of catholic Christians, and we declare the rest to be foolish madmen who uphold the disgrace of heretical dogma; neither shall their meeting-houses receive the name of churches. Besides the divine condemnation, we by the will of heaven are further moved to inflict the penalties of revenge.

A year later the Second General Council was held at Constantinople. That city had been the seat of government for fifty years, and an attempt was made to raise the see above the apostolic sees of Alexandria and Antioch.

---

[1] E. Gibbon, *Decline and Fall*, edit. J. B. Bury, 1909.

DOCUMENT 97——Council of Constantinople: Canon 3.
    A.D. 381.
    (*P.L.* 67. 77.)

The bishop of Constantinople shall have the privileges of honour after the bishop of Rome, because it is new Rome.

(Gore 102 note; Chapman 85A.)

During this council, Gregory Nazianzen resigned the bishopric of Constantinople and the following Lent he composed the *Poem on his Life.*

DOCUMENT 98——Gregory Nazianzen, *Carmen de Vita Sua,*
    Part 1.   A.D. 382.
    (*P.G.* 37. 1068.)

Lines 562–72. Truly nature has not given us two suns; but she has given us two Romes, as lights of the whole world, an old dominion and a new; the one differs from the other as the latter outshines the East and the former the West. But the beauty of the one balances exactly in the scales with the beauty of the other. Regarding the faith which they uphold, the ancient Rome has kept a straight course from of old, and still does so, *uniting the whole West* by sound teaching, as is just, since *she presides over all* and guards the universal divine harmony.

(Chapman 39A.)

In our next Document Rome defines her view of papal and patriarchal authority as against the upstart claims of new Rome (see Doc. 97). The date 382 is upheld by many eminent scholars from Baronius[1] to Kidd[2] and Jalland.[3] The western view insists that the importance of a see depends on its apostolic origin, and not on the civil rank of the city. In the West, Canon 3 of Constantinople "remained unrecognized until, on the foundation of a Latin patriarchate at Constantinople, 1204, the Lateran Council of 1215 allowed that see the second rank in Christendom".[4]

DOCUMENT 99——Council of Rome, A.D. 382, *Post has omnes.*
    (*P.L.* 13. 374.)

After all these writings of the prophets, evangelists, and apostles which we set out above, and on which, by God's grace,

[1] *P.L.* 13. 374.
[2] *Roman Primacy,* 69.
[3] *Leo,* 321 n.
[4] Kidd, *Hist. Ch.,* 2. 288.

the Catholic Church is founded, we think this should also be noticed : that though all the catholic churches diffused throughout the world are but one bridal chamber of Christ, yet the holy Roman church has been set before the rest by no conciliar decrees, but has obtained the primacy by the voice of our Lord and Saviour in the gospel : "Thou art Peter and upon this rock . shall be loosed in heaven." There is added also the society of the most blessed apostle Paul, "a chosen vessel", who was crowned on one and the same day, suffering a glorious death, with Peter in the city of Rome, under Caesar Nero; and they alike consecrated the above-named Roman church to Christ the Lord, and set it above all others in the whole world by their presence and venerable triumph.

The first see of the apostle Peter is therefore the Roman church, "not having spot or wrinkle or any such thing".

But the second see was consecrated at Alexandria, in the name of blessed Peter, by his disciple Mark the evangelist; and he, being directed by S. Peter into Egypt, preached the word of truth, and perfected a glorious martyrdom.

And the third see of the most blessed apostle Peter is at Antioch, which is held in honour because he lived there before he came to Rome, and there, first, the name of the new race of Christians arose.   (Chapman 85.)

CHAPTER XIII

MELETIUS

WE are told by two eminent Roman Catholic historians, Fleury[1] and Hefele,[2] that Meletius presided at the council of Constantinople in A.D. 381, until he died. This council was later recognized as the Second General Council. The evidence for his presidency is the fact that he was the senior bishop present, and that during his funeral oration at Constantinople, Gregory of Nyssa said: "It was a grievous thing for us to be severed from his fatherly guidance . . . our leader is no more."[3] Further Meletius was in due course canonized as a saint, and is commemorated by the Roman Catholic Church on 12 February.

We have to try to discover whether this recognized catholic leader and saint was ever excommunicated by the Roman see, and if so whether he died out of communion with the Pope. It is a long story, which has to be unravelled from the histories of Socrates, Sozomen, and Theodoret, and from the letters of Jerome, Basil, and others.

In the year 326 Eustathius bishop of Antioch, a firm catholic, was slandered by the Arians and ejected from his see.[4] He was followed, 326–360, by five Arian bishops in succession. During this period certain catholics, known as Eustathians, were without a bishop, and were led by their priest Paulinus.[5] But the majority of the catholics kept in communion with the Arian bishops, in obedience to the advice of Eustathius[6] and "in expectation of some favourable change".[7]

In January 361 Meletius succeeded Eudoxius as bishop of Antioch. He had been consecrated bishop of Sebaste by the Arians in 357 and had also been bishop of Beroea.[8] But at his enthronement at Antioch, the emperor Constantius was present and demanded exposition of Proverbs 8. 22, whereupon the new bishop boldly came out as a sound catholic. Jerome, writing twenty-one years later, says that he made a sudden change of faith.[9] He was promptly banished and another

---

[1] *Histoire Ecclésiastique*, 18. 1.
[2] 2. 344.   [3] *P.G.* 46. 852.
[4] Athan. *Hist. Arian.* 4; Theodoret, *H.E.* 1. 21. For the date see H. Chadwick in *J.T.S.*, Jan. 1948, p. 35.
[5] Theodoret, *H.E.* 3. 2.
[6] Chrysostom, *Hom. in Eustathium* § 4 (*P.G.* 50. 604).
[7] Theodoret, *H.E.* 2. 27.
[8] Socrates, *H.E.* 2. 44.
[9] *Chron. ad Ann.* 365 (*P.L.* 27. 503).

Arian, Euzoïus, was put in his place.[1] The emperor died in November, and the following March a council was held at Alexandria, at which reunion at Antioch was considered. Meantime Lucifer, a bishop from Sardinia, visited Antioch and "took the improper course of consecrating Paulinus as bishop".[2] Lucifer later created a schism of his own. "Meletius soon returned from exile",[3] and for the next nineteen years, besides the Arian bishop, Meletius and Paulinus were rival bishops, both believing the catholic faith. The position was especially serious because Antioch was the third or fourth see in Christendom.[4] This was the state of affairs when Jerome came to Antioch in 373, and when he wrote his two famous letters to the Pope in 375,[5] letters which may have decided Damasus to support Paulinus, as we see he does in the next Document. For Jerome calls Meletius "the offspring of the Arians", and calls his followers *campenses*, the nickname they received when forced to worship in the fields.

DOCUMENT 100——Damasus, *Ep.* 3 (*Per filium meum Vitalem*).
    A.D. 375.
  (*P.L.* 13. 356.)

Damasus to his most beloved brother Paulinus. By my son Vitalis, I directed to you a letter, in which I left everything to your discretion. And through Petronius the presbyter, I briefly indicated that, just as he set out, I was rather upset. And so lest any scruple should remain in you, and lest your wise caution should deter those who would perhaps want to be joined to the Church, we are sending you a statement of faith, not so much for yourself, who share the communion of the same faith, as for those who, by subscribing to it, may wish to be joined to you, that is, to us through you, most beloved brother. Further if my son Vitalis, mentioned above, and those with him, should desire to be brought into the flock, they ought first to subscribe to that exposition of faith which was affirmed by the pious will of the Nicene fathers. (Gore 130.)

On the other hand, Basil, bishop of Caesarea in Cappadocia, recognized now by all as a saint, gave his support to Meletius.

[1] Theodoret, *H.E.* 2. 27.
[2] Ibid. 3. 2; Jerome, *Chron. ad Ann.* 366.
[3] Socrates, *H.E.* 3. 9.
[4] Docs. 97. 99.   [5] Docs. 117, 118.

DOCUMENT 101——Basil, *Ep.* 214, to Count Terentius. A.D.
375.
(*P.G.* 32. 785; *P.N.F.* 8. 253B ‡.)

2. A further rumour has reached us, that you are in Antioch and are transacting the business in hand with the chief authorities. And beside this, we have heard that the brethren who are with Paulinus are discussing with your excellency about union with us; and by "us" I mean those who are of the party of the man of God, Meletius the bishop. I hear also that they are circulating a letter of the Westerns, assigning to them the episcopate of the church in Antioch, but which misrepresents Meletius, the admirable bishop of the true Church of God. I do not wonder at this. They are totally ignorant of affairs here; the others, though they seem to know, give an account to them in which party is put before truth. But it is not unlike them, either to be ignorant of the truth, or to conceal the reason which led the blessed bishop Athanasius to write to Paulinus. But your excellency has on the spot those who are able to tell you accurately what passed between the bishops in the reign of Jovian, and from them we beg you to get information. We accuse no one; we pray that we may have love to all, and "especially towards the household of faith". *We congratulate those who have received the letter from Rome.* And inasmuch as it is a grand testimony in their favour, we only hope it is true and is confirmed by the facts. *But we shall never be able to persuade ourselves on these grounds to ignore Meletius,* or to forget the church under him, or to treat as petty, and of little importance to the true religion, the questions which originated the division. I shall never consent to give in merely because somebody is elated at receiving a letter from men, even if it had come down from heaven itself. But if he does not agree with the sound doctrine of the faith, I cannot look upon him as in communion with the saints. (Chapman 98B.)

Now it is clear from Document 100 that the Pope held communion with Paulinus, and the question is, whether he could do so without thereby excommunicating his rival Meletius. Can one be in communion with two rival bishops of the same see? Dom P. Maran, the Benedictine biographer of Basil,[1] thought not. "Basil, in this same epistle 214, denied that he could persuade himself 'either to ignore Meletius or to forget the church over which Meletius presided'. Therefore not unjustly he denied that communion could be held with Paulinus; since in fact one could not hold with him, without rejecting Meletius, who was the sole legitimate bishop of Antioch."[2] On the other hand Dom Chapman asserts that "It is certain that neither St Meletius nor St Flavian was ever formally excommunicated by the apostolic see".[3] Chapman's plea is that both the Pope and Meletius were in communion with Basil, and therefore through him with one another.[4] This was not the first time the bishops of Rome and Caesarea had been in sharp opposition (see Stephen and Firmilian in Doc.48). Two years later Basil reaffirms his loyalty to Meletius.

DOCUMENT 102——Basil, *Ep.* 258, to Epiphanius. A.D. 377. (*P.G.* 32. 949; *P.N.F.* 8. 295A ‡.)

3. As to the church at Antioch . The right reverend Meletius was the first to speak boldly for the truth, and "fought that good fight" in the days of Constantius. Therefore my church has felt strong affection towards him, for the sake of that brave and firm stand, and has held communion with him. I, therefore, by God's grace have held him to be in communion up to this time; and if God will, I shall continue to do so. . . . *We have never accepted communion with anyone of those who have since been introduced to the see, not because we considered them unworthy, but because we saw no ground for the condemnation of Meletius.* (Chapman 98B.)

While in 375 Meletius was not in actual communion with Rome, it has been argued that papal communion must have been restored to him before he died. Evidence for this is found in the two historians Theodoret and Socrates. For five months from the death of Valens in August 378 to the appointment of Theodosius in January 379, the emperor Gratian ruled over the East as well as over the West. It was, according to Theodoret, during this period[5] that he legislated in

[1] A.D. 1730.　[2] *P.G.* 32. 22, 23.
[3] *S.E.P.*, 95.　[4] Chapman, 98B.
[5] *H.E.* 5. 1.

favour of the Roman see (Doc. 95). About seventy years later the historian writes as follows:

DOCUMENT 103——Theodoret, *H.E.*, Book 5.   A.D. 450.
  (*P.G.* 82. 1197; Bagster 274 ‡.)

2. [Gratian] at once displayed the piety for which he was conspicuous, and consecrated the first-fruits of the empire to the King of all. He enacted a law enjoining that the pastors who had been banished should be recalled and restored to their flocks, and that the houses of God should be given up to those who held communion with Damasus, who was bishop of Rome

Gratian sent out with the edict Sapor, a famous general, and he ordered him to expel from the sacred folds the preachers of the Arian blasphemy as if they were wild beasts, and to restore the best shepherds to the divine flocks. In every nation this was done without friction, but in Antioch, the leading city of the East, trouble arose as follows.

3. As we said before, those who held to the apostolic doctrines were divided. . .   When General Sapor arrived and published the imperial edict, Paulinus obstinately asserted that he belonged to the party of Damasus.   .   Then Meletius, the mildest of all men, thus kindly and gently addressed Paulinus: "As the Lord committed to me the care of this flock, and you have received the charge of another, and our little ones are in devout communion with one another, let us, O friend, join our flocks, and make an end of the fight for leadership. Let us feed our sheep and minister to them together. If the central seat causes strife, I will undertake to dispel that. Let us place the holy gospel upon it, and let us seat ourselves on each side of it. If I die first, you, O friend, will become the only ruler of the flock. Should your death occur before mine, I will, as far as I am able, tend the flock alone." So gently and kindly spoke the divine Meletius, but Paulinus did not agree. The officer, after reflecting on what had been said, handed over the churches to the great Meletius. Paulinus continued to govern the sheep who had originally seceded.   (Chapman 98B.)

It appears from this that Sapor believed Meletius to be in communion with the Pope, and that Theodoret, a native of Antioch, took that view. Socrates, writing a little nearer the time, gives a different version of these events. He was not, however, a native of Antioch.

DOCUMENT 104——Socrates, *H.E.*, Book 5. A.D. 434.
(*P.G.* 67. 569; Bagster 368 ‡.)

5. At this time, party spirit arose at Antioch in Syria because of Meletius. We have already remarked that Paulinus the bishop of Antioch, because of his eminent piety, was not sent into exile. But Meletius, after being restored by Julian, was again banished by Valens and later recalled by Gratian. When he returned to Antioch, Paulinus was already an aged man; the partisans of Meletius therefore tried at once to place him hastily on the throne with Paulinus. And when Paulinus declared that it was contrary to the canons to admit a coadjutor who had been ordained by the Arians, the people grew violent and prepared to enthrone him in one of the churches outside the city. Much party spirit was stirred up by this, but in time the people were pacified by the following arrangements. Those who might be elected as bishop met together, six in number including Flavian. These men were bound by an oath not to seek the bishopric if one of the bishops should die, but to allow the survivor to occupy the see of the deceased. And so by these pledges schism was healed and unity restored. But the Luciferians separated themselves from the rest, because Meletius, who had been ordained by the Arians, was admitted to the episcopate. The affairs in Antioch being thus settled, Meletius was obliged to go to Constantinople.

(Chapman 98B.)

If we elect to follow this earlier account, instead of that of Theodoret, there are different grounds for assuming that Meletius was restored to communion with the Pope, namely, that unity being restored, the two bishops would no longer be rivals but in communion with one another, and so also with Rome. Moreover after September 379 there could no longer be any doubt at Rome about the orthodoxy of Meletius, for in that month he presided at a council of 153 bishops at Antioch who signed *The Tome of the Westerns*, a document drawn up at Rome condemning Arian and other heresies. The name of Meletius bishop of Antioch heads the list of signatures.[1]

But the Anglicans Puller[2] and Kidd[3] were both confident that the Pope still refused to recognize Meletius, in spite of his manifest adherence to the truth; for a few months later Damasus wrote a synodal letter to Paulinus again. This letter condemned the heresies, and included a special clause about bishops who change their sees and who lose their sees when absent.

DOCUMENT 105——Damasus, *Ep.* 4, to Bishop Paulinus (*Post concilium Nicaenum*).   A.D. 380.
   (*P.L.* 13. 360.)

9. Those who have migrated from church to church we hold to be alien from our communion, until they return to those cities in which they were first appointed. If while any is travelling about, another is ordained in his place, then he who forsook the city is deprived of the priestly office until his successor rest in peace.

Meletius had changed his see from Sebaste to Beroea, and from Beroea to Antioch. His rival was appointed during his exile,[4] and the papal document is addressed to this rival. So § 9 above appears to be aimed at Meletius and certainly covers his case. Thus if we have interpreted this document rightly, we find that, as late as the year 380, Meletius was still regarded as out of communion with Rome, in spite of his manifest orthodoxy in faith. He died in May or June of 381, and Rivington[5] sets out to prove that he was actually in communion with Rome before he died. He appeals to two documents from the church in North Italy,[6] which was of course in full communion with Pope Damasus, and these two documents may fairly be considered to express the opinions of the western church. An example of complete agreement between the sees of Rome and Milan is shown in Docs. 115 and 116.

On the death of Meletius, Flavian was at once appointed in his place, in violation[7] of the agreement, mentioned in Doc. 104, that the survivor of the two rivals should become sole bishop of Antioch. That this agreement is not an invention of Socrates is shown by the reference to it in our next Document. In this the Italian bishops state that they "have long since received letters from both parties" at Antioch, which was taken by Rivington[8] to mean that they had been in communion with Paulinus and Meletius.

[1] *P.L.* 13. 353.
[2] Page 333.
[3] *Hist. Ch.*, 2. 271.
[4] Sozomen, *H.E.* 5. 12.
[5] Pages 263–268.
[6] Docs. 106 and 107.
[7] Sozomen, *H.E.* 7. 11.
[8] Page 267, and note 2.

DOCUMENT 106——Council of Aquileia, *To the Emperors* (*Quamlibet*). 3 September 381.

In Ambrose, *Ep.* 12. (*P.L.*[1] 16. 988; *L.F.* 47. 71 ‡.)

The holy council assembled at Aquileia, to the most gracious and Christian emperors and most blessed and most glorious princes, Gratian, Valentinian, and Theodosius.

4. The envy of the devil is never at rest, and so we hear that in the East there are, among the catholics themselves, frequent quarrels and warring discords. We are upset in our minds, because we have learnt that there are many innovations, and that people are now being treated unfairly who ought to have been supported, men who have always preserved our communion. We refer to Timothy, bishop of the church of Alexandria, and Paulinus, bishop of the church of Antioch, who have always maintained unbroken communion with us. These are said to be put in great anxiety by the dissensions of other people whose faith was in former times undecided. We would indeed wish that these people, if possible, and if they are recommended by an unmutilated faith, *should be added to our fellowship*,[2] but in such a way that their own rights be preserved to those colleagues who have enjoyed our communion from of old. Our care for them is not superfluous, first because the fellowship of communion should be clear of all offence, and again because *we have long since received letters from both parties, and particularly from those who were divided in the church of Antioch.*

5. Indeed if the irruption of the enemy had not hindered, we should have sent there some of our own number to take the office of umpires and referees, for diffusing peace again, should it be possible. But because the desires which we formed at the time failed to be accomplished owing to the troubles of the state, we presume that our petitions have been presented to your pieties,[3] in which, in accordance with a compact of the parties, we have requested[4] that on the death of one the rights of the church might remain in the possession of the survivor,

---

[1] Migne has two editions of the works of Ambrose. My references are to the 1845 edition.

[2] *ad consortia nostra optemus adjungi.*

[3] *oblatas pietati vestrae opinamur preces nostras.*   [4] *poposcimus.*

and no other ordination should be attempted[1] by force. And therefore we beg of you, most clement and Christian princes, to give orders that a council of all catholic bishops be held at Alexandria, that they may more fully discuss among themselves and define the persons to whom communion is to be imparted, and with whom it is to be maintained.

Rivington believed that to receive "letters from both parties" was the same as to be in communion with both parties. He therefore had to explain why these western bishops wished that the Meletians should be added to their fellowship, though apparently already in communion with them. His theory was that communion had been broken since the death of Meletius, on account of the appointment of Flavian, which was contrary to the agreement. Although there is nothing in the above letter to show that the writers had heard of the death of Meletius, there was time, about three months, for the news to have reached Aquileia from Constantinople, a distance of 1,000 miles by land and 1,400 by sea. Another letter from the same bishops shows that by the late autumn at any rate they had definitely heard of Flavian's appointment.

DOCUMENT 107——Ambrose, *Ep*. 13, *To Theodosius I* (*Sanctum animum tuum*).   About December 381.
   (*P.L.* 16. 990; *L.F.* 47. 74 ‡.)

Ambrose and the other bishops of Italy, to the most blessed emperor and most gracious prince Theodosius.
   1. . . Your majesty! We groan, perhaps with too much grief, but not without sufficient reason, that it has proved easier to get heretics expelled than to establish agreement among the catholics. For the extent of the confusion that has lately arisen is indescribable.
   2. We wrote to you not long ago[2] that since the city of Antioch had two bishops, Paulinus and Meletius, both of whom we regarded as true to the faith, there should be unity, peace, and concord between them, without any breach of church order; or at least that if one of them died before the other, no one should be put in the place of the deceased while the other lived. But now on the death of Meletius, while

---

[1] *attentaretur*.
[2] *dudum* : probably in May 381 (not Doc. 106).

Paulinus is still alive, whom fellowship, derived from our predecessors without interruption, testifies to have remained in our communion, another person is said to have been not so much supplied as super-added into the place of Meletius, contrary to right and to ecclesiastical order.

Puller[1] did not think that bishops were necessarily in communion with those from whom they received letters. He argued that by the late autumn the Italian bishops, having heard of the death of Meletius and the appointment of Flavian, say so clearly, and protest. But in their September letter, though they refer to the agreement, they make no mention of the recent breach of it, and therefore had not heard about this. And so when in their September letter they suggest that certain people in Antioch "should be added to our fellowship", they must be referring to Meletius and his flock, and therefore Meletius was still out of communion with the West when he died,[2] "so that communion with the Roman see is not necessary to membership in the Catholic Church".[3]

[1] Page 320, n. 3.
[2] Puller, 347–350.
[3] Kidd, *Hist. Ch.*, 2. 283.

CHAPTER XIV

THE TIME OF POPE SIRICIUS

Pope Damasus died in December 384 and was succeeded by Siricius, who occupied the Roman see until 399. The works of his contemporary John Chrysostom are considered in Chapter XVI. The nine documents in this chapter fortunately require little comment. The first is by the Pope himself, who announced his appointment to an elderly metropolitan bishop in Spain by the earliest extant papal decretal.[1]

I. SIRICIUS

Document 108—Siricius, *Ep.* 1, to Himerius, Bishop of Tarragona (*Directa ad decessorem*).   11 February 385.
 (*P.L.* 13. 1132.)

1.   In view of our office, we are not free to dissemble or to keep silent, for our zeal for the Christian religion ought to be greater than anyone's. We bear the burdens of all who are heavy laden, or rather *the blessed apostle Peter bears them in us, who in all things, as we trust, protects and defends those who are heirs of his government.*

2. At the beginning of your page, you have observed that many who were baptized by the wicked Arians are hastening to the catholic faith, and that they wish to be rebaptized by one of our brethren: this is illegal, being forbidden by the apostle,[2] by the canons,[3] and *in a general order sent to the provinces by my predecessor Liberius* of revered memory, after the quashing of the Ariminum council. As has been laid down in synod, we admit these persons, in common with Novatianists and other heretics, into the congregation of catholics, only through the invocation of the sevenfold Spirit, by the laying on of hands of a bishop. All the East and West keep this rule; and in future

---

[1] Kidd, *Hist. Ch.* 2. 328, and Dionysius Exiguus (*P.L.* 67. 231).
[2] ? Eph. 4. 5.
[3] See Doc. 60 § 8.

it is by no means fitting that you, either, should deviate from this path, if you do not wish to be separated from our college by sentence of the synod.

3. . . . Up to now there have been enough mistakes of this kind. In future all priests must keep the above rule who do not wish to be torn away from the solid apostolic rock upon which Christ built the universal Church.

20. We have explained, as I think, dearest brother, all the matters of which you complained, and to every case which you have referred, by our son Bassian the presbyter, to *the Roman Church, as to the head of your body*, we have I believe returned adequate replies. And now we urge the mind of your brotherhood more and more to observe the canons and keep the decretals which have been framed, so that what we have replied to your inquiries you may bring to the notice of all our fellow bishops, and not only of those who are in your diocese: but let what we have profitably ordained be sent, with your letters also, to all the Carthaginians and Baeticans, Lusitanians and Gallicians, and to those in the provinces adjoining your own. And though *no priest of the Lord is free to be ignorant of the statutes of the apostolic see*, or of the venerable provisions of the canons, yet it would be more useful, and, on account of the seniority of your priesthood, a very high honour for you, beloved, if those things which have been written generally, and to you especially by name, were brought by your care to the notice of all our brethren; so that what has been profitably drawn up by us, not without consideration, but with care and great caution and deliberation, may remain inviolate, and that the way may be stopped for all excuses in future, which are now open to no one among us.

(Gore 90; Chapman 38B, 94B, 114A.)

II. AMBROSE ON THE PRIMACY OF PETER

The famous Ambrose, bishop of Milan 374–397, was the outstanding bishop of the western church at this period. His book on the incarnation really belongs to the time of Damasus, but is given here along with the other extracts from his writings.

DOCUMENT 109——Ambrose, *Liber de Incarnationis Dominicae Sacramento.* A.D. 381.
(*P.L.* 16. 826.)

32. This man who at first was silent, as he teaches that we ought not to repeat the words of the wicked, when he heard: "Who do ye say that I am?", at once mindful of his place, assumed the primacy: undoubtedly a primacy of confession, not of honour; *a primacy of faith, not of rank.* That is to say, "Now let no one surpass me".

DOCUMENT 110——Ambrose, *Expositio in Lucam*, Book 10. A.D. 390.
(*P.L.* 15. 1848.)

175. There is no doubt, therefore, that Peter believed, and that he believed because he loved, and loved because he believed. Consequently he is also made sad, because he is asked yet a third time: "Lovest thou me?" For he about whom there is a doubt is questioned, but the Lord is not in doubt, and he was asking the question, not in order to get information, but in order to teach *him whom he was leaving for us, as a vicar of his love,* seeing that he was to be raised into heaven. For thus you find "Simon, son of John, lovest thou me?" Likewise "Lord, thou knowest that I love thee", and Jesus says, "Feed my lambs". In full self-awareness, Peter testifies to a love not assumed for the occasion, but long since known to God. For who else is there that could easily make this profession about himself? And for that very reason, he alone of all men makes it: *he is placed before all men*; for love is greater than all.

(Chapman 59A.)

DOCUMENT 111——Ambrose, *Enarratio in Psalmum XL.* A.D. 395.
(*P.L.* 14. 1082.)

30. . Again there was Peter, and he followed him when he was led by the Jews to the house of Caiaphas, chief of the synagogue. That is Peter to whom he said, "Thou art Peter and

upon this rock I will build my Church". *Where therefore Peter is, there is the Church.* Where the Church is, there is no death but eternal life. And he also adds, "And the gates of hades shall not prevail against it, and I will give to thee the keys of the kingdom of heaven". Against blessed Peter, neither has the gate of hades prevailed, nor the gate of heaven shut, but on the contrary he has destroyed the forecourt of hades and thrown open the heavenly one.

DOCUMENT 112——Ambrose, *Enarratio in Psalmum XLIII.*
   A.D. 397.
   (*P.L.* 14. 1109.)

40.   Peter is sifted, as he is driven on to deny Christ. He falls into temptation, speaking like a man full of chaff.   . In the end he wept and washed away his chaff, and by those temptations, he was worthy that Christ should intervene for him.   . At length, after being tempted by the devil, Peter is set over the Church. And so the Lord indicated beforehand that which happened later, namely that he chose him as shepherd of his flock; for he said to him, "When thou art converted, strengthen thy brethren". And so the holy apostle Peter is converted to good fruit, and sifted like wheat, that he with the saints of the Lord might be one bread which should be our food.   (Chapman 59.)

III. ASTERIUS, BISHOP OF AMASEA IN PONTUS

DOCUMENT 113——Asterius, *On the Chief Holy Apostles, Peter and Paul.* A.D. 395.
   (*P.G.* 40. 273.)

Homily 8. In order that he may show his power, God has endowed none of his disciples with gifts like Peter. But, having raised him with heavenly gifts, he has set him above all. And, as *first disciple and greater among the brethren*, he has shown, by the test of deeds, the power of the Spirit. The first to be called, he followed at once.   *The Saviour confided to this man, as some special trust, the whole universal Church,* after having asked him three times "Lovest thou me?". And *he received the world in charge*, as one flock one shepherd, having heard, "Feed my lambs"; and the Lord gave, *wellnigh in his own stead*, that most faithful disciple to the proselytes as a father, and shepherd and instructor.   (Chapman 47A, note 3.)

IV. AMBROSE ON THE ROMAN CHURCH

DOCUMENT 114——Ambrose, *Explanatio Symboli ad Initiandos.* (*P.L.* 17. 1158.)

Nothing is to be taken away from the apostolic writings, and nothing is to be added to them; and in the same way we must expunge nothing from the creed drawn up and handed down by the apostles, nor must we add anything to it. *This is the creed which the Roman church holds, where Peter, the first of the apostles, sat, and thither he brought the common decision.*[1]   (Chapman 72A.)

DOCUMENT 115——Siricius, *Ep.* 7, to the Church of Milan. A.D. 390. (*P.L.* 13. 1171; *L.F.* 47. 281 ‡.)

4. Therefore in accordance with the apostolic precept,[2] since they preached other than what we received, it was the one sentence of us all, presbyters, deacons, and all the clergy, that Jovinian, Auxentius, Genialis, Germinator, Felix, Plotinus, Martian, Januarius, and Ingeniosus, who were found to be promoters of the new heresy and blasphemy, should be condemned by the divine sentence and our judgement, and remain permanently outside the Church. I have sent this letter, not doubting that your holiness will observe it.

DOCUMENT 116——Council of Milan, A.D. 391, *To Siricius.* Ambrose, *Ep.* 42.   (*P.L.* 16. 1124; *L.F.* 47. 282 ‡.)

To their lord, their dearly beloved brother, Pope Siricius; Ambrose, Sabinus, Bassianus, and the rest send greeting.

[1] *communem sententiam eo detulit.*   [2] Gal. 1. 8.

1. In your holiness' letter we recognized the viligance of a good shepherd, for you faithfully guard the door which has been entrusted to you, and with pious care watch over the fold of Christ, being worthy to be heard and followed by the sheep of the Lord. Knowing therefore the lambs of Christ, you will easily discover the wolves, and meet them as a wary shepherd, so as to keep them from scattering the Lord's flock by their unbelieving life and dismal barking.

2. We praise you for this, our lord and brother dearly beloved. . . .

5. But if they will not believe the doctrines of the priests, let them believe Christ's oracles, let them believe the admonitions of angels who say "For with God nothing is impossible". Let them believe the apostles' creed *which the Roman church has always kept undefiled.* .

14. And so you are to know that Jovinian, Auxentius [etc.] ., whom your holiness has condemned, have also been condemned by us, *in accordance with your judgement.*

(Chapman 72A.)

CHAPTER XV

JEROME

JEROME was born of catholic parents in the hilly country of modern Yugoslavia. The earliest authority, Prosper,[1] puts the date of his birth in 331. But the biographer F. Cavallera,[2] after thorough investigation, fixes the year as 347. We quote writings which extend over thirty-eight years of his life. He came to Rome about 354 for secular education, when Liberius was Pope. About 363, he was baptized under the same bishop, and always regarded himself as a member of the Roman church. After considerable travelling he reached Antioch in Syria in 373, where there were three or more rival bishops (see Chapter XIII). The following year he retired to the desert east of Antioch for solitude, but he could not thereby escape the troubles of the Antioch schism; hence his two letters to Pope Damasus, which like all his writings are full of quotations from and allusions to Holy Scripture.

DOCUMENT 117——Jerome, *Ep.* 15, to Pope Damasus. A.D. 375.
(*P.L.*[3] 22. 355; *P.N.F.* 6. 18A ‡.)

1. Since the East, dashed against itself by the accustomed fury of its peoples, is tearing piecemeal the undivided tunic of Christ, woven from the top throughout, and foxes are destroying the vine of Christ, so that among the broken cisterns which have no water it is hard to locate the sealed fountain and the enclosed garden, I have considered that *I ought to consult the chair of Peter,* and the faith praised by the mouth of the apostle, asking now food for my soul, from the place whence I received the garment of Christ. Neither the vast expanse of ocean, nor all the breadth of land which separates us could preclude me from seeking the precious pearl. "Wherever the body is, there

[1] *Chronicum Integrum, P.L.* 51. 576.
[2] *Saint Jérôme,* t. 2, p. 10 (Louvain, 1922).
[3] Migne has two editions of Jerome's works. My references are to the 1845 edition.

will the eagles be gathered together." Now that evil children
have squandered their patrimony, you alone keep your heri-
tage intact. There the fertile earth reproduces a hundredfold
the purity of the Lord's seed. Here the corn, cast into the
furrows, degenerates into darnel or wild oats. It is now in the
West that the sun of justice rises; whilst in the East Lucifer who
fell has set his seat above the stars. "Ye are the light of the
world." "Ye are the salt of the earth." Ye are vessels of gold
and silver. Here the vessels of clay or wood await the iron rod
and eternal fire.

2. Yet though your greatness terrifies me, your kindness
attracts me. From the priest I ask the salvation of the victim;
from the shepherd, the safety of the sheep. Away with envy!
The canvassing of the Roman height recedes. I speak with the
successor of the fisherman, with the disciple of the cross.
Following none in the first place but Christ, *I am in communion
with your beatitude, that is with the chair of Peter. On that rock I
know the Church is built. Whoever shall eat the Lamb outside this
house is profane. If any be not with Noah in the ark, he shall perish in
the flood.* And because for my sins I have migrated to this solitude, where Syria borders on the barbarians, and I cannot
always at this great distance ask for the Holy One of the Lord
from your holiness, therefore I follow here your colleagues the
Egyptian confessors; and under these great ships, my little
vessel lies hid. Vitalis I know not, Meletius I reject; I ignore
Paulinus. *Whoso gathereth not with thee scattereth*, that is, he who
is not of Christ is anti-Christ.

3. Now, alas, after the creed of Nicaea, after the decree of
Alexandria joined to the West, the new expression of three
hypostases is required of me, a Roman, by that progeny of
Arius, the Campenses! What new Paul, doctor of the nations,
has taught this?

4. Decide, I beseech, if you please, and I will not fear to
acknowledge three hypostases. If you order it, let a new creed
be compiled after the Nicene, and the orthodox will confess in
like words with the Arians. . . . Well might Ursinus[1] be joined
to your beatitude, Auxentius[2] to Ambrose. Far be this from

[1] Rival Pope.   [2] Arian bp of Milan before Ambrose.

the faith of Rome. May the devout hearts of the people drink
no such sacrilege. Let us be satisfied to say one substance, three
persons subsisting, perfect, equal, coeternal. Let us drop three
hypostases, if you please, and hold one. It is no use using
different words in the same sense. .   *But if you think right that,
with explanations, we should say three hypostases, we do not refuse. .   .*

5. Wherefore I beseech your holiness, by the crucified
Saviour of the world, that you will write and authorize me to
say or refuse the hypostases.   Likewise *inform me with
whom I ought to communicate* at Antioch; for the Campenses are
joined to the heretical Tarsenes, and desire nothing but to
preach three hypostases in the old sense, *as if supported by the
authority of your communion.*   (Gore 115, 116; Chapman 77.)

DOCUMENT 118——Jerome, *Ep.* 16, to Pope Damasus.
     A.D. 375.
     (P.L. 22. 358; *P.N.F.* 6. 20B ‡.)

2. I therefore, who received Christ's robe in Rome, am now
detained in the border waste of Syria. And, lest you think I
received this sentence from another, I inflicted my own punishment. But as the heathen poet says: "They change sky, not
mind, who cross the sea." The untiring foe follows me behind,
so that now I wage fierce wars in the desert. On the one side
storm the raging Arians, upheld by worldly power. On the
other, a church, torn in three parts, tries to seize me. The
authority of ancient monks who dwell around rises against me.
Meantime I cry: "*He who is joined to Peter's chair is mine.*"
Meletius, Vitalis, and Paulinus *say that they adhere to you.* If one
of them asserted this, I could believe him. Now either two are
lying or all. Therefore I implore your blessedness by the cross
of the Lord, by the essential glory of our faith, the passion of
Christ, that you who follow the apostles in honour will follow
them in worth. May you sit in judgement on a throne with the
twelve. In old age, may another gird you with Peter: may you
gain with Paul the heavenly citizenship, if you write and *tell me
with whom I ought to communicate in Syria.* Despise not a soul for
which Christ died.   (Gore 116; Chapman 77B.)

The doctrine implied in these two letters seems to be: Pope Damasus is the successor of Peter sitting in his chair (*Ep.* 15. 1, 2). The chair of Peter is the rock on which the Church is built (15. 2). To follow Christ is to be in communion with the Pope, and therein lies the only security (15. 2). The Roman church bears fruit a hundredfold, because her faith is reliable (15. 1). Three of the rival claimants to the see of Antioch all profess to cleave to the Pope (*Ep.* 16. 2). The Pope is asked to say which of the rivals is the true bishop (15. 5; 16. 2). The Pope is asked to give a definite ruling on the wording of the creed, and, if he thinks fit, to alter the Nicene creed (15. 4).

On the above letters of Jerome, Puller says: " Of course no catholic would dream of departing from the general teaching of the Fathers in order to adhere to the exaggerated statements of one young man in sore perplexity."[1] Denny writes more or less to the same effect.[2] Kidd says that *Epistle* 15 "was the letter of a young man in a hurry".[3] (Jerome was not less than twenty-eight years old.) Gore also discounts the terms of this letter in view of what he believes to be Jerome's changed attitude towards the papacy in later years. We must proceed to examine the evidence for and against this view.

Jerome returned to Antioch in 379. In the meantime the Pope had made it clear that he accepted Paulinus as the true bishop (Doc. 100), and Jerome was ordained priest by him. He proceeded via Constantinople back to Rome in 382, and became secretary to the Pope. About this time he records in his Chronicle that the Pope previous to Damasus had subscribed to heresy.

DOCUMENT 119——Jerome, *Chronicon ad Ann.* 352.   A.D. 382. (*P.L.* 27. 683.)

Liberius was ordained the 34th bishop of the Roman church, and when he was driven into exile for the faith, all the clergy took an oath that they would not recognize any other bishop. But when Felix was put in his place by the Arians, a great many foreswore themselves; but at the end of the year they were banished, and Felix too; for Liberius, giving in to the irksomeness of exile and *subscribing to the heretical and false doctrine,* made a triumphal entry into Rome.

In Rome was the small and rigid sect of Luciferians, founded by Lucifer who had been largely responsible for the continuance of the

---

[1] Page 162.   [2] Pages 286, 287.   [3] *Hist. Ch.,* 2. 322.

schism at Antioch.[1] In writing against this sect, Jerome discusses the dispute between Stephen, bishop of Rome, and Cyprian on the question of rebaptism,[2] and points out that Stephen's view prevailed. § 9 of this work was quoted by Pope Leo XIII in *Satis Cognitum* § 14, but the term "high priest" appears to be used of any bishop as distinct from a priest.

DOCUMENT 120——Jerome, *Contra Luciferianos.* A.D. 383.
   (*P.L.* 23. 165; *P.N.F.* 6. 324B ‡.)

9. . . The safety of the church depends on the dignity of the high priest. If to him is not given a certain independence and eminence of power, there will be made in the church as many schisms as there are priests. This is the reason that without chrism and the command of a bishop, neither presbyter nor deacon has the right to baptize.

23. Cyprian of blessed memory tried to avoid broken cisterns, and not to drink of strange waters; and therefore, rejecting heretical baptism, he summoned his African synod in opposition to Stephen, who was the blessed Peter's 22nd successor in the see of Rome. They met to discuss this matter, but the attempt failed. At last those very bishops who had together with him determined that heretics must be rebaptized reverted to the old custom, and published a fresh decree. . .

25. If, however, those who were ordained by Hilary, and who have lately become sheep without a shepherd, are disposed to allege scripture in support of what the blessed Cyprian left in his letters, advocating the rebaptizing of heretics, I beg them to remember that he did not anathematize those who refused to follow him. . .

27. . Hilary himself confesses that Julius, Mark, Sylvester,[3] and the other bishops of old alike welcomed all heretics to repentance; and further, to show that he could not justly claim possession of the true custom, the council of Nicaea also, to which we referred not long ago, welcomed all heretics with the exception of the disciples of Paul of Samosata.

[1] See p. 133.   [2] See Chapter IX.
[3] Three Popes, 314 to 352.

28. I might spend the day in speaking to the same effect, and dry up all the streams of argument with the single sun of the Church. (Gore 135 note; Chapman 37A, 57A note.)

During the last year of Damasus' life, 384, Jerome wrote violently against the clerical and Christian society of Rome.[1] The Pope died on 11 December, and Jerome was disappointed that he did not succeed him. The following year "he abandoned Rome in disgust",[2] went to Palestine, and settled in Bethlehem in 386.

DOCUMENT 121——Jerome, *Ep.* 45, to Asella. August, A.D. 385.
  (*P.L.* 22. 481.)

2. I am called an infamous slippery turncoat, and a liar deceiving by the art of Satan. One would attack my walk and my laugh; another objected to my expression; a woman would suspect something in my simplicity. With such people I have lived nearly three years. .

3. Before I became acquainted with the household of the saintly Paula, the whole city re-echoed my praises. Almost everyone concurred in judging me worthy of the episcopate. My words were on the lips of the late Damasus. I was called holy, humble, eloquent. . .

6. I write this in haste, dear lady Asella, as I go on board ship, grieving and in tears; and I thank my God that I am held worthy of the world's hate. Pray that from Babylon I may return to Jerusalem. . I was a fool who wished to "sing the Lord's song in a strange land", and left mount Sion to seek the help of Egypt.

It is after this departure from Rome that Gore believes Jerome's attitude to the papacy to have changed. The date of the next Document is uncertain, but Gore and Chapman agree that it may have been written in 386.[3]

DOCUMENT 122——Jerome, *Ep.* 146, to Evangelus. A.D. 386.
  (*P.L.* 22. 1192; *P.N.F.* 6. 288A ‡.)

1. We read in Isaiah, "A fool will speak folly". I am told that someone has been mad enough to put deacons before

[1] *Ep.* 22 § 28 (*P.L.* 22. 413).   [2] Gore, 116.
[3] Gore, *Church and Ministry*, edit. 1936, p. 157, n. 3; Chapman, 77A note.

presbyters, that is, bishops. For when the apostle plainly teaches that presbyters are the same as bishops, what happens to the server of tables and widows that he sets himself up arrogantly over those at whose prayers the body and blood of Christ are made? . That afterwards one was chosen to preside over the rest, this was done as a remedy for schism, lest anyone should rend the Church of Christ by drawing it to himself. Besides at Alexandria, from Mark the evangelist until the episcopates of Heraclas and Dionysius, the presbyters always chose one of their number, and placing him in a higher rank called him bishop. . . . For what does a bishop do which a presbyter does not, except ordain? It is not the case that there is one church at Rome, and another in all the world besides. Gaul and Britain, Africa and Persia, India and the barbarians worship one Christ and observe one rule of truth. *If you ask for authority, the world outweighs the city. Wherever there is a bishop, whether at Rome or Gubbio, or Constantinople or Rhegium, or Alexandria or Tanis, his worth is the same, and his priesthood is the same.*[1] The power of riches or the lowliness of poverty does not make him a higher or a lower bishop. But all are successors of the apostles.

2. But you say, "How is it that at Rome a presbyter is ordained on the recommendation of a deacon?" Why bring forward to me the custom of one city? Why in the laws of the Church do you appropriate a paltry case which has given rise to pride? The rarer a thing is, the more it is sought. In India pennyroyal is more costly than pepper. Deacons, being few, are made honorable; presbyters in the mass are made contemptible. But even in the church of Rome, presbyters sit and deacons stand; although bad habits have gradually crept in, so that I have seen a deacon, in the absence of a bishop, sit among the presbyters, and at social gatherings give blessings to them. Those who act thus must learn that they are wrong.

(Gore 116, 117; Chapman 75-77.)

Gore claims that Jerome says in effect that "the episcopate at Rome has no more authority than any other episcopate" and that the letter "indicates that the authority of the Roman see rested for Jerome on what is variable in a theologian—on sentiment, on expedience, on feeling—not on what is invariable, the basis of doctrinal authority".

Chapman replies: "Who doubts that St Jerome is right in saying that the bishop of Gubbio is as much a bishop as his metropolitan, the bishop of Rome? . . . And who does not see that this very argument implies that they differ in jurisdiction, while they are equal in bishopship? . . If St Jerome had really argued that the bishop of Tanis was not subject to the bishop of Alexandria, he would have been contradicting the Council of Nicaea,[1] which confirmed the patriarchal rights of Alexandria and Antioch."

We must now see what evidence about his views on papal authority we can glean from Jerome's later works. We saw in Doc. 120 § 9 that he considered loyalty to the bishop the best safeguard against schism. But apparently the authority of the bishop is by ecclesiastical custom rather than by divine law. The purpose of it is the avoidance of schism.

DOCUMENT 123——Jerome, *In Epistolam ad Titum.* A.D. 387. (*P.L.* 26. 562.)

On Titus 1. 5:   It was decreed in the whole world that one of the presbyters should be elected to be placed above the others, to whom the whole care of the church should belong, and the seeds of schism should be destroyed.   . so let bishops remember that it is rather by custom than by the truth of the Lord's direction that they are greater than presbyters.

For the same reason, the avoidance of schism, Peter was appointed by Christ as head of the apostles.

DOCUMENT 124——Jerome, *Adversus Jovinianum*, Book 1. A.D. 392. (*P.L.* 23. 247; *P.N.F.* 6. 366a ‡.)

26.   . . But you say that the Church was founded upon Peter: although elsewhere the same is attributed to all the apostles, and *they all receive the keys* of the kingdom of heaven, and the strength of the Church depends on them all alike, yet *one among the twelve is chosen so that when a head has been appointed, there may be no occasion for schism.* But why was not John chosen,

[1] See Doc. 62.

who was a virgin? Deference was paid to age, because Peter was the elder: one who was a youth, I may say almost a boy, could not be set over men of advanced age; and that the good Master, who was bound to remove every occasion of strife among his disciples, . . . might not seem to afford a ground for jealousy in appointing the young man whom he had loved. Peter was an apostle, and John was an apostle; the first married, the second a virgin. But Peter was only[1] an apostle, while John was an apostle and an evangelist and a prophet.

(Chapman 53A note.)

So according to Jerome a primate was necessary even among the apostles, and a bishop was found to be necessary for the avoidance of schism among priests. Hence Chapman claims that he must have believed in the necessity of a universal primacy.[2]

DOCUMENT 125——Jerome, *In Epistolam ad Galatas*, Book 2, Preface. A.D. 389.
(*P.L.* 26. 355.)

Would you know, O Paula and Eustochium, how the apostle designates each province by its own qualities? To this day remain the same traces of virtues and of errors. Of the Roman people the faith is praised.[3] Where else do people run with the same eagerness and in such crowds to the churches or to the tombs of the martyrs? Where does the Amen so resound like the thunder of heaven, shaking the empty temples of the idols? Not that the Romans have any other faith than that of all the churches of Christ, but in them is greater devotion and simplicity in believing. Again they are reproved for laxity and pride. For laxity as follows : "I beseech you, brethren, mark them which are causing divisions[4]   ." (Chapman 71B.)

In his *De Viris Illustribus*, a sort of *Who's Who* of the Catholic Church, Jerome commends Polycrates, bishop of Ephesus, for standing up against the Roman bishop of his day, he makes the Roman clergy under Zephyrinus responsible for the lapse of Tertullian, and he again records the fall of Pope Liberius.

---

[1] *tantum.*   [2] *S.E.P.*, 110.
[3] Rom. 1. 8.   [4] Rom. 16. 17.

DOCUMENT 126——Jerome, *De Viris Illustribus.* A.D. 392.
   (*P.L.* 23. 657; *P.N.F.* 3. 372A ‡.)

45. Polycrates, bishop of the Ephesians, with other bishops of Asia who, in accordance with some ancient custom, celebrated the passover with the Jews on the 14th of the month, wrote a synodical letter[1] *against* Victor, bishop of Rome, in which he says he follows the authority of the apostle John and of the ancients. From this we make the following brief quotations, "As for us, then, we keep the day inviolate. . . Therefore I for my part, brethren, who number sixty-five years in the Lord . . am not frightened by threats. For those better than I have said, 'We must obey God rather than men'".[2] I quote this to show through a small example the genius and authority of the man.

53. Tertullian.   He was a presbyter of the Church until middle life; afterwards, driven by the envy and abuse of the clergy of the Roman church, he lapsed to the doctrine of Montanus,[3] and mentions the new prophecy in many of his books.

97. Fortunatian, a native of Africa, was bishop of Aquileia during the reign of Constantius; he composed brief commentaries on the Gospels, written in a rustic style, and he was hated because, when Liberius, bishop of Rome, was driven into exile for the faith, he first tempted him and weakened him, and then urged him to subscribe to heresy.[4]

About this time Jerome thinks it necessary to warn the Roman church against the errors and excesses of Jovinian. In this Document the "rock" of Matt. 16. 18 is not interpreted as the chair of Peter, as in Doc. 117 § 2, but as Christ himself.

DOCUMENT 127——Jerome, *Adversus Jovinianum*, Book 2.
      A.D. 393.
      (*P.L.* 23. 350; *P.N.F.* 6. 415A ‡.)

37. . . . Was there no other province in the whole world to receive the gospel of pleasure, and into which the serpent

---

[1] A.D. 190.
[2] Jerome translates the whole letter as it is given by Eusebius in *H.E.* 5. 24 §§ 2–7 (see Doc. 11).
[3] A.D. 200.   [4] A.D. 357.

might insinuate itself, except that which was founded by the teaching of Peter upon the rock Christ.[1] Idol temples had fallen before the standard of the cross and the severity of the gospel; now on the contrary lust and gluttony try to overthrow the solidity of the cross.

38. . Mighty city, mistress city of the world, city of the apostle's praises, show the meaning of your name. Rome is either strength in Greek, or height in Hebrew. Lose not the excellence your name implies: let virtue lift you up on high; do not let sensuality debase you.

Early in the fifth century, Jerome was engaged in a dispute with Rufinus, bishop of Aquileia, over some translations of the *First Principles* of Origen. In the next Document, he is writing to two Roman senators, but his words are as if addressed to Rufinus.

DOCUMENT 128——Jerome, *Ep.* 84, to Pammachius and Oceanus. A.D. 400.
(*P.L.* 22. 750; *P.N.F.* 6. 180A ‡.)

9. Whoever you are who are thus preaching new doctrines, I beseech you to spare the ears of the Romans, spare the faith of a church which an apostle has praised. Why after 400 years do you try to teach us Romans doctrines of which we have known nothing until now? Why do you proclaim in public, opinions which Peter and Paul refused to profess? Until now, no such teaching has been heard of, and yet the world has become Christian. (Chapman 72A.)

Many extracts from the *Apology against Rufinus* are quoted by Chapman in *Studies on the Early Papacy*.[2] They are intended to show that Jerome was as firm a believer in the papacy when he wrote this *Apology* as when he wrote to Pope Damasus twenty-five years before. The Popes who followed Damasus were Siricius, 384–399, and Anastasius, 399–402.

---

[1] Another MS. reads "the rock of Christ".
[2] Pages 124–127.

DOCUMENT 129——Jerome, *Apologia contra Rufinum*, Book 1.
    A.D. 402.
    (*P.L.* 23. 400; *P.N.F.* 3. 485A ‡.)

4. . He says, "The Latin reader will find nothing here discordant from our faith" What faith is this which he calls his? Is it the faith by which the Roman church is distinguished? Or is it the faith which is contained in the works of Origen? *If he answers "the Roman", then we* [both] *are catholics* since we have adopted none of Origen's errors in our translations.

10. . . . The consciences of a great many people have been wounded by the book which you have published under the name of the martyr[1]; they give no heed to the authority of the bishops who condemn Origen, since they think that a martyr has praised him. *Of what use are the letters of* the bishop Theophilus or of *the Pope Anastasius*, who follow out the heretic in every part of the world, *when your book passing under the name of Pamphilus is there to oppose their letters*, and the testimony of the martyr can be set against the authority of the bishops?

    (Chapman 71B, 72A.)

Rufinus also joins with his opponent in praising the faith of the Roman church.

DOCUMENT 130——Rufinus, *Commentarius in Symbolum Apostolorum*. A.D. 410.
    (*P.L.* 21. 339; Morison[2] 4.)

3. I believe in God the Father Almighty. But before I begin to discuss the exact meaning of these words, I think it is here not unsuitable to mention that in various churches certain additions to this clause are to be found. This, however, we do not observe to be the case in the church of the city of Rome. The reason is, I imagine, that *no heresy has ever had its origin there*.   (Chapman 72A.)

Having stated in Doc. 124 that Peter was by Christ's ordinance head of the apostles, Jerome goes on to maintain that he was the author and prime mover in the decree for Gentile Christians of Acts 15. 20.

[1] Pamphilus, who died in 309.
[2] E. F. Morison, *Rufinus: A Commentary on the Apostles' Creed*, London, 1916.

DOCUMENT 131——Jerome, *Ep.* 112, to Augustine.   A.D. 404.
   (*P.L.* 33. 255; M.D. 6. 284 ‡.)

7. When there had been much disputing, Peter rose up, with his wonted readiness, and said, "Men and brethren   . we shall be saved even as they".[1] And to his opinion the apostle James and all the elders together gave consent.

8. These quotations should not be tedious to the reader, but useful both to him and to me, as proving that, even before the apostle Paul, Peter had come to know that the law was not to be in force after the gospel was given; nay more, that *Peter was the prime mover in issuing the decree* by which this was affirmed. Moreover Peter was of so great authority that Paul has recorded in his epistle "Then after three years I went up to Jerusalem to see Peter".[2]   . proving that he would not have had confidence in his preaching of the gospel if he had not been confirmed by the consent of Peter and those who were with him. . . . No one can doubt, therefore, that *the apostle Peter was himself the author of that rule* which he is accused of breaking.   (Chapman 60A.)

Finally, Jerome in his old age writes to the Roman virgin Demetrias, who had fled to Carthage when Rome was sacked in A.D. 410.

DOCUMENT 132——Jerome, *Ep.* 130, to Demetrias.   A.D. 414.
   (*P.L.* 22. 1120; *P.N.F.* 6. 269B ‡.)

16. I have all but passed over the most important point of all. While you were still quite small, Bishop Anastasius of holy and blessed memory ruled the Roman church. In his days a terrible storm of heresy came from the East and strove first to corrupt and then to undermine that simple faith which an apostle has praised. However, the bishop, rich in poverty and as careful of his flock as an apostle, at once smote the noxious thing on the head, and stayed the hydra's hissing. Now I have reason to fear—in fact a report has reached me to this effect—that the poisonous germs of this heresy still live and sprout in the minds of some to this day. I think, therefore, that I ought

[1] Acts 15. 7–11.   [2] Gal. 1. 18.

to warn you, in all kindness and affection, to *hold fast the faith of the saintly Innocent*, the son of Anastasius and his successor in the apostolic see; and not to receive any foreign doctrine, however wise and discerning you may take yourself to be.   (Chapman 77ʙ, 78ᴀ.)

Jerome died on 30 September 420.

CHAPTER XVI

JOHN CHRYSOSTOM

THIS great saint and eloquent preacher was born at Antioch about 347. At the age of twenty-two he was baptized by Meletius and the following year was admitted to minor orders. There followed eleven years of ascetic and monastic life, at the end of which he was forced by ill health to abandon "the life of angels", and so returned to Antioch. Just before going to the council of Constantinople in 381, Meletius ordained him deacon, and after five years the next bishop, Flavian,[1] raised him to the priesthood, and soon gave him scope for his preaching ability, which he used unsparingly from 387 to 398. On 26 February 398 he was consecrated to the see of Constantinople by Theophilus, bishop of Alexandria. He nobly set about the exacting task of reforming the corruptions of his church and clergy, and thereby made many ferocious enemies. These enemies secured Theophilus as their leader, and at the height of his trouble Chrysostom wrote to Pope Innocent and to the bishops of Aquileia and Milan asking for their aid.[2] After two attempts had been made on his life, he was exiled in 404. He died in Pontus on 14 September 407; after he had received Holy Communion, his last words were "Glory be to God for all things. Amen".

The homilies of Chrysostom are cited extensively by Chapman[3] to show the great preacher's belief in the primacy of Peter.

DOCUMENT 133——Chrysostom, *Homily on 2 Timothy 3. 1.*
  (*P.G.* 56. 275.)

4. . The apostles do not see their own affairs, but those of others, all together and each separately. *Peter, the leader of the choir, the mouth of all the apostles, the head of that tribe, the ruler of the whole world, the foundation of the Church,* the ardent lover of Christ; for he says "Peter, lovest thou me more than these?" I speak his praises that you may learn that he loves Christ, for the care of the slaves is the greatest proof of love to the Lord.

[1] Palladius, *Vita* § 5 (*P.G.* 47. 19). But Socrates, *H.E.* 6. 3, says it was Evagrius, successor to Paulinus and rival to Flavian.
[2] *P.G.* 47. 8–12.
[3] *S.E.P.,* Chapter 4.

It is not I who say these things, but the beloved Lord. "If thou lovest me," he says, "feed my sheep." Let us see whether he has the primacy of a shepherd.　　　　　(Chapman 48B note.)

DOCUMENT 134——Chrysostom, *On Matthew*, Homily 54.
　　(*P.G.* 58. 534; *L.F.* 15. 731 ‡.)

2.　　"And I say unto thee, Thou art Peter and upon this rock I will build my Church", that is on the faith of his confession. Thus he shows many will believe and raises his mind and makes him shepherd.　. Do you see how he himself leads Peter to high thoughts of him, and reveals himself and shows that he is the Son of God by these two promises? For those things which are peculiar to God alone, namely to forgive sins, and to make the Church immovable in such an onset of waves, and to declare *a fisherman to be stronger than any rock* while all the world wars against him, these things he himself promises to give; as the Father said, speaking to Jeremiah, that he would set him as a column of brass and as a wall—but him for one nation, *this man for all the world.* I would ask those who wish to lessen the dignity of the Son, which gifts were greater, those which the Father gave to Peter, or those which the Son gave to him? The Father gave to Peter the revelation of the Son, but the Son gave him to sow that of the Father and of himself throughout the world; and *to a mortal man he entrusted the authority over all things in heaven, giving him the keys*, who extended the Church throughout the world and declared it to be stronger than heaven.　　　　　(Gore 86.)

DOCUMENT 135——Chrysostom, *On Penitence*, Homily 5.
　　(*P.G.* 49. 308.)

2. . . After that grave fall (for there is no sin equal to denial), after so great a sin, he brought him back to his former honour, and entrusted him with *the care of the universal Church*, and, what is more than all, he showed us that he had a greater love for his master than any of the apostles, for he saith, "Peter, lovest thou me more than these?"

(Chapman 48A, note 1.)

DOCUMENT 136——Chrysostom, *On John*, Homily 88.
   (*P.G.* 59. 478; *L.F.* 36. 790 ‡.)

   1.   . He says to him "Feed my sheep". Why does he pass
over the others and speak about these to him? He was the
chosen one of the apostles, the mouth of the disciples, the head
of the choir; for this reason Paul went up to see him rather
than the others. And also, to show him that he must now have
confidence, since the denial was done away, he entrusts him
with the primacy[1] of the brethren; and he does not bring
forward the denial, or reproach him with the past, but says:
"If you love me, rule the brethren,[2] and now show the fervent
love which you have always shown, and in which you
rejoiced, and now give for my sheep the life which you said you
would lay down for me." . . . And if anyone would say "*How
did James receive the chair of Jerusalem?*", I would reply that he
appointed *Peter a teacher not of the chair, but of the world.*   .

   2. . .   And he [Christ] did this[3] to withdraw them [Peter
and John] from the unseasonable sympathy for each other; for
since *they* were about to receive the charge of the world, it was
necessary that they should no longer be closely associated
together.   (Gore 88; Chapman 58B.)

   The translation of the verb προΐστημι by "rule" follows the
English Bible[4] and is accepted by Puller.[5] *L.F.* has "preside over".
Gore points out the honour which Chrysostom does to John and Paul.
At the end of the last Document we see that John as well as Peter was
to receive the charge of the world; and further:

DOCUMENT 137——Chrysostom, *On John*, Homily 1.
   (*P.G.* 59. 25; *L.F.* 28. 2 ‡.)

   1.   . The Son of thunder, the beloved of Christ, the pillar
of the churches throughout the world, *having the keys* of heaven,
who drank the cup of Christ, and was baptized with his
baptism, who lay upon the master's bosom, with much confidence this man now comes forward to us.   (Gore 88.)

---

[1] προστασίαν.   [2] προΐστασο τῶν ἀδελφῶν·
[3] John 21. 22.   [4] Rom. 12. 8.
[5] Page 125.

DOCUMENT 138——Chrysostom, *On Genesis*, Homily 24.
  (*P.G.* 53. 211.)

4.   The merciful God is wont to give this honour to his servants, that by their grace others may acquire salvation; as was agreed by the blessed *Paul, that teacher of the world* who emitted the rays of his teaching everywhere.   (Gore 88.)

The most striking of Chrysostom's ideas on Peter's primacy is that he might, if he had wished, have appointed a successor to Judas Iscariot on his sole authority.

DOCUMENT 139——Chrysostom, *On the Acts of the Apostles*, Homily 3.
  (*P.G.* 60. 33; *L.F.* 33. 37 ‡.)

1.   . "And in those days", it says, "Peter stood up in the midst of the disciples and said". Both as being ardent, and as having been put in trust by Christ with the flock, and as having precedence in honour,[1] he always begins the discourse. .

Why did he not ask Christ to give him some one in the room of Judas? It is better as it is. For in the first place, they were engaged in other things; secondly, of Christ's presence with them the greatest proof that could be given was this: as he had chosen when he was among them, so did he now being absent. Now this was no small matter for their consolation. But observe how Peter does everything with the common consent, nothing imperiously.

2.   . And so at the beginning he said, "Men and brethren, it is necessary to choose from among you". He defers the decision to the whole body, thereby both making the elected objects of reverence, and keeping himself clear of all invidiousness with regard to the rest. ".   . One must be ordained to be a witness with us of his resurrection", that their college might not be left mutilated. Then *why did it not rest with Peter to make the election himself?*[2] What was the motive? This, that he might

[1] Another reading is "as first of the choir".
[2] Migne's text has: "Why then? Did it not rest with Peter to make the election himself? Certainly" (καὶ πάνυ γε). Migne follows Montfaucon, but *L.F.* follows more reliable MSS.

not seem to bestow it of favour. And besides, he was not yet endowed with the Spirit. "And they appointed two, Joseph called Barsabbas, who was surnamed Justus, and Matthias." Not "he appointed them"; but it was he that introduced the proposition to that effect, at the same time pointing out that even this was not his own, but from of old by prophecy; so that he acted as expositor, not as preceptor.

3.   "Men and brethren .   " Here is forethought for providing a teacher: here was the first who ordained a teacher. He did not say, "We are sufficient". So far was he beyond all vainglory, and he looked to one thing alone. *And yet he had the same power to ordain as they all collectively.* But well might these things be done in this fashion, through the noble spirit of the man, and considering that prelacy was not then an affair of dignity, but of care for the governed. This neither made the elected to become elated, for it was to dangers they were called, nor those not elected to make a grievance of it, as if they were disgraced. But these things are not done in that way nowadays; no, quite the contrary. For observe, they were 120, and he asks for one out of the whole body; with good right, *as having been put in charge of them*; for to him had Christ said, "And when thou art converted, strengthen thy brethren".

(Gore 80 note, 88, note 1; Chapman 58B, 60B.)

These last words are of special interest, because in Luke 22. 32 the words "thy brethren" must refer to the other apostles; so that according to this homily Peter had charge of the other ten apostles, with the power to add one. Gore sends us to Salmon,[1] who casts doubts on the authorship of this series of homilies, and quotes Erasmus[2]: "I could write better stuff if I were dead drunk." But Gore refers to the series in another context (see Doc. 149).

There are three other passages on Luke 22. 31, 32. Luke wrote: "Simon, Simon, behold Satan desired to have you that he might sift you as wheat: but I have prayed for thee that thy faith fail not: and when thou art converted, strengthen thy brethren." Chrysostom sometimes misquotes, and so misses the point that Satan desired to have all the apostles, but Christ's prayer was for Peter (*On Psalm 129* in *P.G.* 55. 375; *Homily on Meeting More Often* in *P.G.* 63. 466). According to these passages Christ prayed specially for Peter because

[1] *Infallibility*, 2nd ed., 1890, p. 344 n.
[2] A.D. 1530. *Erasmi Epistolae* (ed. P. S. Allen) 8. 344.

of his future pre-eminence. But in *On Matthew*, Homily 82 (*P.G.* 58. 741) he quotes accurately and gives two other reasons for the prayer, namely that Peter's fall was the most serious, and that they were all weak.

In Doc. 136, Chrysostom contrasts James' position as bishop of Jerusalem with that of Peter as teacher of the world. But in dealing with the council of Jerusalem (Acts 15. 6-29), he points out that James speaks last, and he seems to imply that he had higher authority than Peter; incidentally he confuses Simeon, the author of the *Nunc Dimittis*, with Simon Peter.

DOCUMENT 140——Chrysostom, *On the Acts of the Apostles*, Homily 32.
   (*P.G.* 60. 236; *L.F.* 35. 443 ‡.)

2. Notice how Peter ends[1] on a fearful note. He does not preach to them from the prophets, but from current events of which they were witnesses. Of course these add their witness and strengthen the word by what has now happened. And notice, *he first allows the question to be moved in the Church, and then speaks.*[2]   (Chapman 50B note.)

DOCUMENT 141——The Same, Homily 33.
   (*P.G.* 60. 239; *L.F.* 35. 452 ‡.)
   "And after they had held their peace, James answered

1. This man was bishop, as they say, and so he speaks last, and the saying is fulfilled, "In the mouth of two or three witnesses shall every word be established".   "Men and brethren," he says, "hearken unto me." Notice the moderation of the man. His also is a fuller speech, for it completes the matter under discussion. "Symeon", he says, "declared": in Luke,[3] when he prophesied "how first God did visit the Gentiles"[4]

2. There was no arrogance in the Church. Peter speaks after Paul, and no one silences him. James waits patiently; he does not start up. Neither John nor the other apostles say anything; they kept silence, for *James was invested with the chief rule*, and they think this was no hardship, for their soul was clean from

[1] Acts 15. 11.   [2] Acts 15. 7.
[3] Luke 2. 32.   [4] Acts 15. 14.

the love of glory. Peter certainly spoke more emphatically, but James more mildly; for it is necessary for one in high authority to leave what is unpleasant for others to say, while he himself appears in the milder part.

One more reference to Peter must be given.

DOCUMENT 142——Chrysostom, *On the Inscription of the Acts*, II. (*P.G.* 51. 86.)

6. . . In speaking of S. Peter, the recollection of another Peter[1] has come to me, the common father and teacher, who has inherited his prowess, and also obtained his chair. For this is the one great privilege of our city, Antioch, that it received the leader of the apostles as its teacher in the beginning. For it was right that she who was first adorned with the name of Christians, before the whole world, should receive the first of the apostles as her pastor. But though we received him as teacher, we did not retain him to the end, but *gave him up to royal Rome*. Or rather we did retain him to the end, for though we do not retain the body of Peter, we do retain the faith of Peter, and retaining the faith of Peter we have Peter.

(Chapman 92A.)

Chapman gives the following passages to witness that "as a fact he [Chrysostom] is enthusiastic about Rome".[2]

DOCUMENT 143——Chrysostom, *Contra Judaeos et Gentiles*. (*P.G.* 48. 825; *S.E.P.* 96.)

9. . They who were dragged hither and thither, who were despised and bound with fetters, and who suffered all those thousand torments, in their death are more honoured than kings; and consider how this has come to pass: in the most regal city of Rome, to the tomb of the fisherman and the tentmaker run emperors and consuls and generals.

[1] Flavian, bp of Antioch, 381–404.
[2] *S.E.P.*, 95.

DOCUMENT 144——Chrysostom, *On the Epistle to the Romans*, Homily 32.
>   (*P.G.* 60. 678; *L.F.* 7. 504 ‡.)

2.   Where the seraphim praise and the cherubim do fly, there we shall see Paul with Peter, as chief and leader of the choir of the saints, and shall enjoy his generous love. For if when here he so loved men that when he might have departed to be with Christ, he chose to be here, much more will he there display a warmer affection. I love Rome even for this, although indeed one has other grounds for praising it, both for its greatness, its antiquity, its beauty, its numbers, its power, its riches, and its victories in war. But I let all these things pass, and bless it for this reason, that he both wrote to them when living, and loved them so much, and spoke to them when he was with them, and there ended his life. And so indeed the city is more famous for this than for all the other things. And as a body great and strong, it has two shining eyes,[1] the bodies of these saints. The heaven is not so bright, when the sun sends forth his rays, as is the city of Rome, sending out these two lights into all the world. Thence Paul will be caught up, thence Peter   . What two crowns has the city about it, with what golden chains it is girded, what fountains it has! Therefore I admire the city, not for its much gold, not for its columns, not for any other phantasy, but for these pillars of the Church.

Dom Chrysostom Baur, who has made an exhaustive study of Chrysostom's life and writings, tells us that in his copious works "there is no clear and direct message in favour of the primacy of the Pope".[2] How then was unity to be preserved? Chrysostom's answer is that the Holy Ghost was given to bind us together "by the glow of charity".[3]

DOCUMENT 145——Chrysostom, *On the Epistle to the Ephesians*, Homily 9.
>   (*P.G.* 62. 72; *L.F.* 6. 207 ‡.)

3.   . To this end was the Spirit given, that he might unite those who are separated by race and by different manners.

[1] Cp. Leo I: "O Rome . . . these are thy fathers . . . like twin lights of the eyes" (Doc. 242 §§ 1, 7).
[2] *Catholic Encyclopaedia*, 8. 457A.
[3] See E. B. Pusey, *Eirenicon* (1865), p. 52.

And how then is this unity preserved? "In the bond of peace." This cannot exist in strife and discord. "For", he says, "where there are strifes among you, and jealousy, and divisions, are ye not carnal, and walk after the manner of men?" For as fire, when it finds dry pieces of wood, works up all together into one blazing pile, but, when the wood is wet, does not act at all or unite the pieces; as, in the same way, no cold substance can strengthen this union, but generally speaking any warm one can: thus it is that the glow of charity is produced; by the bond of peace, he wishes to bind us all together.

DOCUMENT 146——The Same, Homily 11.
   (*P.G.* 62. 85; *L.F.* 6. 228 ‡.)

   4.   . If therefore we desire to partake of that Spirit which is from the Head, let us cleave to one another. For there are two kinds of separation from the body of the Church: the one when we wax cold in love, the other when we dare to do things unworthy of our membership; for in either way we cut ourselves off from the fullness. . .

   5.   . . Therefore I assert and protest that to make a schism in the Church is no less an evil than to fall into heresy.   I speak not of you who are present, but of those who are deserting from us. This act is adultery.   (Gore 128.)

Denny [1] thinks that the last words above refer to the continuance of the schism at Antioch after the death of Meletius. Homily 9 does not touch the question of Church government and could be used to justify many forms of protestantism. But Pusey says, "This unity, derived from our Blessed Lord as head of the Church, is imparted primarily through the Sacraments".[2] To Chrysostom too the sacraments are essential "because the soul has been locked up in a body", and to him the sacrament of unity is Holy Communion.

DOCUMENT 147——Chrysostom, *On Matthew*, Homily 82.
   (*P.G.* 58. 743; *L.F.* 34. 1090 ‡.)

   4.   . For if you had been without body, he would have delivered the unembodied gifts bare; but because the soul has

___

[1] Page 346.   [2] *Eirenicon* (1865), p. 54.

been locked up in a body, he gives you in things sensible the things that the mind perceives. How many now say, "Would that I could see his form, the mark, the clothes, the shoes"! Behold! you see him, you touch him, you eat him. And you indeed wish to see his clothes, but he gives himself to you, not only to see, but also to touch and eat and receive within.

(Chapman 118B.)

DOCUMENT 148——Chrysostom, *On the First Epistle to the Corinthians*, Homily 24.
(*P.G.* 61. 200; *L.F.* 4. 327 ‡.)

2. . "The bread which we break, is it not the communion of the body of Christ?" Why did he not say "the participation"? Because he intended to express something more, and to point out how close was the union, in that we communicate not only by participating and partaking, but also by being united. For as that body is united to Christ, so also are we united to him by this bread. Why did he add, "which we break"? For although in the Eucharist one may see this done, yet on the cross not so, but the very contrary; "for a bone of him", it is said, "shall not be broken". But what he did not suffer on the cross, this he suffers in the oblation for thy sake, and bears to be broken in two that he may fill all.

(Chapman 118B.)

Finally, in the confusion of those times, especially acute at Antioch, how was the inquiring heathen to choose between the Christian sects? Chrysostom's answer seems to be "Follow the Bible and use your judgement".

DOCUMENT 149——Chrysostom, *On the Acts of the Apostles*, Homily 33.
(*P.G.* 60. 243; *L.F.* 35. 463 ‡.)

4. . The pure life gets many false pretenders: no man would care to imitate the man of vicious life; no! but the man of monastic life. What then shall we say to the heathen? There comes a heathen and says, "I wish to become a Christian, but

I know not whom to join: there is much fighting and faction among you, much confusion; which doctrine am I to choose?" How shall we answer him? "Each of you", says he, "asserts, 'I speak the truth'." No doubt; this is in our favour. For if we told you to be persuaded by arguments, you might well be perplexed; but if we bid you believe the Scriptures, and these are simple and true, the decision is easy for you. If any agree with the Scriptures, he is the Christian; if any fight against them, he is far from this rule. "Which am I to believe, knowing as I do nothing at all from the Scriptures? The others also allege the same thing for themselves. What then if the other come and say that the Scripture has this, and you that it has something different, and you interpret the Scriptures diversely, dragging their sense?" "And you then," I ask, "have you no understanding, no judgement?" "And how should I be able?" says he; "I do not even know how to judge your doctrines. I wish to become a learner, and you are making me already a teacher."   (Gore 50, 51 note; Chapman 36ʙ note.)

Chapman comments "Those who are outside [the Church] must use their own judgement to find the truth" as Chrysostom suggests, but "if once they submit to her [the Church's] claims, by the use of reason and the gift of faith, they cannot exercise their private judgement any further with regard to those truths which she proposes for their acceptance."

CHAPTER XVII

AUGUSTINE

In the last quarter of the fourth century, Augustine arose to be the outstanding teacher of his time, and the most prolific Christian writer of the first five centuries. This famous saint was born in Numidia in 354; he was baptized at Milan in 387 and returned to Africa the following year. He was bishop of Hippo from 397 to 430 when he died. His extant works fill fifteen volumes of Migne's *Patrologia*. In this chapter we quote from his expositions of the Bible, and from his anti-Donatist writings.

I. THE PRIMACY OF PETER

Augustine taught that "Peter was the first of the apostles", and that, on account of this primacy, he represents the Church or bears the image or figure of the Church in almost every place where he is mentioned in the New Testament. He represents the Church in his boldness and strength, also in his weakness and defects. Cases of the latter are an answer to the rigorism of the Luciferians, who seceded from the Church because of her alleged laxity.

DOCUMENT 150——Augustine, *De Agone Christiano*. A.D. 396.
(*P.L.* 40. 308; *L.F.* 22. 184 ‡.)

32. . . . Nowhere ought the heart of mercy to be so strong as in the Catholic Church, that, as a true mother, she neither proudly trample on her sons when in sin, nor scarcely pardon them on amendment. For not without cause among all the apostles does *Peter sustain the person of this Catholic Church*, for unto this Church were the keys of the kingdom of heaven given, when they were given to Peter; and when it is said unto him, it is said unto all: "Lovest thou me?"; "Feed my sheep". Therefore the Church Catholic ought willingly to pardon her sons upon their amendment and confirmation in godliness, when we see that Peter himself, bearing her person, both when

he had tottered on the sea, and when with carnal feeling he had called the Lord back from suffering, and when he had cut off the servant's ear with a sword, and when he had three times denied the Lord himself, and when afterwards he had fallen into superstitious dissembling, had pardon granted unto him, and after amendment and strengthening attained at the last to the glory of the Lord's suffering.   . Many of the bishops who in that persecution had consented to the perfidy of the Arians were corrected and chose to return into the Catholic Church, condemning what they had believed or pretended to believe. These the Catholic Church received into her maternal bosom, like Peter after his tears for his denial, when admonished by the crowing of the cock, or as the same, after his evil dissembling, was put right by the voice of Paul.

(Chapman 51A note.)

DOCUMENT 151——Augustine, *Enarratio in Psalmum CVIII.* A.D. 415.
(*P.L.* 37. 1431 ; *L.F.* 37. 208 ‡.)

1.   Some things are said which seem to relate especially to the apostle Peter, and yet are not clear in their meaning unless referred to the Church, which he is acknowledged to have represented in a figure, *on account of the primacy which he bore among the disciples.* Such is "I will give unto thee the keys of the kingdom of heaven", and other similar passages; so Judas represents those Jews who were Christ's enemies.

(Gore 89; Chapman 50B, 58A.)

DOCUMENT 152——Augustine, *In Joannis Evangelium* 56. A.D. 416.
(*P.L.* 35. 1788; *L.F.* 29. 722 ‡.)

1. .   "Then he comes to Simon Peter", as if he had already washed some others, and after them had come to the chief. *Who is ignorant that the first of the apostles is the most blessed Peter?* But we are not therefore to understand that he came to him after others, but that he began from him.

(Chapman 47A, 78A.)

DOCUMENT 153——Augustine, *Sermo* 76.
  (*P.L.* 38. 479; *L.F.* 16. 215 ‡.)

2. For men, wishing to be built upon men, said "I am of Paul—and I of Apollos, I of Cephas", that is Peter. And others who *did not wish to be built upon Peter but upon the rock* "But I am of Christ". But when the apostle Paul realized that he was chosen and Christ despised, he said "Is Christ divided? Was Paul crucified for you? Were you baptized in Paul's name?". As not in Paul, so neither in Peter, but in the name of Christ, that Peter might be built upon the rock, not the rock upon Peter.

3. Therefore this same Peter, *called blessed by the rock*, bearing the figure of the Church, *holding the chief place in the apostleship*, shortly after he heard he was blessed, now heard that he was Peter, now heard that he was to be built upon the rock.

4. .. The apostle Paul says, "Now we who are strong should bear the burdens of the weak". When Peter says, "Thou are the Christ, the Son of the living God", he represents the strong; but when he fears and totters, and wishes that Christ should not suffer, fearing the death, and not recognizing the life, he represents the weak ones of the Church. In that one apostle then, that is Peter, in the order of the apostles first and principal, in whom the Church was figured, both kinds were to be represented, that is both the strong and the weak, because the Church is not without both.

(Gore 89; Chapman 51A and note, 54A.)

DOCUMENT 154——Augustine, *Sermo* 149.
  (*P.L.* 38. 802; *L.F.* 20. 691 ‡.)

7. For Peter in many places in the Scriptures appears to represent the Church; especially in that place where it was said "I give to thee the keys . . shall be loosed in heaven". What! did Peter receive these keys, and Paul not receive? Did Peter receive and John and James not receive, and the rest of the apostles? Or are not the keys in the Church where sins are daily remitted? But since in a figure Peter represented the Church, what was given to him singly was given to the Church.

(Gore 89; Chapman 51A note.)

DOCUMENT 155——Augustine, *Sermo* 295.
  (*P.L.* 38. 1349.)

2. As you know, the Lord Jesus chose his disciples before his passion, whom he named apostles. Among these *Peter alone almost everywhere deserved to represent the whole Church*. Because of that representation of the whole Church which *only he bore*, he deserved to hear "I will give to thee the keys of the kingdom of heaven". For these keys not one man but the unity of the Church received. Here therefore the excellence of Peter is set forth, because he represented that universality and unity of the Church, when it was said to him "I give to thee" what was given to all. For that you may know that the Church did receive the keys of the kingdom of heaven, hear elsewhere what the Lord said to all the apostles, "Receive the Holy Ghost" and forthwith "Whose soever sins ye remit they are remitted unto them, and whose soever sins ye retain they are retained". *This pertains to the keys*, of which it was said "Whatsoever ye shall loose on earth shall be loosed in heaven, and whatsoever ye shall bind on earth shall be bound also in heaven". But this he said to Peter, that you may know that Peter then represented the person of the whole Church. Hear what is said to him, what to all the faithful saints .

4. Deservedly also, after his resurrection, the Lord commended his sheep to Peter himself to feed; for he was not the only one among the disciples who was thought worthy to feed the Lord's sheep, but when Christ speaks to one, unity is commended—and to Peter for the first time, because Peter is first among the apostles.   (Chapman 51A note.)

According to Augustine then, Peter represents the Church. Gore says "This is an interpretation of our Lord's words to St Peter which we can all accept, and which is quite intelligible. It is quite distinct from the mediatorial view,[1] according to which St Peter is something which the apostles are not, and the source to them of what they are."[2]
  Chapman replies that Augustine "never thought of saying anything so absurd as that Peter was representative of the Church *when he was called the rock upon which the Church is built*[3]—as though the Church

[1] See Leo, Doc. 238.   [2] Page 89.   [3] Chapman's italics.

could be founded on itself!"[1] Actually Augustine usually maintained
that by the "rock", in Matt. 16. 18, our Lord was referring to himself, as in Doc. 153 above. I believe the only known instance of his
referring the "rock" to Peter is in the next Document.

DOCUMENT 156——Augustine, *Retractations*, Book 1, Chapter
   21.   A.D. 427.
   (*P.L.* 32. 618.)

1. [In my first book against Donatus] I mentioned somewhere with reference to the apostle Peter that "the Church is
founded upon him as upon a rock". This meaning is also sung
by many lips in the lines of blessed Ambrose, where, speaking
of the domestic cock, he says: "When it crows, he, the rock of
the Church, absolves from sin." But I realize that I have since
frequently explained the words of our Lord: "Thou art Peter
and upon this rock I will build my church", to the effect that
they should be understood as referring to him whom Peter
confessed when he said: "Thou art the Christ, the Son of the
living God", and as meaning that Peter, having been named
after this rock, figured the person of the Church, which is built
upon this rock and has received the keys of the kingdom of
heaven. For what was said to him was not "Thou art the rock",
but "Thou art Peter". But the rock was Christ, having confessed whom (even as the whole Church confesses) Simon was
named Peter. *Which of these two interpretations is the more likely to
be correct, let the reader choose.*   (Gore 86; Chapman 51.)

NOTE ON THE PATRISTIC INTERPRETATION OF MATT. 16. 18

It will be seen from the limited evidence supplied in these pages
that the fathers interpreted the famous "rock" text in various ways.
An exhaustive study of the subject was made about 270 years ago by
John de Launoy.[2] As regards the period from Tertullian to Leo, he
found thirteen writers who taught that the Church was built upon
Peter, six who said it was built upon the apostles or their successors,
twelve who said it was built upon the faith which Peter confessed
(Matt. 16. 16), and three who interpreted the rock as Christ himself.

[1] Page 54A.
[2] *Opera*, tome 5, pt 2, pp. 101–114 (edit. 1731).

Augustine is in all four classes. From our own Documents we make the following analysis:

1. The rock is Peter: Tertullian, Doc. 12 § 22; Cyprian, Docs. 37, 41, 43, 44, 46; Firmilian, Doc. 49 § 17; Ambrose, Doc. 111; Augustine, Doc. 156; Philip in Doc. 220; Leo, Doc. 239 § 4; Paschasinus in Doc. 256, p. 307.

2. The rock is the faith confessed by Peter: Hilary, Doc. 78 § 36; Chrysostom, Doc. 134; Cyril, Doc. 224; Leo, Doc. 238 § 2.

3. The rock is the saints or the bishops: Origen, Doc. 32 § 11; Cyprian, Doc. 35.

4. The rock is Christ: Jerome, Doc. 127; Augustine, Docs. 155, 158.

5. The rock is the chair of Peter: Jerome, Doc. 117 § 2.

6. The rock is Peter's successors: Augustine, Doc. 163.

In his work on John's Gospel, Augustine follows Cyprian (Doc. 37) in saying that Peter personified unity.

DOCUMENT 157——Augustine, *In Joannis Evangelium* 118.
    A.D. 416.
    (*P.L.* 35. 1949; *L.F.* 29. 1037 ‡.)

4. . Just as the apostles who formed the exact number of twelve, in other words parted into four parts of three each, when all were questioned only Peter replied "Thou art the Christ, the Son of the living God", and to him it was said "I will give to thee the keys of the kingdom of heaven", as if he alone received the power of binding and loosing: seeing then that one so spake on behalf of all, and received the gift along with all, as if personifying the unity itself; one for all because there is unity in all.   (Chapman 51A note.)

Gore thought that after the resurrection "no peculiar dignity" was committed to Peter: he was merely "reinstated in the apostolic commission that his threefold denial might be supposed to have lost him".[1]

DOCUMENT 158——Augustine, *In Joannis Evangelium* 123.
    A.D. 416.
    (*P.L.* 35. 1967; *L.F.* 29. 1073 ‡.)

5. But first the Lord asks what he knew, not once but a second and a third time, whether Peter loved him; and just as

[1] Gore, 81.

often he has the same reply, that he is loved, while just as often he gives Peter the same charge to feed his sheep. The threefold denial is renounced by a threefold confession, that the tongue may serve love no less than fear, and imminent death may not seem to have drawn out more from the voice than the present life. Let it be the office of love to feed the Lord's flock, if it was the signal of fear to deny the Shepherd.   (Gore 81.)

In the next tractate we are told in effect that Peter represents the Church militant, and John the Church triumphant, though both are sharers in both as are all the faithful.

DOCUMENT 159——Augustine, *In Joannis Evangelium* 124. A.D. 416.
   (*P.L.* 35. 1975; *L.F.* 29. 1089 ‡.)

7. .   These two states of life [the life of faith and the life of sight] were symbolized by Peter and John, each of them one; but in this life they both walked by faith, and they will both enjoy that eternal life through sight. For the whole body of the saints, therefore, inseparably belonging to the body of Christ, and for their safe pilotage through this stormy life, did Peter, the first of the apostles, receive the keys of the kingdom of heaven for binding and loosing sins. And for the same congregation of the saints did John the evangelist recline on the breast of Christ, in reference to the perfect repose in the bosom of that mysterious life to come. For it is not the former alone, but the whole Church that binds and looses sins; nor did the latter alone drink at the fountain of the Lord's breast, to utter again in preaching those truths of the Word in the beginning, God with God, and those other sublime truths, the divinity of Christ, and the Trinity and Unity of the whole Godhead, which are yet to be seen in the kingdom face to face, but meanwhile, till the Lord comes, are only to be seen in a mirror and in a riddle; but the Lord has himself diffused this very gospel throughout the whole world, that everyone of his own may drink from it, according to his capacity.   (Gore 82 note.)

II. THE SUCCESSORS OF PETER

Augustine taught that Peter was the first bishop of Rome.

DOCUMENT 160——Augustine, *Contra Litteras Petiliani*, Book 2.
A.D. 402.
(*P.L.* 43. 300; M.D. 3. 325 †.)

118. . . If all men throughout the world were such as you most vainly accuse them of being, what has the *chair* of the Roman church done to you, *in which Peter sat, and in which Anastasius sits to-day*; or the chair of the church of Jerusalem, in which James sat, and in which John sits to-day, with which we are connected in catholic unity, and from which you have severed yourselves by mad fury?   (Chapman 78A note.)

The successors of Peter are the bishops of Rome.

DOCUMENT 161——Augustine, *Ep.* 53: Fortunatus, Alypius, and Augustine to Generosus.   A.D. 400.
(*P.L.* 33. 196; M.D. 6. 192 †.)

2. If the lineal succession of bishops is to be considered, with how much more benefit to the Church do we reckon from Peter himself, to whom, as bearing in a figure the whole Church, the Lord said: "Upon this rock I will build my Church, and the gates of hell shall not conquer it"! For to Peter succeeded Linus, Clement, Anacletus, Evaristus, Alexander, Sixtus, Telesphorus, Iginus, Anicetus, Pius, Soter, Eleutherius, Victor, Zephyrinus, Calixtus, Urban, Pontian, Antherus, Fabian, Cornelius, Lucius, Stephen, Xystus, Dionysius, Felix, Eutychian, Gaius, Marcellinus, Marcellus, Eusebius, Miltiades, Sylvester, Mark, Julius, Liberius, Damasus, Siricius, Anastasius. In this order of succession no Donatist bishop is found. But, unexpectedly, they sent from Africa an ordained man, who, presiding over a few Africans in Rome, propagated the title of Mountain Men or Cutzupits.
(Chapman 24A, 78A.)

Chapman comments: "Like Optatus[1] before him he [Augustine] uses a list of Roman bishops as a witness against the Donatists. . . . He not only asks 'Who is unaware that most blessed Peter is the first of the Apostles?'[2] but he tells us that this primacy remained in the Roman Church."

DOCUMENT 162——Augustine, *Ep.* 43, to Glorius, etc. A.D. 397. (*P.L.* 33. 163; M.D. 6. 143 †.)

7. . . . Carthage was also near the countries over the sea, and distinguished by illustrious renown, so that it had a bishop of more than ordinary influence, who could afford to disregard a number of conspiring enemies because he saw himself joined by letters of communion both to the Roman church, *in which the primacy of an apostolic chair always flourished,*[3] and to other lands from which the gospel came to Africa itself; and he was prepared to defend himself before these churches, if his enemies tried to alienate them from him.   It was a matter concerning colleagues who could reserve their entire case to the judgement of other colleagues, especially of *apostolic churches*.

19.   . . As if it might not have been said, and most justly said to them [the Donatists]: "Well, let us suppose that these bishops who decided the case of Caecilian at Rome were not good judges; there still remained *a plenary council of the universal Church*, in which these judges themselves might be put on their defence, so that, if they were convicted of mistake, their decisions might be reversed."   (Chapman 78A and note.)

These bishops whose decisions might have been reversed by a general council were Miltiades of Rome and eighteen others (see Doc. 56). Other portions of Augustine's 43rd letter are quoted in Doc. 57.

In our next two Documents Rome is not mentioned, but succession from Peter is called the rock on which the Church is built, and is regarded as one of the ways by which the true Church may be identified.

---

[1] Doc. 84 § 3.   [2] Doc. 152.
[3] *in qua semper apostolicae cathedrae viguit principatus.*

DOCUMENT 163——Augustine, *Psalmus contra Partem Donati.*
A.D. 393.
(*P.L.* 43. 30.)

Why! a faggot that is cut off from the vine retains its shape.
But what use is that shape, if it is not living from the root?
Come, brothers, if you wish to be engrafted in the vine. It is
grievous when we see you thus lying cut off. Number *the priests
even from that seat of Peter.* And in that order of fathers see who
to whom succeeded: *that is the rock* which the proud gates of
hades do not conquer. All who rejoice in peace, only judge
truly.   (Chapman 51B, 78A.)

DOCUMENT 164——Augustine, *Contra Epistolam Manichaei.*
A.D. 395.
(*P.L.* 42. 175; M.D. 5. 100 ‡.)

5.   . . There are many other things which rightly keep me
in the bosom of the Catholic Church. The consent of peoples
and nations keeps me, her authority keeps me, inaugurated by
miracles, nourished in hope, enlarged by love, and established
by age. *The succession of priests keeps me, from the very seat of the
apostle Peter* (to whom the Lord after his resurrection gave
charge to feed his sheep) down to the present episcopate. And
so, lastly, does the name itself of catholic, which not without
reason, amid so many heresies, the Church has alone retained;
so that though all heretics wish to be called catholics, yet when
a stranger asks where the Church is, no heretic will venture to
point to his own chapel or house. Such in number and in
importance are the precious ties belonging to the Christian
name which keep a believer in the Catholic Church.
                                             (Chapman 78A note.)

Thomas Aquinas tells us that since our Lord "was about to withdraw his corporal presence from the Church, it was necessary that he
should commit someone who in his place should have the care of the
universal Church".[1] To refute such a view, Gore appeals to Augustine.

[1] *Contra Gentiles*, 4. 76 (edit. 1786, tom. 18, p. 477A). Quoted by Leo XIII,
Satis Cognitum § 11.

DOCUMENT 165——Augustine, *Enarratio in Psalmum LVI.*
A.D. 415.
(*P.L.* 36. 662; *L.F.* 30. 79 ‡.)

1. .. And since the whole Christ is head and body, which truth I do not doubt that you know well, the head is our Saviour himself, who suffered under Pontius Pilate, who now, after he is risen from the dead, sits at the right hand of the Father; but his body is the Church: not this church or that, but diffused over all the world, nor that only which exists among men living, for those also belong to it who were before us and are to be after us to the end of the world. For the whole Church, made up of all the faithful, because all the faithful are members of Christ, has its head, which governs the body, situate in the heavens; though it is separated from sight, yet it is bound by love.   (Gore 34, 197; Chapman 22A.)

Gore comments that "local Churches, associated in fellowship on earth, find their necessary centre of unity, in common with the Church in paradise, at no lower point than in the glorified Christ". But, Von Hügel would ask, need Augustine's faith in Christ as invisible head of the whole Church have prevented him from believing in a vicegerent on earth as head of the Church militant? The Church militant is a visible body. Why not a visible head? If the bishop of Hippo was the visible head of the 5,000 souls in his diocese, why should not Pope Innocent have been a visible head of all the faithful on earth?[1]

III. THE UNITY OF THE CHURCH

Augustine's views on schism are concisely stated in a passage quoted by both Leo XIII[2] and Gore.

DOCUMENT 166——Augustine, *Contra Epistolam Parmeniani,*
Book 2. A.D. 400.
(*P.L.* 43. 69.)

25. We offer these examples from Holy Scripture, to show clearly that there is nothing more serious than the sacrilege of schism. There is no just necessity for cutting up the unity.
(Gore 128.)

[1] See F. Von Hügel, *Petrine Claims*, 12.
[2] *Satis Cognitum* § 10.

How is this precious unity to be maintained? Döllinger[1] pointed out that in the seventy-five chapters of Augustine's treatise on unity "there is not a word on the necessity of. communion with Rome as the centre of unity. He urges all sorts of arguments to show that the Donatists are bound to return to the Church, but of the Papal Chair, as one of them, he knows nothing". Gore refers us to "a remarkable chapter on the division of Judah and Israel". Here Augustine claims that in spite of the fact that the kingdom of Israel set up rival shrines in Bethel and Dan,[2] they were "by no means . . . an heretical sect"; for sixty or seventy years later they still had Jehovah's prophets, and there were still 7,000 men who maintained the true faith.[3]

DOCUMENT 167——Augustine, *De Unitate Ecclesiae.* A.D. 402.
    (*P.L.* 43. 416.)

33. . . . They relate that ten tribes seceded and were surrendered to a servant of Solomon, but two remained for Solomon's son to the kingdom of Jerusalem. "So now", the Donatists say, "the whole world has fallen away, and we like those two tribes have remained in God's temple, that is, in the Church. Also, though very many disciples followed the Lord Jesus Christ, when seventy-two fell away, only twelve remained with him." By these and similar examples, heretics try to commend their fewness, while in the case of the saints of the Church they cease not to rail at the multitude spread over the whole world.   . But since the Donatists imagine that they are to be compared to those two tribes which remained with Solomon's son, let them read, and they will repent of having chosen this comparison. For the two peoples are chronicled in the Scriptures after this manner. The tribes that were near to Jerusalem are called Judah; the others, which were more numerous and separated with the subject of Solomon, are called Israel. Let them read what the prophets say about each of the two kingdoms: how they say that Judah was more wicked than Israel,[4] so that the turning away of Israel was justified by the sins of backsliding Judah, that is, that the sins of the latter were so grave that by comparison the former must be pronounced righteous.

[1] *The Pope and the Council*, E.T., 1870, p. 89.
[2] 1 Kings 12. 29.   [3] 1 Kings 19. 18.   [4] Ezek. 16. 51.

But neither the sins of this kingdom nor those of that were any hindrance to righteous men, who are found to have existed in each of them. For even in that kingdom which they assume to be an object lesson of damnation, namely Israel, there were holy prophets. There was the outstanding prophet Elijah, not to mention others; and to him moreover it was said "I have left to me 7,000 men which have not bowed the knee to Baal". For this reason that part of the people is by no means to be reckoned as having been an heretical sect. For God has ordered those same tribes to separate off, not in order that the faith, but that the kingdom might be divided, and that in this way punishment might be meted out to the kingdom of Judah. But *God never orders a schism* to be formed. For because all over the world kingdoms are commonly divided, for that reason the unity of Christendom is also divided, since in each part is found the Catholic Church. (Gore 139 note.)

Gore admits that Augustine "did not even contemplate the possibility of the Church permanently losing the fellowship of intercourse and love". But he "was not a prophet of the future". He thought erroneously that the Church could never perish anywhere "where she had once been founded, so as to require restoration or refounding from some other part".

Doc. 167 continued. (*P.L.* 43. 425.)

45. . . Surely good seed does not at all need sowing again, inasmuch as from the time at which it was sown it grows on until the harvest. If you say that what the apostles sowed has perished in those parts and that the sowing must therefore be done again from Africa, the answer will be: "Read that to us from the divine oracles." (Gore 139.)

There was among the Donatists a scholar called Tichonius, who saw the absurdity of excluding the vast body of scattered Christians from the pale of the true Church, but failed to see that his own sect was schismatic. Parmenian, a leading Donatist, who hated the idea that universality was a test of truth, succeeded in suppressing him. The position of Tichonius was unique, and Augustine condemned it as illogical.

DOCUMENT 168——Augustine, *Contra Epistolam Parmeniani*,
    Book I. A.D. 400.
    (*P.L.* 43. 33.)

1.   Now there has come into our hands a letter written
by Parmenian, who was once a Donatist bishop, to Tichonius,
who certainly has a keen intellect and copious eloquence, but
is a Donatist. I have decided at the request, nay the orders, of
my brothers, to reply, in what follows, to that letter of Parmenian, chiefly on account of certain evidence from the
Scriptures which he wrongly interprets. For Tichonius, being
bombarded on all sides by all the voices of the sacred pages,
*has woken up and has seen the Church of God diffused over the whole
world,* just as was foreseen and predicted concerning it so long
ago through the hearts and mouths of the saints. And, having
seen this, he has even undertaken to show and to assert, even
in opposition to his own sect, that no man's sin, however
grievous and monstrous, establishes an exception to the promises of God; and that no godlessness of churchmen implies
that the promises of God concerning the Church that is to be
spread even to the ends of the world, will be cancelled.

    Tichonius, therefore, though he argued this energetically
and eloquently, and with many great and manifest evidences
from the Holy Scriptures shut the mouths of those who contradicted him, did not see what logically he ought to have
seen, namely that those Christians in Africa belong to the
Church which is spread throughout the world; and that they,
to be sure, are not linked with those who are schismatics from
the world, but through communion are linked with the world
itself. Now Parmenian and the rest of the Donatists saw that
this was logical and they preferred to take an obstinate line
against the perfectly obvious truth which Tichonius was
asserting, rather than to admit it and be prevailed over by the
African churches which rejoiced in the communion of that
unity which Tichonius was asserting to exist, and from which
they had separated. And indeed Parmenian at first thought
that he must, as it were, castigate him in a letter; but after
doing that he [now] makes him out to be expelled from their
congregation. Accordingly I have decided to reply in this

work to that letter of Parmenian which he wrote to him, reproving him for proclaiming that the Church was spread over all the world and warning him not to dare to do so.

(Chapman 23B note, 120B.)

DOCUMENT 169——Augustine, *Ep.* 93, to Vincent.   A.D. 408.
   (*P.L.* 33. 343; M.D. 6. 431 ‡.)

44. .   Tichonius is the man whom Parmenian checked by his reply, and deterred from writing such things; but he did not refute the statements themselves, but, as I have said above, silenced him by this one thing, that while saying such things concerning the Church which is diffused throughout the world, and while admitting that the sins of others within its unity do not defile anyone else, he none the less withdrew from the contagion of the Africans, because of their being traditors, and was in the party of Donatus.   (Chapman 23B note.)

Wiseman[1] claimed that Augustine condemned Anglicans in advance, in that the English church, by being separated from Rome, was separated from the churches diffused throughout the world.

DOCUMENT 170——Augustine, *Contra Epistolam Parmeniani*,
      Book 3.   A.D. 400.
   (*P.L.* 43. 101.)

24.   It is certain to the whole world that it is an act of praiseworthy forbearance to tolerate evil men, lest, unknown, good men may be condemned. Therefore the whole world's secure verdict is [securus judicat orbis terrarum][2] that they are not good who *divide themselves* from the whole world, in whatever part of the world.

28. . . . We hold unshaken and firm that no good men can separate themselves from it [the Church]; that is, that although they may have to endure evil men, known to themselves, no good men, wherever they may be, can *on their own account*

---

[1] *Dublin Review*, 7. 153, Aug. 1839.
[2] Quoted J. H. Newman, *Apologia*, Everyman's Library, 1912, p. 121.

separate, by the rash sacrilege of schism, from the good who are living far off and unknown. And, in whatever part of the world this has been done, or is done, or shall be, while the other distant parts of the earth are ignorant that it has been done, or why it has been done, and yet continue in the bond of union with the rest of the world, let this be considered quite certain, that none could have so acted, unless they had been either furious with swelling pride, or insane with livid envy, or corrupted by worldly advantage, or perverted by carnal fear.

(Chapman 120B.)

Wiseman:[1] "Here then is a general rule applicable ... to all future possible divisions in the Church. Those cannot be possibly right who have separated themselves from the communion of distant churches which remain still connected in the bond of unity. Whatever plea may be set up of corruption or abuses, the true ground of separation will be one of those pointed out by the great St Augustine." And he thinks that three of the four grounds were present among the English leaders in the time of Henry VIII. Salmon points out that Augustine was dealing with the Donatists who claimed to be the entire Church. Anglicans (like Tichonius) make no such claim. Augustine's words must not be used as a principle that the majority is always right "provided only that they stick together like sheep".[2] This would be unscriptural,[3] and was certainly untrue in the days when "the Nicene faith stood condemned by acclamation, and the whole world groaned in surprise to find itself Arian".[4]

IV. DE BAPTISMO

Augustine's treatise on baptism against the Donatists is so frequently quoted in our controversy that I deal with it separately. Its author is fully acquainted with the dispute between Stephen and Cyprian about the baptism of heretics.[5] He saw that Cyprian was wrong to rebaptize heretics, and Stephen right in refusing to do so. He regarded Stephen's as the primitive custom (5 § 36), but he does not condemn Cyprian for his error, for at that time the consent of the whole Church had not yet "declared authoritatively, by

[1] Op. cit., 154.
[2] *Infallibility*, 1888, p. 268. See also T. A. Lacey, *Catholicity*, 135–149.
[3] Matt. 7. 13, 14.
[4] Jerome, *Adv. Lucif.* § 19 (*P.L.* 23. 172).
[5] See Chapter IX.

the decree of a general council, what practice should be followed in this matter" (1 § 28). He commends Cyprian for maintaining communion with those who disagreed with him, and by inference condemns Stephen as uncharitable for wanting to sever communion with those who did practise rebaptism (5 § 36).

DOCUMENT 171——Augustine, *De Baptismo contra Donatistas*,
   Book 1. A.D. 401.
   (*P.L.* 43. 114; M.D. 3. 11 ‡.)

9. In the next place, that I may not seem to rest on mere human argument (since there is so much obscurity in this question that in earlier ages of the Church, before the schism of Donatus, it has urged great men, and bishops endowed with great charity, so to dispute and doubt among themselves, saving the peace, that the various statutes of their councils in their districts long differed from each other, till at length *the best opinion was established, to the removal of all doubts, by a general council of the whole world*), I therefore bring forward clear proofs from the gospel.

28. We come at last to the blessed martyr Cyprian, of whose authority the Donatists carnally flatter themselves they are possessed, whilst by his love they are spiritually overthrown: at that time, before the consent of the whole Church had declared authoritatively, *by the decree of a general council*, what practice should be followed in this matter, it seemed to him, in common with about eighty of his fellow bishops of the African churches, that every man who had been baptized outside the communion of the Catholic Church should, on joining the Church, be baptized anew. And I take it that the reason why the Lord did not reveal the error in this, to a man of such eminence, was that his pious humility and charity in guarding the peace and health of the Church might be made known and might be noticed, so as to serve as an example of healing power, so to speak, not only to Christians of that age, but also to those who should come after. For when a bishop of so important a church, himself a man of so great merit and virtue, endowed with such excellence of heart and power of eloquence, entertained an opinion about baptism different from that which

was to be confirmed by a more diligent searching into the truth (though many of his colleagues held what was not yet made manifest by authority, but was sanctioned by the past custom of the Church, and afterwards embraced by the whole catholic world), yet under these circumstances he did not sever himself, by refusal of communion, from the others who thought differently, and indeed he never ceased to urge on the others that they should "forbear one another in love, endeavouring to keep the unity of the Spirit in the bond of peace". For so, while the framework of the body remained whole, if any infirmity occurred in certain of its members, it might rather regain its health from their general soundness than be deprived of the chance of any healing care by their death in severance from the body. . .

. But as he with imperfect insight into the mystery was careful to preserve charity with all courage and humility and faith, he deserved to come to the crown of martyrdom; so that, if any cloud had crept over the clearness of his intellect from his infirmity as man, it might be dispelled by the glorious brightness of his blood.

(Gore 119, 134; Chapman 57B note.)

DOCUMENT 172——The Same, Book 2.
(*P.L.* 43. 126; M.D. 3. 32 ‡.)

2. Cyprian speaks as follows in his letter to Quintus "For even Peter . ."[1] Here is a passage in which Cyprian records what we also learn in Holy Scripture, that the apostle *Peter, in whom the primacy of the apostles shines* with such exceeding grace, was corrected by the later apostle Paul, when he adopted a custom in the matter of circumcision at variance with the demands of truth. If it was therefore possible for Peter in some point to walk not uprightly according to the truth . why might not Cyprian against the rule of truth, which afterwards the whole Church held, compel heretics or schismatics to be baptized afresh? I suppose there is no slight to Cyprian in comparing him with the apostle Peter in respect of his crown

[1] See Doc. 44 § 3.

of martyrdom; rather I ought to be afraid lest I am slighting Peter. Who can be ignorant that *the chief apostolate is to be preferred to any episcopate?* But even if *the dignity of their sees differs,* the glory of martyrdom is one. .

3. "When on the first of September   Cyprian said to judge our acts therein." [1]

4.   . You are wont indeed to challenge us with the letters of Cyprian, his opinion, his council; why do you claim his authority for your schism and reject his example when it makes for the peace of the Church? But who cannot know that the sacred canon of Scripture, of both the Old and New Testament, is confined within its own limits, and that it stands above all later letters of the bishops, so that about it we can hold no manner of doubt or dispute as to whether what is written in it is true or right; but that the letters of bishops which have been or shall be written since the closing of the canon are liable to be refuted, either by discourse of someone wiser, or by the weightier authority and more learned prudence of other bishops, or by councils; and that those councils which are held in the several districts or provinces must yield without doubt to the authority of plenary councils which are formed for the whole Christian world; and that even of the plenary councils the earlier are often corrected by the later, when by some experiment things are brought to light which were concealed, and that becomes known which lay hid . .?

5.   . Nor should we dare to assert any such thing, were we not supported by the unanimous authority of the whole Church, to which he, Cyprian, would without doubt have yielded, if at that time the truth of this question had been established by the investigation and decree of a general council.

6.   Cyprian walking by this, by the most persistent tolerance, not by shedding blood, but because it was shed in unity .   came by confession of martyrdom to angelic light, and if not before, at least then, acknowledged the revelation on that point on which, while yet in error, he did not prefer the maintenance of a wrong opinion to unity.

[1] Doc. 47, A.D. 256.

7.　　Why have you separated? I suppose to avoid perishing by communion with evil men. How then was it that Cyprian and so many of his colleagues did not perish? For though they believed that heretics and schismatics did not possess baptism, yet they chose rather to communicate with them when they had been received into the Church without baptism (although they believed that their flagrant and sacrilegious sins were yet upon their heads) than to be separated from unity. Cyprian said "judging no one, nor depriving anyone of the right of communion, if he should think differently".[1]

8.　　. Behold, I see in unity Cyprian and others his colleagues who, on holding a council, decided that those who have been baptized without the communion of the Church have no true baptism, and that therefore it must be given them when they join the Church. But again, behold I see in the same unity that certain men think differently in this matter, and that, recognizing in those who come from heretics and schismatics the baptism of Christ, they do not venture to baptize them afresh. All of these catholic unity embraces in her motherly breast, bearing each one's burden in turn, and endeavouring to keep the unity of the Spirit in the bond of peace, till God should reveal to one or other of them any error in their views.

12.　　which custom coming I believe from the tradition of the apostles (as many things which are not found in their letters, or in the councils of their successors, yet, *because they are preserved throughout the whole Church*, are believed none the less to have been handed down and approved by them).

(Gore 119, 134, 135; Chapman 42A, note 1.)

DOCUMENT 173——The Same, Book 5.
(*P.L.* 43. 192; M.D. 3. 142 ‡.)

31.　　But the custom which is opposed to Cyprian may be supposed to have had its origin in apostolic tradition, as there are many things which the universal Church holds, and therefore are fairly believed to have been enjoined by the apostles, *which do not appear in their writings.*

[1] Doc. 47.

36. I do not wish to go over again what Cyprian poured out in irritation against Stephen, as it is not to the point.   But Stephen thought that we should even hold aloof from those who tried to upset the primitive custom in the matter of receiving heretics; whereas Cyprian, moved by the difficulty of the question itself, being largely endowed with a holy heart of love, thought that we should remain at unity with those who differed. Therefore although he was moved to brotherly indignation, yet the peace of Christ prevailed in their hearts that in such a dispute no evil of schism should arise between them.   (Gore 135; Chapman 42A, note 1, 57 note.)

DOCUMENT 174——The Same, Book 7.
   (*P.L.* 43. 242; M.D. 3. 226 ‡.)

102. It is safe for us not to advance with any rash opinion about things which have been neither started in a local catholic council nor completed in a plenary one, but to assert, with the confidence of a fearless voice, that which, under the government of our Lord God and Saviour Jesus Christ, *has been confirmed by consent of the universal Church.*

CHAPTER XVIII

POPE INNOCENT I

INNOCENT I was Pope from 402 to 417; during this time, Rome was besieged by Alaric in 408, and captured and pillaged in 410. Anglican writers say that Innocent was one of the originators of the papacy,[1] that "his episcopate is a landmark in the development of the papal theory",[2] and that the chaotic condition of the civil power gave him his opportunity.[3] It seems as if in Doc. 179 this Pope is claiming universal jurisdiction. We have to ask ourselves whether this was a new claim, or whether the Pope was just establishing explicitly what the Church had always implicitly held. We must also inquire how contemporary writers regarded the claim.

Our first Document shows the Pope claiming authority throughout the West, and it implies that churches founded by apostles other than Peter are not under his jurisdiction.

DOCUMENT 175——Innocent, *Ep.* 25, to Decentius, bishop of Eugubium (*Si instituta*). 19 March 416.
(*P.L.* 20. 552.)

2. Who does not know or observe that it [the church order] was delivered by Peter the chief of the apostles to the Roman church, and is kept until now, and ought to be retained by all, and that nothing ought to be imposed or introduced which has no authority, or seems to derive its precedents elsewhere?— especially since it is clear that in all Italy, the Gauls, Spain, Africa, Sicily and the adjacent islands, no one formed these churches except those whom the venerable apostle Peter or his successors made priests. Or let them discover that any other apostle be found to have been or to have taught in these provinces. If not, they ought to follow that which the Roman church keeps, from which they undoubtedly received them first; but while they are keen on foreign statements, they seem to neglect the head of their institution.

1 Denny, 318.   2 Kidd, *Hist. Ch.*, 3. 101.
3 Milman, *Hist. of Latin Christianity*, 1. 111 (1867).

In those days Britain was one of the Gauls, that is a country which "ought to follow that which the Roman church keeps".

Our main interest in this and the next chapter is the heresy of Pelagius. Pelagianism, which is unconsciously held by a vast number of Englishmen, exaggerates free will so as to make the grace of God not necessary to salvation. The authors of this heresy were Pelagius and Celestius. They visited Africa in 410, and in 411 Celestius was condemned and excommunicated by the council of Carthage. Pelagius went to Palestine, and there he was accused by two Gallican bishops, Heros and Lazarus, but the accusers failed to attend the investigation, and Pelagius was acquitted in December 415. An adverse report of these proceedings was written by Heros and Lazarus and carried to Africa by Orosius, a Spanish priest. The councils of Carthage and Mileve considered the matter in 416, and then wrote to the Pope.

DOCUMENT 176——Council of Carthage, A.D. 416, *To Innocent.*
June 416.
Augustine, *Ep.* 175. (*P.L.* 33. 759; *S.E.P.* 140 ‡.)

1. We had come according to custom to the church of Carthage, and a synod was held for various affairs, when our fellow presbyter, Orosius, gave us letters from our holy brothers and fellow priests, Heros and Lazarus, which we enclose. These having been read, we perceived that Pelagius and Celestius were accused of being authors of a wicked error, which must be anathematized by all of us. And so we asked that all that had been done with regard to Celestius here in Carthage about five years ago should be gone through. This having been read, as your holiness can perceive from the acts which we append, although the decision was clear by which so great a wound was shown to have been cut away from the Church by an episcopal judgement, yet we thought good, by a common deliberation, that the authors of this persuasion (although it was said that this Celestius had arrived since then at the priesthood), unless they openly anathematized these things, should themselves be anathematized in order that, if their own salvation cannot, at least that of those who have been or may be deceived by them may be procured, when they know the sentence against them.

2. *This act, lord brother, we thought right to intimate to your holy*

charity, in order that to the statutes of our mediocrity might be added the authority of the apostolic see to protect the safety of many, and to correct the perversity of some. For the object of those men with their damnable arguments is, not so much by defending free will as by exalting it into blasphemous arrogance, to leave no room for the grace of God, whereby we are Christians, and whereby the very exercise of our wills becomes really free, when they are set free from the tyranny of carnal lusts, as the Lord says "If the Son shall make you free, then indeed you shall be free".

3. [In support of grace they quote eight passages from Paul and then proceed.] There is no time to quote countless such passages which we would like to collect from Holy Scripture; and we fear lest, by repeating to you these very things which you preach with more grace from an apostolic see, we should seem to act unfittingly. But we do so because, being more infirm, the more zeal we show in preaching God's word, the more constant and bold are the attacks of the heretics.

4. If, therefore, Pelagius seems to your holiness to have been justly absolved by the episcopal acts which are said to have been transacted in the East,[1] at all events the error itself and the impiety, which now has many asserters in different places, ought to be anathematized by the authority of the apostolic see also. For let your holiness consider and feel with us, in your pastoral heart, how baneful and deadly for Christ's sheep is that which of necessity follows from their sacrilegious disputes.

6.   And so, even if Pelagius and Celestius have amended, or deny that they ever held such opinions, or deny to be theirs whatever writings are brought as evidence against them, and if there is no way of convicting them of falsehood, yet in general whoever asserts, dogmatizes, and affirms that human nature in itself can be sufficient for itself for the avoidance of sin and the performance of the commandments of God, is found to be an enemy of God's grace, which is more fully declared by the prayers of the saints. And whoever denies that infants, through the baptism of Christ, are set free from perdition, and obtain

---

[1] Synod of Diospolis (Hefele, 2. 450–455).

eternal salvation, let him be anathema. And further, whatever else happens, we do not doubt that your reverence, after perusing the episcopal acts which are said to have been drawn up in the East in this same cause, will make such a judgement that we shall all rejoice in the mercy of God.   (Chapman 78B.)

These sixty-nine bishops are clear that their former condemnation of Celestius was correct (§ 1), but since he and Pelagius have been acquitted in the East (§ 4), they must be made to renounce their errors openly (§ 1), otherwise it will appear that the heresy itself is approved. They urge the Pope to support them in this, because of his wide authority (§ 2). Their own preaching, based on Paul, is ineffectual (§ 3). The Pope, having before him the acts of the synod which acquitted Pelagius and Celestius, will be in a better position to decide whether they were rightly acquitted (§ 6). At all events the heresy itself must be overthrown (§ 4).

DOCUMENT 177——Council of Mileve, A.D. 416, *To Innocent.*
    June 416.
    Augustine, *Ep.* 176.   (*P.L.* 33. 763; *S.E.P.* 141 ‡.)

1. Since God has by a special gift of his grace set you in the apostolic see, and has given such a man to our times,[1] so that it could rather be imputed to us as a fault of negligence, if we withheld from your reverence whatever is to be furnished for the Church, than that you should be able to receive the same with contempt or neglect, we beseech you to apply your pastoral care to the great peril of the weak members of Christ.

2. A new and most pernicious heresy is trying to raise its head. The enemies of Christ's grace try, by their ungodly arguments, to deprive us of the Lord's Prayer, in which, as the Lord taught us, we say "Forgive us our debts, as we forgive our debtors". [The council justifies its opposition to the heresy by seven more New Testament texts.]

3. We omit many other things which they deal with against Holy Scripture.   . In insinuating these things to your apostolic breast we have no need to say much, or to pile up

1 The precise meaning of this long sentence is obscure. The translation is literal.

words about such an impiety, since doubtless they will move you, so that you will be unable to refrain from correcting them, that they may creep on no further.   .

4. The authors of this most pernicious error are said to be Pelagius and Celestius, whom, indeed, we should prefer to be cured in the Church, rather than that they should be cut off from the Church, if no necessity compels. One of them, Celestius, is even said to have arrived at the priesthood in Asia. Your holiness is better informed by the church of Carthage about what was done against them a few years ago. Pelagius, as the letters of some of our brethren say, is in Jerusalem, and is said to have deceived many there. Many more, however, who have been able to examine his views more closely, are fighting against him for the grace of Christ, and for the catholic faith, but especially your holy son, our brother and fellow priest Jerome.

5. We consider that by the help of the mercy of our Lord God, who deigns[1] both to direct your counsel and to hear your prayers, those who hold such perverse and pernicious opinions will more easily yield to *the authority of your holiness, drawn from the authority of Holy Scripture,* so that we may be rather congratulated by their correction, than saddened by their ruin. But whatever they themselves may choose, your reverence perceives that at least those many who are deceived and entangled by them must be cared for immediately and quickly. We write this to your holiness from the council of Numidia, imitating our colleagues of the church and province of Carthage, who we understand have written on this matter to the apostolic see, which your blessedness adorns.

(Chapman 78B.)

This letter comes from sixty-one bishops, including Augustine. It gives less information than the one from Carthage, but presses the same point, that the Pope must condemn the heresy to prevent its spreading (§ 3). It hints that the Palestine synod was deceived by Pelagius (§ 4). The heretics will more readily yield to the Pope (§ 5). But why? Because his authority is drawn from the authority of the Bible. There are two views on what this means. Dr Bright[2] thinks it means that the Pope will condemn the heresy on scriptural grounds,

---

[1] One MS. has "will deign".   [2] *Roman See*, 1896, p. 127.

as the council has done in § 2. But Chapman[1] says there must be more in it than that. If the authority of the Pope and that of the episcopate are both drawn from the same source, why should one have more weight than the other? He is sure the passage means that papal authority is based on the primacy of Peter as revealed in the Bible. He finds this to be the contemporary African view by combining the following passages from Augustine: "Who is ignorant that the first of the apostles is the most blessed Peter?" (Doc. 152); "Who can be ignorant that the chief apostolate is to be preferred to any episcopate?" (Doc. 172 § 2); "the Roman Church, in which the primacy of an apostolic chair always flourished" (Doc. 162).

It was of the utmost importance to secure papal condemnation of the heresy, and so the letters of the two councils are supported by a long private letter to the Pope, from five leading African bishops.

DOCUMENT 178——Aurelius, Alypius, Augustine, Evodius, and Possidius, *To Innocent.* A.D. 416.
Aug. *Ep.* 177. (*P.L.* 33. 764; *S.E.P.* 143 ‡.)

1. We send to your holiness letters from the two councils of the provinces of Carthage and Numidia, signed by no small number of bishops, against the enemies of Christ's grace. . . . Therefore the family of Christ which says "When I am weak, then am I strong", and to which the Lord says "I am thy salvation", with suspense of heart, with fear and trembling, waits for the help of the Lord also, by the charity of your reverence.

2. We have heard that there are some in the city of Rome, where he [Pelagius] lived long, who favour him for various reasons, some clearly because he is said to have persuaded them, but more because they do not believe him to hold such views, especially as it is boasted that ecclesiastical acts were drawn up in the East, where he is living, by which he is declared innocent. If indeed the bishops pronounced him catholic, we must believe that it was for no other reason than because he said he acknowledged the grace of God.

[1] *S.E.P.*, 143n.

3. It is not a question of Pelagius only, but of so many others of whose verbosity and contentiousness .   the world is full. Therefore either he should be sent for to Rome by your reverence and carefully examined as to what grace he means when he admits (if he does admit) that men are by grace aided to avoid sin and live justly, or else this must be transacted with him by letter. And when it is proved that he means that grace which is taught by ecclesiastical and apostolic truth, then without any scruple of the Church, without any lurking ambiguity, he must be absolved, and then we must really rejoice in his acquittal.

14. If they [his supporters] know that the book which they think or know to be his has been anathematized and condemned by himself on the authority of catholic bishops, and especially that of your holiness, which we do not doubt will be of greater weight with him, we think they will not dare further to disturb simple Christian breasts.   . And so we thought it preferable to send to your blessedness a letter written by one of us to the same [Pelagius]. This letter is a reply to one which Pelagius had sent to the writer (by a certain deacon, an oriental but a citizen of Hippo) to justify himself. We consider it better that you should deign to send it to him yourself, and we ask you to do so, for then he is less likely to scorn to read it, as in it he will consider the sender more than the writer.

17. No doubt your blessedness will judge of the other accusations in the same way as the acts [of the two councils], and we assume that your kindness of heart will pardon us for having sent to your holiness a longer letter than you might perhaps have wished. For we do not pour back our little stream for the purpose of replenishing your great fountain; but in these times of severe testing .   we wish this to be proved by you, *whether our littleness flows from the same head of waters as your abundance*, and by your reply to be consoled, because we share in common the one grace.   (Chapman 78B.)

In the above letter the authority of the Pope is further emphasized (§ 14). The authority as stated is not inconsistent with universal jurisdiction. But the writers, fearing Pelagius may have infected even Rome (§ 2), do not hesitate to tell Innocent how his authority should be used (§ 3). They close on a note of somewhat abject humility.

To all three letters the Pope replied in the following January.

DOCUMENT 179——Innocent, *Ep.* 29, to the Council of Carthage (*In requirendis*). 27 January 417.
Aug. *Ep.* 181. (*P.L.* 33. 780; *S.E.P.* 146 ‡.)

1. In inquiring about those things which should be handled with all care by priests, and especially by a true, just, and catholic council, by preserving, as you have done, *the example of ancient tradition*, and by being mindful of the discipline of the Church, you have truly strengthened the vigour of our religion, no less now in consulting, than before in passing sentence. For you decided that *it was proper to refer to our judgement*, knowing what is due to the apostolic see, since all we who are set in this place desire to follow the very apostle from whom the very episcopate and whole authority of this name has emerged; following whom, we know how to condemn the evil and to approve the good. So also, you have by your priestly office preserved *the institutions of the fathers*, and have not spurned that which they decreed by a sentence not human but divine, that *whatever is done, even though it be in distant provinces, should not be ended until it comes to the knowledge of this see*, that by its authority the whole just pronouncement should be strengthened, and that from there the other churches (like waters proceeding from their natal sources and flowing through the different regions of the world, the pure streams of an uncorrupt head) should take up what they ought to enjoin, whom they ought to wash, and whom that water, worthy of pure bodies, should avoid as defiled with uncleansable filth.

2. I congratulate you, therefore, dearest brothers, that you have directed a letter to us by our brother and fellow bishop Julius, and that while caring for the churches which you rule, you also show your concern for the advantage of all, and that *you ask for a decision which may benefit all the churches of the world*

together; so that the Church, being established in her rules, and confirmed in this decree of just proclamation against such errors, may be unable to tolerate those men.

(Chapman 78B.)

DOCUMENT 180——Innocent, *Ep.* 30, to the Council of Mileve
     (*Inter caeteras*).   27 January 417.
     Aug. *Ep.* 182.   (*P.L.* 33. 784; *S.E.P.* 147 ‡, and editor.)

2. It is therefore with due care and fitness that you consult *the secrets of the apostolic office* (that office, I mean, to which belongs, besides those things that are outside, the care of all the churches) as to what opinion should be held on doubtful matters, following the form of the ancient rule which, you and I know, has ever been kept in the whole world. But this I pass by, because I am sure your prudence is aware of it: for how could you by your actions have confirmed it, unless you knew that answers to questions always flow through all provinces from the apostolic spring? Especially as often as *questions of faith* are to be ventilated, I think all our brothers and fellow bishops ought to refer *to none but Peter*, that is to the author of their name and office, even as your affection has now referred [to us], a matter which may benefit all churches in common throughout the whole world. For they must needs be more cautious when they see the inventors of these evils, on the report of two synods, cut off by the decree of our sentence from ecclesiastical communion.

3. Therefore your charity will do a double good; for you will obtain the grace of having observed the canons, and *the whole world will share your benefit.*[1] For who among catholics will choose any longer to hold conversation with Christ's enemies? . . .

6. We declare that Pelagius and Celestius, that is the inventors of new doctrines which, as the apostle said, are wont to produce no edification, but rather utterly empty questionings, should by the authority of apostolic vigour be deprived of ecclesiastical communion, until they recover from the snares

1 From this point to the end of the Doc. the translation is by the editor.

of the devil, by whom they are held prisoners according to
their own choice; and that meanwhile they should not be
received within the Lord's fold, because, following the course
of a crooked way, they have themselves chosen to desert.

(Gore 43 note; Chapman 78B, 95A.)

The Africans in their letters had given no indication of why they
believed the Pope to have so much authority, but Innocent is clear
that his authority is derived from "the institutions of the fathers".
He claims, too, that the other churches derive their authority from
Rome, that it is for Rome to decide on doubtful matters, and that
Rome's decision is for the whole Church. I think the opening words
of Doc. 180 are the earliest indication we have of the Vatican claiming
to possess inside information not available to the Church at large.[1]

Anglicans say that the Pope is bluffing. He develops a new theory
of his own authority, and then claims ancient precedent for it.[2]
Chapman[3] replies that the theory was not new; there was plenty of
ancient precedent for it. Most of the evidence is lost, but there remains
the evidence that Pope Callistus, A.D. 220, claimed to be "bishop
of bishops"[4] (Doc. 18 § 1), that Pope Stephen, A.D. 256, "insists
that he holds his succession from Peter" (Doc. 49 § 17), that Pope
Damasus, A.D. 371, claimed that papal opinion ought to be sought
before all other (Doc. 93), and that Pope Siricius, A.D. 385, said that
Peter acted in the Popes, and that every "priest" must know what
Rome decrees (Doc. 108). There is no evidence that the African
bishops regarded the claims of Innocent as out of place; in fact contemporary documents suggest the contrary. For example:

DOCUMENT 181——Augustine, *Ep.* 186: Alypius and Augustine
to Paulinus.[5]   A.D. 417.
(*P.L.* 33. 816.)

2. . . . After a letter had reached us from the East, quite
openly pushing the [Pelagian] heresy, it was now our duty not
to fail the Church in any way, by any episcopal authority
whatever; accordingly reports were sent on this matter from

1 Langen, *Geschichte der Römischen Kirche*, 1. 737. Cp. Irenaeus, Doc. 9. 3
§ 1; Tertullian, Doc. 12 § 26; Augustine, Doc. 172 §§ 4, 12, and Doc. 173
§ 31; and 2 Esdras 14. 26.
2 Bright, *Roman See*, 129; Denny, 318.
3 *S.E.P.*, 149.
4 But this may refer to Agrippinus, bishop of Carthage. See p. 26.
5 Bishop of Nola near Naples.

two councils, those of Carthage and Mileve, to the apostolic
see. .   We also wrote to the late Pope Innocent, in addition
to the reports of the councils, a private letter,[1] in which we
dealt more fully with the same question. To all he wrote back
to us *in the manner that was right and proper for the pontiff of the
apostolic see.*   (Chapman 79A.)

DOCUMENT 182——Augustine, *Sermo* 131.   23 September 417.
    (*P.L.* 38. 734; *L.F.* 20. 592 ‡.)

    10.   "For being ignorant of God's righteousness, and
wishing to establish their own, they have not submitted to the
righteousness of God." My brethren, have compassion with
me. When you find such men, do not hide them; have no mis-
directed mercy. Refute those who contradict, and those who
resist bring to us. For already two councils on this question
have been sent to the apostolic see; and replies have also come
from there. The cause is finished[2]; would that the error might
sometime be finished also!   (Chapman 79B.)

    The importance of Innocent's replies (Docs. 179, 180) is shown by
the repeated reference to them during the next twenty years. See
Docs. 187 § 1, 188, 190 §§ 10–11, 191 § 8, 192 § 5, 195, 197, 198,
230 § 57, 231, 232, 233 § 88.

        [1] Doc. 178.   [2] Cp. Doc. 196.

CHAPTER XIX

POPE ZOSIMUS

I. CELESTIUS AND PELAGIUS

SIX weeks after writing his replies to the African church, Pope Innocent died, and was succeeded by Zosimus. The African bishops had condemned Celestius and Pelagius on the written evidence of Heros and Lazarus. The new Pope regarded these two bishops as "unknown men, and aliens who had obtained their sees in Gaul by unworthy means",[1] and he was ready to regard their evidence as unreliable. The heretics too were unwilling to take their sentence lying down. First Celestius came to Rome and handed in a written confession of faith.

DOCUMENT 183——Celestius, *Libellus*. A.D. 417.
In Augustine, *De Pecc. Orig.* 26 and 5 and 6. (*P.L.* 45. 1718; M.D. 12. 69 and 51 ‡.)

1. If indeed any questions have arisen beyond the faith, on which there might be much dissension, I have not passed judgement as the originator of any dogma, as if I had definite authority for this; but whatever I have derived from the fountain of the apostles and prophets, *I have offered for approval to the judgement of your apostolate*; so that if by chance any error of ignorance has crept in, human as we are, *it may be corrected by your sentence.*

2. Infants ought to be baptized for the remission of sins, according to the rule of the universal Church, and according to the meaning of the gospel; we readily admit this, for the Lord has determined that the kingdom of heaven should only be conferred on the baptized; and since the resources of nature do not possess it, it must necessarily be conferred by abundance of grace.

3. We did *not* say that infants therefore must be baptized

---

[1] Zosimus, *Ep.* 2 § 4 (*P.L.* 20. 651).

for the remission of sins in order *that we might seem to affirm original sin*,[1] which is very alien from catholic sentiment. But because *sin is not born with a man*, it is subsequently committed by the man; for it is shown to be *a fault, not of nature*, but of the will. It is fitting, indeed, to confess this lest we should seem to make different kinds of baptism; and it is necessary to lay down this first, lest by the occasion of the mystery, evil should, to the disparagement of the Creator, be said to be conveyed to man by nature, before it has been committed by man.

(Chapman 79B, 80A.)

In spite of the preamble of deference to the Pope, no one denies that this document is heretical, for it openly repudiates original sin (§ 3). The Pope examined Celestius on it in the basilica of S. Clement, and then wrote as follows to the African bishops:

DOCUMENT 184——Zosimus, *Ep.* 2, to Aurelius and the African Bishops (*Magnum pondus*).   September 417.
   (*P.L.* 20. 649.)

1. Great matters demand a great weight of examination, that the level of judgement be not less than the matters dealt with. In addition there is the authority of the apostolic see, to which the decrees of the fathers ordained a particular reverence in honour of S. Peter. We must therefore pray, and pray without ceasing, that by the continued grace and unceasing help of God, from this fountain the peace of the faith and of catholic brotherhood may be sent unclouded into the whole world.   .

2. The priest Celestius came to us for examination, asking to be acquitted of those charges on which he had been wrongfully accused to the apostolic see. And although we were distracted by a great weight of ecclesiastical business, we put it all on one side, so that you would not have to wait for information, and we sat for the examination in the basilica of S. Clement, who was imbued with the learning of the blessed apostle Peter.

[1] *peccatum ex traduce.*

3. We discussed all that had been done before, as you will learn from the acts attached to this letter. Celestius being admitted, *we caused to be recited the pamphlet which he had handed in*, and not content with this, we repeatedly inquired of him whether he spoke from his heart or with his lips the things which he had written.

6. In the present case we have decided nothing hurriedly or immaturely, but we make known to your holinesses our examination upon *the unfettered faith of Celestius*.[1] The earlier libellus, written by him in Africa, ought to be evidence in his favour against those who boast on unexamined rumours. Wherefore within two months either let those come forward who can show *that he now believes otherwise than the contents of his pamphlets* and confession, or let your holinesses recognize nothing of doubt to be remaining in that which he henceforward openly and manifestly professes.

7. I have therefore admonished Celestius himself, and other priests present at the time from various places, that these little snares of questions and silly contests, which do not build, but destroy, spring from that contagious curiosity which there is when each man abuses his natural capacity.

(Chapman 80A.)

Zosimus next considered the statement of faith which Pelagius had sent to Pope Innocent, but which arrived after his death. The bulk of this document is orthodox, but there are evasive passages on free will and baptism.

DOCUMENT 185——Pelagius, *Libellus Fidei.* A.D. 417.
(*P.L.* 45. 1718.)

7. We acknowledge one baptism, which we assert ought to be celebrated in the same form of words for infants as for adults. If a man lapses after baptism, we believe he can be saved by penitence.

13. We confess free will, but we say [men] always need God's help, and we condemn those who say with the Manichaeans that man cannot avoid sin, as well as those who assert with Jovinian that man cannot sin.

---

[1] *super absoluta Celestii fide.*

14. This is the faith, most blessed Pope, which we have learned in the Catholic Church, which we have ever held and hold. If we have by chance set down aught in it unskilfully or without due caution, *we desire to be corrected by you, who hold both the faith and the see of Peter. If, however, this our confession is approved by the judgement of your apostolate, then whoever desires to blacken me will not prove that I am a heretic, but that he himself is unskilful or evil-minded or not a catholic.*

(Chapman 80A.)

After reading the above, the Pope wrote again to Africa, and the opening words of his letter confirm that he failed to detect heresy in the pamphlet of Celestius. He makes it quite clear that, during his interview with him, Celestius had stuck to his libellus (Doc. 183). In spite of this the Pope had declared his faith to be unfettered (Doc. 184 § 6), and does so again in this following letter (§ 2).

DOCUMENT 186——Zosimus, *Ep.* 3, to Aurelius and the African Bishops (*Postquam a nobis*). 21 September 417. (*P.L.* 20. 654; *S.E.P.* 163 †, and editor.[1])

1. After the presbyter Celestius had been heard by us and had professed plainly the sentiments of the faith, and had *confirmed the statements of his libellus* with repeated protestations, we wrote fully of him to your charity.

2. And now, behold, we have received a letter from Praylius, bishop of Jerusalem, . . who intervenes most earnestly in the cause of Pelagius. The same Pelagius has also sent a letter of his own, containing his complete purgation, and he has appended a profession of faith, what he holds and what he condemns, without any deceit, so that all difficulties of interpretation may cease. These were publicly read; all *their contents corresponded with what Celestius had produced previously*, and were in the same sense and tenor. Would that any of you, dear brothers, could have been present at the reading of these letters! What joy was there on the part of the holy men present! How they wondered! Scarcely could any refrain even from tears: that such men had been able to dishonour un-

1 §§ 1–3 from *S.E.P.*; § 8 added by editor.

fettered faith. Is there any place where the grace or help of God is left out? . .

3. . . . See! Pelagius and Celestius appear before the apostolic see by their letters and confessions. Where is Heros? Where is Lazarus? Damnable names, making one blush. Where are those young men Timasius and Jacob, who produced writings said to be of Pelagius? When these accused make such professions before the apostolic see, you yourselves judge whether the things reported of them by men of evil character and of no weight, and by vague rumour, should be believed.

8.   . May you judge that those whom false judges were condemning are recognized as having never been torn away from our body[1] and from catholic truth.   Therefore we send for your delight copies of the writings sent by Pelagius. We do not doubt that the reading of them will bring to you joy in the Lord concerning his unfettered faith.

(Chapman 80A.)

The two letters of the Pope, with the minutes of his examination of Celestius, reached Carthage on 2 November, and the bearer informed the deacon Paulinus that Zosimus wished to see him. Evidently this Paulinus had been one of the chief accusers of Celestius in A.D. 411, and had sent a written accusation against him then. After six days he replies, and we get a confused version of the interview Celestius had with the Pope (§ 2).

DOCUMENT 187——Paulinus the Deacon, *Libellus Zosimo oblatus contra Celestium.* 8 November 417.
(*P.L.* 45. 1724; *S.E.P.* 166 ‡.)

1. I beseech justice of your blessedness, Lord Zosimus, venerable Pope. The true faith is never disturbed, certainly not in the apostolic church, in which teachers of false faith are as truly punished as they are easily discovered, that they may die in the evils they have committed, unless they correct them so that in them may be *that true faith which the apostles taught, and which the Roman church holds*, together with all the doctors of the catholic faith. And if . . . these also who are or will be

---

[1] Cp. Doc. 180 § 6.

discovered remain in their perfidy, let them be delivered to the spiritual sword to be destroyed; just as the other leaders of heresy, long ago *judged by the apostolic see, or by the fathers,* were expelled from the bosom of the Catholic Church, and given over to eternal death. So let it be with Pelagius and Celestius, who were condemned by your predecessor, the late Pope Innocent, if they reject the true faith and remain in their perverse doctrine.

2. Following his sentence, your blessedness directed to Celestius these words among others, when he was heard by the apostolic see: "Do you condemn everything about the questions which are contained in the libellus of Paulinus?" And in another place: "Are you acquainted with the letters which the apostolic see sent to the brothers and fellow bishops of the African province?" And then: "Do you condemn all that we have condemned, and hold all that we hold?" And again: "Do you condemn all that is flung about in your name?" And again: "Or those things which Paulinus exposed in his pamphlet?" And when he said that I might be proved a heretic by my accusations of himself, you, filled with the Holy Ghost, rejected his wild and quibbling words and by your apostolic authority gave a judgement by which I was declared catholic, and he might be cured if he would. "I do not want you to lead us in a circle; do you condemn all that was objected against you by Paulinus, or spread about by rumour?" To whom is this decision not sufficient? Who would reject a decision so healthy, so worthy, and so pious except one who is astray from the faith? And he who had above confessed that he would condemn whatever was objected against him, if you judged it to be contrary to the faith, hears the word "condemn", and not only does not condemn, but disputes to such great injury of the see. So now the Roman church is no longer ignorant of the character of her plaintiff who has dared in so audacious a spirit to contradict, and not to condemn what your holiness decreed should be condemned.

3. I thank God . that the apostolic see condemned, by the mouth of two pontiffs, the heresy of which I accused Celestius . he has also against him   Cyprian, Ambrose,

Gregory, and Pope Innocent . . . at least he ought certainly to follow you, if he prefers learning the truth to teaching falsehood; he has (which is first) your blessedness, whose sentence he ought to have obeyed, when he heard you say "condemn". . .

4. Wherefore I pray your apostleship to receive this libellus of mine, that I may be able to give thanks to your great see, and to its most just decisions given in my favour. I write it because the subdeacon Basiliscus summoned me verbally at Carthage on 2 November, on behalf of your holiness, with acts of the apostolic see addressed to me, to be present before the apostolic see and the judgement of your holiness, to which it was suggested that I had fled. I would promise not to be absent, if the sentence had been against me and not for me. . . . Let that which could no longer be hid, but has been publicly brought to light, be now cut off by your holiness with the spiritual sword, that the flock of the Lord, which you govern as a good shepherd with anxious care, may no longer be torn by the teeth of this wild beast. (Chapman 80 note.)

There is no doubt that Paulinus rates the judgement of the Pope very high, perhaps regarding him as having unique authority in matters of faith. That is why he is so anxious that Zosimus should not blunder in this case. He did not, however, obey the papal summons to Rome.

The African bishops, 214 of them, met in council and also wrote to the Pope, but only a few lines of what they said have been preserved verbatim. These are as follows:

DOCUMENT 188——Council of Carthage, A.D. 417, *To Zosimus.* November 417.
In Prosper, *Contra Collatorem* 15. (*P.L.* 45. 1808; Kidd, *Docs.* 2. 163.)

We decree that the sentence against Pelagius and Celestius, issued by the venerable bishop Innocent, from the see of the most blessed apostle Peter, *shall stand*, until they shall openly and explicitly confess that the grace of God by Jesus Christ our Lord helps us not only to know, but to do what is right, in every single act; so that, without it, we could not have, think, say, or do anything that pertains to true and holy religion.

We learn more of what the Africans said to the Pope from Doc. 192 § 5.

The winter passes and then the Pope replies. The claims he makes for his see are clear and emphatic. He denies that he had approved every word of the libellus of Celestius. Here is the letter in full; it cannot be translated into readable English.

DOCUMENT 189——Zosimus, *Ep.* 12, to Aurelius and the Council of Carthage (*Quamvis patrum*). 21 March 418. (*P.L.* 20. 676.)

1. Although the tradition of the fathers has assigned such great authority to the apostolic see that *no one would dare to dispute its judgement*, and has kept this always by canons and rules and church order, and in the current of its laws pays the reverence which it owes to the name of Peter, from whom it descends; for canonical antiquity, by the consent of all, has willed such power to this apostle, so that the promise of Christ our God, that he should loose the bound and bind the loosed, is equally given to those who have obtained, with his assent, the inheritance of his see; for he has a care for all churches, especially for this where he sat, nor does he permit any of its privileges or decisions to be shaken by any blast, since he established it on the firm and immovable foundation of his own name, which no one shall rashly attack, but at his peril. Peter then is the head of so great authority, and has confirmed the devotion of all the fathers who followed him, so that the Roman church is established by all laws and discipline, whether human or divine. His place we rule, and we inherit the power of his name; you know this, dearest brothers, and as priests you ought to know it. *Such then being our authority, that no one can revise our sentence*, we have done nothing which we have not of our own accord brought to your notice in our letter, giving this much to our brotherhood, that by consulting together, not because we did not know what ought to be done, or might do something which might displease you as contrary to the good of the Church, but we desired to treat together

with you of a man who, as you wrote, was accused before you, and who came to our see asserting his innocence, not refusing judgement from the former appeal; of his own accord calling for his accusers, and condemning the crimes of which he was falsely accused by rumour. We thought, in fact we know, that his entire petition was explained in the earlier letter which we sent you, and we believed that we had sufficiently replied to those you wrote in answer.

2. But we have unfolded the whole roll of your letter which was sent by Subdeacon Marcellinus. You have understood the entire text of our letter as if we had believed Celestius in everything, and had given our assent, so to speak, to every syllable without discussing his words. Matters which need a long treatment are never rashly postponed, nor without great deliberation must anything be decided on which a final judgement has to be given. So let your brotherhood know that we have changed nothing since we wrote to you, or you wrote to us; but we have left all as it was before, when we informed your holiness of the matter in our letter, in order that the supplication you sent to us might be granted. Farewell.

(Chapman 95A, 115A.)

This letter reached Carthage on 29 April. After writing it the Pope officially condemned the heretics. His sentence is not extant,[1] but some account of it is given by Marius Mercator, who wrote eleven years later. See §§ 4 and 9 below.

DOCUMENT 190——Marius Mercator, *Commonitorium super Nomine Celestii.* A.D. 429.
(*P.L.* 45. 1687; *S.E.P.* 171, 175 †, and editor.[2])

3. The same Celestius, thrown out of Constantinople, quickly went to Rome in the time of the late Bishop Zosimus. He was there questioned (according to our copies of the acts), and being terrified by such an examiner, he gave rise to hope by numerous answers, promising that he condemned those chapters about which he was accused at Carthage. For he was earnestly ordered and expected to do so, and for this reason

[1] But see *P.L.* 20. 693–697.
[2] §§ 4, 9 from *S.E.P.*; §§ 3, 10, 11 added by the editor.

was gently treated by that holy priest, and procured from him a kindly letter to the African bishops, which kindness he still abuses, deceiving the ignorance of many.

4. When the African bishops replied, exposing the whole cause which had been thrashed out there, sending the acts of their councils which had been held about him, whether present or absent, he was then called for a fuller hearing, that he might hasten to fulfil his promise of condemning the aforesaid chapters, and so be absolved from the excommunication he had undergone from the African pontiffs. But not only did he fail to appear, but he fled from Rome, and for this he was condemned by the aforesaid Bishop Zosimus of blessed memory in a very long and complete document. In this document, the chapters of which Celestius was accused are contained, and his whole case, and that of his more depraved master, Pelagius, is narrated. We have copies of these writings, and we note that similar copies were sent to the bishops, to the churches of the East, to the diocese of Egypt, to Constantinople, Thessalonica, and Jerusalem.

[Here follow quotations from Pelagius' writings.]

9. All the above-quoted chapters are contained, as was said, in that letter of the late Bishop Zosimus which is called "Tractoria", *by which Celestius and Pelagius were condemned.* This letter was sent to Constantinople and *throughout the world,* and *was strengthened*[1] *by the subscriptions of the holy fathers.* Julian and his accomplices refused to sign it, and to consent to those fathers. They were deposed not only by imperial laws, but also by decrees of the Church, and banished from all Italy. Many of them came to their senses, and, being corrected of their errors, returned as suppliants to the apostolic see, and being accepted received back their churches.

10. Celestius and Pelagius were not for the first time condemned by Zosimus, of blessed memory, but by his predecessor Innocent, of holy record, by whom Julian had been ordained. And Julian after their condemnation, until the death of Innocent, remained in his communion, and persevered in the sound opinion; and since he communicated with him who had

---

[1] *roborata.*

condemned Pelagius and Celestius, doubtless he himself condemned them; and what he wants now, and what he complains of, we do not know.

11. Now when they were condemned by Innocent of holy record, the position was as follows: after the devastation of Rome, Pelagius was living in Palestine. His books were found by certain studious bishops in which he seemed to have written many various things against the catholic faith. These books were sent to Africa with letters to the fathers and bishops, and they were read at three councils which were summoned. After that *reports were sent to Rome,* and the books were sent there, and *an apostolic ruling was returned to the said councils, excommunicating Celestius and Pelagius.* I have in my hands a copy of these writings.   (Chapman 79A, 117A.)

It would have saved a lot of bother if Mercator had told us the date of this lengthy papal *Tractoria* (see § 9 above). On 30 April the emperors in Ravenna banished Celestius and Pelagius from Rome, and pronounced their heresy criminal.[1] On the next day a full African council enunciated in nine resolutions the catholic doctrine of original sin and of grace.[2] Some Roman Catholics[3] have dated the papal condemnation of the two heretics before the imperial sentence against them, and supposed that the latter was in consequence of the former. They have the support of Possidius,[4] writing nineteen years later. This order of events is accepted by the Anglican scholar, William Bright.[5] But most Anglicans[6] prefer to follow the Gallicans[7] who say that the Pope took his line from the decision of the emperors and the African bishops; and Duchesne[8] is sure that it was the African primate who prevailed on the emperor to issue his decree. There is not much evidence available. We learn from Augustine, two years later, that the Pelagians accused the Pope of changing his mind "driven by fear of a command" (Doc. 192, beginning). This implies that he acted after the imperial decree, and in consequence of it. If the papal sentence had preceded the imperial decree, then Augustine would have been

[1] *P.L.* 45. 1726.   [2] *P.L.* 45. 1728.
[3] Baronius, *Ann.* 418. 19, 23, 24; Chapman, *S.E.P.,* 173n.
[4] Doc. 232.
[5] *Age of the Fathers,* 2. 211.
[6] *D.C.B.,* 4. 1224A; J. C. Robertson, *Hist. Ch.,* 2. 151; Kidd, *Hist. Ch.,* 3. 113.
[7] Quesnel, *P.L.* 56. 980; Tillemont, *Mémoires,* 13. 744; Fleury, *Hist. Ecclésiastique* 23. 50.
[8] Duchesne, 3. 166, n. 3.

able to refute the Pelagian "slander" by simply pointing out the order of events. He does no such thing.

It appears from Zosimus' own letters (Docs. 184, 186) that this Pope made a serious blunder on an important matter of faith, namely original sin, and that he declared a document (Doc. 183) to be orthodox which was in fact heretical, though in a later letter (Doc. 189) he denied that he had approved the whole document. Augustine defends the Pope against the charge of heresy and prevarication. He has before him, besides the papal letters we have seen, also the minutes of the examination of Celestius at Rome which we have only seen in part (Doc. 187 § 2).

DOCUMENT 191——Augustine, *De Peccato Originali.* A.D. 418. (*P.L.* 44. 388; M.D. 12. 52 ‡.)

6. [After quoting the heretical portion of Celestius' libellus (Doc. 183 § 3) he proceeds:] This his opinion Pelagius was afraid or ashamed to bring out to you; but his disciple, without any obscurity, was neither ashamed nor afraid to publish it openly before the apostolic see.

7. But the very merciful prelate of that see, when he saw him carried headlong with such presumption like a madman, until he might recover, if that were possible, preferred to bind him bit by bit by question and answer, rather than to strike him with a severe sentence, which would thrust him down that precipice over which he seemed to be already hanging. I do not say "had fallen", but "seemed to be hanging"; for earlier in the same libellus he had promised before speaking of such questions: "If by chance any error of ignorance has crept in, human as we are, *it may be corrected by your sentence.*"[1]

8. So the venerable Pope Zosimus, holding to this foreword, urged the man, inflated with false doctrine, to condemn what he was accused of by the deacon Paulinus, and to give his assent to the letters of the apostolic see which had emanated from his predecessor of holy memory. He refused to condemn what the deacon objected, but he dared not resist the letters of blessed Pope Innocent, nay, *he promised "to condemn whatever that see should condemn"*.[2] Thus gently treated, as if a madman,

[1] Doc. 183 § 1.   [2] Cp. Doc. 187 § 2.

that he might be pacified, he was still not thought fit to be released from the bonds of excommunication. But a delay of two months[1] was granted, that an answer might be received from Africa, and so an opportunity of recovery was given him by a medicinal gentleness in his sentence. For, indeed, he would be cured, if he would lay aside his obstinate vanity, and attend to what he promised, and would read those letters to which he professed to consent. But after the rescripts were duly issued from the African council of bishops,[2] there were very good reasons why the sentence should be carried out against him, in strictest accordance with equity.

9. . . . For though Pelagius tricked the investigation in Palestine, seeming to clear himself before it, he entirely failed in imposing on the church at Rome (where, as you are aware, he was well known), although he tried even this; but as I said, he entirely failed. For the most blessed Pope Zosimus recollected what his exemplary predecessor had thought of these very proceedings. He considered what was felt about this man by the trusty Romans, whose faith deserved to be spoken of in the Lord, and whose resounding zeal for catholic truth against his error he saw burning harmoniously. The man had lived among them for a long while, and his opinions could not be hidden. . . .

18. This being so, you of course feel that episcopal councils, and the apostolic see, and the whole Roman church, and the Roman Empire, which by God's grace has become Christian, have been most righteously moved against the authors of this wicked error, until they recover from the snares of the devil.

24. . For the time, indeed, Pelagius seemed to say what was agreeable to the catholic faith, but in the end he had no power to deceive that see. Indeed after the replies of the council of Africa, into which province this pestilent doctrine had stealthily made its way, without, however, spreading widely or sinking deeply, other opinions also of this man were, by the care of some faithful brethren, discovered and brought to light at Rome, where he had dwelt for a very long while, and had already engaged in sundry discourses and controversies. In

[1] Doc. 184 § 6. [2] Doc. 188.

order to procure the condemnation of these opinions, Pope Zosimus, as you may read, annexed them to his letter [1] which he wrote *for publication throughout the catholic world.*

(Chapman 80B.)

Augustine's next defence of the Pope is more elaborate and more vehement.

DOCUMENT 192——Augustine, *Contra duas Epistolas Pelagianorum*, Book 2. A.D. 420.

(*P.L.* 44. 573; M.D. 15. 274 ‡.)

5. Moreover, they, the Pelagians, accuse the Roman clergy, writing, "They, driven by the fear of a command, have not blushed to be guilty of the crime of prevarication: contrary to their previous judgement, wherein, by the acts, they had assented to the catholic dogma, they later pronounced that man's nature is evil". Nay, but the Pelagians conceived a false hope that their new and horrible dogma could prevail upon the catholic minds of certain Romans, when those crafty spirits .. were treated with more lenity than the stricter discipline of the Church required. For while so many important ecclesiastical documents were passing to and fro between the apostolic see and the African bishops .. what sort of letter or what decree is found of the late Pope Zosimus in which he declared that we must believe that man is born without any taint of original sin? He certainly never said this; he never wrote it at all. But since Celestius had written this in his pamphlet, merely among those matters on which he confessed he was still in doubt and desired to be instructed   the willingness to amend, and not the falsehood of the dogma, was approved. Therefore his pamphlet was called catholic, because if by chance in any matters a man thinks otherwise than what the truth demands, it reveals a catholic mind not to define them with the greatest accuracy, but to reject them when they are detected and pointed out. . . . This was thought to be the case with him when he replied that *he consented to the letters of the late Pope Innocent, in which all doubt about this matter was*

[1] Doc. 190 § 9.

removed. In order that this might be made fuller and clearer in him, matters were held up until letters should come from Africa, in which province his craftiness had somehow become more clearly known. Eventually these letters came to Rome, declaring that for *slow-witted* and anxious men, it was not sufficient that he confessed his general consent to the letters of Innocent, but that he ought openly to revoke the mischievous statements which he had made in his pamphlet. For if he did not do this, many people of *insufficient intelligence* would be more likely to believe that those poisons of the faith in his pamphlet had been approved by the apostolic see, because it had been affirmed by that see that the pamphlet was catholic, than to believe that the poisons had been amended because of his answer that he consented to the letters of Pope Innocent. . . . But if, which God forbid, it had been judged in the Roman church that those dogmas of Celestius or Pelagius, condemned by Pope Innocent, should be pronounced worthy of approval, the mark of prevarication would rather have to be branded on the Roman clergy for this. To sum up, in the first place the letters of the most blessed Pope Innocent, in reply to the letters of the African bishops, have equally condemned this error which these men are trying to commend to us. Likewise his successor, the holy Pope Zosimus, never said or wrote that this dogma which these men think concerning infants is to be held. Besides, when Celestius tried to clear himself, he bound him by repeated interruptions[1] to consent to the aforesaid letters of the apostolic see. Surely then, provided the stability of the most ancient and robust faith was maintained, whatever in the meanwhile was done more leniently with Celestius was the most merciful persuasion of correction, not the most pernicious approval of wickedness. And since afterwards Celestius and Pelagius were condemned by the repeated authority of the same priesthood, this was the proof of a severity for a while withheld, but at length of necessity carried out, not a violation of that previously known, or a new recognition of truth.

6.   These are the words of the venerable Bishop Innocent to the council of Carthage on this affair   What could be

[1] Doc. 187 § 2.

more clear or more manifest than that judgement of the apostolic see? To this Celestius professed that he assented, when, it being said to him by your holy predecessor, Zosimus, "Do you condemn all that is flung about in your name?",[1] he himself replied, "I condemn them in accordance with the judgement of your predecessor, Innocent".

(Chapman 79A.)

It was evidently most important to uphold the prestige of the Roman see and to get the Pope to condemn heresy and support the truth, but there is no question of letting him decide what the truth is. If the Roman clergy should fall into error, the truth itself would not be compromised. On Augustine's defence of the Pope, Tillemont remarks: "Since Zosimus afterwards amended the error, which he had been able to make owing to deception, the charity of Augustine, who was not writing a history, in which he would have been obliged to represent things just as they were, covers this mistake with a modest silence. He describes what was praiseworthy in him, since he honoured him as the first bishop, and he excuses the rest as far as possible, that is as far as the truth allowed him."[2]

II. JULIAN

A few more documents on the Pelagian troubles must be given. They take us beyond the time of Zosimus, and are concerned with Julian, who was the son of a bishop,[3] and, when a widower, was himself consecrated bishop of Eclanum, in the region of Naples, by Pope Innocent.[4] He became the leader of eighteen Italian bishops who refused to sign against Celestius and Pelagius, and were deposed, excommunicated, and banished. These documents further emphasize the respect felt by catholics and heretics alike for the Roman see as guardian of the faith.

DOCUMENT 193——Julian of Eclanum, *Libellus Fidei*, to
Zosimus. A.D. 418.
(*P.L.* 45. 1735; *S.E.P.* 180, and editor.[5])

16. We have written and sent this to your holiness, as it appears to us according to the catholic rule. If you think we ought to hold otherwise, write us a reply. But if it is impossible

---

[1] Doc. 187 § 2.   [2] *Mémoires*, 13. 726 (A.D. 1710).
[3] *P.L.* 45. 1035.   [4] Doc. 190 § 10.
[5] § 16 from *S.E.P.*; § 17 added by editor.

to contradict us, and yet some wish to stir up scandal against us, we declare to your holiness that we appeal to a plenary council.

17. But one thing we particularly urge on your holiness, namely that you should not regard it as done as a criticism of yourself that through fear of God we dare not sign a condemnation of men in their absence, because we have learnt from the Scriptures that the human will ought not to be put before the commands of God.   (Chapman 81 note.)

The writer does not appeal to a council from the decision of the Pope, but neither does he regard the hoped-for consent of the Pope as of sufficient weight by itself.

Augustine replies to Julian and his fellow exiles in four books dedicated to Pope Boniface, who succeeded Zosimus in December 418. We have seen part of this work already (Doc. 192).

DOCUMENT 194——Augustine, *Contra duas Epistolas Pelagianorum*, Book 1.   A.D. 420.
(*P.L.* 44. 550; M.D. 15. 237 ‡.)

1.   You [Pope Boniface] who mind not high things, however *loftily you are placed*, did not disdain to be a friend of the lowly, and to return ample love. . . I have ventured to write to your blessedness about these things which are now claiming the episcopal attention to viligance on behalf of the Lord's flock.

2.   . Since the heretics do not cease to growl at the entrances to the Lord's fold, and on every side to tear open the approaches so as to plunder the sheep redeemed at such a price; and since the pastoral watch-tower is common to all of us who discharge the episcopal office (although you are pre-eminent therein *on a loftier height*), I do what I can in respect of my small portion of the charge, as the Lord condescends to grant me, by the aid of your prayers, to oppose their pestilent and crafty writings. . . .

3.   . These words .   I determined to address especially to your holiness, not so much for your learning as for your examination, and, *if perchance anything should displease you, for your correction.*   (Chapman 80A note.)

DOCUMENT 195——Augustine, *Contra Julianum Pelagianum*,
   Book 1. A.D. 422.
   (*P.L.* 44. 648.)

13. Do you think they are therefore to be despised, because
they are all of the western church, and we have mentioned no
eastern bishop? What are we to do, since they are Greeks and
we are Latins? *I think you ought to be satisfied with that part of the*
world in which the Lord willed to crown the first of his apostles with a
glorious martyrdom. If you had been willing to hear blessed
Innocent, the president of that church, you would then have
freed your perilous youth from the Pelagian snares. For what
could that holy man answer to the African councils except
what from of old *the apostolic see and the Roman church with the*
rest steadfastly holds? Yet you charge his successor with the
crime of prevarication, because he would not go against the
apostolic doctrine, and the sentence of his predecessor.
Take care how you reply to S. Innocent, who has no view on
this matter except that of those men, western fathers, to whom
I have introduced you, in case it is of any use. He himself sits
with these too, after them in time though *before them in place.*

(Chapman 79.)

DOCUMENT 196——The Same, Book 3.
   (*P.L.* 44. 704.)

5. Necessity therefore compelled that we should, at least
by our assembly, crush their immodesty, and restrain their
audacity. In truth *your cause is anyhow finished by a competent*
decision of bishops in common.[1] There is no more need of examination with you, but merely to make you acquiesce in the sentence,
or to restrain your turbulence.

DOCUMENT 197——The Same, Book 6.
   (*P.L.* 44. 842.)

37. How is it that you, in your persistent depravity, accuse
Zosimus, of blessed memory, bishop of the apostolic see, of

[1] Cp. Doc. 182.

prevarication? *He did not go back from his predecessor, Innocent,* whom you feared to name; but you preferred Zosimus, because he first dealt leniently with Celestius, since the latter, in these your statements, said that if anything was displeasing he was prepared to correct it, and promised to consent to the letters of Innocent.   (Chapman 80B.)

DOCUMENT 198———Augustine, *Opus Imperfectum contra Julianum,* Book 6.   A.D. 430.
(*P.L.* 45. 1520.)

11.   . Since you persist in asserting that freedom, acting rightly or wrongly, cannot perish through sheer misuse, let the blessed Pope Innocent, pontiff of the Roman church, answer. Replying on your affairs to the episcopal councils of Africa he said, "Having experienced free will   .".[1] *Do you see what the catholic faith does through its minister?*   (Chapman 79A.)

[1] Innocent, *Ep.* 29 § 6 (*P.L.* 20. 586).

CHAPTER XX

APIARIUS AND ANTONY

THIS chapter is concerned with the right of bishops and priests to appeal to Rome, and the authority of the Sardican canons which we quoted in Chapter XI, Section III, which grant such a right to bishops. These canons enacted in A.D. 342 were unknown to the church in North Africa seventy-six years later. That church had a law which Monseigneur Duchesne, rightly or wrongly, thought actually forbade appeals to Rome.[1]

DOCUMENT 199——Council of Carthage, 13 June 407: Canon 11.
African Code[2] 105. (*P.L.* 67. 216.)

Whoever, having been excommunicated in Africa, creeps into communion overseas, shall be cast out of the clergy.

The matter was brought to a head by the case of Apiarius,[3] which lasted into the time of three Popes. Apiarius was an African priest who for some offence was excommunicated by Urban, bishop of Sicca, and thereupon went to Rome, where he appealed to Pope Zosimus, at the same time accusing Urban of gross evil. This took place before 1 May 418, and according to Hefele one of the canons of the council on that date was passed probably as a protest against the action of Apiarius.[4]

DOCUMENT 200——Council of Carthage, 1 May 418: Canon 17.
African Code 125. (*P.L.* 67. 221; *P.N.F.* 14. 502 ‡.)

It also seemed good that presbyters, deacons, or other inferior clergy, in the causes which they had, if they questioned

[1] Duchesne, 3. 169.
[2] A collection of African canons of this period made by Dionysius Exiguus in the sixth century.
[3] The documents on this case are collected in Turner, 561–622.
[4] Hefele, 2. 463.

the judgement of their bishops, should be heard by the neighbouring bishops (having been invited by them with the consent of their own bishops), and they should settle whatever is between them. But if they should think to appeal from these, they shall not appeal except to African councils, or to the primates of their provinces. But he who thinks to appeal overseas shall be received in communion by no one in Africa.

It will be seen that the above canon makes no reference to the appeal of bishops.

Apiarius returned to Africa accompanied or followed by three papal legates, the leader of whom was an objectionable man called Faustinus, bishop of Potentia. They arrived with "commands and letters"[1] from Zosimus to the African church; and among their papers was a commonitory in which they were instructed to negotiate on the question of the appeal of bishops to the Pope, and the excommunication of Bishop Urban, or his summoning to Rome, if he did not reform his ways (Doc. 202 § 3).

After some preliminary talks, the papal legates attended the plenary council of Africa on 25 May 419. The acts of this council are given by Migne in *P.L.* 67. 181–224, and there is an English translation of them in *P.N.F.* 14. 441–443. See also Hefele, 2. 465–476. As most of the relevant points were brought out in the council's letter to the Pope (Doc. 202), we need not reproduce the minutes here.

The president was Aurelius, primate of Carthage, and 217 African bishops attended. The proceedings opened with the reading of the Nicene canons, but Faustinus was bored by this and asked that they should get on with the Pope's points at once. The council agreed, and it soon appeared that Zosimus was basing his claim to hear the appeal of bishops on Canon 5 of Sardica (Doc. 69 § 5), and that he was under the impression that that canon was Nicene. The Africans had never heard of the canon before Faustinus appeared on the scene, and Alypius, bishop of Tagaste, pointed out that there was nothing of the kind in their copies of the Nicene canons. He promised, however, that the canon Faustinus had read, allowing appeals to Rome by bishops, would be observed in Africa, until such time as authentic copies of the Nicene canons could be obtained from the East. The whole council said, "What was decided at Nicaea has our approval", and Jocundus, bishop of Suffitula, who had apparently been asleep, woke up and gave his testimony to the same effect.

The rest of the day was mainly occupied in reading many of the African canons, old and new. One of the new canons was as follows:

[1] See the council's letter to Boniface: Boniface, *Ep.* 2 § 1 (*P.L.* 20. 752).

DOCUMENT 201——Council of Carthage, 25 May 419: Canon 1.
   African Code 28.   (*P.L.* 67. 192; *P.N.F.* 14. 456 ‡.)

It also seemed good that presbyters, deacons, or other inferior clergy, in the causes which they had, if they questioned the judgements of their bishops, should let the nearby bishops, with the consent of their own bishop, hear them, and let the bishops who have been consulted judge between them. But if they should think to appeal from these, they shall not appeal to oversea judgements, but to the primates of their own provinces, *as has often been determined about bishops*. But he who shall think to appeal across the sea shall be received to communion by no one in Africa.

The above canon covers the same ground as Canon 17 of the year before (Doc. 200), with the addition of the words "as has often been determined about bishops". The question is: What had often been determined about bishops? The Anglicans, following Tillemont [1] and Van Espen,[2] say that it means that the African church had frequently forbidden its bishops to appeal to authorities overseas, including Popes. To this Roman Catholics reply that there is no canon known which forbids bishops to appeal to Rome.[3] On this view the new clause in the canon does not refer to oversea appeals at all.[4] "The clerics are being given the same rights which had often been granted to bishops to appeal to their primates."[5] But there is no known canon giving bishops the right to appeal to the primates of their provinces. It must be admitted that the wording of the canon is inconclusive, but since, in this same council, Africa had just granted temporary permission for its bishops to appeal to Rome (Doc. 202 § 5), it would seem that such appeals were not the normal thing. Against such an assumption, the Roman Catholics bring forward a letter from the aged Augustine to Pope Celestine, which we will consider in its chronological order (Doc. 207). Before that, comes the letter of the African council to Pope Boniface.

DOCUMENT 202——Council of Carthage, 31 May 419, *To Boniface (Quoniam Domino placuit)*.
   In Boniface, *Ep.* 2.   (*P.L.* 20. 752; *P.N.F.* 14. 506 ‡.)

To the most blessed lord and honourable brother, Boniface; Aurelius, Valentine of the first see of Numidia, and others

---

[1] *Mémoires*, 13. 1037 (A.D. 1710).
[2] *Jus Ecclesiasticum*, tom. 3, p. 300 (A.D 1753).
[3] Ballerini: *P.L.* 55. 570.   [4] Hefele, 2. 470.
[5] *S.E.P.*, 195.

present with us to the number of 217 from the council of all Africa.

2. Apiarius the presbyter, about whose ordination, excommunication, and appeal no small scandal arose not only at Sicca, but also in the whole African church, was restored to communion after seeking pardon for all his errors. Before this, Bishop Urban of Sicca without hesitation corrected what in him seemed to need correction. But we were bound to consider the peace and quiet of the Church, not only for now, but also for the future; and since many such things had happened before, we were obliged to guard against the same or even worse hereafter. We therefore agreed that Apiarius should be removed from the church of Sicca, retaining only the honour of his rank, and that he should officiate as a presbyter wherever else he would and could, and he received a letter to this effect. On his written petition, we granted this without difficulty.

3. But before this case was thus closed, among other things which we discussed daily, it was reasonable that, during the proceedings, we should ask our brothers, Bishop Faustinus, and Philip and Asellus, to bring forward the business with which they had been charged. They proceeded to make a verbal statement, but when we urged that they should present it in writing, then they produced a commonitory. This was read to them and set down in the minutes, which they are bringing to you. In this they were bidden to treat of four things with us, first about *the appeal of bishops to the pontiff of the Roman church*, secondly that bishops should not sail unsuitably to court, thirdly the hearing of the causes of presbyters and deacons by nearby bishops, if they had been wrongfully excommunicated by their own, and fourthly concerning the bishop Urban, that he should be excommunicated or even sent to Rome, unless he had corrected what seemed to need correction.

4. As to the first and third points, namely that bishops should be allowed to appeal to Rome, and that the cases of clerics should be settled by the bishops of their own provinces, we have already taken care to insinuate, in our letter last year to the late Bishop Zosimus, that we were willing to observe them for a little while without injury to him, until an inquiry

into the statutes of the council of Nicaea. And now we pray your holiness to cause us to observe the acts drawn up by the fathers at Nicaea, and to enforce among yourselves there those things which they brought in the commonitory: that is, [here follow Canon 5 of Sardica (Doc. 69 § 5) and Canon 14[1] of the same].

5. The above have been inserted in the acts of the most accurate copies of the Nicene council, until the arrival of authentic copies. If these canons (just as they were decreed, and as they are contained in the commonitory which our brothers alleged was sent to us by the apostolic see) were only observed by you in Italy, then we should be compelled neither to tolerate what we will not now mention, nor to bear the intolerable. But we believe that with the help of the mercy of our Lord God, while your holiness presides over the Roman church, we shall no longer suffer from this insolence, and that we, who are not arguing, shall be treated with brotherly love, as we ought to be treated. And you will also realize, according to the wisdom and justice which the Most High has given you, what is due, if by chance the Nicene canons are other than you suppose. For though we have read many copies, we have never read, in the Latin copies, that which you sent to us in the aforesaid commonitory. So too, because we can find them in no Greek text here, we desire the canons to be brought to us from the eastern churches, where it is said the authentic copies are available. For this end, we beg your reverence to be pleased to write in person to the pontiffs of those parts, namely of Antioch, Alexandria, and Constantinople, and to any others also if it shall please your holiness, that thence there may come to us the same canons decreed by the fathers at the city of Nicaea, and thus you will confer, by the help of the Lord, a great benefit upon all the churches of the West. For who can doubt that the copies of the Nicene council gathered in the Greek empire are most accurate, which though collected from so diverse and such noble Greek churches are found to agree when compared? Until this is done, the rules laid down in the aforesaid commonitory, about the appeals of bishops to the

[1] Hefele, 2. 148.

Roman pontiff, and about the conclusion of the cases of clerics by the bishops of their own provinces, *we undertake to observe until the proof arrives*, and we trust, God willing, that your blessedness will help us in this. (Gore 115.)

About six months later, copies of the Nicene canons arrived from Alexandria and Constantinople. The canons Zosimus had quoted were not among them, and the Africans forwarded these documents to Boniface on 26 November 419. When Zosimus had claimed the right to interfere with the African church, he based his claim on the canons of the Church, and the Africans met him on these grounds. The next Pope, writing to Thessalonica, adopts a different tone.

In 379 Gratian had ceded Dacia and Macedonia to the eastern empire. Pope Damasus appointed the bishop of Thessalonica as his vicar in these provinces. In 419, a Corinthian, Perigenes, consecrated to Patrae, was not received by that church, but soon after was asked for by the church of Corinth. The 16th canon of Antioch [1] empowered the provincial synod to sanction the episcopate of Perigenes at Corinth, but Boniface chose to intervene to this end.

DOCUMENT 203——Boniface, *Ep.* 5, to Rufus, Bishop of
    Thessalonica (*Credebamus*). 19 September 419.
    (*P.L.* 20. 762.)

1. . . As you have loyally said in your letters, the most blessed apostle *Peter watches with his eyes* in what manner you exercise the office of rector. He who was appointed shepherd of the Lord's sheep in perpetuity cannot but be very close to you, cannot but watch over any church, no matter where it is situated, in which we have laid a foundation-stone of the universal Church. (Chapman 95A.)

In 421 Atticus, bishop of Constantinople, obtained from Theodosius II a law attaching the sees of Illyria to the patriarchate of Constantinople. In the following Documents we see how the Pope replied.

DOCUMENT 204——Boniface, *Ep.* 13, to Rufus, Bishop of
    Thessalonica (*Retro majoribus*). 11 March 422.
    (*P.L.* 20. 776.)

2. . To the synod which is said to be due to meet illegally at Corinth about the case of our brother and fellow bishop,

[1] Hefele, 2. 71.

Perigenes, whose state, we wrote, can in no way whatever be disturbed, we have dispatched such a writing, that the brethren one and all may understand, first that they ought not to have met in council without your knowledge; secondly that there is to be no revision of our decision. For *it has never been lawful to reconsider what has once been settled by the apostolic see.* In this document, as was fitting, we upheld the deference due to your holiness, as your grace will learn on reading it.

(Chapman 115A.)

DOCUMENT 205——Boniface, *Ep.* 14, to the Bishops of Thessaly (*Institutio universalis*). 11 March 422.
(*P.L.* 20. 777; Jalland, *Papacy*, 276.)

1. The universal ordering of the Church at its birth took its origin from the office of blessed Peter, in which is found both its directing power and its supreme authority. From him as from a source, at the time when our religion was in the stage of growth, all churches received their common order. This much is shown by the injunctions of the council of Nicaea, since it did not venture to make a decree in his regard, recognizing that nothing could be added to his dignity: in fact it knew that all had been assigned to him by the word of the Lord. *So it is clear that this church is to all churches throughout the world as the head is to the members, and that whoever separates himself from it becomes an exile from the Christian religion, since he ceases to belong to its fellowship.*

DOCUMENT 206——Boniface, *Ep.* 15, to Rufus and the other Bishops of Macedonia, etc. (*Manet beatum*). 11 March 422.
(*P.L.* 20. 782; Jalland, *Papacy*, 275.)

5. . Since the occasion demands it, if you will please examine Canon Law,[1] you will find what is the second see after the Roman church and what is the third. This group [of sees] has been canonically set apart, so that the bishops of

[1] Doc. 62 § 6; Doc. 99.

other churches, though sharing one and the same episcopal status, may realize that there are those to whom they ought to be obedient in a bond of love for the sake of ecclesiastical discipline. . . None has ever been so rash as to oppose the apostolic primacy, *the judgement of which may not be revised*; none rebels against it, unless he would be judged in his turn.

To return to Africa: we suggested above[1] that the granting by the African church of a temporary right for its bishops to appeal to Rome (Doc. 202 § 5) implies that such appeals were abnormal. We must now look at the evidence by which this argument is refuted.

In the year 422 Augustine, aged 68, wanted a bishop for the town of Fussala in his district (Aug. *Ep.* 209 § 2).[2] He chose a suitable priest, and asked his aged primate to come a long way for the consecration, but when the old man arrived, the candidate declined the office, and Augustine, in order not to make the primate's journey fruitless, unwisely presented for consecration a lector called Antony, who was duly appointed bishop of Fussala (§ 3). This appointment was disastrous, as Antony turned out to be an intolerable tyrant, and a swindler (§ 4). For the sake of the people, he had to be deprived of his jurisdiction by a council of nearby bishops, who, however, allowed him to retain his rank (§ 5). To make matters worse, Antony prevailed on the primate of Numidia who had consecrated him " to believe all his statements, and to commend him as altogether blameless to the venerable Pope Boniface" (§ 6). He asserted that if he was fit to be a bishop at all, he was fit to be bishop of Fussala (§ 7). It is not clear that he actually went to Rome, but he certainly was in touch with Pope Boniface. The Pope was more cautious than the primate: he acquitted Antony with the saving clause "if he has truthfully told us the facts". Rumours were going round that the decision of the Pope to reinstate Antony was to be enforced by the civil sword. The people of Fussala were moved to write a letter of protest to the new Pope, Celestine, who succeeded in September 422. Augustine also writes to Celestine, and it is from his letter that we learn the story.

DOCUMENT 207——Augustine, *Ep.* 209, to Celestine. A.D. 423. (*P.L.* 33. 955; M.D. 13. 387 ‡.)

6. . . . With crafty eloquence he, Antony, persuaded our aged primate, a most venerable man, to believe all his statements, and to commend him as altogether blameless to the venerable Pope Boniface. But why should I rehearse all the

---

[1] Page 226. [2] *P.L.* 33. 953.

rest, seeing the same venerable old man must have reported the whole affair to your holiness?

7.   . He, Antony, proclaims: "Either I ought to sit in my own see, or I ought not to be a bishop."   .

8. There are cases on record in which *the apostolic see, judging, or confirming the judgement of others,* [sanctioned decisions] by which persons were for offences neither deposed from their episcopal office, nor left altogether unpunished. I will not look into those very remote from our time; I shall mention recent cases. Let Priscus, a bishop of the province of Caesarea, proclaim: "Either the office of primate ought to be open to me as to others, or I ought not to remain a bishop." Let Victor, another bishop of the same province, with whom, when involved in the same penalty as Priscus, no bishop beyond his own diocese holds communion, let him, I say, protest: "Either I ought to have communion everywhere, or I ought not to have it in my own district." Let Lawrence,[1] a third bishop of the same province, speak, and in the precise words of this man exclaim: "Either I ought to sit in the chair to which I have been consecrated, or I ought not to be a bishop." But who will censure these judgements, unless he supposes either that all offences should be overlooked, or that all should be punished in one way?

9. Since, then, with pastoral and vigilant caution, the most blessed Pope Boniface has put in his letter about Bishop Antony the words, "if he has truthfully told us the facts", receive now the course of events which in his pamphlet he kept back, and also the things which were done after the letter of that man of blessed memory had been read in Africa; and in the mercy of Christ extend your aid to men imploring it more earnestly than he does from whose turbulence they desire to be freed. For either from himself, or at least from very frequent rumours, threats are held out that the courts of justice, and the public powers, and military force are to execute the decision of the apostolic see; and so these unhappy men, being now catholic Christians, dread severer treatment from a catholic bishop, than they dreaded from the laws of catholic

---

[1] Bp of Icosium.

emperors when they were heretics. Do not permit these things to be done, I implore you by the blood of Christ, by the memory of the apostle Peter, who has warned those placed over Christian people against violently lording it over the brethren.[1] I commend to the gracious love of your holiness both the catholics of Fussala, my children in Christ, and also Bishop Antony, my son in Christ, for I love both. *I do not blame the people of Fussala for bringing to your ears a just complaint against me* for imposing on them a man whom I had not proved, and who was in age at least not yet established, by whom they have been so afflicted.

Here then are definite cases of interference by the Pope in the affairs of the African church. Augustine gives no hint that they are unusual, and he actually implores the Pope to reverse the decision of the primate of Numidia, which was the province concerned. Can it then be said that the Pope did not possess a primacy of jurisdiction over Africa, or that there was no right of appeal by African bishops to Rome? Anglicans have argued: first, in the case of Antony himself, the fact that the threat of civil intervention had to be employed to carry into effect the Pope's decision shows that his interference was not accepted as of divine right by the African church.[2] Secondly, three recent cases of appeals to Rome by the African bishops, Priscus, Victor, and Lawrence (§ 8), may all have been allowed under the temporary agreement of the year 418 (Doc. 202 § 4). Denny[3] assumes this conjecture to be a fact. The only other mention that we get of any of these three bishops is that Lawrence signed the minutes of the council of Carthage in 419 as legate of his province.[4] One might suppose that this agreement would have ended in November 419, when copies arrived from the East proving that oversea appeals were not allowed by the Nicene canons. This means that the three bishops must have all got into trouble and taken their grievances to Rome within the space of eighteen months, and the case of Lawrence must have been dealt with in six months. This is not impossible, but Puller[5] follows Tillemont[6] in prolonging the agreement to the time of our next Document, in which the African bishops rubbed it in that appeals to Rome were not allowed by the Nicene canons (Doc. 208 § 4). The ground for this theory is that although the letter of the 419 council implies that the temporary agreement would end as soon as "the proof arrives" (Doc. 202 § 5), yet in the discussion that preceded the letter, the council had agreed that if the Nicene canons failed to justify the Roman claim to hear appeals, the agreement

[1] 1 Peter 5. 3.   [2] See Puller, 195.   [3] Page 306.
[4] *P.L.* 67. 224.   [5] Page 189.   [6] *Mémoires*, 13. 865.

would be discussed in another synod,[1] not that it would be annulled. Lastly, Puller[2] argued that those bishops who were dealt with by the Pope long ago may have been bishops in Italy, where the Pope was metropolitan.[2]

In the last Document, Augustine, as always,[3] shows respect to the papacy. But our next Document, written to the same Pope by a plenary African council, was not signed by the aged bishop of Hippo, and it reveals a different tone. Apiarius had broken out again; he had again appealed to Rome, and Faustinus, more obnoxious than ever, had again turned up in Carthage as papal legate.

DOCUMENT 208——Council of Carthage, A.D. 424,[4] *To Celestine (Optaremus).*
African Code 138. (*P.L.* 50. 423; *P.N.F.* 14. 509 ‡.)

To the lord and beloved and honourable brother Celestine, from Aurelius, Palatine, Antony, Totus, Servusdei, Terence, Fortunatus, Martin, Januarius, Optatus, Ceticius, Donatus, Theasius, Vincent, Fortunatian, and the rest assembled at Carthage in the general council of Africa.

1. We could wish that, just as your holiness intimated to us your joy at the arrival of Apiarius in your letter sent to us by our fellow presbyter Leo, so could we also reply with joy about his acquittal. The cheerfulness on both sides would be more certain, and would appear less hasty, if it had followed the hearing of the case. On the arrival of Bishop Faustinus, we assembled a council, and we believed that he had been sent with that man in order that, as by his help Apiarius had formerly been restored to the priesthood, so now he might by his labours be acquitted of the grave crimes charged against him by the people of Tabraca. But the course of examination by our council discovered such enormous crimes of his that they were too much even for the patronage and pleading which Faustinus substituted for judgement and justice. For first he resisted the whole council, and inflicted many insults, as if asserting the privileges of the Roman church, and wishing that he should be received into communion by us, because

1 *P.L.* 67. 186.   2 Page 195, n. 1.
3 See Docs. 162, 178 § 17, 191, 192, 194, 195.
4 A.D. 424: Hefele, 2. 480. A.D. 425 or 426: Coustant, *P.L.* 50. 422; Ballerini, *P.L.* 56. 121.

your holiness, believing him to have appealed, though unable to prove it, had restored him to communion. But such an action was not lawful, as you will realize better by reading the minutes. After a most laborious inquiry lasting three days, during which in the greatest affliction we investigated the various charges, God, the judge, strong and patient, cut short the obstructions of Bishop Faustinus, and the evasions of Apiarius himself, by which he tried to hide his foul enormities. For his disgusting obstinacy was overcome, by which he hoped to conceal all this dirty mire through an impudent denial; and our God so pressed his conscience, publishing even to men the secret crimes which he was already condemning in his swinelike heart, that in spite of his crafty denial, he broke forth into a confession of all the crimes with which he was charged, and of his own accord convicted himself of every kind of incredible infamy, and changed into groans even our hope by which we believed and wished that he might be cleared of such shameful blots, only that this our sadness was mitigated by one consolation, that he released us from the labour of a longer inquiry, and by a reluctant confession had applied some sort of remedy to his wounds, even though an unwilling one, lord brother.

2. Therefore with all due respect we earnestly beseech that in future you do not readily admit to a hearing persons coming hence, or further choose to receive to communion those who have been excommunicated by us, because you, venerable sir, will readily perceive that this has been defined even by the Nicene council. For though this seems there to be forbidden for the inferior clergy, or the laity, how much more did it wish the same to be observed in the case of bishops, lest those who are suspended from communion in their own province might seem to be restored to communion hastily or improperly by your holiness!

3. Let your holiness reject, as is worthy of you, that impudent sheltering with you of presbyters and lower clergy, because by no definition of the fathers has the church of Africa been deprived of this, and the Nicene decrees have plainly committed not only the clergy of inferior grade but the bishops

themselves to their own metropolitans. For they prudently and justly perceived that all business should be concluded in the place where it arose; and *they did not think that the grace of the Holy Ghost would be lacking in any province for the priests of Christ to discern wisely the right, and to hold it firmly*, especially since whoever thinks he is wronged by any judgement may appeal to the council of his province, or even to a general council; unless by chance there is anyone who believes that God can inspire *a single individual* with justice, and refuse it to *numberless priests assembled in council*. And how will the oversea judgement itself be valid, since it will be impossible to send thither the necessary witnesses, either on account of sex, or old age, or many other impediments?

4. For we have found in no patristic council that anyone should be sent from the side of your holiness, because, with regard to what you sent us by Bishop Faustinus as contained in the Nicene council, we can find nothing of the kind in the more authentic copies of that council, which we have received from Cyril, bishop of Alexandria, and from Atticus, prelate of Constantinople, and which we formerly sent .   to Bishop Boniface, your predecessor.

5. And further, do not send your clerical executors. Whoever wishes you to send them, do not comply, lest we should seem to introduce the smoky pride of the world into the Church of Christ, which offers the light of simplicity, and the day of humility, to those who desire to see God.

6. For now that the miserable Apiarius has been removed out of the Church of Christ for his horrible crimes, we are confident that through the uprightness and moderation of your holiness, Africa, without injury to brotherly love, will no longer have to endure our brother Faustinus. Lord and brother, may our Lord long preserve your holiness to pray for us!

(Gore 115.)

In their letter to Pope Boniface, the African bishops had said that, as far as they knew, the Nicene canons granted no right to bishops or others to appeal to Rome (Doc. 202 § 5). Now, having received reliable copies of the canons, they confirm this (§ 4) and further assert (§ 2) that such appeals are actually forbidden by Canon 5 of

Nicaea (see Doc. 62 § 5). They censure the Pope for using canons that are not genuine, to support his claim to interfere, but they stretch the Nicene canon to include bishops, which it does not do. They claim that the canon means "that all business should be concluded in the place where it arose" (§ 3), a phrase which looks back beyond Nicaea to Cyprian (Doc. 38 § 14).

Kidd's summing up of this angry letter is as follows: "Thus Africa vindicated its right, in matters of ecclesiastical order, to remain *sui juris*, while continuing in the unity of the Faith and without breach of communion. She recognized the primacy of the Roman See, so long as Rome made no claim to a primacy of jurisdiction. Coelestine accepted the situation."[1] Chapman had previously argued: If the Africans denied the Pope "all real jurisdiction in Africa, why did they take any notice of his repeated absolution of Apiarius? Why were they not indignant at his threatening to excommunicate, or summon to Rome, one of their bishops? Why did they not treat Faustinus, whose embassy was not authorized even by the Sardican canon, as a mere messenger, instead of the representative of a superior? Why did they not write to the Pope that he had no power to judge cases of appeal from Africa, whether of bishops or clerics? Why did not they add that to send clerical *executores* would be absurd, as they did not recognize their authority?"[2]

[1] *The Roman Primacy*, 105.   [2] *S.E.P.*, 205.

CHAPTER XXI

THE COUNCIL OF EPHESUS, 431

ROMAN CATHOLICS and Anglicans have both sought to use the council of Ephesus in support of their views. Chapman infers that the history of the council proves "that the Pope is indeed the head; he deposes the bishop of Constantinople, he is of greater authority than the council",[1] and also that the council admitted the supremacy of the Pope.[2] On the other hand Denny cites quotations from the acts and letters of the synod to show that in the year 431 the supreme authority in the Church was that of a universal council of bishops.[3]

When Augustine died, the bishops of the four chief sees were Celestine of Rome, Cyril of Alexandria, John of Antioch, and Nestorius of Constantinople. Nestorius was appointed in 428 and began his episcopate by persecuting heretics by means of the civil power; he proceeded to create a stir by criticizing the term "Mother of God", Θεοτόκος, as applied to our Lady. One of his friends went so far as to say, "It is impossible for God to be born of a woman".[4] In his first recorded sermon[5] Nestorius quotes John 3. 6, and shows that he was anxious to safeguard the humanity of Jesus, and to avoid making Mary into a goddess. His opponents saw in his teaching a depreciation of the divinity of Christ, and of the wonder and glory of the incarnation. And contemporaries observed that this attitude comes easily to those who have sympathies with Pelagianism, which depreciates the power of grace.[6] Cyril saw in the criticism of the title Θεοτόκος a denial of the divinity of Mary's Son, and he wrote an encyclical letter to that effect,[7] and thus the battle was joined on the doctrine of the incarnation between these two great eastern sees.

The Pope first heard of the controversy by the circulation of Nestorius' sermons in Rome early in 429, and he wrote to Cyril for information. He received two letters from Nestorius,[8] but over a year passed before he heard from Cyril.

---

[1] Page 91A.
[2] Page 114.
[3] Pages 170–179.
[4] Socrates, *H.E.* 7. 32.
[5] *Sermo* 1 § 7 (*P.L.* 48. 761).
[6] See Prosper, Doc. 230 § 58, and Cassian, *De Incarn. Christi*, 1. 3 (*P.L.* 50. 21).
[7] *Ep.* 1 § 4 (*P.G.* 77. 13).
[8] *P.L.* 50. 438–444.

DOCUMENT 209——Cyril of Alexandria, *Ep.* 11, to Celestine.
   About April 430.
   (*P.G.* 77. 80.)

Cyril sends greetings in the Lord to the most holy and beloved-of-God, the father Celestine.

1. . It would be more agreeable if we could keep silence, but God demands of us vigilance, and ancient church custom requires me to inform your holiness. . I have hitherto observed a profound silence, and have written neither to you nor to any other fellow priest on him who now is in Constantinople and governs the church there, because haste in such a case is a fault; but now that the evil has come to a climax, I feel bound to speak and explain all that has occurred.

3. .. The people now refuse to assemble at church with him [Nestorius], except a few light-headed ones, and those who take the opportunity to flatter him. Almost all the monasteries along with their archimandrites and many of the senate have stopped going to church for fear of receiving injury to their faith. . . .

5. Your holiness is also to know that we have all the oriental bishops with us; all are shocked and grieved, especially the bishops of Macedonia.

7. I was unwilling openly to sever communion with him until I had laid these facts before you. Deign therefore to decide what seems right,[1] whether we ought to communicate at all with him, or to tell him plainly that no one communicates with a person who holds and teaches what he does. Further the purpose of your holiness ought to be made known by letter to the most religious and God-loving bishops of Macedonia, and to all the bishops of the East, for we shall then give them, according to their desire, the opportunity of standing together in unity of soul and mind, and lead them to contend earnestly for the orthodox faith which is being attacked.

8. With reference to the matter in hand, our fathers, who have said that the Holy Virgin is Mother of God, are involved in the condemnation, along with us who are here to-day. For

---

[1] τυπῶσαι τὸ δοκοῦν.

although he did not like to do this[1] with his own lips, yet by sitting and listening to another, namely Dorotheus, he has encouraged him to do it, for immediately on leaving the throne, he communicated him at the holy mysteries.

9. And that your holiness may be well informed about his opinions, and about those of the fathers, I send you the books with the passages marked. I have had them translated as well as could be done at Alexandria. I also send you, by Possidonius, the letters I have written.   (Chapman 88A.)

The Pope, with the letters of both sides before him, called a council at Rome in August and himself approved of the word Θεοτόκος.

DOCUMENT 210——Celestine, *Address to the Council of Rome,*
   A.D. 430 (*Recordor beatae*).
   (*P.L.* 50. 457.)

1. I remember that on Christmas Day the late Ambrose made all the people sing with one voice to God: "O come, Redeemer of the nations, show forth the virgin birth; let every age marvel; such a way befits God."[2] Did he not say that "such a way befits God"? Therefore this agrees well with the meaning of our brother Cyril, when he calls Mary "Mother of God". "Such a way befits God." It is God whom the Virgin brought forth by the aid of almighty power.

This council condemned the teaching of Nestorius, and the Pope wrote to this effect to Cyril, Nestorius, and others.

DOCUMENT 211——Celestine, *Ep.* 11, to Cyril of Alexandria
   (*Tristitiae nostrae*).   11 August 430.
   (*P.L.* 50. 463.)

3. . . . If he, Nestorius, persists, an open sentence must be passed on him, for a wound, when it affects the whole body, must be cut away at once. For what has he to do with those

1 i.e. deny that Mary was Mother of God.
2 Ambrose, *Hymnus* 4 (*P.L.* 16. 1473).

who are of one mind, he who considers that he alone knows best, and dissents from our faith? Let those therefore remain in our communion whom this man has excluded from communion for opposing him; and tell him that he himself will be unable to retain our communion, if he continues in his way of error, opposing the apostolic teaching.

4. And so, *appropriating to yourself the authority of our see, and using our position,*[1] *you shall with resolute severity carry out this sentence,* that either he shall within ten days, counted from the day of your notice, condemn in writing this wicked assertion of his, and shall give assurance that he will hold, concerning the birth of Christ our God, *the faith which the Romans, and the church of your holiness,* and the universal religion holds; or if he will not do this (your holiness having at once provided for that church) he will know that *he is in every way removed from our body.*

5. We have written the same to our brothers and fellow bishops John, Rufus, Juvenal, and Flavian, so *our judgement* about him, or rather *the divine sentence of our Christ,* may be known.   (Chapman 88b.)

DOCUMENT 212——Celestine, *Ep.* 13, to Nestorius (*Aliquantis diebus*).   11 August 430.
      (*P.L.* 50. 483; Fleury[2] 3. 27 †.)

11. Take heed that unless you teach, about Jesus Christ our God, what the Roman, Alexandrian, and universal Catholic Church holds, and what up to your time was held by the holy church of Constantinople; and if within ten days after the receipt of this you do not openly and in writing condemn this impious novelty, which tends to undo what the ancient Scriptures join, you are excluded from the communion of the whole Catholic Church. We have directed this our sentence to be taken by my son, the deacon Possidonius, with all the documents, to the holy pontiff of the city of Alexandria, my fellow priest, that he may act in our room; and that our decree may be known to you and to all our brethren.

---

1 *auctoritate igitur tecum nostrae sedis ascita, nostrae vice usus.*
2 M. Fleury, *Ecclesiastical History,* E. T. by J. H. Newman, 1844.

Another of Celestine's letters, in a similar style, was to the
bishop of Antioch,[1] who in a friendly letter[2] urged Nestorius to yield.
But Cyril, instead of trying to reclaim the wandering sheep by kindness, sent him the famous *Cum Salvator*, in which he seems to regard
the condemnation as a joint affair of the councils of Rome and
Alexandria.

DOCUMENT 213——Cyril of Alexandria, *Third Letter to Nestorius*
(*Cum Salvator*).   November 430.
Cyril, *Ep.* 17.   (*P.G.* 77. 108; Kidd, *Docs.* 2. 256 †.)

2. Take notice then that in conjunction with the holy synod
which was assembled in great Rome, under the presidency of
our most pious and religious brother and fellow minister, Bishop
Celestine, we conjure and counsel you, in this third letter also,
to abstain from these mischievous and perverse doctrines, which
you both hold and teach, and to adopt in place of them the
orthodox faith delivered to the churches from the beginning
by the holy apostles and evangelists, who were both eye-
witnesses and ministers of the word. And unless you do this by
the time prescribed in the letter of our aforementioned most
pious and religious brother and fellow minister, Celestine,
bishop of the church of the Romans, know that you have
neither part nor lot with us, nor place nor account among the
priests and bishops of God. For it is impossible that we should
bear to see the churches thus thrown into confusion, and the
lay people scandalized, and the orthodox faith set aside, and
the flocks scattered abroad by you who ought rather to preserve them in safety, if you were, like us, a lover of sound
doctrine, treading in the religious footsteps of the holy fathers.
But with all, both laity and clergy, who have been excommunicated or deposed for faith's sake by your religiousness, we
all are in communion. For it is not just that those who hold the
true faith should be wronged by your sentence, for having
rightly withstood you. For this same thing you did signify in
your letter to our most holy fellow bishop Celestine, bishop of
great Rome.   .

5. There is then one Christ and Son and Lord, not as though
he were a man connected with God simply by a unity of dignity

[1] *P.L.* 50. 465.   [2] Mansi, 4. 1061.

or authority, for equality of honour does not unite natures: Peter and John are *equal in honour* in that they are apostles and holy disciples, but the two are not one.

(Gore 87; Chapman 88B.)

This letter enclosing the Pope's letter to Nestorius was crossed in the post by letters from the emperors, summoning a general council for 7 June 431.

DOCUMENT 214——The Emperors Theodosius and Valentinian, *To Cyril.* A.D. 430.
(Mansi 4. 1112.)

We wish the sacred doctrine to be discussed and examined in a holy synod, and that which seems to conform to the right faith to be ratified, whether those who are defeated are granted indulgence by the fathers or not. Further we by no means permit the cities and churches to be disturbed; but since we do not allow the doctrine to remain in dispute, *they ought to be judges of this affair who preside over the priesthood everywhere*, and through whom we ourselves are or shall be professing the truth.

DOCUMENT 215——The Emperors Theodosius and Valentinian, *To Cyril and to all Metropolitans.* Constantinople, 19 November 430.
(Mansi 4. 1113; Fleury 3. 41 †.)

Your piety therefore will do well, as soon as the approaching feast of Easter shall be passed, to repair to Ephesus so as to be ready by the day of Pentecost; you will bring with you such bishops as you shall think necessary, providing that a sufficient number remain to conduct the business of the province, and that so many as shall be sufficient may come to the council. . . In the meantime no one shall introduce privately any innovation until the holy synod be assembled and until *the common sentence of the same is given by all.*

The writers seem to regard the forthcoming council as supreme in the dispute, but they had not yet heard of the papal condemnation.

On 7 December the letters of Celestine and Cyril (Docs. 212, 213) were handed to Nestorius. The ten days allowed by the Pope therefore expired on 17 December, but apparently there was no question of abandoning the council. Chapman[1] says that "the Pope approved of the meeting of the council and . . . intended Nestorius to be granted a fresh trial". This is true, but does not explain why the council went ahead regardless of the papal sentence. The Pope's letters[2] approving the council were not written till May 431, and did not reach Ephesus till after the council had begun. Kidd[3] says that "Coelestine acquiesced" in the council. When Cyril heard about the proposed council, he found it necessary to ask the Pope whether Nestorius should appear as a member, or as a culprit already condemned by papal sentence. We learn this from Celestine's reply.

DOCUMENT 216——Celestine, *Ep.* 16, to Cyril of Alexandria
     (*Intelligo sententiam*).   7 May 431.
     (*P.L.* 50. 501.)

1. . . . We are replying briefly to your holiness.

2. You ask whether the holy synod ought to receive a man who condemns what it preaches; or, because the time of delay has elapsed, whether *the sentence already delivered* is in force. Concerning this matter let us consult the Lord in whose worship we are united. Will he not answer us straightway through the prophet, "I do not desire the death of one who dies"; and through the apostle Paul that he "willeth all men to be saved and come to know the truth"? Never is a quick repentance displeasing to God in any man.   (Chapman 88B.)

SESSION I

Cyril of Alexandria presided at the council, and is described in the acts as also holding the place of the Pope. But Chapman admits that he presided because he himself was the senior bishop present.[4] This is a stale controversy; for as long ago as 1595, Francis of Sales had asserted that "St Cyril presided as legate and lieutenant of Pope Celestine".[5] This was answered by de Launoy about eighty years later.[6]

[1] Page 89A.
[2] Doc. 216 and within Doc. 219.   [3] *Roman Primacy*, 107.
[4] Page 89.
[5] *Les Controverses*, E.T., 221.
[6] *Opera*, tom. 5, pt 2, p. 581 (edit. 1731).

DOCUMENT 217——Council of Ephesus: First Session. 22 June
    431.
    (Schwartz, Tom. 1, Vol. 1, pt 2, p. 3.)

In the most holy church which is called Mary, there were
present the bishops Cyril of Alexandria, who also held the
place of Celestine, the most holy and devout archbishop of the
Roman church; and Juvenal of Jerusalem and Memnon of
Ephesus; Flavian of Philippi, also representing Rufus, most
reverend bishop of Thessalonica

One hundred and fifty-eight bishops were present. Nestorius is
cited three times to attend. The creed is read, and then Cyril's
second letter to Nestorius,[1] in which he explains his doctrine of the
incarnation. Cyril then asks for approval of the letter, which is given
by 127 bishops speaking in turn. Among them:

Doc. 217 continued.   (Schwartz 14.)

Theodotus, bishop of Ancyra, said: "The letter of our most
religious and pious father,[2] the bishop Cyril, shows clearly and
openly the exposition of the faith by the 318 holy fathers who
met at Nicaea."

The bishops who have not spoken approve the letter by assent.
Then the letter of the Pope to Nestorius (Doc. 212) and the third
letter of Cyril to Nestorius (Doc. 213), in which he carries out the
Pope's instructions, are both read, but not discussed. After more
evidence a letter from Capreolus, bishop of Carthage, is read.

Doc. 217 continued.   (Schwartz 53 and *P.L.* 53. 845.)

".   Taught by the vigour of ancient authority, you have
driven from your midst the new doctrines which were not
formerly heard by the ears of the Church, and you have withstood any new and similar mistakes. Let not these things be
revived which the Church has previously opposed, and,
recently rejecting, has defeated *by the authority of the apostolic see*,
and by the unanimous decision of priests, lest a voice long since
swept away might appear to be renewed under the pretext of

---

[1] *Ep.* 4 (*P.G.* 77. 44).   [2] Cp. below, p. 246.

fresh discussions. . . For whoever desires that his decrees concerning the catholic faith should be permanent must confirm his opinion, not by his own authority, but *by the judgement of the ancient fathers*; so that in this way, corroborating his opinions partly by the decrees and sentences of the ancients and partly by those of the moderns, he may show that he asserts, teaches, and holds the one truth of the Church."

On the proposal of Cyril, it was agreed by all that this letter be inserted in the acts, since it "contains a most lucid expression of opinion". The council then passed sentence.

Doc. 217 continued.   (Schwartz 54; *P.N.F.* 14. 218 †.)

The holy synod said: "As, in addition to other things, the impious Nestorius has not obeyed our citation, and did not receive the holy bishops who were sent by us to him, we were compelled to examine his ungodly doctrines. We discovered that he had held and published impious doctrines in his letters and treatises, as well as in the discourses which he delivered in this city, and which have been testified. Urged of necessity thereto by the canons, and because of the letter[1] of our most holy father[2] and fellow servant Celestine, the bishop of the Roman church, we have come with many tears to this sorrowful sentence against him, namely that our Lord Jesus Christ, whom he has blasphemed, decrees by the holy synod that Nestorius be excluded from the episcopal dignity, and from all priestly communion." [198 signatures.]

(Chapman 89B, 90A.)

The canon to which they refer is the 73rd "Apostolic", which condemns a culprit who does not appear after three citations.[3]

The following day the above sentence was delivered to Nestorius in a rude note referring to him as "the new Judas".[4] During the week sermons were preached and letters were written including one by Nestorius to the emperors.[5] Then on Saturday the bishop of Antioch arrived with about fifteen bishops. These, with others of the same opinion already in Ephesus, immediately held a private meeting and decreed as follows:

[1] καὶ ἐκ τῆς ἐπιστολῆς.   [2] Cp. above, p. 245.   [3] Hefele, 1. 487.
[4] Schwartz, 64; Mansi, 4. 1228.   [5] Mansi, 4. 1232.

DOCUMENT 218——Conciliabulum at Ephesus.   27 June 431.
  (Mansi 4. 1268; Hefele 3. 57 †.)

The holy synod assembled at Ephesus by the grace of God
and the command of the pious emperors declares: We should
indeed have wished . . to hold a synod in peace, but since
you held a private meeting amongst yourselves from an heretical, insolent, and obstinate disposition, although we were
already nearby, and since you have filled both the city and the
holy synod with confusion, in order to prevent the examination
of your Apollinarian, Arian, and Eunomian heresies, and have
not waited for the arrival of the holy bishops of all regions   .
therefore shall you, Cyril of Alexandria, and you, Memnon of
this place, know that you are deposed and dismissed from all
priestly functions as the originators of the whole trouble.   .
You others who gave your consent are excommunicated, until
you acknowledge your fault and reform, accept anew the
Nicene faith without foreign addition, anathematize the heretical propositions of Cyril, which are clearly repugnant to the
teaching of the evangelists and apostles, and in all things
comply with the order of the emperors, who require a peaceful
and more accurate consideration of the questions of faith.

The above document was signed by John of Antioch and forty-two
other bishops, among them Theodoret of Cyrus, the historian.

SESSION II

The papal legates reached Ephesus a month after the time decreed
by the emperors, and explained that they had been held up by a
storm. They brought with them a letter from Celestine, which was
read in synod. From this letter Denny concludes that even the Pope
himself held that the supreme government of the Church was
episcopal: "The 'One Episcopate' succeeds to the 'One Apostolate'
in power and obligations."[1] On the other hand Tixeront thinks that
Celestine "said it was not his intention that Nestorius be judged
again; the decision of the Roman Council sufficed; the Council of
Ephesus had merely to promulgate that sentence and make it
ecumenical".[2] See § 5 of the letter below.

[1] Page 176. See also Kidd, *Hist. Ch.,* 3. 245.
[2] *History of Dogmas,* E. T., 3. 45.

DOCUMENT 219——Council of Ephesus: Second Session.
Friday, 10 July 431.
(Schwartz, Tom. 1, Vol. 1, pt 3, p. 53; editor, and *P.N.F.*
14. 219A †.)

In the episcopal residence of Memnon, there were present the bishops Cyril of Alexandria, who also held the place of Celestine, the most holy and blessed archbishop of the Roman church; Juvenal of Jerusalem; Memnon of Ephesus; Flavian of Philippi, who also kept the place of Rufus, most reverend bishop of Thessalonica; and Theodotus of Ancyra in Galatia I; and all as related before. Then those who came from the West entered and sat down: the most reverend bishops Arcadius and Projectus, and also the most beloved of God, Philip, a presbyter and legate of the apostolic see.

Philip said: "We bless the holy and adorable Trinity that our lowliness has been deemed worthy to attend your holy synod. For a long time ago our most holy and blessed Pope Celestine, bishop of the apostolic see, through his letter[1] to the holy and most pious man, Cyril, bishop of Alexandria, *gave judgement concerning the present cause* and affair, which letter has been shown to your holy assembly. And now again, for the corroboration of the catholic faith, he has sent through us letters to all your holinesses, which you will bid to be read with becoming reverence and to be entered on the ecclesiastical minutes."

Arcadius and Projectus, bishops and legates of the Roman church, said: "May it please your blessedness to give order that the letter of the holy and ever-to-be-mentioned-with-veneration Pope Celestine, bishop of the apostolic see, which has been brought by us be read, from which your reverence will be able to see what care he has for all the churches. . ."

And afterwards the most holy and beloved-of-God Cyril, archbishop of the church at Alexandria, spoke as is next in order. He said: "Let the letter of the most holy and most blessed Celestine, bishop of the apostolic see of Rome, be read to the holy synod with due honour." Siricius, notary of the holy catholic church of the city of Rome, read it. And after it

[1] Doc. 211.

had been read in Latin . . . all the most reverend bishops asked that it should be read in Greek. . . Arcadius and Projectus . . said: "The letter has been translated into Greek, and if you so command, let it be read." . Peter, presbyter of Alexandria and senior notary, read:[1]

1. A synod of priests gives witness to the presence of the Holy Ghost. For true is that which we read, since the truth cannot lie, to wit, the promise of the gospel: "Where two or three are gathered together in my name, there am I in the midst of them." And since this is so, if the Holy Ghost is not absent from so small a number, how much more may we believe he is present when so great a multitude of holy ones are assembled together! .

2. . For he wills that *all of us should perform that office which he thus entrusted in common to all.* We must needs follow our predecessors. Let us all, then, undertake their labours, since we are the successors in their honour. And we show forth our diligence in preaching the same doctrines that they taught, besides which, according to the admonition of the apostle, we are forbidden to add aught. For the office of keeping what is committed to our trust is no less dignified than handing it down. . We must strive in common to keep the faith which has come down to us to-day through the apostolic succession. For we are expected to walk according to the apostle. For now, not our appearance, but our faith is called in question.

3. . Let us be unanimous, thinking the same thing, for this is expedient; let us do nothing out of contention, nothing out of vain glory; let us be in all things of one mind, of one heart, when the faith which is one is attacked. . . .

5. Owing to our anxiety, we have sent our holy brethren and fellow priests, who are at one with us and are most approved men, Arcadius and Projectus, the bishops, and our presbyter, Philip, that they may be present at what is done and *may carry out what things have been already decreed by us.* To the performing of which we have no doubt that your holinesses

---

[1] The Latin version of this letter is *Ep.* 18 of Celestine: *Spiritus Sancti* (*P.L.* 50. 505).

will assent *when it is seen that what has been decreed is for the
security of the whole Church.* 8 May 431.

And all the most reverend bishops at the same time cried
out: "This is a just judgement. To Celestine, the modern
Paul! To *Celestine, the guardian of the faith! To Celestine, of one
mind with the synod!* To Celestine the whole Synod offers its
thanks! One Celestine! One Cyril! One faith of the Synod!
One faith of the world!"

Projectus, the most reverend bishop and legate, said: "Let
your holinesses consider the form of the writings of the holy
and reverend Pope Celestine, the bishop, who has exhorted
your holinesses (not as if teaching the ignorant, but as reminding
them that know) that those things which *he has long ago defined,*
and now thinks it right to remind you of, you may command
to be carried out to the uttermost, according to the canon of
the common faith, and according to the use of the Catholic
Church."

Firmus, the bishop of Caesarea in Cappadocia, said: "The
apostolic and holy see of the most holy bishop Celestine has
previously *given a decision* and formula in this matter, through
the writings which were sent to the most God-beloved bishops,
to wit, to Cyril of Alexandria,[1] and to Juvenal of Jerusalem,
and to Rufus of Thessalonica, and to the holy churches both of
Constantinople and of Antioch. This we have also followed
and . . . we carried into effect the formula, having pronounced
against him a canonical and apostolic judgement."

Arcadius, the most reverend bishop and legate, said:
"Although our sailing was slow, and contrary winds hindered
us, so that we did not know whether we should arrive at our
destination as we hoped, nevertheless by God's good providence . . .

". . Wherefore we desire to ask your blessedness that you
command that we be taught what has been *already decreed by
your holinesses.*"

Philip, presbyter and legate of the apostolic see, said: "We
offer thanks to the holy and venerable synod, that when the
letter of our holy and blessed Pope had been read to you, you

[1] Doc. 211.

holy members by your holy voices *joined yourselves to the holy head also by your holy acclamations.* For your blessedness is not ignorant that the blessed apostle Peter is head of the apostles and of the whole faith. We insignificant ones have now arrived after a stormy voyage and much hardship, and we request you give an order that those matters dealt with in this holy synod before our arrival be put before us, so that we too may ratify the decisions, in agreement with the opinion of our blessed Pope and of this holy assembly here present."

Theodotus, bishop of Ancyra, said: "*By the letter of the most religious bishop Celestine,* and by the coming of your holinesses, *the God of the universe has shown the sentence of the synod to be just.* For you have shown the zeal of the most holy and reverend bishop Celestine, and his care for the pious faith. And since, very reasonably, your reverence wishes to learn, from the minutes of the acts, what has been done about the deposition of Nestorius, your reverence will be fully convinced of the justice of the sentence, and of the zeal of the holy synod, and the harmony of the faith which the most pious and holy bishop Celestine has proclaimed with a great voice. Of course, after your full conviction, the rest shall be added to the acts."

(Chapman 89B, 90.)

We notice that when the bishops cheered the Pope's letter, they said that he agreed with the council, but Philip the legate is careful to explain that the cheering really meant that the bishops agreed with the Pope, their "holy head". The bishop of Ancyra thought that the papal letter proved that the sentence against Nestorius had been right.

SESSION III

The next day the bishop of Jerusalem opened the proceedings by asking whether the papal legates had read the minutes of the first session, and had understood them. Philip replied first.

DOCUMENT 220——Council of Ephesus: Third Session. Saturday, 11 July 431. (Schwartz, ibid., p. 59; *P.N.F.* 14. 223A †, and editor.)

Philip, presbyter and legate of the apostolic see, said: "We have read the acts and we have learnt what your holy synod has done in the case of Nestorius. From the minutes we find that everything has been carried out according to the canons and the discipline of the Church. And although it may be useless, we also seek from your honour that the documents read in your synod may now again be read to us also, so that we may follow the formula of the most holy Pope Celestine (who committed this care to us) and of your holiness, and may be able *to confirm the decisions.*"

Arcadius seconded this motion, and under the direction of the bishop of Ephesus, the condemnation of Nestorius was read again.

Doc. 220 continued.   (Schwartz 60.)

Philip, presbyter and legate of the apostolic see, said : " *There is no doubt, and in fact it has been known in all ages, that the holy and most blessed Peter, prince and head of the apostles, pillar of the faith, and foundation of the Catholic Church, received the keys of the kingdom from our Lord Jesus Christ, the Saviour and Redeemer of the human race, and that to him was given the power of loosing and binding sins : who, even to this time and always, lives and judges in his successors. Our holy and most blessed Pope Celestine the bishop is according to due order his successor and holds his place,* and he sent us to supply his presence in this holy synod which the most humane and Christian emperors have convened, bearing in mind and continually guarding the catholic faith. For they both have kept and are now keeping intact the apostolic doctrine handed down to them from their most pious and humane grandfathers and fathers of holy memory.   . Accordingly *the decision of all the churches is firm, for the priests of the eastern and western churches are present* in this priestly gathering either themselves or certainly by their legates.   'And his bishopric, another will take'. Wherefore Nestorius knows that he is alienated from the communion of the priests of the Catholic Church."

The opening words of the above speech were quoted by the Vatican Council of 1870 as coming from the council of Ephesus.[1] Twenty-six years later this was corrected by Pope Leo XIII, who quoted the

[1] *Pastor Aeternus* § 2: C. Butler, *Vatican Council*, 2. 280.

words as from Philip the legate, but pointed out that no voice was raised to dispute the papal claims made in the speech.[1] A recent Anglican writer has countered this by saying: "It is not the custom of Eastern bishops . . . to protest against the claims of Rome, when Rome is on their side. In such cases silence does not of itself imply consent."[2] It is probable, though not certain from his words, that Philip intended to imply that the Pope was the only successor of Peter. But compare the Pope's own words in § 2 of his letter read the day before.[3] Towards the end of his speech, Philip says that the condemnation of Nestorius is irrevocable, because the gathering is representative. Speeches by the other two legates followed, and then:

Doc. 220 continued.   (Schwartz 62 ; *P.N.F.* 14. 224A.)

Cyril, bishop of Alexandria, said: "The professions which have been made by Arcadius and Projectus, the most holy and pious bishops, and also by Philip, the most religious presbyter of the Roman church, are clear to the holy synod. For they have made their profession in the place of the apostolic see, and of the whole of the holy synod of the God-beloved and most holy bishops of the West. Consequently let those things which were *defined by the most holy Celestine,* the God-beloved bishop, be carried into effect, and the vote cast against Nestorius the heretic by the holy synod which met in the metropolis of Ephesus be agreed to unanimously; for this purpose let there be added to the acts already prepared the proceedings of yesterday and to-day, and let them be shown to their holinesses, so that by their subscriptions according to custom, *their canonical agreement with all of us* may be shown."

Arcadius, the most reverend bishop and legate of the Roman church, said: "According to the acts of this holy synod, we necessarily confirm their doctrines with our signatures."

The holy synod said: "Since Arcadius and Projectus, the most reverend and most religious bishops and legates, and Philip, the presbyter and legate of the apostolic see, have said that they are of the same mind with us, it only remains that they redeem their promises and confirm the acts with their

---

[1] *Satis Cognitum* § 13.
[2] H. E. Symonds, C.R., *The Church Universal and the See of Rome,* London, 1939, p. 122.
[3] See above, p. 249.

signatures, and then let the minutes of the acts be shown to them."

Philip, presbyter and legate of the apostolic see: "I have undersigned the minutes."

Arcadius, bishop and legate of the apostolic see: "I have signed the sentence against Nestorius which pronounces him to be the author of schism and heresy and every blasphemy and impiety."

Projectus, bishop and legate of the apostolic see: "I have signed *the just judgement of this holy and ecumenical synod*, assenting to all things, just as we have been informed through the acts, concerning the deposition of the impious Nestorius."

(Chapman 90B, 91A, 95A.)

DOCUMENT 221——Council of Ephesus, *To the Emperors Theodosius and Valentinian.* 11 July 431.
(Schwartz, ibid., p. 63; Fleury 3. 97 †.)

Most Christian Emperors! The God of all, having approved and accepted your pious care and earnestness, has stirred up the zeal of the western holy bishops to avenge the injury done to Christ. For though the length of the journey prevented the multitude of the holy bishops from coming to us, yet they assembled together, the most holy and pious Celestine, bishop of great Rome, presiding. And now they have approved with one accord our sentence concerning the faith, and those who differed they have pronounced to be cut off from the priesthood. And before the assembly of this synod, *Celestine, bishop of great Rome, showed* [the same opinion] *by his letter*[1] to Cyril, beloved of God, bishop of the great city of Alexandria, whom he appointed to act in his place. And now once more *he has confirmed this* by another letter[2] which he sent to the holy synod convened by Your Majesties in the city of Ephesus. He sent this letter by Arcadius and Projectus, most holy bishops, and Philip, most religious presbyter of great Rome, who represent Bishop Celestine. Moreover these men who came made known to us, by a letter to this our synod, *the opinion of*

[1] Doc. 211.   [2] Within Doc. 219.

the holy council of the whole West; they declared that they were likeminded with us in faith and religion, and they decreed the same as we and put it in writing. We inform Your Majesties of their agreement with us, that your pieties may rest assured that the judgement which went out from us is *the one common sentence of the whole world.*

The bishops ask that they may be allowed to go home. They have suffered from poverty, sickness, old age, and death. "Since the whole world is unanimous, except for the few who prefer the friendship of Nestorius to religion",[1] a new bishop of Constantinople should be appointed. The letter is signed by Cyril and all the bishops present.

DOCUMENT 222———Council of Ephesus, *To Celestine.*   17 July
   431.
   (*P.L.* 50. 512; *P.N.F.* 14. 237A ‡.)

The holy synod which by the grace of God was assembled at Ephesus, to the most holy and reverend fellow minister Celestine, health in the Lord.

1. The zeal of your holiness for piety, and your care for the right faith, so dear and pleasing to God the Saviour of us all, are worthy of all admiration. For it is your custom in such great matters to make trial of all things, and *to support the churches which you have made your own care.* But since it is right that all things which have taken place should be brought to the knowledge of your holiness, we are writing of necessity to inform you that, by the will of Christ, the Saviour of us all, and in accordance with the orders of the most pious and Christ-loving emperors, we assembled together in the metropolis of the Ephesians.

5. .   There were sitting with us the most reverend bishops Arcadius and Projectus, and with them the most holy presbyter Philip, all of whom were sent by your holiness, who gave to us your presence and filled the place of the apostolic see.   .

6. When there had been read in the holy synod what had been done touching the deposition of the most irreligious

---

1 Schwartz, ibid., p. 64, line 27.

Pelagians .   and those inclined to like errors, *we also con-sidered it right that the decisions of your reverence concerning them should stand strong and firm.*[1] And we are unanimous in holding them deposed. And, that you may know accurately all things that have been done, we have sent you a copy of the acts and of the subscriptions of the synod. We pray that you, dearly beloved and most longed-for, may be strong and mindful of us in the Lord.

[1] Cp. Doc. 188.

CHAPTER XXII

THE TIME OF POPE SIXTUS III

POPE CELESTINE died in 432 and was succeeded by Sixtus, who occupied the Roman see for eight years. During this period Vincent of Lerins wrote his *Commonitory*, a unique work to be considered in the next chapter. Other writers of the time include Cyril of Alexandria, Prosper of Aquitaine, Possidius of Africa, Praedestinatus, and the Greek historian Socrates.

I. CYRIL OF ALEXANDRIA

We have already seen (Doc. 213) that writing to Nestorius, Cyril declared Peter and John to be equal in honour. In our next Document we see that Thomas is called a universal teacher, and that our Lord's words "Feed my lambs" are regarded as restoring Peter to his apostolic office, which he had forfeited by his denial.

DOCUMENT 223——Cyril of Alexandria, *Commentary on John's Gospel*, Book 12.

On John 19. 25.   (*P.G.* 74. 661 ; *L.F.* 48. 633 †.)

No marvel if a woman fell into such an error, when even Peter himself, the elect [1] of the holy disciples, was once offended when Christ plainly told him that he would be betrayed.

On John 20. 28.   (*P.G.* 74. 733 ; *L.F.* 48. 690 †.)

The blessed Thomas without flinching confessed his faith in him, saying, "My Lord and my God". . . . To him who held this faith he says, at the end of the Gospel, "Go, make disciples of all nations". And if he bids him who was so minded teach all the nations and appointed him to instruct the world in his mysteries, he wishes us to have a like faith.

---

[1] πρόκριτος.

On John 21. 15–17.   (*P.G.* 74. 749; *L.F.* 48. 702 †.)

For the wondrous Peter, overcome by uncontrollable fear, denied the Lord three times. Christ heals the error done, and demands in various ways the threefold confession. . . . For although all the holy disciples alike fled .   . still Peter's fault in the threefold denial was in addition, special and peculiar to himself.   Therefore by the threefold confession of blessed Peter, the fault of triple denial was done away. Further by the Lord's saying "Feed my lambs", we must understand a renewal as it were of the apostleship already given to him, washing away the intervening disgrace of his fall, and the littleness of human infirmity.

(Gore 81 ; Chapman 48A note, 58A.)

Chapman [1] finds evidence for Cyril's belief in the primacy of Peter in his use of certain words to describe him. In the above Document Peter is "the elect of the holy disciples". On John 6. 68 we get "All speak by one, the chief" [2] (τοῦ προύχοντος). In the next two Documents he is called "the chosen one", and "the leader".

DOCUMENT 224——Cyril of Alexandria, *On the Holy Trinity*, Dialogue 4.
   (*P.G.* 75. 865.)

The divine Word pronounced Peter, the chosen one [3] of the holy apostles, to be blessed. For when, in the parts of Caesarea called Philippi, the Saviour asked "Who do men say that the Son of man is?"   . he cried out saying "Thou art the Christ, the Son of the living God", and speedily received the reward of his true conception about him, Christ saying "Blessed art thou   .", calling, I imagine, nothing else the rock, in allusion to his name, but the *immovable and stable faith* of the disciple on which the Church of Christ is founded and fixed without danger of falling.

---

1 Page 48A note.   2 *P.G.* 73. 613.
                3 τὸν ἔκκριτον.

DOCUMENT 225——Cyril of Alexandria, *Commentary on Luke's Gospel.*

On Luke 22. 31, 32.   (*P.G.* 72. 916.)

31. .   Therefore, passing over the other disciples, he comes to the leader [1] himself, and he says "Often Satan wished that he might sift you as wheat", for proof and trial. For it is Satan's way to attack those of good repute.

32. . Therefore when the Lord had hinted at the disciple's denial in the words that he used, "I have prayed for thee that thy faith fail not", he at once introduced a word of consolation, and said: "And do thou, when once thou art converted, strengthen thy brethren." That is, "*Be thou a support and a teacher of those who through faith come to me*". Again, marvel also at the insight of that saying and at the completeness of the divine gentleness of spirit. For so that he should not reduce the disciple to despair at the thought that after his denial he would have to be debarred from the glorious distinction of being an apostle, he fills him with a good hope, that he will attain the good things promised. In fact he says "And when thou art converted, strengthen thy brethren". O loving kindness! The sin was not yet committed, and he already extends his pardon and sets him again in his apostolic office.

(Chapman 59A.)

As regards the primacy of Rome, Cyril tells us that the Pope of his day confirmed the acts of the council of Ephesus.

DOCUMENT 226——Cyril of Alexandria, *Ep.* 40, to Acacius of Melitene.   A.D. 434.

(*P.G.* 77. 201.)

. . If anyone brings you a letter purporting to have been written by Philip, most reverend presbyter of the Roman church, and reading just as if the most holy bishop Sixtus had resented the deposition of Nestorius, and had helped him, do not believe it. For he [Sixtus] wrote in harmony with the holy synod, and confirmed all its acts, and is in agreement with us.

(Chapman 114B note.)

---

[1] κορυφαῖον.

For Cyril's views on Christian unity, Pusey[1] quotes a long extract from his comments on John 17. 21, "That they may all be one". I give a small portion only.

DOCUMENT 227——Cyril of Alexandria, *Commentary on John's Gospel*, Book 11.
   (*P.G.* 74. 560; *L.F.* 48. 550 ‡.)

11. .   Through the mystical communion of his own body, which is one, he blesses those who believe in him, and he makes us one body with himself and with each other. For who shall divide and eject from a natural union with one another those who through the one holy body are bound up into oneness with Christ? For if "we all partake of the one bread", we are all made one body. For Christ cannot be divided; therefore the Church is also called "the body of Christ", and we too are "members in particular", according to the mind of Paul. For we all, being joined to the one Christ through the holy body (in which we have received in our own bodies him, the one and indivisible), owe our membership more to him than to ourselves. And that while the Saviour is accounted the head, the Church is called the rest of the body, as members joined together, Paul will show by the words: [Eph. 4. 14–16].
   (Gore 32 note.)

II. POPE SIXTUS

The Pope expresses his own views on the Roman primacy in a letter to the bishop of Antioch, after the latter had made up his quarrel with Cyril (see Doc. 218).

DOCUMENT 228——Sixtus III, *Ep.* 6, to John, Bishop of Antioch (*Si ecclesiastici*).   17 September 433.
   (*P.L.* 50. 609.)

5.   . Let us at God's bidding rejoice in a good and pleasant thing, for once again we begin as "brethren to dwell together in unity". We wish your holiness to proclaim what

1 *Eirenicon* (1865), pp. 48–51.

you write. From the outcome of this affair you have learnt what it means to be in agreement with us. The blessed apostle *Peter, in his successors, has handed down what he received.* Who would be willing to separate himself from the doctrine of him whom the Master himself instructed first among the apostles? It was not hearsay or selected speech which taught him; he was trained with the others by the mouth of the teacher. He had not to search among writings and writers; he received the original and direct faith which can admit of no dispute, on which we must always meditate, and in which we must abide, so that following the apostles with a pure affection, we may be counted apostolical. (Chapman 94A.)

III. PROSPER

From the remaining Documents in this Chapter, we learn how five contemporary writers saw the Roman primacy in action. Prosper, born in the south of France, was a young layman, zealous for the teaching of Augustine against the Pelagians.

DOCUMENT 229——Prosper of Aquitaine, *Carmen de Ingratis*, Part I.   A.D. 429.
(*P.L.* 51. 96.)

Ll. 33–46: While mad error was spreading such things abroad, and misleading untutored ears with pernicious false-hoods, there was at hand, with God's encouragement, the dutiful devotion of the holy fathers, which was provided throughout the world, and which with one accord destroyed the dreadful foe with heavenly missiles. For at the same time the one Spirit thundered with the same decrees. *First to hew down the oncoming scourge was Rome, the see of Peter, which, having been made capital of the world's pastoral office, holds by religion what-ever it does not hold by arms.* Next, and not lingering behind, sprang forward the guardian of the eastern leaders, and, capturing the originator of the infamous doctrine, con-strained him with a kindly enactment to repudiate his own false teaching, unless he preferred to be separated from the body of Christ, and to be cut off from the congregation of saints. (Chapman 79A.)

About the year 431 Prosper went to Rome to interest Pope Celestine against the semi-Pelagians of Marseilles, who were led by John Cassian. His chief work, *Contra Collatorem*, was written against some writings of Cassian called *Collationes*. Prosper is trying (§ 60) to gain Pope Sixtus over to Augustinian opinions on predestination and irresistible grace.[1]

DOCUMENT 230——Prosper, *Liber contra Collatorem* 21.
    A.D. 432.
    (*P.L.* 45. 1830.)

57.   We do not have to fight against your party afresh, nor have we to begin battles against an unknown foe; the war engines of your party were smashed and fell clattering among those who were sharers, yes, and leaders of their insolence, at the time when Innocent of blessed memory struck the heads of deadly error with the apostolic sword;[2] when the synod of the bishops of Palestine constrained Pelagius to come out with his views, to his own undoing and that of his followers; when Pope Zosimus[3] of blessed memory added the strength of his official support to the decrees of the African councils, and armed the right hands of all prelates with the sword of Peter for the striking down of the ungodly; when Pope Boniface of saintly memory rejoiced at the catholic devotion of the most pious emperors, and made use not only of apostolic but also of imperial edicts against the enemies of God's grace; and when he also, very learned as he was, invoked nevertheless the replies of the blessed Bishop Augustine against the books of the Pelagians.[4]

58.   Moreover the pontiff Celestine of venerable memory (to whom the Lord bestowed many gifts of his grace for the protection of the Catholic Church) knew that to those who have been condemned there should be offered, not an investigation of the judgement, but only the remedy of penitence. Therefore he ordered Celestius (who demanded a hearing as if the matter had not been discussed) to be exiled from the bounds of all Italy. In this way he determined that neither the rulings of

[1] See Augustine, *De Predestinatione Sanctorum* : *P.L.* 44. 959.
[2] Docs. 179, 180.   [3] Doc. 190 § 9.
[4] Doc. 194.

his predecessors, nor the decrees of the synods, should be revocable, so that what once had deserved to be eradicated, should never be allowed a further consideration. And with no less active care he freed the Britains from this same disease, for he shut off from that retreat of the ocean certain enemies of God's grace who were occupying the soil of their birth. And whilst he made the Roman island catholic, he made also the barbarous island Christian, by ordaining a bishop for the Scots.[1] Through this man, too, the eastern churches were purged of the twin plagues, when help was given by the apostolic sword[2] to that most glorious defender of the catholic faith, Cyril, prelate of the city of Alexandria, for the suppression of the Nestorian impiety. In this way even the Pelagians, who were confederate in their known errors, were again laid low.

60. . . . That the snares of the heretics be not perpetuated, we trust that by the protection of the Lord it will come to pass that what he worked in Innocent, Zosimus, Boniface, and Celestine, he will also work in Sixtus, and that in the guardianship of the Lord's flock, there is reserved to this shepherd the special glory of expelling hidden wolves, as they did the open ones.   (Chapman 79A.)

Our next Document, sometimes called *The Syllabus on Grace*, was discovered among the papal archives[3] in the sixth century, and mistakenly appended by Dionysius Exiguus to Celestine's *Epistle* 21; it came to be printed as §§ 4–15 of that letter. Its authorship was assigned by Coustant[4] to Prosper, but the modern view[5] is that it was probably written by Leo the Great, who was archdeacon of Rome at the time.

DOCUMENT 231——*Quia nonulli.*   A.D. 435.
    (*P.L.* 45. 1756.)

4. Whereas not a few who glory in the name catholic linger in the condemned opinions of heretics, whether by wickedness

[1] Palladius.   [2] Doc. 213.
[3] Jalland, *Leo*, 41, n. 31.   [4] *P.L.* 50. 525.
[5] Tixeront, *History of Dogmas*, 3. 279; Duchesne, 3. 199; Kidd, *Hist. Ch.*, 3. 156.

or by inexperience, and presume to dispute with pious champions, and, while they do not hesitate to anathematize Pelagius and Celestius, yet speak against our teachers as those who go beyond the right measure, and whereas *they profess to follow and approve only what the most sacred see of the most blessed apostle Peter, through the ministry of its presidents, has ratified and* taught against the enemies of God's grace, it has become necessary diligently to inquire what the directors of the Roman church have judged concerning the heresy which arose in their times, and what they considered should be held about God's grace, against the most noxious defenders of free will.

At the same time we shall add some decisions of African councils, which without doubt *the apostolic prelates made their own when they approved them.* Therefore, in order that those who doubt about any point may be instructed, we make the constitutions of the holy fathers plain in a comprehensive syllabus, by which if anyone is not too contentious, he may recognize that the whole dispute is summed up in the short quotations which follow, and that no reason for contradiction remains to him, if he believes and speaks with catholics.

[Here follow §§ 5–9, which give extracts from *Epp.* 29 and 30 of Pope Innocent, from the *Tractoria* of Pope Zosimus, and from the reply of the African bishops.]

10. For God so works in the hearts of men, and in free will itself, that holy thought, pious counsel, and every motion of good will is from God: whereas through him we can do anything good, without him we can do nothing. Indeed the same doctor, Zosimus, established this declaration when he spoke in support of divine grace to the bishops of the whole world. [Here follows another extract from the *Tractoria*.]

11. Furthermore that which is laid down among the decrees of the Carthaginian synod, as it were *embracing the possession of the apostolic see*: [here follow Canons 3, 4, and 5 of the council of Carthage, 1 May 418].

12. Besides the *inviolable sanctions of the most blessed and apostolic see*, by which the most devout fathers, trouncing enthusiasm for pernicious novelties, have taught us to ascribe to the grace of Christ both the beginning of good will, and any

progress in laudable endeavours, and perseverance therein to
the very end, let us also be mindful of the sacraments of priestly
intercession, which, having been handed down by the apostles,
are celebrated in the same way throughout the world and in
the whole Catholic Church, that the law of prayer may
determine the law of belief.

[§ 13 explains that the uniform ritual and universal practice
of infant baptism imply the need of casting out evil spirits.]

14. Therefore by these ecclesiastical rules, and by documents
selected from divine authority, the Lord helping us we are so
strengthened . . .

15.   . And so, for the establishment of the grace of God
(whose works and honour may by no means be deprecated),
*we believe to be quite enough whatever the writings of the apostolic see
have taught us,* according to the aforesaid rules; so that we absolutely regard as not catholic anything that is seen to be contrary to the decisions we have just quoted.

(Chapman 81B, 82A, 114B.)

The writer clearly believes in the primacy of Rome as guardian of
the faith. All that matters is to discover what the Popes have said.
Other decisions are of interest because the Popes approved them
(§ 4), or because they embraced the papal opinions (§ 11). The
sanctions of the apostolic see are inviolable (§ 12), and are amply
sufficient to establish our faith in divine grace.

IV. POSSIDIUS

Possidius takes us back nearly twenty years to the beginning of the
Pelagian troubles. This African bishop clearly believed that the Pope
had the right to decide the faith for all catholics, and that he exercised
that right.

DOCUMENT 232——Possidius, *Vita Augustini.* A.D. 437.
(*P.L.* 32. 48; Chapman 80.[1])

18. . . . Augustine strove for nearly ten years, writing and
publishing books, and frequently speaking about the Pelagian
errors. And since these heretics were trying to bring the

[1] Chapman's extract begins at the second sentence; I have added the
first.

apostolic see round to their view, African councils of holy bishops also did their best to persuade the holy Pope of the city (first the venerable Innocent, and afterwards his successor, Zosimus) that this heresy was to be abhorred and condemned by catholic faith. And these bishops of so great a see successively branded them, and cut them off from the members of the Church, giving letters to the African churches in the West, and to the churches of the East, and declared that they were to be anathematized and avoided by all catholics. The judgement pronounced upon them *by the Catholic Church of God* was heard and followed also by the most pious emperor Honorius, who condemned them by his laws, and ordered them to be treated as heretics. Wherefore many of them have returned to the bosom of holy Mother Church, whence they had wandered, and are yet returning, as the truth of the right faith becomes known against this detestable error.   (Chapman 80, 81.)

V. PRAEDESTINATUS

It is less clear that Praedestinatus believed a papal sentence against a heretic to be equivalent to condemnation by the Catholic Church, but it is possible to read him in that sense. As an historian he is unreliable. Soter died in 171, but Praedestinatus makes him condemn the Tertullianists, whereas Tertullian flourished in the next century. This is only one example of the writer's inveracity. It is therefore a pity that Chapman uses § 26 as evidence of papal authority in the second century. Writing from the point of view of his own day, Praedestinatus assumed that any heretic would have been condemned by the bishop of Rome.

DOCUMENT 233——Praedestinatus, *De Haeresibus.*   A.D. 440.
     (*P.L.* 53. 596.)

26. The Cataphrygians arose as the twenty-sixth heresy, taking their name from the province whence they came .
holy Soter, Pope of the city, wrote a book against them, and so did Apollonius, the president of the Ephesians, against whom Tertullian, a presbyter of Carthage, wrote. Tertullian always wrote extremely well, but he laid himself open to blame in this

only, that he defended Montanus and attacked the aforesaid Soter, Pope of the city.

86. We read that once upon a time the Tertullianists were condemned by Soter, the Roman Pope. . . .

88. . Opposition of all kinds was charged against Celestius to condemn him, but he argued that he was orthodox in many of these matters, and that he could not be condemned in respect of the rest. Then, when the matter was referred to him by almost all the African bishops,[1] Pope Innocent condemned Pelagius and Celestius.[2] But they, both before and after they were *condemned by the universal Church*, did not stop writing to the effect that man can be without sin, and that Adam did not damage the human race.

(Chapman 66A, 79A.)

VI. SOCRATES

From Rome, Gaul, and Africa, we pass to the East for the evidence of Socrates, a Church historian of Constantinople. He looks back a hundred years to the time of Athanasius.

DOCUMENT 234——Socrates, *Ecclesiastical History*, Book 2.
   A.D. 439.
   (*P.G.* 67. 196; Bagster 119 ‡.)

8. . There were present at this synod of Antioch ninety bishops from various cities. But Maximus, bishop of Jerusalem, who had succeeded Macarius, did not go, remembering that he had been deceived and induced to subscribe to the deposition of Athanasius. Neither was Julius, bishop of great Rome, there, nor did he send a representative, although *the ecclesiastical canon orders that the churches may make no ordinances contrary to the mind of the bishop of Rome*.

15. Athanasius at last reached Italy. . At the same time, Paul of the city of Constantinople, Asclepas of Gaza, Marcellus of Ancyra of Galatia Minor, and Lucius of Adrianople, having been expelled from their churches on various charges, reached royal Rome. Each of these laid his case before Julius, bishop of

[1] Docs. 176, 177, 178.   [2] Docs. 179, 180.

Rome, who, exercising *the privilege of the church in Rome*, fortified them with outspoken letters, and sent them back to the East, restoring to each his proper place, and upbraiding those who had hastily deposed them. They sailed away from Rome, and *trusting to the impresses of Bishop Julius*, they again took possession of their own churches, forwarding the letters to those to whom they were addressed. These people considered themselves treated with indignity by the reproaches of Julius; they assembled in council at Antioch, and dictated a reply to his letters, as the expression of the feeling of the whole synod. *It was not his province, they said, to notice their decisions* in reference to any whom they might wish to expel from their churches, seeing that they had not opposed him when Novatus was ejected from the Church. These things the eastern bishops sent to Julius, bishop of Rome.

17.   When Julius, bishop of Rome, was aware of these fresh plots of the Arians against Athanasius, and had also received the letter of Eusebius, then dead, he summoned Athanasius, having learnt where he was hidden. The letter of the bishops who had previously assembled at Antioch reached him just then, with others from the bishops in Egypt assuring him that the charge against Athanasius was a fabrication. On receipt of these contradictory documents, Julius first replied to the bishops who had written to him from Antioch, complaining of the acrimonious feeling they had shown in their letter, and charging them with a violation of the canons, because they had not summoned him to the council (*the ecclesiastical canon orders that the churches may make no ordinances contrary to the mind of the bishop of Rome*), and saying that they deceitfully perverted the faith.   (Chapman 38B note, 74A note.)

Pope Julius had actually said that "according to the ecclesiastical canon" complaints against Marcellus and Athanasius should have been sent "to us all, so that justice might be determined by all".[1] So the inaccurate comments of Socrates express an eastern opinion of the fifth century. He says that Julius, as bishop of Rome, had the privilege of restoring the leading bishops to their sees, that his primacy was such that the churches might not legislate against his opinion, and that this latter prerogative had been granted by ecclesiastical

[1] Doc. 67 § 35.

canon. This witness of Socrates is the more remarkable, since he disliked the recent policy of the Roman see.

DOCUMENT 235——Socrates, *Ecclesiastical History*, Book 7.
    A.D. 439.
    (*P.G.* 67. 757; Bagster 475 ‡.)

11.   . This Celestine took away the churches from the Novatianists at Rome, and forced their bishop, Rousticula, to hold meetings packed in houses. Until then the Novatianists had flourished greatly at Rome, possessing many churches, well attended. But envy attacked them also, and the Roman episcopate, like that of Alexandria, went beyond the office of the priesthood, to its present state of domination. And from then the bishops would not allow even those who agreed with them to assemble in peace, but took away all they had, only praising them for their agreement. But those in Constantinople did not behave like that.

In view of Cyprian's remarks,[1] quoted by Chapman, to the effect that the Church cannot be divided, it is perhaps not out of place to give here one more extract from Socrates, for he seems to say that it actually was divided in the fourth century.

DOCUMENT 236——Socrates, *Ecclesiastical History*, Book 2.
    A.D. 439.
    (*P.G.* 67. 245; Bagster 151 ‡.)

22. When those convened at Sardica,[2] as well as those who had formed a separate synod[3] at Philippopolis in Thrace, had each done what they considered right, they returned to their own cities. The West therefore was separated from the East, and the boundary of communion between them was the hill called Tisoukis, which belongs to the people of Illyria and Thrace. As far as this hill, there was indiscriminate communion, though the faith happened to be different; but beyond they did not communicate with one another. Such was the confused state of the churches at that time.

---

[1] Doc. 37 §§ 5, 6, 23. See pp. 57–58.
[2] See pp. 99–107.   [3] Doc. 68.

CHAPTER XXIII

VINCENT OF LERINS

In the dispute between Roman Catholics and Anglicans, both sides appeal with confidence to the well-known *Commonitory* of Vincent. His main point is made at the end of the second chapter.

DOCUMENT 237——Vincent of Lerins, *Commonitorium*. A.D. 434.
  (*P.L.* 50. 640; Bindley [1] 26 †.)

2. . . . In the Catholic Church itself we must take great care that we hold that which has been believed *everywhere, always, by all*. For that is truly and properly catholic, as the very force and meaning of the word show, which comprehends everything almost universally. And we shall observe this rule if we follow *universality, antiquity, consent*. We shall follow universality if we confess that one faith to be true which the whole Church throughout the world confesses; antiquity, if we in no wise depart from those interpretations which it is plain that our holy ancestors and fathers proclaimed; consent, if in antiquity itself we eagerly follow the interpretations and decisions of all, or certainly nearly all, priests and teachers alike.

(Gore 39, 45, 58; Chapman 39B.)

The R.C. communion is world-wide, so that there are a number of people everywhere who believe in the universal jurisdiction of the Pope. They claim that this belief is rooted in antiquity, and is based on our Lord's words to Peter. According to Chapman, some of the opinions of Gore, far from fulfilling the rule of Vincent, "are better described by recently, in England and by a few".[2] The Anglican communion is also world-wide with members in every continent. These people affirm their faith in "the Holy Catholick Church" and deny the universal jurisdiction of the Roman see.[3] They claim that such jurisdiction has not got the consent of antiquity, or "anything

[1] T. H. Bindley, *The Commonitory of St Vincent of Lerins*, London, 1914.
[2] Page 40A.
[3] Article 37.

approaching to a consent".[1] Vincent cannot answer our inquiries for us, but he encourages us to pursue them, and he throws light here and there on some aspects of the subject. For example, Roman Catholics often claim as evidence for the truth of their beliefs the fact that they are held by "half the Christians of the world".[2] Vincent does not recognize this claim as valid, for his knowledge of the Arian heresy made him see that almost the whole Church can be infected by a new heresy. The appeal to universality fails, unless it is backed by an appeal to antiquity.

Doc. 237 continued.   (*P.L.* 50. 640; Bindley 27 †.)

3. What, then, will the catholic Christian do if any part of the Church has cut itself off from the communion of the universal faith? What surely but prefer the soundness of the whole body to a pestilent and corrupt member? What if some novel contagion seek to infect *the whole Church*, and not merely a small portion of it? Then he will take care to cling to antiquity, which cannot now be seduced by any fraud of novelty. What if in antiquity itself error be detected on the part of two or three men, or perhaps of a city, or even of a province? Then he will look to it that he prefer *the decrees of an ancient general council*, if such there be, to the rashness and ignorance of a few. But what if some error spring up concerning which nothing of this kind is to be found? Then he must take pains to find out and compare the opinions of the ancients (provided, of course, that such remained in the communion and faith of the one Catholic Church, although they lived in different times and places), conspicuous and approved teachers; and whatever he shall find to have been held, written, and taught, not by one or two only, but by all equally and with one consent, openly, frequently, and persistently, that he must understand is to be believed by himself also, without the slightest hesitation.

(Gore 39, 48, 59.)

Our author explains that when, in the third century, the novelty of rebaptism was introduced, it was the Pope who kept the Church to the ancient ways, and his opinion which prevailed, in spite of the council of Carthage in 256.

[1] Gore, 91.   [2] Chapman, 37A note.

Doc. 237 continued.   (*P.L.* 50. 645 ; Bindley 35 †.)

6.   . But not to labour the point, we will take one such
example, and that a very conspicuous one, from *the apostolic
see*; so that it may be clearer than daylight to everyone with
how great energy, zeal, and argument the blessed successors
of the blessed apostles have always defended the integrity of
the faith they have once for all received. It happened in the
past that Agrippinus, bishop of Carthage, of venerable memory,
was the first of all mortals to think it right to rebaptize, contrary to the divine canon, contrary to the rule of the universal
Church, contrary to the feeling of all his fellow bishops, contrary to ancestral custom and regulations. And this innovation
brought about such an amount of evil that it afforded to all
heretics an example of sacrilege, and even to some catholics an
occasion of error. When, then, all protested against the new-
ness of this practice, and the priests everywhere, each as his
zeal prompted him, opposed it, Pope Stephen[1] of blessed
memory, prelate of the apostolic see, *acting indeed with his
colleagues, but even so before them*, opposed it, thinking it right, as
I imagine, so far to excel all the rest in his devotion to the faith
as *he surpassed them by the authority of his place*. Accordingly, in a
letter which he sent then to Africa, he sanctioned these words :
"Let nothing be innovated beyond what has been handed
down."[2] For that holy and prudent man knew that the policy
of piety does not permit any other rule than that the selfsame
things which have been received as of faith from the fathers
should be taught under seal of faith to the children ; and that
we are bound to follow whither orthodoxy leads us, not to lead
orthodoxy whither we wish ; and that it is the peculiar property of Christian modesty and earnestness not to hand down
to posterity our own fancies, but to preserve what has been received from our forefathers. What, then, was the ultimate issue
of the whole question? Only what was usual and customary.
Antiquity was retained, novelty was repudiated. But perchance
patronage was lacking to the introduction of that novelty. Nay,
it had on its side such force of genius, such floods of eloquence,

[1] A.D. 254–257.   [2] Doc. 48 § 1.

such a number of partisans, so close a resemblance to the truth, such textual support in the Bible (only obviously interpreted in a new and wrong sense), that it seems to me the whole of that combination could not have been destroyed in any other way but by the very essence of the great stir itself—that which began it, that which defended it, that which applauded it— its boasts of novelty! And what validity in the end had that African council or its decrees? None whatever, thanks to God; but the whole affair, like a story, like a dream, like refuse, was effaced, rejected, and trampled under foot.

(Chapman 42A, note 1, 57A note.)

On the dispute about rebaptism see Chapter IX. Roman Catholics say that the present papal claims are a development of the earliest teaching of the Church. In the course of centuries the Church realized the implications of our Lord's words to Peter. Vincent was the first to establish this doctrine of development.

Doc. 237 continued.   (*P.L.* 50. 667; Bindley 89 †.)

22.   . . Still teach the same things that you learnt, so that although you speak in a new way, you do not speak new things.

23. But some one will say perhaps, "Is there, then, to be no religious progress in Christ's Church?" Progress certainly, and that the greatest. For who is he, so jealous of men and so odious to God, who would attempt to forbid it? But progress, mind you, of such sort that it is a true advance, not a change, in the faith. For progress implies a growth within the thing itself, while change turns one thing into another. Consequently the understanding, knowledge, and wisdom of each and all—of each churchman and of the whole Church—ought to grow and progress greatly and eagerly through the course of ages and centuries, provided that the advance be on its own lines, in the same sphere of doctrine, the same feeling, the same senti- ment. The religion of souls should follow the nature of bodies, which, though they develop and unfold their measures in the course of years, yet remain the same as they were. . . . For it is right that those ancient dogmas of heavenly philosophy

should in the process of time be tended, smoothed, and polished. It is not right for them to be changed, maimed, mutilated. They may gain evidence, light, and distinction, but they must keep fullness, integrity, and peculiarity. . . What else had the councils in view in their decrees except that what before was believed in simplicity might thenceforward be believed more intelligently; and that what before was preached coldly might thenceforward be preached more fervently; and that what before was practised carelessly might thenceforward be performed with solicitude? This, I say, and nothing but this, has the Catholic Church ever accomplished by the decrees of her councils when roused by the novelties of heretics—to consign in writing to posterity the truths she had previously received only by tradition, comprising a vast amount of matter in a few words, and often, for the better understanding, never for a new meaning, of the faith, using a new characteristic word.   (Gore 56, 57; Chapman 26B, 27B.)

This chapter on development is interesting and is quoted at even greater length by Gore and Chapman; but it does not help us, for Vincent does not tell us how to decide whether a doctrine is new, or a development of the old. For that decision we must either accept some modern authority, or fall back on our own judgement. In § 3 above our author declares his faith in general councils. He returns to this point frequently, adding that the opinion of a single bishop, however holy, cannot be relied upon.

Doc. 237 continued.   (*P.L.* 50. 674; Bindley 106 †.)

27.   . Likewise in this very antiquity they must first of all prefer to the rashness of one or of a very few *the decrees of a general council* (if such there be); secondly, they must follow what is next best, *the consentient opinions of many and great teachers.*   .

28.   Only the opinions of those fathers are to be collected who holily, wisely, and constantly lived, taught, and *remained in the catholic faith and communion*, or who were happily counted worthy to die in Christ or to be slain for his sake. And yet even these are to be trusted only on this condition, that whatever all or the majority, in one and the same sense, openly,

frequently, and persistently (as if forming a consentient council of teachers) have confirmed by receiving, holding, and handing on, that only is to be received as indubitable, fixed, and settled. Whatever any holy man has held, be he bishop, confessor, or martyr, other than or contrary to all, that must be regarded as in the class of his private opinions, peculiar and personal to himself, altogether lacking the authority of the common, general, and public opinion. Otherwise we should, to the greatest risk of our eternal safety and after the sacrilegious manner of the heretics and custom of the schismatics, be following the erroneous novelties of one man, and setting aside the ancient truth of universally received teaching.

29. . . . First they should ascertain whether anything has been decreed of old by all the priests of the Catholic Church with the authority of a general council; secondly, if any new question has arisen respecting which no such decrees can be found, recourse must be had to the opinions of the holy fathers, of those, that is, who in their own times and places, remaining in the unity of communion and faith, stood forth as approved teachers; and then whatever they shall be found to have held with one mind and consent, that should be judged without any scruple to be the true and catholic doctrine of the church. And lest we should seem to state this more by our own presumption than on the authority of the Church, we have adduced the instance of the holy council which about three years ago was held in Ephesus.   (Gore 48, 59.)

Vincent points out that the general council of Ephesus appealed to the writings [1] of ten bishops of earlier times, among them two Popes.

Doc. 237 continued.   (*P.L.* 50. 680; Bindley 115 †.)

30. These, then, are the men whose writings, whether as judges or as witnesses, were quoted in that council: S. Peter, bishop of Alexandria, a very renowned doctor and most blessed martyr; S. Athanasius, prelate of the same city, a most faithful teacher and most eminent confessor; S. Theophilus, also a bishop of the same city, a man distinguished for

[1] See Mansi, 4. 1184–1196; or Schwartz, Tom. 1, Vol. 1, pt 2, pp. 39–44.

his faith, his life, and his knowledge, whose successor was the venerable Cyril, who now adorns the Alexandrian church. And lest perchance this teaching should be thought to be that of only one city or province, there were added those lights of Cappadocia, S. Gregory of Nazianzus, bishop and confessor, S. Basil of Caesarea, bishop and confessor, and also the other S. Gregory, bishop of Nyssa, most worthy, from his faith, manner of life, integrity, and wisdom, to be the brother of Basil. And then in order that it might be proved that not only Greece, and the East, but also the Western and Latin world always so thought, certain letters were read there of S. Felix the martyr and of S. Julius, both bishops of Rome. And that not only the capital of the world, but its flanks also might yield their testimony to the council's judgement, there were added from the South the blessed Cyprian, bishop of Carthage and martyr, and from the North S. Ambrose, bishop of Milan.

(Gore 41.)

Finally, Vincent justifies the appeal to antiquity in any dispute by showing that it was by this means that contemporary Popes dealt with questions that came their way.

Doc. 237 continued. (*P.L.* 50. 683; Bindley 120 †.)

32. All this would be enough in its cumulative abundance to crush and extinguish every profane heresy; but yet, lest anything should be wanting to the completeness of our contention, we will add at the end a double authority from the apostolic see—one of S. Sixtus, the venerable Pope who now adorns the Roman Church, the other of his predecessor, Pope Celestine of blessed memory, which we have thought it right to insert here. Holy Pope Sixtus says in an epistle which he sent to the bishop of Antioch about Nestorius' case: "Therefore because, as the apostle says, there is one faith, which has evidently been held hitherto, let us believe what ought to be confessed and held." What are the things which ought to be believed and confessed? He goes on, "Let no licence be allowed to novelty, because it is not fitting that anything be added to antiquity. Let not the clear faith and belief of our fathers be

clouded by any admixture of filth".[1] Decidedly apostolical, that he should adorn the belief of the fathers with the light of clearness, and describe profane novelties as a mixture of filth.

But holy Pope Celestine was equally of the same opinion. For he says in his letter which he sent to the priests in Gaul, convicting them of connivance in error because, by their keeping silent, they were abandoning the old faith and suffering profane novelties to spring up: "Deservedly are we to blame, if by our silence we encourage error. Therefore let those who are guilty of this be rebuked. Do not let them have unrestricted liberty of preaching." . . . He goes on . . "If this be true, let novelty cease to assail antiquity".[2] That was the blessed opinion of blessed Celestine—not that antiquity should cease to subvert novelty, but that novelty should cease to attack antiquity.

As long ago as 1696 the Benedictine editor of Augustine's works wrote that "Vincent of Lerins distorts this passage from its true sense, thus opposing Prosper and Hilary, so that he became suspected, by no means unjustly, of the errors of the semi-Pelagians".[3] The point is that in his 21st letter Celestine was approving Prosper and Hilary for upholding the extreme views of Augustine on predestination and irresistible grace, but Vincent regards these views as novelties, and misuses the Pope's words in order to oppose them.[4]

Doc. 237 continued. (*P.L.* 50. 684; Bindley 123 †.)

33. Whoever shall break these apostolic and catholic decrees is bound first of all to insult the memory of S. Celestine, who enjoined that novelty should cease to assail antiquity. Next he must mock the decision of S. Sixtus, who believed that no licence ought to be given to novelty, because it is not fitting that anything should be added to antiquity. He also despises the fixed opinion of blessed Cyril, who loudly praised the zeal of the venerable Capreolus,[5] because he desired the doctrines of the ancient faith to be confirmed and novel inventions to be

1 Sixtus III, *Ep.* 6 § 7 (*P.L.* 50. 609).
2 Celestine, *Ep.* 21 § 2 (*P.L.* 50. 529).
3 *P.L.* 45. 1756, note a.
4 See R. S. Moxon, *Vincentius*, Cambridge, 1915, pp. xxix, xxx, 133.
5 See p. 246.

condemned.[1] Moreover he tramples on the synod of Ephesus, the judgements of the holy bishops from almost the whole of the East.   . Finally such a one despises the whole Church of Christ and her teachers, apostles, and prophets, and especially the blessed apostle Paul, as so much dirt.

(Chapman 82 note.)

[1] See p. 245.

CHAPTER XXIV

LEO THE GREAT

I. THE PRIMACY OF PETER

LEO I was consecrated bishop of Rome on 29 September 440, and on the anniversary of this day he used to preach before about 200 Italian bishops, gathered for the metropolitan synod. Basing his remarks on the well-known Petrine texts in Matthew, Luke, and John, he expounded his theory of Peter's primacy, and of his own authority derived from it.

DOCUMENT 238——Leo, *Sermo* 4 (*Gaudeo, dilectissimi*).
   (*P.L.* 54. 149; Allies[1] 6.)

2. . . It is by far more profitable, and more worthy, to raise the mind's eye to the contemplation of the glory of the most blessed apostle Peter, and to celebrate this day chiefly in honour of him who was watered with so copious streams from the very fountain of all graces that, while *nothing has passed to others without his participation*, yet he received many special privileges of his own. . And yet,[2] out of the whole world, one, Peter, is chosen, who presides both at the call of the Gentiles, and over all the apostles and collected fathers of the Church; so that though there be, among God's people, many priests and many shepherds, yet Peter especially rules all whom Christ also rules originally.[2] Beloved, it is a great and wonderful sharing of his own power which the divine honour bestowed on this man, and if he wished that other rulers should be in common with him, *yet did he never give except through him what he denied not to others*. And then the Lord asks all the apostles what men think of him; and they answer in common so long as they set forth the doubtfulness of human ignorance. "And upon this rock I will build my Church,

---

[1] T. W. Allies, *The See of Peter*, London, 1850.
[2] . . .[2] Quoted Leo XIII in *Satis Cognitum* § 12.

and the gates of hell shall not prevail against it."[1] On this strength, he says, I will build an eternal temple, and the loftiness of my Church, reaching to heaven, shall rise upon the firmness of this faith.[1]

3. . "I will give to thee the keys   loosed in heaven." The right of this power did indeed pass on to the other apostles, and the order of this decree passed on to all the chiefs of the Church; but not in vain was that which was imparted[2] to all *entrusted to one*. Therefore this is commended to Peter separately, because all the rulers of the Church are invested with the figure of Peter. The privilege therefore of Peter remains, wherever judgement is passed from his equity. Nor is there too much severity or indulgence, where nothing is bound, nothing loosed, except what blessed Peter either looses or binds. Again as his passion pressed on, which was to shake the firmness of the disciples, the Lord says, "Simon, behold Satan has desired to have you that he may sift you as wheat, but I have prayed for thee that thy faith fail not, and when thou art converted, confirm thy brethren, that ye enter not into temptation". The danger from the temptation of fear was common to all apostles, and they equally needed the help of divine protection, since the devil desired to harass and shatter all; and yet special care is taken of Peter by the Lord, and he asks specially for the faith of Peter, as if the state of the others would be more certain if the mind of the chief were not overcome. So then in Peter the strength of all is fortified, and the help of divine grace is so ordered that the stability which through Christ is given to Peter, *through Peter is conveyed to the apostles*.

4. Since then, beloved, we see such a protection divinely granted to us, reasonably and justly do we rejoice in the merits and dignity of our leader, rendering thanks to the eternal King, our Redeemer, the Lord Jesus Christ, for having given so great a power to him whom he made chief of the whole Church, that if anything, even in our time, by us be rightly done and rightly ordered, it is to be ascribed to his working, to his guidance,

---

[1] . . . [1] Quoted by Pius IX in *Pastor Aeternus*, preface (C. Butler, *Vatican Council*, 2. 276).

[2] *intimetur*.

unto whom it was said, "And thou, when thou art converted, confirm thy brethren"; and to whom the Lord after his resurrection, in answer to the triple profession of eternal love, thrice said, with mystical intent, "Feed my sheep". And this, beyond a doubt, the pious shepherd does even now, and fulfils the charge of his Lord, confirming us with his exhortations, and not ceasing to pray for us, that we may be overcome by no temptation. But if, as we must believe, he extends this care of his piety to all God's people everywhere, how much more will he condescend to grant his help unto us his children, among whom, on the sacred couch of his blessed repose, he rests in the same flesh in which he ruled! To him, therefore, let us ascribe this anniversary day of us his servant, and this festival, by whose patronage we have been thought worthy to share his seat itself, the grace of our Lord Jesus Christ helping us in all things, who liveth and reigneth with God the Father and the Holy Ghost for ever and ever. Amen.

(Gore 78 note; Chapman 47B.)

DOCUMENT 239——Leo, *Sermo* 5 (*Sicut honor*).
(*P.L.* 54. 153; Jalland, *Leo*[1] 69, 71, 72 †.)

2. . . . For although the pastors, each one singly, preside over their own flocks with a special care and know that they will have to render an account[2] for the sheep entrusted to them, we have a duty which is shared with all; in fact the function of each one is a part of our work: so that when men resort to the see of the blessed apostle Peter from the whole world,[3] and seek from our stewardship that love of the whole Church entrusted to him by the Lord, the greater our duty to the whole, the heavier we feel the burden to rest on us.

4. There is a further reason for our celebration: not only the apostolic but also the episcopal dignity of the most blessed *Peter, who does not cease to preside over his see* and obtains an abiding partnership with the eternal Priest. For the stability

---

[1] I have added some words omitted by Jalland.
[2] Cp. Cyprian, Doc. 45 § 3.
[3] Cp. Irenaeus, *Adv. Haer.* 3. 3 § 2 (Doc. 9).

which the rock himself was given by that Rock, Christ, *he conveyed also to his successors*, and wheresoever any steadfastness is apparent, there without doubt is to be seen the strength of the shepherd. For if to almost all martyrs everywhere, in recognition of their endurance of the martyrdoms which they underwent, this has been granted in order to make their merits manifest, namely that they are able to bring help to those in danger, to banish diseases, to drive out unclean spirits, and to cure countless bodily weaknesses, who so ignorantly or grudgingly estimates the honour of blessed Peter as not to believe that *all parts of the Church are ruled by his care* and enriched by his help? There flourishes and survives still in the chief of the apostles that love of God and men which neither the bars of the prison, nor chains, nor the onslaughts of the mob, nor the threats of a king could terrify, and an unconquerable faith, which waged unceasing warfare, and did not wax cold in defeat.　　　　　　　　　　(Chapman 95A.)

Notice first the idea that the other apostles derived their authority not direct from our Lord, but from him through Peter. Gore[1] says that this teaching is new, but seventy years before, Optatus had pointed out that Peter alone had received the keys,[2] which is a reasonable interpretation of Matt. 16. 19, the force of which is not necessarily weakened by Matt. 18. 18. Notice also the idea that Peter himself lives on in his successors, the bishops of Rome. This idea can be traced back fifty-five years to Pope Siricius,[3] and it is also held by Leo's Italian contemporary, Peter Chrysologus, archbishop of Ravenna.

DOCUMENT 240——Peter Chrysologus, *Ad Eutychem.* February 449.
In Leo, *Ep.* 25. (*P.L.* 54. 743.)

2. . . We exhort you, honourable brother, that you obediently listen to what has been written by the blessed Pope of the city of Rome, since blessed Peter, who lives and presides in his own see, offers the truth of the faith to those who seek. For we, in our zeal for peace and faith, cannot decide questions

---

[1] Page 78.　　　　[2] Doc. 86 § 3.　　　　[3] Doc. 108 § 1.

of faith apart from the consent of the bishop of Rome. May the Lord vouchsafe to preserve your love for us a very long time, our most dear and honoured son.　　(Chapman 95.)

DOCUMENT 241——Peter Chrysologus, *Sermo* 154.
　　(*P.L.* 52. 608.)

. . Just as Peter received his name from the rock, because he was the first to deserve to establish the Church, by reason of his steadfastness of faith, so also Stephen was named from a crown . . the first who deserved to bear witness with his blood. *Let Peter hold his ancient primacy* of the apostolic choir. Let him open to those who enter the kingdom of heaven. Let him bind the guilty with his power and absolve the penitent in kindness.　　(Chapman 47B.)

Preaching on the festival of Peter and Paul, Leo recognizes that the greatness of his see is due to the preaching and martyrdom of both these apostles, but he calls it "the blessed Peter's holy see".

DOCUMENT 242——Leo, *Sermo* 82 (*Omnium quidem*).　29 June.
　　(*P.L.* 54. 422; *P.N.F.* 12. 194B ‡.)

1. . . . Besides that reverence which to-day's festival has gained from all the world, it is to be honoured with special and peculiar exultation in our city, that there may be a predominance of gladness on the day of their martyrdom in the place where the chiefs of the apostles met their glorious end. For these are the men through whom the light of Christ's gospel shone on thee, O Rome, and through whom thou, who was the teacher of error, wast made the disciple of truth. These are thy fathers and true shepherds, who gave thee claims to be numbered among the heavenly kingdoms, and built thee under much better and happier auspices than they by whose zeal the first foundations of thy walls were laid, and of whom the one that gave thee thy name defiled thee with his brother's blood. These are they who have promoted thee to this glory, that being made a holy nation, a chosen people, a priestly and royal state, and the head of the world through the blessed Peter's holy see, thou didst attain a wider sway by divine religion,

than by earthly domination. For although thou wert increased
by many victories, and didst extend thy rule on land and sea,
yet what thy toils in war subdued is less than what the peace
of Christ has conquered.

2. . In order that the result of this unspeakable grace
[the incarnation] might be spread abroad throughout the
world, God's providence made ready the Roman empire,
whose growth has reached such limits that the whole multitude
of nations are brought into close connexion. For the divinely-
planned work particularly required that many kingdoms
should be leagued together under one empire, so that the
preaching of the word might quickly reach to all people, when
they were held beneath the rule of one state. .

3. When the twelve apostles . . . had distributed the world
into parts among themselves . the most blessed Peter, chief
of the apostolic band, was appointed to the citadel of the
Roman empire, that the light of truth which was being displayed for the salvation of all the nations might spread itself
more effectively throughout the body of the world from the
head itself. . .

7. . Of the excellence of these two fathers [Peter and
Paul] we must rightly boast in louder joy, for God's grace has
raised them to so high a place among the members of the
Church, that he has set them like the twin lights of the eyes[1]
in the body whose head is Christ.　　　　　(Chapman 83A.)

II. HILARY OF ARLES

Hilary was bishop of Arles in southern Gaul (429–449), and metropolitan of the province of Vienne. He had attempted to depose two
bishops, one of whom was not in his own province. The Pope, on
hearing their complaints, restored the two bishops and confined
Hilary to his own see.[2]

DOCUMENT 243——Leo, *Ep.* 10, to the Bishops throughout the
　　　　Province of Vienne (*Divinae cultum*).　July 445.
　　　　(*P.L.* 54. 628; *P.N.F.* 12. 8 ‡.)

1. Our Lord Jesus Christ, Saviour of the human race,
instituted the worship of the divine religion, which he wished

---

[1] See Doc. 144.　　　　　　　　　[2] *P.L.* 54. 631–634.

by God's grace to flash upon all nations. . The mystery of his gift the Lord willed to belong to the office of all the apostles, in such a way that he has placed the principal charge on blessed Peter, chief of all the apostles, and *from him, as from the head, wishes his gifts to flow to all the body*:[1] so that anyone who dares to secede from the firmness of Peter may understand that he has no share in the divine mystery. For he wished him who had been received into partnership in his undivided unity to be named what he himself was, when he said: "Thou art Peter and upon this rock I will build my Church"; that the building of the eternal temple by the wondrous gift of God's grace might stand on Peter's solidity, strengthening his Church so surely that neither could human rashness assail it nor could the gates of hell prevail against it.

2. . . . But Hilary has quitted this path so well maintained by our fathers, and has disturbed the position and harmony of the priests by a new presumption.

5. We, however, have done what, God judging, we believe you will approve. After holding council with all the brethren, we have decreed that the wrongfully ordained man should be deposed, and the bishop Projectus abide in his priesthood.

6. A gang of soldiers, as we have learnt, follows the priest through the provinces, and wherever the churches have lost their rightful priests, he makes a disorderly invasion, protected in his presumption by an armed guard. Before this court are dragged for ordination men unknown to the cities over which they are to be set.

7. . Tell him [Hilary] that he is not only deposed from another's rights, but also deprived of his power over the province of Vienne which he had assumed wrongfully. . . . he may now be kept by our command, in accordance with the clemency of the apostolic see, to the priesthood of his own city alone.

(Gore 78 note; Chapman 49B.)

This letter was followed by an imperial decree.

[1] See Doc. 238 § 2.

DOCUMENT 244——Valentinian III, *Certum est.* 8 July 445. In Leo, *Ep.* 11. (*P.L.* 54. 637; Kidd, *Docs.* 2. 282 †.)

The Emperors Theodosius and Valentinian to Aetius, Master of the Military and Patrician.

It is certain that for us the only defence lies in the favour of the God of heaven; and to deserve it our first care is to support the Christian faith and its venerable religion. Inasmuch then as the primacy of the apostolic see is assured, by the merit of S. Peter, who is chief of the episcopal order, by the rank of the city of Rome, and also *by the authority of a sacred synod,* let no one presume to attempt any illicit act contrary to the authority of that see. For then at length will the peace of the churches be maintained everywhere, if the whole body acknowledges its ruler. Hitherto these customs have been observed without fail; but Hilary of Arles, as we are informed by the trustworthy report of that venerable man Leo, Pope of Rome, has with contumacious daring ventured upon certain unlawful proceedings; and therefore the churches beyond the Alps have been invaded by abominable disorders [1] [, of which a recent example particularly bears witness. For Hilary who is called bishop of Arles, without consulting the pontiff of the church of the city of Rome, has in solitary rashness usurped his jurisdiction by the ordination of bishops. He has removed some without authority, and indecently ordained others who are unwelcome and repugnant to the citizens. Since these were not readily received by those who had not chosen them, he has collected to himself an armed band and in hostility has either prepared a barrier of walls for a blockade or embarked on aggression. Thus he has led into war those who prayed for peace to the haven of rest. Such men have been admitted contrary to the dignity of the empire and contrary to the reverence due to the apostolic see; and after investigation they have been dispersed by the order of that pious man the Pope of the city. The sentence applies to Hilary and to those whom he has wickedly ordained. *This same sentence would have been valid through the Gauls without imperial sanction; for what is not*

[1] See n. 1 on p. 287.

allowed in the Church to the authority of so great a pontiff? Hilary is allowed still to be called a bishop, only by the kindness of the gentle president; and our just command is, that it is not lawful either for him or for anyone else to mix church affairs with arms or to obstruct the orders of the Roman overseer].[1] By such deeds of daring, confidence in, and respect for, our empire is broken down. Not only then do we put away so great a crime; but in order that not even the least disturbance may arise amongst the churches, nor the discipline of religion appear in any instance to be weakened, we decree by this eternal law that it shall not be lawful for the bishops of Gaul or of the other provinces, contrary to ancient custom, to do aught without the authority of the venerable Pope of the eternal city. And whatever the authority of the apostolic see has sanctioned, or may sanction, shall be the law for all; so that if any bishop summoned to trial before the pontiff of Rome shall neglect to come, he shall be compelled to appear by the governor of that province. Those things which our divine parents conferred on the Roman church[2] are to be upheld in every way. Wherefore your illustrious and eminent magnificence is to cause what is enacted above to be observed in virtue of this present edict and law

(Chapman 47B.)

Kidd sees in this edict "the crowning proof that the papacy at Rome—as distinct from the primacy of the Apostolic See in Christendom—is the creation of the state".[3] The Ballerini brothers[4] were of the opinion that Hilary had interfered where he had no jurisdiction, and therefore his action was void. A later R.C. writer says, "As to the invocation of the secular arm to enforce religious discipline, its prudence in a variety of cases may be questioned, but the right to do so has always been claimed, and from time to time exercised, ever since the conversion of Constantine made it a possibility".[5] Jalland writes: "The competence of the bishop of Arles to exercise metropolitical rights within the province of *Viennensis* might not have been questioned, nor his error on the side of rigour in the administration of penitential discipline seriously regarded, if he had been content to

---

[1] [. . .][1] Kidd omits these lines in his translation.
[2] See Doc. 95.
[3] *Hist. Ch.*, 3. 358, 359.
[4] See their long reply, in *P.L.* 55. 533. to Quesnel's *Dissertation*.
[5] H. I. D. Ryder, *Catholic Controversy*, 67, 68 (5th edition, 1882).

confine his activity within a sphere which, from Leo's standpoint, constituted its proper limit. But, as it was, Hilary's conduct appeared to amount to a grave menace to the peace and order of the Church, and therefore deserved to be stopped".[1]

III. THE ROBBER SYNOD

In August 449 a second council was held at Ephesus, which Leo later described as "no court of justice but a gang of thieves",[2] whence it is often called the "Robber Synod". It was presided over by Dioscorus, bishop of Alexandria, and to it the Pope sent his legates, and a letter[3] expounding the doctrine of the incarnation. This letter was suppressed by Dioscorus, and the council, besides upholding the Monophysite heresy, also deposed the orthodox Flavian, bishop of Constantinople. Flavian, on hearing the sentence against him, immediately disclaimed the authority of the council, in which he was backed up by one of the papal legates. The minutes of these proceedings are embodied in the acts of Chalcedon (see Doc. 254, p. 300). Other leading bishops deposed by the council were Domnus of Antioch and Theodoret[4] of Cyrus. Flavian died from ill treatment, three days after the sentence, but he had in the meantime dispatched an appeal[5] to the Pope. In due course the Pope heard all about the council from his legates, and at once wrote letters of protest to the emperor Theodosius II.

DOCUMENT 245——Leo, *Ep.* 44, to Theodosius II (*Litteris clementiae*). 13 October 449.
(*P.L.* 54. 827; *P.N.F.* 12. 53A ‡.)

Leo the bishop and the holy synod assembled in Rome, to Theodosius Augustus.

1. From your clemency's letter which, in your love of the catholic faith, you sent some time ago to the see of the blessed apostle Peter, we drew such confidence in your defence of truth and peace, that we thought nothing harmful could happen in so plain and well ordered a matter; especially when those who were sent to the episcopal council which you instructed to be held at Ephesus were so fully taught, that if the Alexandrian pontiff had allowed the writings which they

[1] *Leo*, 123.   [2] *Ep.* 95. 2 (*P.L.* 54. 943).   [3] *Ep.* 28 (*P.L.* 54. 755).
[4] S. G. F. Perry, *Second Synod of Ephesus*, E.T., 258, 363.
[5] E.T.: Church Historical Society, Tract No. 70 (Oxford, 1885).

brought, either to the holy synod or to Bishop Flavian, to be read in the ears of the bishops, by the declaration of the most pure faith, which, since it is divinely inspired, we have received and hold, all noise of disputings would have been hushed, so that neither ignorance could act foolishly any longer, nor jealousy find occasion to do harm. But since private interests are considered under the cover of religion, the disloyalty of a few has brought about what must wound the Church universal. For from no unreliable messenger, but from a most faithful reporter of the facts, namely our deacon Hilary [1] (who, lest he should be forced to subscribe, with difficulty escaped), we have learnt [that the proceedings were irregular and the voting not free]. . . This our delegates from the apostolic see saw to be so blasphemous and opposed to the catholic faith, that no pressure could force them to assent; for in the same synod they stoutly protested, as they ought, that the apostolic see would never receive what was being passed, since the whole mystery of the faith will in fact be torn out (which in your piety's time should not be), unless this foul evil, which exceeds all former sacrilege, is abolished.

3. Because this mystery is being impiously opposed by a few ignorant people, and since our delegates faithfully protested, and Bishop Flavian gave them an appeal in writing, therefore all the churches of our parts, and all the priests, entreat your clemency, with groans and tears, to order a general synod to be held in Italy. This synod will either dismiss or appease all disputes in such a way that there be nobody any longer either doubtful in faith or divided in love. To this synod of course the bishops of the eastern provinces must come, so that if any of them were overcome by threats and injury, and deviated from the path of truth, they may be fully restored by sound means; likewise that they themselves whose case is harder, if they acquiesce in wiser councils, may not fall from the unity of the Church. *And how necessary this request is, after the lodging of an appeal, is witnessed by the canonical decrees passed at Nicaea by the priests of the whole world, which are added below.*

(Gore 111; Chapman 96A.)

[1] Pope from 461 to 468.

On this letter, and the previous one (*Ep.* 43), Gore based his charge against Leo as "distinctly and consciously guilty of a *suppressio veri* at any rate, which is not distinguishable from fraud",[1] and as "strangely blinded in conscience to the authority of truth".[2] The Nicene canons make no reference to appeals to Rome, and the Pope is attempting to use the Sardican legislation (Doc. 69) as if it had Nicene authority. He does this in spite of the fact that Popes Boniface and Celestine had had it brought home to them that the Sardican canons were not Nicene.[3] Jalland[4] is inclined to take a lenient view of the Pope's conduct, thinking that he was unconvinced by the earlier correspondence, since in the Roman manuscripts the Sardican canons still formed part of the Nicene collections.

It is unlikely that the Emperor Theodosius II would have paid heed to Leo's request for another council to undo the evil of the "Robber Synod"; but on 28 July 450 he died and was succeeded by his orthodox sister, Pulcheria, who in less than a month married the soldier-senator Marcian and invested him with the imperial insignia. The relations between the court and the Pope were now amicable, and the following letter of the empress opened the way to the council of Chalcedon.

DOCUMENT 246——The Empress Pulcheria, *To Leo.* A.D. 450. Leo, *Ep.* 77. (*P.L.* 54. 906; Teetgen[5] 253.)

The letter of your blessedness we have received, with all reverence due to a bishop; by which we know that your faith is pure and such as ought with holiness to be held forth in the sacred Church. But I equally, with my lord, the most serene emperor, my spouse, have ever abode, and do still abide therein, turning away from all perverseness, defilement, and evil doing. The most holy bishop, therefore, of glorious Constantinople[6] hath continued in the same faith and worship, and embraces the confession of your apostolic letters, putting away that error arisen from some, which from his own letters, also, your holiness will be able to perceive; and he hath, without delay of any kind, subscribed the letter likewise of catholic faith which your blessedness addressed to the bishop

1 Gore, *St Leo the Great*, London, 1880, p. 114. Cp. W. Bright, *Age of the Fathers*, 2. 496.
2 Gore, *R.C. Claims*, 110.
3 See above, pp. 229, 236.   4 *Papacy*, 312.
5 A. B. Teetgen, *St Pulcheria*, London, 1907.
6 Anatolius, A.D. 449–458.

Flavian of holy memory. And accordingly, let your reverence deign, in whatever way you see good, to signify to all bishops, even of the whole East, of Thrace and Illyricum, as also it hath pleased our lord the most pious emperor, my spouse, that they may be able quickly to muster from the western parts and meet in one city, and there, having formed a council, let them at your invitation proceed to decree about the catholic confession and concerning those bishops who previously held aloof, as the faith and Christian piety may require. Moreover let your holiness know that by the command of our lord and most serene prince, my spouse, the body of Flavian of holy memory has been brought to the most glorious city of Constantinople, and has been duly placed in the basilica of the apostles in which his predecessors were wont to be buried. And likewise, by the authority of his decree, he has ordered those bishops to return who for the same cause of having agreed with the most holy Flavian in the concord of catholic faith had been sent into exile, in order that by the sanction of the council and the decree of the bishops assembled they may be enabled to recover the episcopate and their own churches.

(Chapman 95B.)

IV. SOZOMEN

The Greek historian Sozomen closely follows Socrates (Doc. 234) in his remarks about papal authority in general and Pope Julius in particular.

DOCUMENT 247——Sozomen, *Church History*, Book 3. A.D. 450. (*P.G.* 67. 1052; Bagster 113 ‡.)

8. Athanasius, escaping from Alexandria, came to Rome. Paul, bishop of Constantinople, Marcellus of Ancyra, and Asclepas of Gaza went there at the same time. Asclepas, who was opposed to the Arians, had been accused by them of having thrown down an altar, and Quintian had been appointed in his place. Lucius, bishop of Adrianople, who had been deposed from his office on another charge, was also staying in Rome. The Roman bishop, on learning the accusation

against each one, and finding that they were all like-minded about the doctrine of the council of Nicaea, admitted them to communion as of like orthodoxy. And *alleging that the care for all belongs to him, because of the dignity of the see, he restored each to his own church.*[1] . .

10.   . Julius, learning that Athanasius was not safe in Egypt, called him back to himself. He replied at the same time to the letter of the bishops who were convened at Antioch, for just then he happened to have received it, and he accused them of having secretly introduced innovations contrary to the dogmas of the Nicene council, and of having violated the laws of the Church by not calling him to the synod. For *there is a priestly law, making void whatever is effected against the mind of the bishop of Rome.*   (Gore 101 note ; Chapman 38 note, 74A note.)

V. THEODORET

The witness of the learned Theodoret is interesting. He was born about 393, and at the age of thirty was made bishop of Cyrus, a diocese with 800 tiny parishes, near the upper waters of the Euphrates. He was a zealous bishop and a popular preacher, especially at Antioch, which he often visited.

DOCUMENT 248——Theodoret, *Oratio de Caritate.*
   (*P.G.* 82. 1509.)

[Quoting Luke 22. 31, 32.] "For as I", he says, "did not despise thee when tossed, so be thou a support to thy brethren in trouble, and the help by which thou wast saved do thou thyself impart to others, and exhort them not while they are tottering, but raise them up in their peril. For this reason I suffer thee also to slip, but do not permit thee to fall, [thus] through thee gaining steadfastness for those who are tossed." So this great pillar supported the tossing and sinking world, and permitted it not to fall entirely and gave it back stability, having been ordered to feed God's sheep.

                                        (Chapman 59B, note 1.)

[1] More of this § 8 will be found in Doc. 65.

DOCUMENT 249——Theodoret, *Ep.* 86, to Flavian.   A.D. 448.
  (*P.G.* 83. 1280; *P.N.F.* 3. 282A †.)

   . Dioscorus is turning the see of blessed Mark[1] upside
down ; and this he does, well knowing that the metropolis of
Antioch possesses the throne of the great Peter, who was
teacher of blessed Mark, and first and leader of the choir of
the apostles.

On being deposed by the Robber Synod, Theodoret like Flavian
appealed to Rome.

DOCUMENT 250——Theodoret, *Ep.* 113, to Leo.   A.D. 449.
   Leo, *Ep.* 52.   (*P.L.* 54. 848; *P.N.F.* 12. 55B †.)

   1. If Paul, the herald of the truth, the trumpet of the Holy
Ghost, had recourse to the great Peter, in order to obtain a
decision from him for those at Antioch who were disputing
about living by the law,[2] much more do we small humble folk
run to the apostolic see to get healing from you for the sores
of the churches. For it is fitting that you should in all things
have pre-eminence, since your see possesses many peculiar
privileges.   . Your city has the fullest abundance of good
things from the giver of all good. For she is of all cities the
greatest and most famous, the mistress of the world, and
teeming with people. Besides this she has created an empire
which is still predominant, and has imposed her own name
upon her subjects. But her chief decoration is her faith, to
which the divine apostle is a sure witness when he exclaims
"Your faith is proclaimed in all the world"; and if, immediately after receiving the seeds of the saving gospel, she
bore such a weight of wondrous fruit, what words are sufficient
to express the piety which is now found in her? She has, too,
the tombs of our common fathers and teachers of the truth,
Peter and Paul, to enlighten the souls of the faithful. And this
blessed and divine pair arose indeed in the East, and shed its
rays in all directions, but voluntarily underwent the sunset of
life in the West, from whence now they light up the whole
world. These have rendered your see so glorious: this the

---

[1] Alexandria. See Doc. 99.   [2] Cp. Acts 15. 2 and Gal. 2. 1, 2.

height of your good things. For their God has made their see
bright, since he has settled your holiness in it to send forth the
rays of the true faith.

4.   . After such toils and troubles I am condemned without a hearing.

5. However, I wait for the verdict of your apostolic throne,
and beg and pray your holiness to help me, when *I appeal to
your right and just tribunal,* and to bid me come to you and show
that my teaching follows in the apostolic track.   I beseech
you not to spurn my petition, nor to overlook the insults
heaped upon me.

6. Before all, tell me whether I ought to acquiesce in this
unrighteous deposition or not. *I await your verdict; and if you bid
me abide by my condemnation, I will do so,* and will trouble no one
hereafter, but await the unerring verdict of our God and
Saviour. . .

7. . . I entreat your holiness . . to consider my slandered
position, so falsely attacked, to be worthy of your protection.
Above all I beseech you to defend with all your might the faith
that is now plotted against, and to keep the hereditary doctrine
intact for the churches. So shall your holiness receive from the
bountiful Master a full reward.

(Gore 84 note; Chapman 59B, note 2, 60, 95B.)

DOCUMENT 251——Theodoret, *Ep.* 116, to Renatus the
    presbyter.   A.D. 449.

(*P.G.* 83. 1324; *P.N.F.* 3. 295B †.)

Twenty-six years I have been a bishop; I have undergone countless labours; I have struggled hard for the truth; I
have freed tens of thousands of heretics and brought them to
the Saviour, and now they have stripped me of my priesthood,
and are exiling me from the city. They have no respect for my
old age, or for my hairs grown grey in the truth. Wherefore I
beseech your sanctity to persuade the very sacred and holy
Archbishop Leo to bid me hasten to your council. For that
holy see has precedence of all churches in the world, for many
reasons; and above all for this, that it is *free from all taint of*

heresy, and that no bishop of false opinions has ever sat upon its throne, but it has kept the grace of the apostles undefiled.

Denny argues that as Theodoret had been deposed by the patriarch of Alexandria, and as the patriarchs of Antioch[1] and Constantinople were themselves deposed, he "naturally turned to the only remaining patriarch, him of Rome".[2] But Theodoret says above that he trusts the orthodoxy of the Roman see, and it is probable that he saw himself following in the footsteps of Athanasius.

DOCUMENT 252——Theodoret, *Church History*, Book 2. A.D. 450.

(*P.G.* 82. 996; Bagster 93 †.)

3. With these and similar arguments, they attacked the vacant mind of the emperor and persuaded him to expel Athanasius from the Church. But he, having discovered the plot, withdrew and went to the West. The Eusebians had falsely accused Athanasius to the bishop of Rome (just then Julius was shepherding that church). He therefore, *obeying the law of the Church, summoned the accusers to come to Rome, and called the devout Athanasius to trial.* And he, accepting the call, set out at once; but the false accusers, seeing that the lie would easily be detected, did not go to Rome.

For the sequel to Theodoret's appeal to Rome see the minutes of the council of Chalcedon, Sessions 1 and 8 (Docs. 254, 260).

There is another interesting document belonging to this first half of Leo's pontificate. There was a priest in Marseilles called Salvian, highly esteemed by his contemporaries: "a teacher of bishops",[3] and "the most blessed Salvian the presbyter".[4] He paints a gloomy picture of the church in Gaul at this time, from which Gore quotes three words.

DOCUMENT 253——Salvian, *De Gubernatione Dei*, Book 3. A.D. 439–451.

(*C.S.E.L.* 8. 57; Sanford[5] 92.)

9.   . God commands us all to love one another, but we rend each other in mutual hatred. God enjoins us all to give

[1] S. G. F. Perry, *Second Synod of Ephesus*, 359–363.   [2] Page 187.
[3] Gennadius, *De Scrip. Eccles.* 67 (*P.L.* 58, 1099).
[4] Hilary of Arles, *Sermon on Honoratus* 19 (*P.L.* 50. 1260).
[5] Eva M. Sanford, *On the Government of God*, Columbia Univ. Press, 1930.

our goods to the poor, but we plunder other men's goods instead. God orders every Christian to keep his eyes pure; how many men are there who do not wallow in the filth of fornication? What more can I say? It is a heavy and sorrowful charge that I must bring: the Church itself, which should strive to appease God in all things—what else does it do but arouse him to anger? Except a very few individuals who shun evil, what else is the whole congregation of Christians, but *the very dregs of vice*? How often will you find a man in the Church who is not a drunkard or a glutton or adulterer or fornicator or robber or wastrel or brigand or homicide? And what is worst of all, they commit these crimes endlessly.

(Gore 30.)

Gore's point is that this picture, which could be reproduced from other times and places, does not prevent us from believing that the Catholic Church is Holy. Neither, he contends, need our present unhappy divisions prevent us from believing that the Catholic Church is One.

CHAPTER XXV

THE COUNCIL OF CHALCEDON

WE said in the last chapter that the Robber Synod of Ephesus upheld the Monophysite heresy. This heresy consisted in asserting that our Lord only possessed one nature after the incarnation, whereas the orthodox faith is that God the Son became man, and thereafter the one person Jesus Christ had a divine and a human nature, both natures being perfect and unconfused. The author of the new error was Eutyches, a monk over seventy years old, the head of a monastery near Constantinople. He was condemned, deposed, and excommunicated by his bishop, Flavian, at the council of Constantinople in November 448. But he had friends in high places: his godson Chrysaphius was chief minister of the emperor, and Dioscorus, bishop of Alexandria, was on his side, and in defiance of canon law[1] admitted him to his communion. So again there was war between the great eastern sees of Alexandria and Constantinople. The first round was won by Alexandria at the Robber Synod in August 449, when Flavian was excommunicated and the opinions of Eutyches were upheld. Dioscorus took the liberty of pronouncing excommunication against the Pope,[2] whose important doctrinal letter to Flavian he declined to have read. Then on the death of Flavian, Dioscorus proceeded to consecrate a man called Anatolius in his place.

The death of the Emperor Theodosius II on 28 July 450 altered the course of events, because his sister, Pulcheria, who succeeded him, and her husband, Marcian, were both orthodox. The unpopular Chrysaphius was put to death, and the way was clear for the Fourth General Council, which was held at Chalcedon in October 451. Chalcedon was about a mile from Constantinople, separated from it by the Bosphorus straits. This council held sixteen sessions. The lengthy acts are found in Mansi, 6. 565–1102, 7. 1–453; E. Schwartz, *Acta*, Tome 2. See also Hefele, 3. 298–428; Kidd, *Hist. Ch.*, 3. 315–334; Jalland, *Leo*, 289–310.

Our Documents cover portions of the acts of seven sessions which have been thought to throw light on the position of the Pope. In translating these acts I have occasionally abbreviated, often omitting the (to us) pompous titles given to Church and State officials. As the extracts are rather involved, it may be helpful to notice here the more relevant points. In Sessions I and VIII we have the restoration of

---

[1] Nicene Canon 5 (Doc. 62).   [2] Mansi, 6. 1048

Theodoret to his see by Pope and synod. In Session II doubts are expressed about the orthodoxy of an important papal document and in Session IV these doubts are cleared up. Session III deals with the condemnation of Dioscorus, and in the last two sessions we are concerned with one of the canons.

SESSION I

The seating arrangements in the church of S. Euphemia were like those in a college chapel. There were nineteen imperial commissioners, referred to as "the most glorious judges and senators", who sat before the altar rails facing down the nave. There were 520 bishops [1] present. On the left of the judges, facing across the church, were the three papal legates, Bishops Paschasinus and Lucentius and the priest Boniface. Next to them were Anatolius of Constantinople, Maximus of Antioch, and the bishops of Caesarea in Cappadocia and of Ephesus. These leaders were backed by their suffragans. Those belonging to the patriarchate of Antioch, referred to as Orientals, were a noisy crowd. On the opposite seats were the bishops of Egypt, Palestine, and Illyricum, who intended at first to stand by the decision of the Robber Synod. They were led by Dioscorus of Alexandria, Juvenal of Jerusalem, and Bishop Quintillus, who represented the bishop of Thessalonica.[2]

After some sparring for position the first session settled down to a lengthy reading of the minutes of the synods of Constantinople in 448 and Ephesus in 449, with frequent interruptions. The chief Roman legate took the lead.

DOCUMENT 254——Council of Chalcedon: First Session. 8 October 451.
(Schwartz, Tom. 2, Vol. 1, p. 65.)

Bishop Paschasinus, guardian of the apostolic see, stood in the midst and said: "We received directions at the hands of the most blessed and apostolic bishop of the Roman city, who is head of all the churches, which directions say that Dioscorus is not to be allowed to sit in the assembly, but that if he should attempt to take his seat he is to be cast out. This instruction we must carry out; if now your holiness so commands, let him be expelled or else we leave."

---

[1] Doc. 263 § 1.   [2] Schwartz, Tom. 2, Vol. 1, p. 56.

The judges said: "What special charge do you prefer against the most reverend Bishop Dioscorus?"

And when Dioscorus, the most religious bishop of Alexandria, at the bidding of the judges and of the sacred assembly had sat down in the midst, and the most reverend Roman bishops had also sat down in their own places, and kept silence, Eusebius, bishop of Dorylaeum, stepping into the middle said

This Eusebius was a keen heresy-hunter, and had been deposed along with Flavian at Ephesus in 449.[1] He now asks[2] that the minutes of the Robber Synod be read out, in order to show that Dioscorus was the real heretic. The reading began with the emperor's letter[3] to Dioscorus, dated 3 March 449, by which that council was convened.

Doc. 254 continued.   (Schwartz 69.)

Constantine the secretary said: "The same letter was sent to the other bishops." The most glorious judges and illustrious senate said: "The most reverend bishop Theodoret should take his place in the synod, because *the most holy archbishop Leo restored him to his episcopate*, and the pious emperor decreed his presence at the sacred synod." And, Theodoret coming in, the bishops of Egypt, Illyricum, and Palestine cried out: "Mercy! the faith is destroyed; the canons have rejected him; throw him out, throw out the teacher of Nestorius." The Orientals   cried out: "We were beaten, and signed a blank paper; throw out the Manichaeans, throw out the enemies of Flavian, throw out the enemies of the faith."

[After more clamour] Theodoret came into the middle and said: "I have presented a petition to the rulers of the world in which I set forth the cruelties I have endured; I beg to be examined."

The judges said: "The bishop Theodoret, *having recovered his proper place from the archbishop of Rome*, has now entered as an accuser; wherefore, to avoid confusion, let us finish what we

[1] Schwartz, 191. See below, p. 301.   [2] Schwartz, 66, 67.
[3] Schwartz, 68, 69.

had begun. *The presence of Theodoret shall prejudice no one's cause;* all the claims you have against him, or he against you, shall stand good,　　especially since the bishop of Antioch testifies to his orthodoxy.

So we see that the bishop of Cyrus, deprived by the Robber Synod, is within two years restored by the Pope. Chapman[1] contends that the Pope reversed a sentence passed upon Theodoret twenty years before by the universal council of Ephesus in 431. But the quarrel of Cyril against John of Antioch and Theodoret had only lasted three years.[2] Theodoret had then enjoyed 14 years' peace till 448, when the emperor confined him to his own see. (For the restoration of Theodoret by the council of Chalcedon see Session VIII below.)

After more shouting and shouting back across the church, the reading of the minutes of the Robber Synod continued.

Doc. 254 continued.　(Schwartz 77.)

"On the 8th of August 449, at the synod of Ephesus, at the church called Mary, the bishops present were Dioscorus of Alexandria, Julian, legate of Leo, most holy bishop of the Roman church". And when this was read the Orientals and bishops with them cried out: "He was thrown out; no one acknowledged the name of Leo." Constantine continued reading, "and Juvenal of Jerusalem and Domnus of Antioch and Flavian of Constantinople". And when this was read, the Orientals shouted: "Flavian is entered as if condemned; this is manifest slander; why did not Flavian sit in his own place? Why did he put the bishop of Constantinople fifth?" Bishop Paschasinus said: "See, we, God willing, have placed the lord Anatolius first: these put the blessed Flavian fifth." Diogenes, bishop of Cyzicus, said: "*Because you know the canons.*"

This can only refer to Canon 3 of the council of Constantinople, A.D. 381 (Doc. 97), which assigns the second place in the Church to the bishop of Constantinople. It appears that the chief Roman legate recognized this canon, which his colleague Lucentius in the 16th session repudiated (see below, Doc. 262). The reading of the minutes got under way again, revealing the suppression of the Pope's letter to Flavian and many other irregularities. Embodied in these minutes

---

1 Page 115A.
2 See Theodoret, *Ep.* 171 (A.D. 434): *P.G.* 83. 1484.

were those of the council of Constantinople, A.D. 448, including Flavian's statement of faith. This statement was approved by the Roman legates, Anatolius, Maximus, and others on their side. Whereupon Juvenal of Jerusalem and the other bishops of Palestine and the bishop of Illyricum and four Egyptians crossed over the church.

Doc. 254 continued.   (Schwartz 115.)

Peter, bishop of Corinth, said: "I was not present at the Ephesian synod, for at that time I was not ordained bishop, but I realize, from what has been read, that Flavian's statement does in fact explain the words of Cyril. I have withdrawn my hesitation. When they were read, they informed me more perfectly." And getting up, he crossed over to the other side. The Orientals cried: "*Peter thinks with Peter*; welcome blessed orthodox!"

Dioscorus of Alexandria said: "Flavian was justly condemned, because he said 'After the union, two natures'. I can prove from Athanasius, Gregory, and Cyril in many places that we ought not to say 'After the union, two natures', but 'One incarnate nature of the Word'. I am rejected with the fathers, but I stand by their doctrine. I transgress in nothing. . . And I must request that the rest be read."

The reading continued on into the night, till at last they reached the sentence against Flavian:

Doc. 254 continued.   (Schwartz 191.)

"Dioscorus, bishop of Alexandria, said: 'The holy and great synod of Nicaea, long ago assembled by the will of God, decreed our true and pure faith, and the council which recently assembled here confirmed it and declared that anyone who altered it should be subject to the penalties . Well now you see that Flavian, bishop of Constantinople, here before us, and Eusebius of Dorylaeum have unsettled everything, and are become a scandal to all the churches and to the orthodox everywhere. It is plain then that they have made themselves liable to the punishment decreed by our holy fathers. It follows that Flavian and Eusebius must be deposed from all episcopal and priestly dignity. I therefore pronounce them deposed, and all the bishops shall declare their opinion. Further the emperors will be informed of to-day's proceedings.' Bishop Flavian said: 'I disclaim your authority.'[1] Hilary, deacon of the Roman Church, said: 'It is contradicted.'"

And when this was read, the Orientals and bishops with them shouted: "Anathema to Dioscorus! this hour condemns him; this hour he is damned. Blessed Lord, thou hast avenged him [Flavian]. Orthodox emperor, you have avenged him. Long live Leo! Long live the patriarch!"

(Chapman 92B note, 114B, 115A.)

The judges wound up the session by saying that Dioscorus, Juvenal, and four others who had been leaders at the Robber Synod ought to be deposed.[2]

SESSION II[3]

The six bishops admonished by the judges were absent from the second session,[4] the main interest of which was the reading of the Pope's letter to Flavian which had been suppressed at Ephesus. The orthodoxy of this letter was accepted by the majority, but doubted by a few.

DOCUMENT 255——Council of Chalcedon: Second Session.
    10 October 451.
    (Schwartz, ibid., p. [273]; *P.N.F.* 14. 248A†, and editor.)

When all were seated before the rails of the most holy altar the judges said: ". . . The question now to be investigated, studied, and decided is how to establish the true faith. This is the main purpose of the council.   . Hasten therefore, without fear or favour or enmity, to set forth the pure faith, so that they who do not seem to have understood all these things may be brought to unity by the full knowledge of the truth. For we wish you to know that the most divine and pious lord of the

---

[1] παραιτοῦμαί σε.   [2] Schwartz, 195.
[3] Schwartz reverses the traditional order, which is followed here, of Sessions II and III.
[4] Hefele, 3. 315.

whole earth and ourselves hold the orthodox faith set forth by the 318 and the 150, and what has also been taught by the rest of the most holy and glorious fathers, and thus we believe."

The bishops cried: ". The fathers taught, and in their writings are preserved what they set out, and we cannot say more."

Cecropius, bishop of Sebastopol: "The affairs of Eutyches have been examined, and on them the most holy *archbishop of Rome has given a formula with which we agree*, and we have all subscribed his letter."

The bishops cried: "So say all of us. The things set forth are sufficient; it is not possible to make any other."

The creeds of Nicaea and Constantinople were read with acclamations; then two letters of Cyril, dated 430[1] and 433.[2]

Doc. 255 continued.   (Schwartz [277].)

The most glorious judges and the illustrious senate said: "Let there be read also the letter of the most worthy Leo, archbishop of the royal and elder Rome."

Beronician, the most devout clerk of the sacred consistory, read from a book handed to him by Aetius, archdeacon of the holy church of Constantinople: "Leo to the beloved brother Flavian . . . dated 13 June 449."[3]

After the reading of the above letter, the most reverend bishops cried out: "This is the faith of the fathers; this is the faith of the apostles. So we all believe; so the orthodox believe. Anathema to him who does not so believe! *Peter has spoken these things through Leo.* So taught the apostles. Piously and truly did Leo teach; so taught Cyril; the eternal memory of Cyril! Leo and Cyril taught the same; anathema to him who does not so believe! This is the true faith. So think the orthodox. This is the faith of the fathers. Why were not these things read at Ephesus? Dioscorus hid them."

Part of the foregoing letter, "In order to pay our debt, the invisible nature united itself with the passible, so that, as our

---

[1] *Ep.* 4 (*P.G.* 77. 44).   [2] *Ep.* 39 (*P.G.* 77. 173).
[3] Leo, *Ep.* 28 (*P.L.* 54. 755–782).

salvation required, the one mediator between God and man, the man Jesus Christ, on the one side could die, on the other could not",[1] was *doubted* by the bishops of Illyria and Palestine.

Aetius, archdeacon of Constantinople, read from the late Cyril of Alexandria: "But forasmuch as his own body by the grace of God, as the apostle says, tasted death for every man, he is said to have suffered death for us. It is not that he experienced death as regards his nature, to say or hold which is madness, but that, as I said just now, his flesh tasted death."[2]

Likewise the part which contained: "Each nature in union with the other performs the actions which are proper to it, the Word those which are proper to the Word, the body those which are proper to the body. The one is resplendent with miracles, the other submits to insults"[3] was doubted by the bishops of Illyria and Palestine.

Aetius, archdeacon of Constantinople, read from the late Cyril: "There are some sayings which apply best to God, others to the manhood, and others again hold a middle position, showing that the Son of God is both God and man."[4]

Likewise the part of his letter which contained: "For although in the Lord Jesus Christ there is one person of God and man, yet the glory and the shame which are common to the two natures have different sources. From us he has the manhood which is inferior to the Father; from the Father the divinity equal to the Father"[5] was doubted by the bishops of Illyria and Palestine.

Theodoret, bishop of Cyrus, said: "There is an example of this also from the most blessed Cyril, thus: 'He became man and changed not his properties, but remained what he was. The one, however, is understood as thoroughly dwelling in the other, that is, the divine nature in the manhood.'"[6]

The most magnificent judges said: "After all this, who doubts?"

The most reverend bishops cried out: "No one doubts."

Atticus, bishop of Nicopolis, said: "We beg your magni-

[1] *P.L.* 54. 763.   [2] Cyril, *Ep.* 4 (*P.G.* 77. 48).
[3] *P.L.* 54. 767.   [4] Cyril, *Ep.* 40, to Acacius (*P.G.* 77. 196).
[5] *P.L.* 54. 769, 771.   [6] Cyril, *Scholia* 25 (*P.G.* 75. 1397).

ficence to allow us a few days for quiet consideration of the letter of our master and holy father, Archbishop Leo, who adorns the apostolic see, and the letter of Cyril with the twelve chapters." [1]

The bishops cried out: "If you order inquiry, we request that the fathers meet together."

The judges said: "The assembly is postponed for five days, and in the meantime your reverences shall come to Archbishop Anatolius and consult together concerning the faith."

All the most reverend bishops cried: "So we believe, so all believe; none of us doubt; we have already subscribed."

The judges continued: "You need not all meet, but since it is suitable to persuade all who doubt, let Archbishop Anatolius choose, from the bishops who have signed, those he thinks fit to instruct the doubters."   (Chapman 92B, 95B.)

These doubting bishops were keen supporters of Cyril. Their fear of the Nestorian heresy had caused them to sit on the opposition benches at the opening of the council. They wished to be sure that the Pope's letter was in accord with Cyril's teaching.

SESSION III

Meantime the council proceeds with the formal deposition of Dioscorus, after listening to four complaints against him from his own see. They are of interest because of the titles and position they give to the Pope.

DOCUMENT 256——Council of Chalcedon: Third Session.
      13 October 451.
      (Schwartz, ibid., p. [211].)

"To the most holy and beloved of God and *ecumenical archbishop* and patriarch of great Rome, Leo, and to the holy and ecumenical synod which is assembled at Chalcedon by the will of God and the sacred injunction, from Theodore, deacon of Alexandria.   ."

[1] Cyril, *Ep.* 17 (*P.G.* 77. 120).

(Schwartz [216].)

"To the most holy and most blessed *ecumenical patriarch* of great Rome, Leo, and to the holy and ecumenical synod which by the will of God and the divine command is assembled in the city of Chalcedon, from the wretched Athanasius, formerly presbyter of the great Alexandria, and nephew of the late Archbishop Cyril.   ."

The other two plaintiffs [1] begin their statements in the same manner as the deacon Theodore. Then Dioscorus is cited three times to attend the synod, in accordance with the 74th "Apostolic" canon.[2] He refuses to come and is formally sentenced by the papal legates. They say that the sentence is that of the Pope, who speaks through them and through the synod. But the synod, when sending the notification of his penalty to Dioscorus, does not mention the Pope at all.

Doc. 256 continued.   (Schwartz [224].)

Julian, bishop of Hypaipa, said : "Holy fathers, listen. When Dioscorus held the supreme power at the city of Ephesus for judging between S. Flavian with Bishop Eusebius, and Eutyches, putting forward an opinion which was unfair in every way, he himself led off with an unjust judgement, and all of necessity followed his lead. Now your holinesses hold the supreme power from the most holy Archbishop Leo; and the whole of the sacred council that is assembled by God's grace, and by the decree of our most pious emperors, has heard every one of the injustices committed at Ephesus; and everything done there has become known to your holinesses; and the council has cited Dioscorus, not once or twice, but three times, to appear, but he has absolutely refused to obey. We therefore urge your sanctity who hold, or rather ye who hold, the place of the most holy Archbishop Leo to speak out against him, and to define concerning him the canonical penalties. For we all, and the whole universal council, are voting with your sanctity."

Bishop Paschasinus said : "Again I say, what is the pleasure of your blessedness?"

[1] Schwartz, [213] and [219].   [2] Hefele, 1. 487.

Maximus, bishop of great Antioch, said: "With what your sanctity thinks we agree."

Paschasinus, bishop of Lilybaeum in Sicily, and with him Bishop Lucentius and Boniface, the priest of the church of great Rome, legates of the most holy and most blessed patriarch of great Rome, Archbishop Leo, pronounced: "It has been clearly shown by to-day's and the previous session what Dioscorus, bishop of the great Alexandrian church, dared to do against the order of the canons and church discipline. To pass over much else, he has received back into communion Eutyches, as being of the same opinion as himself, although he had been justly deposed by his bishop Flavian, and this he did in an irregular manner,[1] before he united with the other bishops at the Ephesian synod. But the apostolic see pardoned them for what they did there against their will and they have as far as possible shown obedience to Archbishop Leo and to the universal council.

". . But he, up till now, has proudly persisted in those things for which he ought to have lamented and bowed to the earth. Moreover, he did not allow the letter of the blessed Pope Leo to the late Flavian to be read, though he was often requested, and though he promised on oath, to do so; which not being read, the holy churches throughout the world have suffered scandal and injury. . . . He has ventured to pronounce excommunication against the most holy and pious Leo, archbishop of great Rome. Several complaints against him have been presented to the holy and great synod, and once, twice, and three times he has not obeyed the summons according to the episcopal canons. . . so he has proclaimed the vote against himself. Wherefore *the most holy and blessed Leo, archbishop of the great and elder Rome, through us and through this present most holy council, together with the thrice blessed and all glorious Peter the apostle, who is the rock and support of the Catholic Church and the foundation of the orthodox faith, has stripped him of the episcopal and all priestly dignity.* Assuredly, therefore, this most holy and great synod will vote upon the aforesaid Dioscorus according to the canons."

---

[1] See Nicene Canon 5 (Doc. 62).

Anatolius, bishop of royal Constantinople, new Rome, said: "*Considering all matters in the same way as the apostolic see, I vote with it* about the condemnation of Dioscorus, who was bishop of the great city of Alexandria, who has proved himself unworthy of all priestly office by disobeying in all things the canons of the fathers, and by not choosing to obey when three times canonically summoned."

The Latin acts give 188 more speeches confirming the sentence. Here are three examples.

Doc. 256 continued. (Schwartz, Tom. 2, Vol. 3, pp. [307], [310], [329].)

Theodore, metropolitan bishop of Tarsus, said: "Dioscorus has alienated himself from priestly worth by receiving Eutyches into his communion, contrary to rule, when he had been condemned by Flavian   whence he has been justly condemned by the greatest sees, as well of great Rome as of new Rome, by Leo and Anatolius, archbishops of the most holy churches, with whom I agree, and I have so spoken, judging him to be alien from all pontifical ministry."

Peter, metropolitan bishop of Gangra, said: "On the condemnation of Dioscorus, I consent to what the apostolic see and the holy fathers have decided."

Euphrates, bishop of Eleutherna, said: "I agree with the holy fathers on the condemnation of Dioscorus, formerly bishop of Alexandria, and *I judge* him to be alien from all priestly ministry."

And when all the most holy bishops had spoken, they signed thus:

Here follow the signatures of only 252 bishops, so that apparently about half of them did not sign.

Doc. 256 continued.   (Schwartz, Tom. 2, Vol. 1, p. |237|.)

The holy, great, and universal council which by the grace of God, according to the oracle of our pious and beloved emperors, assembled at Chalcedon, a city of Bithynia, in the martyry of the most holy and victorious martyr Euphemia, to Dioscorus.

Learn that on 13 October you were deposed from the episcopate, and made a stranger to all church order, by the holy and ecumenical synod, on account of your disregard of the divine canons and your disobedience to this holy and ecumenical synod, and on account of the other crimes of which you have been found guilty; for even when called to answer your accusers three times by this holy and great synod, according to the divine canons, you did not come.   (Chapman 91.)

SESSION IV

At the fourth session the judges were back in their places in order that the faith might be further considered, and especially Leo's letter to Flavian which had been read a week before.[1] The doubting bishops had in the meantime been instructed by the papal legates.

DOCUMENT 257——Council of Chalcedon: Fourth Session.
     17 October 451.
     (Schwartz, ibid., p. [288]; Fleury 3. 358 ‡.)

The judges said: "Let the council now declare what seems good concerning the faith.   ."

On behalf of the papal legates, Bishop Paschasinus said: "As the holy and universal council holds fast and follows the rule of faith which was set forth by the 318 at Nicaea, it also confirms the faith set forth by the 150 gathered at Constantinople at the bidding of the late emperor Theodosius the great. Moreover the exposition of the creed set forth at the council of Ephesus by the late Cyril, in which Nestorius was condemned, is likewise welcomed. And in the third place the writings of that blessed man Leo, *archbishop of all the churches,*

[1] See Doc. 255.

who condemned the heresies of Nestorius and Eutyches, show what the true faith is. Likewise the holy synod holds this faith: this it follows; nothing further can it add, nor can it take anything away."

When this had been translated into Greek, the bishops cried: "So we all believe, so we were baptized, so we baptize; so we have believed, so we now believe."

The judges said: "Since we see that the holy gospels have been placed alongside of your holiness, let each one of the bishops here assembled declare *whether the epistle of archbishop Leo is in accordance* with the exposition of the 318 fathers of Nicaea, and with the decrees of the 150 fathers afterwards assembled in the royal city."

Anatolius, bishop of Constantinople, said: "The letter of the most holy Archbishop Leo agrees with the creed of the 318 holy fathers of Nicaea, and of the 150 who afterwards assembled at Constantinople and confirmed the same faith, and with the proceedings at Ephesus of the ecumenical synod (under the blessed Cyril, who is among the saints) which condemned Nestorius. I therefore agree to it, and have willingly signed."

The papal legates said: "It is plain, and there can be no doubt, that the one faith of the most blessed Pope Leo agrees with the faith of the 318 fathers of Nicaea and with that of the 150 at Constantinople, and with the definitions set forth at Ephesus . . and in no way differs. Therefore the letter of the most blessed Pope, which expressed that faith on account of the error of Eutyches, is seen to be of the same sense, and also of one spirit with that creed."

Maximus, bishop of Syrian Antioch, said: "The letter of Leo, most holy archbishop of royal Rome, agrees with the expositions of the 318 holy fathers of Nicaea and of the 150 of Constantinople, new Rome, and with the exposition of faith by Bishop Cyril in Ephesus, and I have signed it."

[Sixty-two other bishops spoke to the same effect. I give three specimens.]

John, bishop of Sebaste, in the first Armenia, said: "As I see it, the meaning of the letter of Leo, bishop of the Romans, agrees with the faith of the 318 and of the 150 afterwards

assembled at Constantinople, and with the exposition of
Ephesus at the deposition of the ungodly Nestorius, at which
blessed Cyril presided, and I have signed this same letter."

Seleucus, bishop of Amasea, said: "We have found the
synodical letter of our most holy father Cyril to be in harmony
with the faith of the 318 holy fathers. Likewise we have found
the letter of the most holy Archbishop Leo to agree with the
318 and with those who agree with Cyril."

John, bishop of Germanicia Augusta on the Euphrates,
said: "In the faith of the 318 .   . and of the 150   . we have
been baptized and baptize. And having found what was set
forth by S. Cyril and confirmed in the former council of
Ephesus, as indeed the letter of the most holy Archbishop Leo,
to be in harmony with this, we have signed it.

[On behalf of 31 bishops of Illyria] Sozon, bishop of
Philippi, read from a chart: "We keep the faith of the 318
holy fathers, which is our salvation, and to it we devote our
lives; nowhere do we disagree with the faith of the 150, and
we follow in all things the decrees and definitions of the first
synod of Ephesus, at which Celestine and Cyril were leaders;
and we are fully convinced that the most holy father and archbishop Leo is most orthodox. But that which in his letter
appeared doubtful has been explained to us by the papal
legates.   . For when by your authority we assembled with
Anatolius, bishop of Constantinople,   they banished our
doubts. For they rejected all who separate the flesh of our
Lord and Saviour Jesus Christ from his Godhead, and who
do not say that the divine and human existed in him from the
Holy Virgin Mary, Mother of God, unmingled, unchanged,
and undivided. With this we are satisfied; we agree that the
letter accords with all that the fathers have proclaimed, and
we have signed it." All the Illyrians with one voice said:
"We all agree."

[On behalf of 16 bishops of Palestine] Bishop Ananias read from a chart: "We all have always kept the faith of the 318 and we do keep it, and thereto we devote our life. We follow without disagreement that of the 150, and agree with the decrees and definitions of the late Cyril at the first synod of Ephesus. But when the letter of Leo, archbishop of Rome, was read to us, we accepted the greater part as correct. But some parts seemed to express a certain separation and division, and so we hesitated to accept them.   We learnt, however, from the representatives of Archbishop Leo, that they admit no separation of our Lord and Saviour Jesus Christ, but confess one and the same Lord and Son of God. And now we think, if your greatness permits, that these things should be put on record for the benefit of the whole world." All the aforesaid bishops said: "So say all of us and agree."

[There were 44 more speeches like that of Maximus of Antioch.]

The judges said: "The other bishops will state whether they agree that what has been said accords with the sayings of the holy fathers."

All the most reverend bishops shouted: "We are all agreed. We all cling together. We all believe alike. We all think these things. Thus we think   Long live the emperors! The five[1] also have subscribed to the faith. As Leo, so they think. Long live the emperors!"   (Chapman 117A.)

We see then that, before accepting the Pope's exposition of the faith, the bishops assured themselves that it agreed with the creeds and other statements of doctrine which they regarded as authentic. Now it was defined by Pope Pius IX in the Vatican council of 1870 "that it is a dogma divinely revealed: that the Roman Pontiff, when he speaks *ex cathedra*, that is, when in discharge of the office of Pastor and Doctor of all Christians, by virtue of his supreme Apostolic authority, he defines a doctrine regarding faith or morals to be held by the Universal Church, by the divine assistance promised to him in blessed Peter, is possessed of that infallibility with which the Divine Redeemer willed that His Church should be endowed for defining doctrines regarding faith or morals; and that therefore such defini-tions of the Roman Pontiff are irreformable of themselves and not

1 Five bishops formerly associated with Dioscorus.

from the consent of the Church".[1] Further we are told by Pope Leo XIII that this definition is retrospective: "no newly conceived opinion is set forth, but the venerable and constant belief of every age".[2] It is therefore important to know whether Leo's letter was a pronouncement *ex cathedra* or not. Roman Catholic scholars disagree on this point. Tixeront thinks that "this letter has always been regarded as a dogmatic document of the first order. . . . S. Leo wishes neither to discuss nor to explain; he pronounces and he judges".[3] But Bellarmine holds that "Leo had sent his letter to the council, not as containing his final and definite sentence, but as an instruction, assisted by which the bishops might form a better judgement".[4] Jalland [5] suggests that we allow Leo to decide the point as follows:

DOCUMENT 258——Leo, *Ep.* 93, to the Council of Chalcedon.
   26 June 451.
   (*P.L.* 54. 937; *P.N.F.* 12. 70A ⁺⁄₊.)

2. And so, dearest brothers, let all attempts to call in question the divinely inspired faith be entirely put down, and the vain unbelief of heretics be laid to rest, and do not let that be defended which may not be believed, since in accordance with the evangelical decrees, the voices of the prophets, and the teaching of the apostles, with the greatest fullness and clearness in the letter which we sent to the late Bishop Flavian, *it has been made clear what is* the devout and genuine confession upon the mystery of the incarnation of our Lord Jesus Christ.

Chapman held that "St Leo apparently meant his 'tome' to Flavian as an infallible utterance, but in the case of a document of that length I do not see that he could have complained if the Fathers of Chalcedon had objected to the wording here and there as ambiguous or misleading. As a fact, St Leo thought it was the devil who made some bishops ask for explanations!"[6] To support this he cites part of the next Document.

[1] *Pastor Aeternus* § 4: C. Butler, *Vatican Council*, 2. 295.
[2] *Satis Cognitum* § 15.
[3] *Histoires des Dogmes*, Deuxième Edition, 3. 86. I refer to the French because E.T. seems faulty here.
[4] *De Conciliorum Auctoritate*, 2. 19: *Op.* 2: 270A (edit. 1872).
[5] *Leo*, 302.
[6] Chapman, 117A.

DOCUMENT 259——Leo, *Ep.* 120, to Theodoret of Cyrus (*Remeantibus*). 11 June 453. (*P.L.* 54. 1046; *P.N.F.* 12. 87A ‡.)

1. On the return of our brothers and fellow priests whom the see of blessed Peter sent to the holy council, we ascertained, beloved, the victory you and we together had won, by help from above, over the blasphemy of Nestorius and the madness of Eutyches. Wherefore we glory in the Lord, chanting with the prophet: "Our help is in the name of the Lord, who hath made heaven and earth": who has allowed us to sustain no harm in our brethren, but has corroborated, by the irrevocable assent of the whole brotherhood, *what he had before defined by our ministry*, to show that what had before been enacted by the first see of all, *and received by the judgement of the whole Christian world*, had truly proceeded from himself, that in this too the members may agree with the head. And herein our cause for rejoicing grows when we see that the more fiercely the foe assailed Christ's servants, the more did he afflict himself. For lest the assent of the other sees, to that which the Lord of all has appointed to precede the rest, might seem mere complaisance, or lest any other evil suspicion might creep in, some were found to dispute our decisions. And while some, *instigated by the author of dissension*, rush forward into a war of contradiction, a greater good results from his evil, under the dispensation of the author of all goodness. For the gifts of divine grace are sweeter to us when they are not gained without great toils, and continued peace through idleness is liable to seem a lesser good than one which is restored by labours. Besides, the truth itself shines more brightly, and is more bravely upheld, when *what the faith had already taught* is afterwards confirmed by further inquiry. And finally the merit of the priestly office gains much in lustre, where the authority of the higher is preserved, so that the liberty of the inferiors is thought to be in no way diminished. And the result of a discussion contributes to God's greater glory when the debaters exert themselves with confidence in overcoming the gainsayers, that what of itself is proved wrong may not seem to be passed over in prejudicial silence.   (Chapman 117A and note.)

About 250 years ago, long before the Vatican council, Bishop Bossuet[1] used the above letter to argue against papal infallibility. He points out that Leo himself stresses that his tome was "corroborated by the irrevocable assent of the whole brotherhood", "received by the judgement of the whole Christian world", and "confirmed by further inquiry". And so he assumes that according to Leo the consent of the Church must be added before a papal judgement on the faith can be regarded as irrevocable. This, however, does not give weight to Leo's words that before all these consents God had already laid down the faith through the ministry of the Pope. Further, "Satan's attack" on the Illyrian and Palestinian bishops did not succeed. They were put right by the papal legates, and Leo is sure that the whole discussion redounded to the greater glory of God.

SESSION VIII

During the first session it was stated by the judges that the Pope had restored Theodoret to his bishopric; and they gave that as a reason for his taking his place in the council. His opponents shouted against this and were scarcely pacified by the judges' saying that "the presence of Theodoret shall prejudice no one's cause" (Doc. 254). He was suspected of being a Nestorian, and had been condemned as such at the Robber Synod. In spite of the papal restoration, the council of Chalcedon makes certain that he is not a heretic before it restores him.

DOCUMENT 260——Council of Chalcedon: Eighth Session.
    26 October 451.
    (Schwartz [368]; Hefele 3. 356 $\ddagger$.)

The bishops cried: "Theodoret must anathematize at once."

Theodoret stepped forward at once: "I have presented a petition to the emperor and a paper to the legates of Archbishop Leo, and if you wish, let it be read, that you may know how I think."

The bishops cried: "We will have no reading; anathematize Nestorius at once."

Theodoret said: "By God's grace I was brought up by orthodox priests, and rightly instructed, and I have also taught rightly and reject not only Nestorius and Eutyches, but every man who does not rightly think."

---

[1] *Gallia Orthodoxa*, 61: *Oeuvres*, 9. 40A (Paris, 1836).

The bishops, interrupting, cried: "Say clearly 'Anathema to Nestorius and his doctrines, anathema to Nestorius and his friends!'"

Theodoret said: "In truth I say nothing, unless I know that it is pleasing to God. First I assure you that neither do I think of a city, nor do I desire honour, nor am I here for such, but because I have been slandered. I came to prove that I am orthodox, and that I anathematize Nestorius and Eutyches, and all who confess two Sons."

The bishops, interrupting, cried: "Say openly 'Anathema to Nestorius and those who think with him!'"

Theodoret said: "If I have not explained how I believe, I say nothing, but I do believe."

The bishops, interrupting, cried: "He is a Nestorian heretic; throw him out."

Theodoret said: "Anathema to Nestorius, and to him who does not call the Holy Virgin Mary 'Mother of God', and who divides into two Sons the one only begotten Son! And I have signed the rule of faith, and the letter of Archbishop Leo, and so I think. And after all this, may you be saved!"

The judges said: "Every remaining doubt about the beloved Theodoret is removed, for he has anathematized Nestorius in your presence, and has been favourably received by Archbishop Leo, and has readily accepted the definition of faith which your pieties have accepted, and has also subscribed the letter of the aforesaid most holy Archbishop Leo. It remains that, by the exercise of your reverences' vote, he receive back his church, as the most holy Archbishop Leo has thought right."

All the bishops cried: "Theodoret is worthy of the see. The orthodox to the Church! The Church takes back the shepherd. . Long live Archbishop Leo! Leo has judged with God. The people take back the orthodox. Worthy of the see! The Church restores Theodoret to the episcopate."   (Chapman 115A.)

SESSION XV

On the last day of October, in the absence of the judges and papal legates, the council passed what came to be called the 28th canon, which has caused so much controversy in ancient and modern times.

DOCUMENT 261——Council of Chalcedon: Fifteenth Session. 31 October 451.

(*P.L.* 67. 93.)

Canon 28. We, following in all respects the rules of the holy fathers and recognizing the canon[1] of the 150 most religious bishops just recited, do also define and vote for the same things respecting the privileges of the most holy church of Constantinople, new Rome. For to the throne of the elder Rome, because that was the imperial city, the fathers naturally rendered[2] the first honours; and moved by the same consideration, the 150 most religious bishops assigned equal honours to the most holy throne of new Rome, judging with reason that the city which is honoured with the government and senate, and enjoys equal privileges with the elder royal Rome, should also be magnified like her in ecclesiastical matters, being second after her: so that the metropolitans only, of the Pontic, and Asian, and Thracian dioceses, and moreover the bishops of the aforesaid dioceses who are among the barbarians, shall be ordained by the above-mentioned most holy throne of the most holy church of Constantinople. Clearly each metropolitan of the aforesaid dioceses, with the bishops of the province, is to ordain the bishops of the province as has been declared by the divine canons;[3] but the metropolitans themselves of the said dioceses shall, as has been said, be ordained by the archbishop of Constantinople, after the usual election has been reported to him.

(Gore v, 102; Chapman 86A and note 2.)

Modern disputes have turned on the meaning of ἀποδίδωμι. This verb appears forty-eight times in the New Testament, frequently in connexion with the payment of debts, and almost always with the meaning of giving back or rendering what is due. Such are the first translations given by Liddell and Scott. None the less Kidd translates *gave*[4] or *conceded*,[5] which suggests that the Roman primacy was not of apostolic origin, but had been assigned by some later fathers. See also Gore, p. 102, who, however, abandoned the translation *gave* in his tenth edition.[6] But some R.C. scholars are prepared to accept the

[1] See Doc. 97.   [2] ἀποδεδώκασι.
[3] Nicene Canons 4 and 6. See Doc. 62.
[4] Kidd, *Docs.*, 2. 300.   [5] *Roman Primacy*, 145.
[6] *R.C. Claims*, 10th edition, preface.

translation "The fathers *gave* [or *decreed*] the first honours to Rome". They explain it in two ways which are mutually exclusive. A. Westall [1] says that the fathers referred to are Peter and Paul. He thinks that the framers of the canon got this idea from Leo himself, who wrote, "These are thy fathers . . . who have promoted thee to this glory".[2] Elsewhere the council calls the Pope "an interpreter to all of the voice of blessed Peter".[3] Duchesne does not agree; he thinks that the fathers referred to are bishops, not apostles, and so he is forced to the opinion that those who wrote this canon were mistaken in their views about the origin of the Roman primacy.[4]

SESSION XVI

Controversy about the main purport of Canon 28 began the very next day. The attempt to give the bishop of Constantinople a wider jurisdiction was resisted by the papal legates, when they, with the imperial judges, returned to the council on 1 November. Paschasinus led off with a complaint that the proceedings of the day before, in the absence of the Roman legation, were uncanonical. The archdeacon of Constantinople replied that the legates had been asked to stay but declined. The whole affair he said was above board. The judges then ordered the acts to be read, and Canon 28 (Doc. 261) was recited together with 192 episcopal signatures, among them that of Theodoret, who like the others remarks, "Having determined, I signed".[5]

DOCUMENT 262——Council of Chalcedon: Sixteenth Session.
    1 November 451.
    (Schwartz [453]; *P.N.F.* 14. 292B ‡.)

Lucentius, bishop and legate of the apostolic see, said: "In the first place your excellency should notice that it was brought about by the circumstances of the holy bishops, who were forced to sign the said canons."

The bishops cried: "No one was forced!"

Lucentius said: "It seems that the decrees of the 318 have been passed over, and that mention has only been made of those of the 150 which are not among the synodical canons,[6]

---

1 *Dublin Review*, Vol. 132, Jan. 1903, pp. 100–114.
2 Doc. 242 § 1.   3 Doc. 263 § 1.
4 *Churches Separated from Rome*, E.T., 131.
5 Schwartz, [452]. Cp. Gore, 103, n. 2.
6 Cp. Doc. 254 above, p. 300.

(and which were made, as they acknowledged, eighty years ago).[1] If during those times they experienced the benefit, why do they now seek what is not canonical?"

Aetius, archdeacon of Constantinople, said: "If they have received any instructions on this head, let them be expressed."

Boniface, a Roman legate, said: "The most blessed and apostolic bishop among other things gave us this order. (And he recited from a chart) 'The rulings of the holy fathers shall with no rashness be violated or diminished. Let the dignity of our person in all ways be guarded by you. And if any influenced by the power of his own city should undertake to make usurpations, withstand this with suitable firmness'."

The judges said: "Let each party quote the canons."

Paschasinus, bishop and legate, read: "The canon of the 318 holy fathers: 'The Roman church always had the primacy. Let Egypt therefore so hold itself that the bishop of Alexandria have the authority over all, for this is also the custom of the Roman bishop. So too he who is established at Antioch. And in the other provinces let the privileges of the churches be preserved.   .'"

Constantine, the secretary, read from a book handed to him by Aetius, archdeacon of Constantinople: "The canon of the 318 holy fathers: 'Let the ancient customs prevail, those of Egypt so that the bishop of Alexandria shall have jurisdiction over all, since this also is the custom of the bishop in Rome [etc. as in Doc. 62].'"

The same secretary read from the same book: "The decision of the second synod: these things the bishops decreed who assembled in Constantinople . . 'The bishop of Constantinople shall have the privileges of honour after the bishop of Rome, because it is new Rome'."[2]

The judges said: "Let the bishops of Asia and Pontus who have signed the tome just read say whether they signed willingly, or were compelled by any necessity."

And these coming into the middle, Diogenes, bishop of Cyzicus, said: "Before God I signed of my will."

[1] (. . .) Latin text only. See Schwartz, Tom. 2, Vol. 3, p. [548].
[2] Canons 1, 2 and 3 of Constantinople, A.D. 381. See Doc. 97.

[Twelve others spoke to the same effect, and then:]
The remaining bishops cried: "We signed willingly."

The judges said: "From what has been done, and from everything laid down, we observe that the primacy of all and the chief honour according to the canons is to be kept for the beloved archbishop of old Rome, but that the reverend archbishop of the royal Constantinople, which is new Rome, is to enjoy the honour of the same primacy, and to have the power to ordain the metropolitans in the dioceses of Asia, Pontus, and Thrace.   ."

The bishops cried out: "This is a just sentence; so we all say. These things please us all. This is a just judgement. Establish the proposed decree.   Let us go.   We all say the same."

Bishop Lucentius said: "The apostolic see gave orders that all things should be done in our presence [or Latin version: "The apostolic see ought not to be humiliated in our presence"] [1]; and therefore whatever was done yesterday in our absence, against the canons of the court, we beseech your highness to order it to be rescinded. But if not, let our protest be recorded in the minutes, and pray let us know clearly what we are to report to that most apostolic bishop who is the ruler of the whole Church, so that he may be able to speak out about the insult to his own see, and about the upsetting of the canons."

The judges said: "The whole council has approved what we proposed."   (Gore 101 note, 102; Chapman 86B, 87A note.)

Our main interest in this session is concisely put by Hefele: "The prerogative assigned to the church of Constantinople is, in spite of the opposition of the Roman legate, decreed by the synod."[2] Notice also the two versions of the Nicene Canon 6. The version read by Paschasinus appears to come from an Italian codex known as *The code of Ingilram*, bishop of Teate, which C. H. Turner[3] assigns to the fourth century. Jalland[4] thinks that the opening words, "The Roman church

[1] Schwartz, Tom 2, Vol. 3, p. [552].   [2] Hefele, 3. 428.
[3] Turner, 103, 121.
[4] *Papacy*, 309.

always had the primacy", refer to the primacy in Italy, and may have been inserted about A.D. 370 owing to the loss of prestige suffered by Rome under Pope Liberius, and owing to the increasing importance of the see of Milan. The two oldest Latin versions follow the Greek text.

It is a question whether the true version of the canon was really read by the secretary after the Roman version. It does not help the case for Canon 28 of Chalcedon, which was under discussion, but merely emphasizes the nakedness of the land as far as the see of Constantinople is concerned. Consequently the Ballerini [1] and Hefele [2] say it was interpolated into the acts. The Ballerini bring forward the Latin MS. *Codex Julianus*, which omits the passage. They are followed by the Jewish historian Erich Caspar,[3] and more recently by Jalland.[4] On the other hand the acts of Chalcedon clearly state that both versions were read one after the other, and certain Anglicans [5] have supposed that the reading of the correct version was for the purpose of correcting the version of the Roman legates which exalts the primacy of the Roman church.

[1] *P.L.* 56. 48.   [2] Hefele, 3. 425.
[3] *Geschichte des Papsttums*, Erster Band, p. 523 (A.D. 1930).
[4] *Papacy*, 309, n. 4.
[5] W. Bright, *Age of the Fathers*, 2. 546; H. R. Percival in *P.N.F.* 14. 293ᴮ; B. J. Kidd, *Roman Primacy*, 147.

CHAPTER XXVI

LEO AFTER CHALCEDON

THE 28th canon of Chalcedon (Doc. 261) figures largely in the later correspondence of Pope Leo. Our last seven Documents all refer to it, and are all mentioned by Chapman.

DOCUMENT 263——Council of Chalcedon, *To Leo*.   A.D. 451. Leo, *Ep.* 98.   (*P.L.* 54. 952; *P.N.F.* 12. 72A ‡.)

1.   "Teaching them to observe all things whatsoever I commanded you".[1] You have kept this command, which is like a golden cord leading down from the author of it to us. You are set as an interpreter to all of the voice of blessed Peter, and to all you impart the blessings of that faith. And so we too, wisely taking you as our guide in all that is good, have shown to the sons of the Church their inheritance of the truth. We have not given our instruction singly and in secret, but with one mind and agreement we have made known the confession of the common faith. We were all delighted at the spiritual food which Christ supplied to us through your letter; we revelled in it as at an imperial banquet and we seemed to see the heavenly Bridegroom actually present with us. For if where two or three are gathered together in his name, he has said that he is in the midst of them, must he not have been much more particularly present with 520 priests who preferred to their country and their ease the spread of knowledge about him? Of all these you were the chief, as head to members, showing your goodwill in matters of organization. The faithful emperors were eager to renew the doctrinal fabric of the Church and presided for the sake of good order, just like Zerubbabel to Joshua in the matter of the temple at Jerusalem.

1 Matt. 28. 20.

322

2. The enemy would have been like a wild beast outside the fold .   if the late pontiff of the Alexandrians had not thrown himself to him for a prey.   . By his terror-won votes he acquitted Eutyches, who had been condemned for heresy, and restored to him the dignity which your holiness had taken away from him as unworthy of it. And, like the strangest of wild beasts, he fell upon the vine which he found in the finest condition, uprooted it, and planted that which had been cast out as unfruitful. He cut off those who acted like true shepherds, and he placed over the flocks those who had shown themselves to be wolves. Besides all this he extended his fury even against *him who had been charged with the custody of the vine by the Saviour—we refer to your holiness*—and he intended to excommunicate one who was zealous to unite the body of the Church.

4. We mention further that we have made certain other decisions also for the good management and stability of church affairs, as we are persuaded that your holiness will accept and ratify them when you are told. The long prevailing custom which the holy church of God at Constantinople had of ordaining metropolitans for the provinces of Asia, Pontus, and Thrace we have now ratified by the vote of the synod, not thereby adding anything to the see of Constantinople, but to provide for the good order of the metropolitan sees, because of the frequent disorders that arise when their bishops die.

We have also ratified the canon[1] of the 150 holy fathers who met at Constantinople   which declares that after your most holy and apostolic see, the see of Constantinople shall have privileges, being placed second; for we are persuaded that, with your usual interest, you have often extended that apostolic radiance of yours even to the church of Constantinople also. This you will increase many times by sharing your own good things ungrudgingly with your brethren. And so deign, most holy and blessed father, to embrace as your own, and as lovable and agreeable to good order, the things we have decreed, for the removal of all confusion, and the confirmation of church order. For the legates of your holiness,

[1] Doc. 97.

the most holy bishops Paschasinus and Lucentius, and with them the godly presbyter Boniface, tried hard to resist these decisions, wishing that this good work also should start from your foresight, so that the establishment of discipline, as well as of faith, should be credited to you. But we, regarding our most devout and Christian sovereigns, who delight therein, and the illustrious senate, and, so to say, the whole capital, recognized as fitting the confirmation of the honour by this universal council, and we confidently endorsed it, as if it were initiated by your holiness, as you always hasten to cherish us, knowing that every success of the children redounds to the parents. We therefore beg you to honour our decision by your assent, and as we have yielded agreement to the head in noble things, so may the head also fulfil what is fitting for the children. Thus will our pious emperors be respected, who have ratified your holiness' judgement as law, and the see of Constantinople will receive its recompense for having always displayed such loyalty on matters of religion towards you, and for having so zealously linked itself to you in full agreement. But that you may know that we have done nothing for favour or in hatred, but as being guided by the divine will, we have informed you of the whole scope of our actions, to strengthen our position and to ratify and establish what we have done.

(Gore 103; Chapman 86, 87.)

Notice four points in this letter. The Pope is the mouthpiece of Peter, and imparts Peter's faith to all (§ 1). The Pope was the head of the council of Chalcedon. His letter was spiritual food supplied by Christ (§ 1). The Pope has been charged with the care of the Church by our Lord (§ 2), and his care for others extends to Constantinople (§ 4). The papal legates resisted Canon 28, desiring that the initiative should come from the Pope, who is asked to honour the council's decision by his assent.

The emperor and the bishop of Constantinople were equally anxious that the 28th canon should receive papal approval, but the style of their writing differs from that of the council, and Anatolius gives a different reason for the resistance of the legates, namely that they did not know the Pope's mind. Both these writers deal first with the agreement reached on matters of faith, and then come to the point.

DOCUMENT 264——The Emperor Marcian, *To Leo.* 18
December 451.
> Leo, *Ep.* 100. (*P.L.* 54. 974; Jalland, *Leo* 318, and
> editor.)

3. After that, this decision was actually made, so that
the resolution of the 150 most holy bishops in the time of
the divine Theodosius the Elder concerning the honour of the
venerable church of Constantinople, and the recent prescrip-
tion of the holy synod on the same subject, should be upheld
intact: namely that, after the apostolic see, the bishop of the
city of Constantinople receives the second place, because the
said most glorious city is called Rome the Younger. Let your
holiness think fit to add personal assent also to this part, even
though the most reverend bishops who met together at the
holy synod as representatives of your devoutness have voted
against it. For they absolutely forbad anything to be settled
concerning this venerable church by the synod.

4. . And we beg that your devoutness will also give
instructions that those things which the holy synod has decreed
be observed for ever. Other things by hand. May God preserve
you for many years, most holy and devout father.

(Chapman 87B.)

DOCUMENT 265——Anatolius, Bishop of Constantinople, *To
Leo.* A.D. 451.
> Leo, *Ep.* 101. (*P.L.* 54. 982.)

4. . . . As there was no doubt that your holiness and your
church possessed still higher honour, the synod willingly confirmed the canon of the 150 fathers that the bishop of Constantinople should have the next rank after the most holy
Roman see, since Constantinople is new Rome. And they further decreed that he should ordain the metropolitans of the
provinces of Pontus, Asia, and Thrace, the bishops under them
being ordained by their own metropolitans, a decree by which
the see of Constantinople lost several rights of ordination which
it had exercised for sixty or seventy years.

5. But when all things were going well, and were joyfully concluding, the most pious bishops Paschasinus and Lucentius and the most reverend presbyter Boniface (who had often been informed by us about this same matter), not knowing the intention of your holiness which you have towards the holiest church of Constantinople, after the sacred synod had signed and by subscription confirmed this decree, scorn the synod, and without cause throw the assembly into confusion, setting this see at nought, and bringing much occasion of insolence on me and on this most holy church of Constantinople. Moreover these decrees had been drawn up in accordance with the will of our most pious emperors, the most magnificent and glorious judges of the council assisting by pronouncing the definition of the holy synod to be secure. . God is witness that we on our part, both before and after their arrival, were careful in all things which pertain to your glory and honour, and this being clear, it is also evident that similar honour and reverence was accorded to them. And in accordance with your dignity, *the sacred synod has remitted this decree to your holiness, that we may obtain approval and confirmation from you*; and we implore you, O most holy one, that this be made effective by you. For the throne of Constantinople has your apostolic throne as its father.   (Chapman 87B.)

Leo had no doubt that his legates had understood his instructions, and he resists the new legislation with all his power, basing his objections on the fact that it is contrary to the 6th canon of Nicaea. This he does in three letters sent to Constantinople in May 452, and in his letter to the empress he formally cancels the 28th canon of Chalcedon, by the authority of Peter.

DOCUMENT 266——Leo, *Ep.* 104, to the Emperor Marcian
     (*Magno munere*).   22 May 452.
     (*P.L.* 54. 993; *P.N.F.* 12. 75A ‡.)

2. Now that these things about which so great a number of priests assembled have been brought to a good and desirable end, I am surprised and grieved that the peace of the universal Church, which had been divinely restored, is again being

disturbed by a spirit of ambition. For although my brother Anatolius seems of necessity to have consulted himself in forsaking the error of those who ordained him, accepting the catholic faith by a healthy correction, yet he should have taken care not to mar, by any depravity of desire, that which he is known to have obtained by your kindness. For we, having regard to your faith and intervention, wish to be kind rather than just towards him, though his beginnings were suspicious on account of those who consecrated him.   . Anatolius the bishop detracts greatly from his proper merits by desiring undue aggrandizement.

3. Let the city of Constantinople have, as we desire, its glory, and, under the protection of God's right hand, long enjoy the rule of your clemency. Yet things secular stand on a different basis from things divine, and there can be no sure building save on that rock which the Lord has laid for a foundation. He that covets what is not his due loses what is his own. Let it be enough for him that by the aid of your piety, and *by my gracious favour*, he has obtained the bishopric of so great a city. Let him not disdain a royal city, though he cannot make it an apostolic see; and let him on no account hope that he can rise by doing injury to others. For the privileges of the churches determined by the canons of the holy fathers, and fixed by the decrees of the Nicene synod, cannot be overthrown by any unscrupulous act, nor can they be disturbed by any innovation. And in the faithful execution of this task by the aid of Christ, I am bound to display an unflinching devotion; for it is a charge entrusted to me, and it tends to my condemnation if the rules sanctioned by the fathers and drawn up under the guidance of God's Spirit at the synod of Nicaea for the government of the whole Church are violated with my connivance, which God forbid, and if the wishes of a single brother have more weight with me than the common good of the Lord's whole house.

4. .   With earnest entreaty, I pray and beseech your piety to refuse assent to this monstrous attack against Christian unity and peace, and to curb effectively the obnoxious greediness of my brother Anatolius. (Chapman 87B.)

DOCUMENT 267——Leo, *Ep.* 105, to the Empress Pulcheria
   (*Sanctis et Deo*). 22 May 452.
   (*P.L.* 54. 998; *P.N.F.* 12. 76B ‡.)

2. My brother and fellow bishop Anatolius, not sufficiently
considering your grace's kindness and *the favour of my assent*,
whereby he gained the priesthood of the church of Constantinople, instead of rejoicing at what he had gained, has been
inflamed with undue desires beyond the measure of his rank,
believing that his intemperate ambition could be advanced by
the assertion that certain persons had signified their assent
thereto by an extorted signature; in spite of the fact that my
brethren and fellow bishops who represented me, faithfully and
laudably expressed their dissent from these attempts, which
are doomed to speedy failure.

. For it is alleged that connivance at this sort of thing has
been going on for about sixty years, a fact which the aforesaid
bishop supposes will help his cause.

3.   Indeed resolutions of bishops which are repugnant
to the rules of the holy canons composed at Nicaea, in conjunction with the loyalty of your faith, *we dismiss as invalid, and
by the authority of Peter, the blessed apostle, we absolutely disannul
by a general decree* in all ecclesiastical cases, obeying those laws
which the Holy Ghost defined by the 318 bishops for the pacific
observance of all priests, in such sort that even if a much greater
number were to pass a different decree from theirs, whatever
was opposed to their constitution would have to be held in
no respect.   (Chapman 87B, 115A.)

DOCUMENT 268——Leo, *Ep.* 106, to Anatolius (*Manifestato*).
   22 May 452.
   (*P.L.* 54. 1003; *P.N.F.* 12. 78A ‡.)

2.   It seems that this time is opportune for the see of
Alexandria to lose the privilege of the second place, and for
the church of Antioch to be deprived of its right to the third
rank,[1] with the result that when these places are subjected to
your law, all metropolitan bishops are stripped of their rightful

[1] See Doc. 99.

office.   The Nicene council has been divinely endowed with so great a privilege that if ecclesiastical decisions are approved, whether by few or many, whatever is inconsistent with its decrees is altogether devoid of authority.

5.   Your purpose is in no way supported by the writing of certain bishops given, as you allege, sixty years ago, and *never brought to the knowledge of the apostolic see* by your predecessors. And this transaction, which from its outset was doomed to fall through, and has long since done so, you now wish to bolster up by useless means which are too late, namely by extracting from the brethren an appearance of consent, which their tired modesty presented to you to their own injury.

The rights of provincial primates may not be overthrown, nor may metropolitan bishops be defrauded of privileges based on antiquity. The see of Alexandria may not lose any of that dignity which it merited through S. Mark the evangelist, and disciple of blessed Peter, nor may the splendour of so great a church be obscured by another's clouds, Dioscorus having fallen through his persistence in impiety. The church of Antioch too, in which first, at the preaching of the blessed apostle Peter, the Christian name arose, must continue in the position assigned it by the fathers, and, being set in the third place, must never be lowered therefrom. For the see is on a different footing from the holders of it; and each individual's chief honour is his own integrity. And since that does not lose its proper worth in any place, how much more glorious must it be when placed in the magnificence of the city of Constantinople, where many priests may find, through your observance, both a defence of the canons of the fathers, and an example of uprightness!   (Chapman 87B.)

In this last letter the Pope misrepresents the 28th canon, which carefully safeguards the rights of metropolitan bishops. Further, if the Pope had really never heard of Canon 3 of Constantinople (Doc. 97), this is an argument against a fourth-century date for our Doc. 99, which seems to be the Roman reply to that canon. But see the remark of Leo's legate at the first session of Chalcedon, and the reply of Diogenes.[1]

[1] Doc. 254, p. 300.

The Pope's letter to Theodoret, which we have already seen (Doc. 259), was written about a year after this; and so we come to our last Document, the reply of Anatolius to Leo, saying that the confirmation of Canon 28 of Chalcedon was reserved to the Pope.

DOCUMENT 269——Anatolius, *To Leo.* April 454.
    Leo, *Ep.* 132. (*P.L.* 54. 1084.)

4. As for those things which the universal council of Chalcedon recently ordained in favour of the church of Constantinople, let your holiness be sure that there was no fault in me, who from my youth have always loved peace and quiet, keeping myself in humility. It was the most reverend clergy of the church of Constantinople who were eager about it, and they were equally supported by the most reverend priests of those parts, who agreed about it. Even so *the whole force and confirmation of the acts was reserved for the authority of your blessedness.* Therefore let your holiness know for certain that I did nothing to further the matter, having always held myself bound to avoid the lusts of pride and covetousness.

(Chapman 87B, 88A.)

The somewhat "abject"[1] humility of this letter would have been more impressive if the writer had not delayed his reply for two years. It seems too that his statement about reserving confirmation to the Pope was insincere.[2] Leo refused to confirm the canon, but his refusal had no practical effect, as Chapman points out. "The long prevailing custom which the holy church of God at Constantinople had of ordaining metropolitans for the provinces of Asia, Pontus, and Thrace"[3] "went on as before".[4]

[1] Chapman, 87B.	[2] See Jalland, *Leo*, 346.
[3] Doc. 263 § 4.	[4] Chapman, 88A.

INDEX OF DOCUMENTS

INDEX OF SCRIPTURE REFERENCES
IN THE DOCUMENTS

CHRONOLOGICAL INDEX OF THE BISHOPS OF ROME

For references to four later popes see General Index.

GENERAL INDEX

For many persons within the period 96–454 dates are given in brackets. A stretch of years covers tenure of office as shown, but in some cases only the year particularly dealt with is given.

Abercius, bp of Hierapolis (180), 30
Acacius, bp of Militene (434), 259, 304n.
Aetius, archdn of Constantinople (451), 303, 304, 319
Africa, 23, 41, 61, 181
Agrippinus, bp of Carthage (210), 26, 68, 70, 272
Alaric, 194
Alcibiades, 35
Alexandria, 21, 42, 44, 93, 97, 98, 103, 129, 131, 154, 228, 293n., 305, 306, 328; and see Councils
Alypius, bp of Tagaste (419), 225
Ambrose, bp of Milan (374–97), 143–7, 149, 210, 240, 276
Ambrosiaster (370), 121–3
Anatolius, bp of Constantinople (449–58), 290n., 298, 305, 308, 310, 327, 328
Antioch, 3, 43, 93, 96n., 97, 129, 131, 132, 134, 137, 150, 162, 171, 228, 293, 295, 328; and see Councils
Anti-popes, 31–43, 84, 117, 118, 149, 151
Antonian, African bp (252), 40
Antonine, emp. (138–61), 21
Antony, bp of Fussala (423), 231–3
Apelles, 21, 73
Apiarius, African priest, 224, 227, 234, 236
Apollonius, bp of Ephesus (210), 266
Apostles' Creed, 159
"Apostolic" Canons, 4th cent., 93, 246, 306
Apostolic churches, 9–11, 22, 194
Appeals, 100, 101, 224–7, 231, 294
Aquileia, 139, 162
Aquinas, T., 182
Arabia, 43

Arcadius, bp and papal legate (431), 248, 249, 252, 253, 255
Arianism, 82, 92, 99, 102–4, 106–13, 115, 132, 133, 136–8, 142, 149–51
Asia, 15, 16, 24
Asterius, bp of Amasea (395), 145
Athanasius, bp of Alexandria (328–73), 80, 81, 94–6, 102–4, 108–12, 114, 134, 267, 275, 291, 292, 295, 301
Atticus, bp of Constantinople (406–25), 229, 236
Augustine, bp of Hippo (396–430), 86, 87, 173–93, 199, 200, 203, 204, 215–23, 231–4, 261, 262n., 265
Aurelius, bp of Carthage (391–430), 199, 208, 225, 226
Auxentius, bp of Milan (355–74), 149

Bacchus, F., 12
Bacchylus, bp of Corinth (190), 15
Ballerini, 226n., 234n., 287n., 321
Baptism, 38, 67–78, 90, 188–93, 205, 207, 265, 272
Baronius, C., 215n., 130
Basil, bp of Caesarea in Cappadocia (370–9), 124–6, 134, 135, 276
Basilides, Spanish bp (254), 64–6
Batiffol, P., 3, 56, 66, 72
Baur, C., 169
Bellarmine, R., 313
Benson, E. W., 26, 55, 78
Bethlehem, 153
Bévenot, M., 52, 56
Bible, 273
  authority of, 191, 198, 199
"Bishop of bishops", 26, 72
Bishops, the, 3, 4, 49, 53, 57, 62, 63

Councils:—*continued*

Nicaea, A.D. 325...92, 102, 112, 115, 126, 155, 228, 235, 289, 290, 292, 301, 303, 309–11, 327, 328

Philippopolis, A.D. 342...99, 269

Rome, A.D. 313...85
A.D. 340...96, 106
A.D. 371...126
A.D. 378...127
A.D. 380...138
A.D. 382...130

Sardica, A.D. 342...99–107, 269

Councils various, A.D. 357–9...115

General, 181, 189, 191, 193, 271, 274, 275

Coustant, P., 234n., 263

Crescens, bp of Cirta (256), 72

Cyprian, bp of Carthage (248–58), 37–40, 49–80, 117, 152, 188–93, 210, 237, 276, 281n.

Cyril, bp of Alexandria (412–44), 236–40, 242–8, 250, 253, 255, 257–60, 263, 276, 300, 301, 303–6, 310, 311

Cyril, bp of Jerusalem (348), 115

Decentius, bp of Eugubium (416), 194

Decius, emp. (249–51), 37, 49

Denny, E., xvi, 56, 57, 106n., 151, 170, 194n., 203n., 233, 238, 247, 295

Development, xvii, 273

Dianius, bp of Caesarea in Cappadocia (340–62), 96

Dionysius, bp of Alexandria (247–65), 42–4, 67, 79–82, 154

Dionysius, bp of Corinth (171), 6

Dionysius Exiguus, 263

Dionysius, metropolitan of Italy (355), 109

Dioscorus, bp of Alexandria (444–51), 288, 293, 297–302, 305, 306, 308, 309, 323, 329

Divided Christians, 12

Divided Church, xv, 42, 57, 58, 64, 78, 114, 125, 172, 183, 185, 269

Doctrinal confusion, 115, 125, 126

Döllinger, I. von, 36, 69, 184

Domnus, bp of Antioch (440–52), 288, 300

Donatism, 84, 117, 177, 181, 184–6, 189

Donatist anti-popes, 118

Donatists and Anglicans, 120, 187

Donatus, bp of Carthage (247), 60

Donatus, bp of Casae Nigrae, 85, 86

Donatus the Great (342), 99, 177, 189

Duchesne, L., 61, 215n., 224, 263n., 318

Easter, 14–19, 75, 90, 102, 243

Ephesus, 11, 15, 22; and see Conciliabulum and Councils

Ephrem the Syrian, 116

Erasmus, D., 166

2 Esdras, 203

Eucharist, 3, 4, 23, 63, 65, 171, 265

Eusebians, 94–6, 99, 103, 109, 295

Eusebius, bp of Caesarea in Palestine (314–40) and historian, 6, 7, 14, 18, 24, 25, 31, 41n., 44n., 48, 82, 84, 87, 90

Eusebius, bp of Dorylaeum (451), 299, 301, 302, 306

Eusebius, bp of Nicomedia (339), 94

Eusebius, bp of Vercellae (355), 109

Eustathius, bp of Antioch (326), 132

Eutyches (451), 297, 303, 307, 310, 323

Faustinus, bp of Potentia (419), 225, 227, 234, 235

Felicissimus, African deacon (252), 50, 58

Felix, anti-pope (355), 151

Felix, bp of Buslacene (256), 72

Felix, Spanish bp (254), 64–6

Filocalian Catalogue, A.D. 354...36, 62n.

Firmilian, bp of Caesarea in Cappadocia (256), 43, 57, 75

Firmus, bp of Caesarea in Cappadocia (431), 250

Flacillus, bp of Antioch (333–42), 96

Flavian, bp of Antioch (381), 135, 137, 138, 140, 141, 168n.

Flavian, bp of Constantinople (446–9), 288, 289, 291, 297, 299–303, 307, 313

Paul of Samosata, bp of Antioch (260–70), 82, 152
Paulinus, African deacon (417), 209, 210, 216
Paulinus, bp at Antioch (362–88), 132–4, 136–41, 149, 150
Paulinus, bp of Nola (417), 203
Paulinus, bp of Trèves (355), 109
Pelagianism, A.D. 416–31…196, 205, 238, 256, 261–3, 265
Pelagius, British monk, 195–203, 205, 207–11, 214–17, 219, 262, 264, 267
Pelagius II, 53
Percival, H. R., 321n.
Perigenes, bp of Corinth (419–35), 229, 230
Persecution, 5, 40, 49, 84, 92
Peter, apostle, 1, 5, 6, 9, 21–3, 27, 31, 45–61, 63, 68–70, 76, 83, 90, 91, 98, 100, 105, 111, 115–23, 129, 131, 142, 144–6, 155–60, 162–9, 173–9, 180, 190, 194, 202, 206, 211, 212, 229, 233, 243, 251–3, 257–9, 261, 262, 264, 279–86, 288, 293, 301, 303, 307, 312, 318, 322, 328, 329
Peter, bp of Alexandria (380), 129, 275
Peter, bp of Corinth (451), 301
Philadelphia, 4
Philip, apostle, 15
Philip, priest and papal legate (431), 248–55, 259
Phillips, G., 93n.
Phrygians, see Montanists
Pius IX, 280n., 312
Polycarp, bp of Smyrna (110–56), 6, 10, 15, 17, 22
Polycrates, bp of Ephesus (190), 15, 157
Pompey, bp of Sebrata (256), 72, 73
Pontus, 9, 14, 21, 43, 162
"Pope" as title, xvii, 26
Possidius, bp of Calama (437), 199, 265
Praxeas, 25
Praylius, bp of Jerusalem (417), 208
Prestige, G. L., 36n.
Primus, bp of Corinth (150), 8
Principalitas, 12, 22
Prisca, Montanist prophetess, 25

Proclus, 25
Projectus, bp and papal legate (431), 248–50, 253, 255
Prosper of Aquitaine (429), 148, 238n., 261–3, 277
Prudentius, poet (400), 37
Pulcheria, empress (450), 290, 297
Puller, F. W., xvi, 12n., 39n., 49, 52, 61, 72, 75, 138, 141, 151, 233, 234
Pusey, E. B., 63, 112, 169n., 170, 260

Quesnel, P., 101, 215n., 287n.
Quintus, Mauritanian bp (255), 40, 68, 69

Renouf, P. le P., 108
Reunion, xviii
Rivington, L., xvi, 12n., 19n., 52, 61, 66, 87, 138, 140
Robertson, J. C., 215n.
Rufinus, bp of Aquileia (410), 158, 159
Rufus, bp of Thessalonica (410–31), 229, 230, 241, 245, 248
Ryder, H. I. D., 287n.

Sabellius (218), 34, 82
Sabinus, Spanish bp (254), 64–6
Salmon, G., 74, 166, 188
Salvian, priest of Marseilles, 295
Schwartz, E., 302n.
Secret mysteries, 9, 20, 21, 202, 203
Simon Magus, 9, 90
Smyrna, 3, 6, 15
Socrates, historian (439), 99n., 133n., 137, 238n., 267–9
Sozomen, historian (450), 95, 138n., 291
Spain, 8, 64, 142
Succession, episcopal, 22, 49, 154, 182
Symonds, H. E., 253
Syria, 5, 22, 30, 35, 43, 150

Tatian (150), 29
Telfer, W., 100n.
Tertullian, priest of Carthage (200), 20–8, 61, 66, 157, 203n., 266

Made in the USA
Las Vegas, NV
13 October 2021

32257883R00203